Maternalism Reconsidered

International Studies in Social History

General Editor: Marcel van der Linden
Published in association with the International Institute of Social History, Amsterdam

MATERNALISM RECONSIDERED

Motherhood, Welfare and Social Policy in the Twentieth Century

Edited by

Marian van der Klein
Rebecca Jo Plant
Nichole Sanders
and
Lori R. Weintrob

Berghahn Books
New York • Oxford

Published in 2012 by
Berghahn Books
www.berghahnbooks.com

Library of Congress Cataloging-in-Publication Data

Maternalism reconsidered : motherhood, welfare and social policy in the twentieth
century / [edited by] Marian van der Klein ... [et al.].
  p. cm. – (International studies in social history)
  Includes bibliographical references and index.
  ISBN 978-0-85745-466-9 (hardback : alk. paper) – ISBN 978-0-85745-467-6
(ebook)
  1. Motherhood–History–20th century. 2. Mothers–History–20th century. 3.
Social policy–History–20th century. 4. Public welfare–History–20th century. I.
Klein, Marian van der.
  HQ759.M37365 2012
  306.874'3–dc23

                                                    2011041080

British Library Cataloguing in Publication Data

A catalogue record for this book is available from the British Library

Printed in the United States on acid-free paper

ISBN: 978-0-85745-466-9 (hardback)
ISBN: 978-0-85745-467-6 (ebook)

CONTENTS

CHAPTER 1

INTRODUCTION
A New Generation of Scholars on Maternalism

Rebecca Jo Plant and Marian van der Klein

Today as much as ever, mothers and motherhood are categories to be reckoned with in political debates. In nations across the globe, policymakers and commentators discuss whether mothers should be compensated for the care work they perform; whether women should be offered incentives to prevent population decline, or, alternately, be pressured to slow population growth; whether governments should take special measures to protect women due to their reproductive capacity; and to what extent, if any, mothers tend to vote *en bloc*. Regardless of the type of governmental regime and the role envisioned for mothers, the language that politicians and bureaucrats employ when addressing questions related to mothers and children often seems remarkably similar and strikingly familiar. Though their appeals are frequently dismissed as empty political rhetoric, they echo longstanding gendered discourses that have deep roots in both cultural beliefs and material life.

Since the late nineteenth century, calls for child and maternal welfare programmes and mothers' rights have emanated from all quarters of the globe, sometimes successfully, sometimes in vain. They have been advanced by liberals and conservatives, feminists and anti-feminists, men and women, a wide variety of religious groups and democratic, fascist and communist regimes. Moreover, as the celebration of Mother's Day in various countries reveals, discourses of motherhood not only encompass

Notes for this chapter begin on page 17.

economic and political issues, but are also embedded in cultures of esteem and honour. In seeking to understand the myriad ways in which mother-hood has figured within public life and social provisions, many scholars have embraced the paradigm of maternalism. It is this slippery construct that the essays in this volume attempt to analyse, test and refine.

'Maternalism' as an Analytical Category

In the early 1990s, scholars first began employing 'maternalism' as an analytical tool that helped to explain the emergence of modern welfare states in the U.S. and Western Europe. This literature was part of a broad-er trend among feminist scholars toward reassessing the gendered origins of welfare states. Indeed, two of the first and most influential edited col-lections to reflect this new scholarly movement – Linda Gordon's *Women, the State, and Welfare* (1990), which focuses on the U.S., and Gisela Bock and Pat Thane's *Maternity and Gender Policies* (1991), which focuses on Western Europe – did not advance the concept of maternalism.[1] Yet both volumes raised issues that would emerge as central concerns of the first wave of scholars who embraced and promoted the maternalist para-digm. Central among these issues was the role that women's voluntary organizations played in pressing for and implementing welfare measures. Rejecting the concept of the 'patriarchal' welfare state as overly simplistic and ahistorical, along with social control models that left little room for agency, numerous scholars began to devise more nuanced ways of con-ceptualizing women's relationships – as both advocates and beneficiaries – to welfare measures in different national contexts.

Several factors helped to fuel the burgeoning interest in motherhood, public policy and the state. During the 1970s and into the 1980s, many feminist scholars neglected women's roles in the formation of modern welfare states, focusing instead on the relationship between women and the labour market. This resulted in a tendency to marginalize questions of motherhood – a tendency that historians and social and political scientists subsequently sought to correct. Moreover, by the 1990s, people both within and outside the academy had increasingly acknowledged the fact that, despite significant gains in the workforce, many women continued to struggle with their own personal 'maternal dilemma' – the difficulty of balancing motherhood and individualism.[2] This growing recognition probably influenced the types of questions that scholars asked and the general climate in which feminist scholarship developed. Finally, and per-haps most critically, the restructuring of welfare policies in various nations – and the potentially ominous consequences for mothers and children –

prompted many scholars to turn their attention to the historical roots and ideological underpinnings of such systems.

It is perhaps not surprising that academics in the United States – where maternalist reform had been a powerful force in the early twentieth century and where attacks on the welfare state surged in the late twentieth century – pioneered the scholarship on maternalism. In a widely cited 1990 article that compared maternal welfare provisions in the United States, Great Britain, France and Germany, historians Seth Koven and Sonya Michel introduced the concept of maternalism to welfare scholarship, defining it as 'ideologies that exalted women's capacity to mother and extended to society as a whole the values they attached to that role: care, nurturance and morality'.[3] Soon thereafter, historians Molly Ladd-Taylor, Linda Gordon, Robyn Muncy and political scientist Theda Skocpol all charted a middle-class women's movement that emerged around the turn of the century and managed to exert a surprising degree of influence in an era when women still lacked the vote. As they and other scholars demonstrated, the efforts of Progressive Era maternalist reformers resulted in the establishment of mothers' pensions in numerous states, the 1912 founding of a federal Children's Bureau and the 1921 passage of the Sheppard-Towner Infancy and Maternity Protection Act, which provided expectant mothers with health information and support from professionally trained nurses.[4] Meanwhile, European scholars began identifying similar women's movements prior to World War II in Germany, France, Scandinavia and, to a lesser extent, in Great Britain.[5] Maternalism quickly became a familiar category of analysis for studying developments in these regions and drawing attention to the gendered character of welfare states.[6]

The introduction of the concept of maternalism has enriched both the field of gender history and the history of welfare states. Historians of maternalism not only widened the niche occupied by widows and orphans in welfare history, but also made clear that a discourse grounded in normative gender roles could still be about agency, and in fact had historically been used to promote social change. In other words, they showed that women's quest for social justice could no longer be considered the exclusive province of 'equal rights feminism'. As a paradigm, maternalism also helped to attenuate the emphasis on oppression, which had long been prominent in women's history, especially in the history of mothers and housewives. Behind victims, scholars began to discern recipients of benefits and politically savvy female reformers. Finally, the concept of maternalism served to advance the field of welfare history by highlighting the close interaction between the public and private sectors that characterized the early phases of welfare state formation in many nations. As Eirinn

Larsen has noted, because the rubric of maternalism places 'the activism of private organizations ... on equal footing with the action of political parties, trade unions, and official bureaucrats', it led researchers to 'notice and integrate the contributions of those who did not have formal political rights'. Thus, the concept of maternalism helped to 'challenge both the state-centrism and the limited definition of "politics"' that had previously characterized the history of welfare states.[7]

The readiness with which scholars latched on to 'maternalism' suggests that many found it to be a highly useful concept – one that filled a linguistic void in its capacity to describe certain movements and policies more accurately than other available terms. 'Maternalism' offered a way of discussing and analysing women's varied associational and political activities without becoming overly fixated on the loaded question of what can or cannot be properly designated 'feminist'.[8] Today, some scholars prefer to define maternalism as a particular form of feminism, one that highly values and seeks support for women's roles as caregivers. Others, however, define maternalism much more broadly, as an ideology that posits motherhood as a social and civic role, but one that lacks intrinsic political content.[9] To their minds, maternalism could serve conservative, even reactionary ends just as readily as it could accommodate support for suffrage and other feminist demands. Both of these perspectives are reflected in the essays featured here.

While such competing perspectives on maternalism reflect the differing views of individual authors, they also suggest the ways in which distinctive national contexts, historical experiences and historiographies have led scholars to ask different questions and assume different attitudes toward maternalism. In the United States, discussions of maternalism tend to be more immediately political, due at least in part to the intense debates over welfare 'reform', ongoing struggles over maternity leave and the seemingly endless debate over how – or even if – women should combine employment and motherhood. Perhaps as a result, American scholars often feel compelled either to defend or criticize maternalist paradigms. In Europe, historians of maternalism tend to be more preoccupied with the phenomenon's unsavoury historical connotations: maternalist movements are often associated with fascist practices or outmoded, politically conservative views on issues pertaining to sex and reproduction.[10] Generally speaking, scholars of Latin America regard maternalism in a more favourable light. They tend to portray it as compatible with (and at times even inseparable from) feminism or broader movements for social justice.[11] It is also notable that maternalist movements in Latin America appear to have been even more tightly connected to children's well-being than was the case in Europe and the United States. For example, whereas the leading maternalist organizations in the United States boasted names like the National Congress of Mothers or the General Federation of Women's Clubs, the most prominent organization in Brazil – described by Maria Lúcia Mott in Chapter 9 – was called the *Cruzada Pró Infância* (Pro-Childhood Crusade).

As these varying perspectives suggest, the meaning of 'maternalism' has not become clearer over time. To the contrary, the term has been defined in a variety of competing ways from the outset, and the confusion surrounding it has only multiplied in recent years. For instance, scholars of welfare states have often defined 'maternalism' in relation to equal rights feminism; that is, they have viewed it as a distinct ideology that has provided women with an alternative, less controversial foundation for political mobilization, or as a set policies that focus specifically on women and children (in contrast to 'paternalist' policies directed at men as workers and/or breadwinners). A quite separate stream of literature, which focuses on the experiences of domestic workers, uses 'maternalism' to characterize individual relationships situated within the domestic realm, rather than voluntary movements and state interventions. According to this usage, 'maternalism' has historically allowed elite women to assert their authority over less powerful women within a domestic context, while cloaking that authority in the mantle of maternal concern. Judith Rollins appears to have been the first scholar to employ the term in this manner; she argued that employer–employee relationships in the Boston area were shaped by 'rituals of deference and maternalism'.[12] Subsequently, other scholars of domestic workers, in countries ranging from Lebanon to South Africa, have described 'maternalism' as a means by which female employers have maintained class and racial boundaries and perpetuated inequality.[13] Writing about Sri Lankan housemaids in Lebanon, Nayla Moukarbel puts it baldly: 'Maternalism presupposes a relationship of domination, and not just one of protection and care. The emphasis the female employer puts on the emotional aspect of the relationship is, in fact, a form of manipulation.'[14] These scholars depict 'maternalism' in unambiguously negative terms, yet they are describing a very different phenomenon to scholars who have analysed 'maternalism' as a critical component of emerging welfare states.

Even when the focus is narrowed to literature concerning policies and politics, the wide range of ways in which 'maternalism' is currently being used can be dizzying. Historians of maternalist welfare movements have typically employed it to refer simultaneously to programmes designed to improve the plight of mothers and children and to female activism aimed at securing said policies and programmes. But others have used 'maternalism' to describe myriad political movements in which women have pressured governments or pursued social reforms unrelated to welfare policies. For example, historians and other scholars have applied the term to *las madres de La Plaza Mayo*, the Argentine women who famously protested the 'disappearance' of their loved ones under the military dictatorship of Jorge Rafael Videla.[15] Malathi de Alwis has analysed a similarly maternalist movement – the Sri Lankan Mothers' Front, which mobilized in the 1990s to demand 'a climate where we can raise our sons to manhood, have our husbands with us and lead normal women's lives'.[16] U.S. scholars have identified as 'maternalist' movements ranging from the anti-nuclear group Women Strike for Peace to the breastfeeding advocacy group La Leche League to the environmental activism of the Love Canal Homeowners' Association.[17] Given that women in all these cases portrayed their activism as an expression or extension of their maternal role, the designation 'maternalist' seems entirely appropriate. But here again, this body of literature bears only a tenuous relationship to the scholarship on welfare states.

In recent years, scholars who focus on state policies toward women and children have also extended, modified and challenged the concept of maternalism in new ways. The essays in this volume are exemplary in this regard. Broadly speaking, one can point to three major developments in the historiography on maternalism and the welfare state. First is the growing interest in studying how states have sought to construct men's and women's roles in relation to one another. Thus, whereas many earlier studies concentrated primarily on 'women and the welfare state', more recent scholarship has emphasized the gendered character of welfare states more broadly. Indeed, some researchers have argued that it is necessary to move 'beyond maternalism' in order to explore more comprehensively the ways that varied governmental regimes have intervened in families or mobilized familial imagery for political ends. In their edited collection *Families of a New World: Gender, Politics, and State Development in a Global Context*, Lisa Pollard and Lynne Haney contend that 'maternalism' tends to obscure the ways in which the state also sought to shape men's roles and behaviour.[18] In a related manner, Marian van der Klein's essay in this volume (Chapter 3) interrogates Skocpol's distinction between 'maternalist' and 'paternalist' states by showing how maternalist policies, even in the U.S., were always constructed in relation to the concept of a male breadwinner. Given that mothers' pensions in the U.S. were designed to compensate for the lost wages of the male breadwinner, she asks, does it really make sense to view them as so different from so-called 'paternalist' European social insurance programmes? In line with historians Jane Lewis and Alice Kessler-Harris, van der Klein concludes that, in both Europe and the United States, the breadwinner and the homemaker proved to be mutually dependent and mutually reinforcing categories.[19]

These are clearly instructive insights, yet many scholars in this volume and elsewhere have nonetheless found it appropriate to retain 'maternalism' as a tool for analysing policies or programmes that emphasized issues of motherhood and maternity, even as they also take heed of men's roles. For instance, Lara Campbell's essay (Chapter 6) demonstrates how working-class Canadian mothers mobilized to demand state support for the complementary roles of housewife and breadwinner. As one of the women she cites demanded, 'Why should our children and I be denied having a good husband and father in our home?' Likewise, Rebecca Jo Plant's essay (Chapter 7) shows how American 'war mothers' derived their status from their son's contributions to the war effort during World War I; because mothers were so closely identified with their children, the soldier's and mother's 'sacrifice' tended to be conflated, so as to become almost one and the same. Drawing on Christine Erickson's terminology, Plant identifies war mothers' advocacy for an unusual federal programme that would benefit war mothers and widows as a form of 'patriotic maternalism'.[20]

A second development in the literature on maternalism entails new attempts to conceptualize 'the state' and the process of policymaking. In their previously mentioned article, Koven and Michel argued that an analysis of policy outcomes cast doubt on the efficacy of maternalism as a political strategy. They argued that 'weak' states like the U.S., and to a lesser extent Great Britain, ended up with comparatively less generous maternal welfare provisions than France and Germany, even though they boasted comparatively more powerful women's movements. In contrast, 'strong' states like France and Germany – characterized by well-developed central bureaucracies – ended up with more generous welfare provisions, despite the fact that these nations had weaker women's movements. In Chapter 2 of this volume, Sonya Michel notes that, were she and Koven to revisit the same subject today, 'Instead of looking at the specific nature of central states, we would look at the specific nature of welfare state regimes that were either in place or in formation in each society'. Indeed, scholars have increasingly recognized that the state alone did not create social policy; rather, policy often emerged from a complex interplay between state actors and civil society. Even before scholars like Peter Baldwin argued for the need to move beyond the strong/weak state typology, historians concerned with the gendered dimensions of welfare states had begun to reframe the issue in more complex and nuanced terms, such as dirigiste/corporatist states versus liberal/deferring/delegating states.[21] In doing so, many scholars have drawn on the work of Gøsta Esping-Andersen, who developed a typology that distinguished between liberal, conservative-corporatist and social-democratic welfare regimes.[22] Many recent assessments of maternalism emphasize the importance of groups outside the government, including philanthropists, social reformers, industrialists and those involved in private voluntary and religious associations. This trend is evident in several of the essays featured here, including Lori Weintrob's study of private maternity insurance in France (Chapter 4) and Maria Lúcia Mott's study of women's philanthropic efforts in Brazil (Chapter 9).

Finally, a third development in the literature on maternalism is the emergence of a more global perspective that incorporates regions beyond North America and Western Europe, and one that includes not only comparative analysis, but also an emphasis on transnational exchange. Though historians first used the term to conceptualize nascent welfare states in the liberal democracies of Western Europe and North America, they have more recently begun to test its applicability to other, more authoritarian regimes. Two essays in this volume, Elisabetta Vezzosi's study of maternal-infant health programmes in fascist Italy (Chapter 10) and Yoshie Mitsuyoshi's account of pronatalist policies implemented by the Soviets in Western Ukraine (Chapter 11), are representative of this trend.[23] There has also been a growing recognition that the movement for maternalist welfare policies was a truly international one. Beginning in the late nineteenth century, maternal and child welfare advocates met regularly at international conferences – such as the 1935 Pan-American Child Congress, analysed by Nichole Sanders in Chapter 8 – to hammer out responses and solutions to the problems created by industrial capitalism. Reformers did not simply turn to the well-known U.S. and German models for inspiration, but rather participated in a much broader exchange of ideas: policymakers in the Netherlands looked to France, Mexico and even Chile; the Italians drew on models advanced by the Belgians; Latin American policymakers looked to Russia as well as other models; the Russians appropriated ideas from the French. Finally, new empirical research has increasingly challenged the idea, championed by Theda Skocpol, that the pre-New Deal U.S. welfare system, along with the voluntary movements that supported its construction, were exceptional in their maternalist orientation, as compared to European nations that developed along paternalist lines. Diane Sainsbury, for instance, argues that maternalist activism in Norway equalled or even surpassed that of American women,[24] and Linda Bryder has shown how American reformers concerned with maternal and infant mortality sought inspiration from the remarkable (and remarkably enduring) Plunket Society in New Zealand.[25]

A more encompassing, global perspective is also apparent in scholars' use of the concept of 'maternal imperialism' (or, less typically, 'imperial maternalism') to analyse the ways in which white women imported and sought to impose maternalist ideas on native populations in imperial and settler societies. Among the first scholars to explore this dynamic were Barbara Ramusack and Antoinette Burton, who focused on British women's activities in India.[26] Subsequently, Susan Pedersen analysed what she deemed 'the maternalist moment' in British colonial policy concerning 'child slavery' in interwar Hong Kong. According to Pedersen, in this instance a maternalist approach ultimately prevailed because it proved to be 'the form of female activism most acceptable, even useful, to colonial administrators seeking to demonstrate the benefits of British rule'.[27] In her study of French Indochina during roughly this same time period, Nicola J. Cooper has traced the rise of a maternalist colonial discourse that differed markedly from the prewar discourse, which cast colonization in more masculine, militarist terms. A new tendency to represent France as a 'great, protective Imperial Mother', she argues, contributed to a 'rethinking of the role of women in the empire'.[28] Finally, in her awarding-winning comparative study of settler societies in the U.S. West and Australia, historian Margaret D. Jacobs has shown how maternalist ideology served to justify the removal of indigenous children from their families and how white women reformers assumed a leading role in implementing such policies.[29] Other studies of maternalism in imperial and settler contexts that have explored the dynamic between reformers and the populations they sought to 'uplift' have emphasized the agency of the 'reformed' as well the reformers.[30] However, works like Jacobs' suggest that it was within these contexts, where the cultural and economic differences between the powerful and the subject were at their most pronounced, that the pernicious potential of maternalism became most fully manifest.

Finally, scholars have highlighted the international character of maternalism by analysing movements that developed within non-Western nations. For instance, Sarah Hodges has explored the 'global reach of the politics of maternalism and eugenics' in southern India in the period from 1920 to 1940. She shows how birth control advocates embraced a 'maternalist biopolitics' that linked the ideal of hygienic and 'modern' motherhood to the project of 'nation-building in its broadest sense – not as part of an anti-colonial struggle, but as an articulation of national identity and pride'.[31] Similarly, Firoozeh Kashani-Sabet has shown how, in the early twentieth century, Iranian policymakers and modernists developed their own form of maternalism – one inflected by nationalism and Islam. 'Maternalist ideology placed new controls on women's sexuality and reproductive rights but also fostered welfare programmes that improved the health of women and infants,' Kashani-Sabet concludes. 'As Iran grappled with its social welfare policies in the second half of the 20th century, maternalist ideology would alternately broaden or restrict women's choices in matters of marriage, maternity, and personal hygiene.'[32]

While this general conclusion echoes earlier scholarship that focused on the U.S. and Western Europe, broad similarities regarding the impact of maternalist beliefs and programmes should not obscure the markedly different ways that maternalism developed within particular cultural and geopolitical contexts.

One could conclude, in frustration, that 'maternalism' has been defined in so many ways that it really ought to be retired. Yet perhaps the term's looseness is actually its primary asset. From the outset, scholars of the welfare state have portrayed maternalism as a two-headed concept. According to Michel and Koven, 'it extolled the virtues of domesticity while simultaneously legitimating women's public relationships to politics and the state, to community, workplace and marketplace'.[33] But that is not the only ambiguity it enfolds. Maternalism encompasses economics as well as culture, money as well as sentiments, tradition as well as change. It is about women's movements that sought to enhance the financial position of mothers and children and about women's movements that attempted to use motherhood, with all its powerful connotations, to seek broader social and political reforms. It highlights the connection between elite women's growing participation in the public realm and the emergence of benefits for mothers of the lower classes. It is, in short, a matter of 'practising' mothers and maternal ideals, of state agencies and voluntary organizations, of grassroots movements and expanding governmental power. The very breadth and diversity intrinsic to the concept is what makes it suitable for describing and analysing ambiguities and tensions. In other words, one might agree with Jane Lewis that maternalism is a 'slippery' concept,[34] but one might add that it is also, for this very reason, well suited for investigating slippery historical contexts.

In the end, the imprecision that adheres to the concept of maternalism need not be a fatal flaw so long as the scholar who employs it is clear about her or his own working definition. After all, 'maternalism' is purely an analytical tool: unlike 'feminism' or 'pacifism' or 'socialism' – terms that have also produced protracted debates as to their proper definition – it was not employed by historical actors themselves. It is therefore more 'up for grabs' in the sense that the primary standard for assessing its utility must be its success in illuminating certain historical phenomena rather than its accuracy in categorizing individuals who laid claim to the term themselves. This collection of essays will by no means end the debate over how to define 'maternalism'. If anything, it will only fuel it. But it will offer fresh perspectives on the development and implementation of child and maternal welfare policies and the political controversies that surrounded them. In the process, it will offer a guide to readers who hope to understand how the literature on maternalism and welfare states has evolved since the 1990s and some of the new directions it has assumed in recent years.

History and Contributions to this Volume

All the essays featured here evolved from a conference held at the International Institute of Social History in Amsterdam in 2002, entitled 'Maternalism Reconsidered: Mothers and Method in Twentieth-Century History'.[35] This event assembled scholars from six nations and three continents who had embarked on research projects that required them to engage with the scholarship on maternalism and to assess the concept's value. In the end, it is clear that most authors have chosen to retain the concept, either as an analytic tool or as a descriptive term to identify certain movements and policies.

In contrast to earlier compilations on gender and the welfare state that have focused on the late nineteenth and early twentieth centuries, a majority of the papers featured here concentrate on the post-World War I era. An emphasis on the period of early welfare state formation in Europe and the U.S. is inappropriate for understanding similar developments in other contexts. In Latin America, for example, social reforms also came about as a result of the processes of urbanization and industrialization, but they occurred at a later period and within a different political context. The final essay in this volume, Alma Idiart's account of Infant-Maternity programmes in Argentina (Chapter 12), traces not only the rise of maternalist policies in the 1930s, but also their growing vulnerability under the neo-liberal economic policy of the 1980s and 1990s.

Aside from the two chapters concerning France and the United States, this volume also highlights developments in nations that have not figured prominently in the historiography on maternalism – fascist Italy, the Netherlands, Soviet-occupied Ukraine, Canada, Brazil, Argentina and Mexico. Taken as a whole, it allows the reader to glimpse similarities and differences between, say, Canadian housewives who defended their husbands' right to work in the 1930s and Western Ukrainian mothers who took strategic advantage of Soviet programmes that offered material assistance. It also brings to the fore little-known feminist personalities, such as the austere Dutch Anna Polak, director of the Bureau for Women's Labour, and the dynamic Brazilian Pérola Byington, leader of the *Cruzada Pró Infância*. By showcasing little-known developments, organizations and individuals, our authors offer new empirical findings that will be of interest to scholars who hope to understand maternal and infant policies from a comparative perspective. Other essays – most notably Berteke

Waaldijk's nuanced analysis of Dutch social workers (Chapter 5) – provide fresh theoretical approaches to questions concerning gender, class differences and citizenship.

One thing that stands out is that most of the authors featured here prefer to deploy the concept of maternalism functionally and flexibly. They qualify the term in various ways, referring, for example, to 'state maternalism', 'patriotic maternalism' or 'working-class maternalism'. Most of the authors adhere to Koven's and Michel's basic definition while sometimes also referencing Ladd-Taylor's distinction between 'sentimental' and 'progressive' maternalists. But they generally refrain from attempts to formulate a definition that might be applied in all contexts, choosing instead to leave the debate where it is. Rather than asking *if* maternalism can be applied to new contexts beyond the U.S. and Western Europe in the late nineteenth and early twentieth centuries, these scholars are concerned with *how* the concept can most effectively be used to understand historical phenomena in an international and transnational context.

In Chapter 2, 'Maternalism and Beyond', Sonya Michel surveys how historians of the U.S. have employed the concept of maternalism since its introduction in the early 1990s. While acknowledging the difficulty of differentiating maternalism from other forms of female activism, she suggests that one can do so by focusing on reformers' attitudes toward the poor women whose circumstances they hoped to improve. According to Michel, maternalism was an inherently class- and race-bound ideology; like paternalists, maternalists *condescended* to the poor rather than viewing them as potential allies. Michel also proposes some suggestions as to how scholars might further refine our understanding of variations in the historical evolution of welfare states. Finally, she discusses recent 'neo-maternalist' movements in the United States that have both retained and departed from a 'traditional' maternalist framework.

Historiographical questions are also central to the next chapter, Marian van der Klein's 'The State, the Women's Movement and Maternity Insurance, 1900–1930: A Dutch Maternalism?' which offers a trenchant critique of attempts to draw international comparisons among early welfare states in Europe and the U.S. along with a case study of the campaign for maternity in the Netherlands. In contrast to the U.S., the Netherlands lacked a strong maternalist movement that lobbied for legislation to protect mothers' interests and rights; those who employed maternalist rhetoric tended to be conservative and church-affiliated women concerned with protecting marriage and family life. The organization most active in lobbying for maternity provisions – the National Bureau for Women's Labour – addressed the issue by emphasizing workers' (rather than mothers') rights. But in the end, van der Klein shows, the feminist goal of a premium-free maternity provision – one that would be available to both workers and non-workers, married and unmarried women alike – remained outside the realm of the politically possible.

In Chapter 4, 'Mobilizing Mothers in the Nation's Service: Civic Culture in France's Familial Welfare State, 1890–1914', Lori Weintrob focuses on the subject of maternity protection in France during the Third Republic. Rather than emerging as part of a broader fight for workers' rights, maternity protection here developed as a central component of the quest for national unity. Spurred by fears of depopulation and the threat of socialism, solidarist reformers addressed maternal-child welfare as part of a broader agenda to protect those 'at risk' by mobilising civil society. In particular, Weintrob traces the creation of private maternity insurance funds that, after 1913, collaborated with the state to support mandatory maternity leaves. The state's reliance on private, voluntary associations – often staffed if not led by women –reveals a degree of public–private collaboration in the emerging French welfare state that scholars have tended to overlook. In addition, Weintrob explores an important shift in the realm of cultural representation, as religious maternal imagery gave way to new 'secular, republican and scientific' images of motherhood.

Chapter 5, 'Speaking on Behalf of Others: Dutch Social Workers and the Problem of Maternalist Condescension', brings us back to a central issue raised by Sonya Michel, namely the extent to which condescension toward the poor lay at the heart of the maternalist enterprise. Focusing on the origins of professional social work in the Netherlands during the late nineteenth and early twentieth centuries, Berteke Waaldijk probes the meaning of condescension and how it functioned during a period when both female social workers and their poor female clients lacked full citizenship rights. Portraying themselves as uniquely qualified to understand the needs of poor mothers, female social worker emphasized both their capacity as women to empathize with other women and their capacity as scientifically trained professionals to address the problems of poverty in a sober, rational manner. Yet even as social workers sought to expand their own rights by claiming the authority to speak on behalf of poor women, they also constructed their clients as subjects in their own right – subjects entitled to protections and civil rights that had not been recognized under the old system of charitable giving. Waaldijk thus argues that the 'delicate balance between distance and identification' displayed by middle-class social workers led not only to instances of demeaning condescension, but also to the first attempts to spell out clients' rights 'to privacy, to confidentiality, to a minimum of intervention and interference by agencies and to knowledge about what information was being used in decisions about them'.

The following chapter also addresses the relationship between maternalism and evolving conceptions of citizenship. In '"Respectable Citizens of Canada": Gender, Maternalism and the Welfare State in the Great
Depression', Lara Campbell shows how 1930s Anglo-Canadians increasingly challenged long-standing associations between relief, charity and
dependence by insisting that citizenship should encompass the right to
basic economic security. Embracing the notion of a family wage premised on adequate male breadwinning, working-class housewives assumed
the role of 'militant maternalists', arguing that male unemployment had
eroded their ability to meet their familial obligations. The maternalist
ideology they espoused was free of sentimentalism and grounded in the
material realities of working-class motherhood. However, as Campbell
shows, working-class Anglo-Canadians also tended to define citizenship
in racialized terms: by pointing to their British ancestry, they portrayed
themselves as particularly worthy of aid. Thus, Campbell explores how
radical economic demands, framed in maternalist and familialist rhetoric,
could also reinforce exclusionary racial ideologies.

Chapter 7, 'The Gold Star Mothers Pilgrimages: Patriotic Maternalists and Their Critics in Interwar America', explores a very different form
of maternalist politics. Rebecca Jo Plant shows how, even as progressive
maternalists in the late 1920s faced increasing political resistance in the
U.S., war mothers' associations successfully lobbied for a costly and unprecedented federal programme – government-run pilgrimages that sent
mothers and widows of American servicemen killed in the Great War to
Europe to visit their loved ones' graves. She also discusses critics of the
pilgrimage programme, including African Americans, who protested the
segregation of their gold star mothers and wives; impoverished veterans
and their family members, who felt the monies could be better spent;
peace advocates, who saw the pilgrimage programme as an attempt to
whitewash the carnage and meaninglessness of the war; and cultural critics, who disdained the sentimentality surrounding motherhood. Though
these dissenting voices were marginalized at the time, they ultimately
helped to discredit patriotic maternalism in the eyes of many Americans.
By the time the United States entered World War II, Plant argues, the
cultural and political climate had become less conducive to women's attempts to claim recognition as 'mothers of the nation'.

While Plant highlights the ways in which maternalism could be infused
with nationalist sentiments, Nichole Sanders calls for greater attention to
the transnational character of the movement to enhance maternal-child
welfare. In Chapter 8, 'Protecting Mothers in Order to Protect Children:
Maternalism and the 1935 Pan-American Child Congress', she focuses on
the seventh of a series of maternal-child welfare conferences held under the

auspices of the larger Pan-American Association and which sought to enhance regional cooperation. Sanders argues that the Congress promoted a vision of Latin American maternalism that differed from similar movements in the United States and Western Europe. This difference, she argues, resided in the extent to which Latin American Congress participants explicitly addressed issues of class and race, and because delegates saw their own populations as obstacles to economic and social development, they articulated a vision of child-maternal welfare as a 'civilizing mission'. Delegates viewed mothers as the key to social change; if properly trained by professional social workers, they would raise healthy, modern children. The model promoted by the Pan-American Congress also departed from earlier charitable approaches to social change in Latin America in that it prescribed a strong role for both women and the state.

Some of the attributes that Sanders identifies as representative of Latin American maternalism are further analysed by Maria Lúcia Mott in Chapter 9, 'Maternal and Child Welfare, State Policy and Women's Philanthropic Activities in Brazil, 1930–1945'. Challenging prior scholarship that has dismissed or belittled women's charitable activities, Mott argues that maternalist philanthropic organizations in Brazil constituted a progressive force that has not been properly appreciated by either women's historians or historians of the welfare state. In particular, she examines the role that women played in the creation and administration of the *Cruzada Pró Infância*, an organization founded in 1930 that initially focused on combating infant mortality. Philanthropic entities such as *La Cruzada* emerged from a nineteenth-century 'separate spheres' tradition that defended women's education and charitable activities as an extension of their maternal role, but differed from earlier ventures in that they were neither tied to the Catholic Church nor administered by elite women. Pointing to the broad scope of the *Cruzada*'s activities – including campaigns for suffrage, labour reform and programmes for single and working mothers – Mott contends that the *Cruzada* offered many services for poor women that the government could or would not provide at the time.

The next two chapters explore state-backed programmes within authoritarian contexts that have rarely been considered in the literature on maternalism. In 'Maternalism in a Paternalist State: The National Organization for the Protection of Motherhood and Infancy in Fascist Italy', Elisabetta Vezzosi explores government-backed attempts to improve maternal-infant health under Mussolini. Provocatively, Vezzosi argues that women's attempts to turn the fascist politicization of motherhood to their own advantage can be viewed as a form of maternalism – one in which mothers expressed their needs through unorganized resistance and by wielding indirect influence on state welfare policies. Vezzosi argues that the government's emphasis on pronatalism created opportunities for some women: it facilitated the emergence of female networks and led to the professionalization of occupations such as nursing and social work, while also granting both working and non-working mothers a greater sense of entitlement to assistance. Such benefits came at a high price, however, especially for single mothers who faced significant state intrusion into their private lives. Nevertheless, Vezzosi argues that the fascist-era agency helped pave the way for a more modern social welfare system and laid the groundwork for 'postwar opportunities and scenarios for a new kind of female citizenship'.

In 'Maternalism, Soviet-Style: The Working "Mothers with Many Children" in Post-war Western Ukraine', Yoshie Mitsuyoshi shows how the USSR promoted mother-child welfare as part of a larger Sovietization campaign designed to counter Ukrainian nationalism. The Soviets' attempts to modernize motherhood, which included improving medical facilities and awarding medals and cash benefits to 'mothers of many children', sought to legitimize the fiercely resisted Soviet presence. Yet these policies proved relatively uncontroversial, and sometimes even popular, in part because Ukrainian women welcomed the badly needed assistance, and in part because the glorification of motherhood could easily be reconciled with pre-Soviet cultural values. Like Vezzosi, Mitsuyoshi argues that women responded to the politicization of motherhood in a highly pragmatic manner, taking advantage of programmes that offered material benefits that could ease their burdens while often disregarding or resisting their ideological dimensions.

Finally, in the last chapter, 'The Origins and Transformations of the Infant-Maternity Health and Nutritional Programmes in Argentina', Alma Idiart examines the Infant-Maternity Programmes (IMPs) in Argentina. Idiart contends that the state created IMPs and other health initiatives in part to undercut the power of the elite female-headed charity, the *Sociedad de Beneficencia*. She further shows how the concept of motherhood itself has been more narrowly redefined over the course of the twentieth century. One effect of neo-liberalism, she argues, has been to reduce motherhood to its strictest biological function – that is, only pregnant or nursing women would be eligible for aid, thereby excluding other mothers in need of assistance. Although the IMPs have largely been spared wholesale dismantling, these changes suggest that maternalism has lost much of its currency in contemporary Argentina.

In summary, this volume showcases innovative work on mothers' rights and the relationship between familial ideologies, nationalism and welfare state formation in European, North American and Latin American contexts during the past two centuries. Building upon existing scholarship, while extending into new geographic and temporal areas, the essays featured here explore how maternalist discourses have been deployed in different nations – by the state, by voluntary agencies and by women themselves – and assess the political and social ramifications that have followed.

Notes

The authors would like to thank Alice Kessler-Harris for inviting Marian van der Klein to Columbia University, where we could meet. Ellen Baker and Barbara Locurto kindly provided an office as well as a laptop. Co-editors Nichole Sanders and Lori Weintrob, along with Frances M. Clarke, Rachel Klein, Marcel van der Linden, Sonya Michel and Berteke Waaldijk, read earlier versions. The introduction has also benefited from comments on a lecture delivered by Marian van der Klein at University College Maastricht and from the critiques of two anonymous readers who reviewed the manuscript.

1. G. Bock and P. Thane (eds). 1991. *Maternity and Gender Policies: Women and the Rise of the European Welfare States, 1880s–1950s*, London and New York: Routledge, 4; and L. Gordon (ed.). 1990. *Women, the State, and Welfare*, Madison: University of Wisconsin Press.

2. Ann Taylor Allen coined the term 'maternal dilemma', which she defines as centred on the question: 'Is it possible to be both a mother and an autonomous individual?' See A.T. Allen. 2005. *Feminism and Motherhood in Western Europe, 1890–1970: The Maternal Dilemma*, New York: Palgrave MacMillan, 1.

3. S. Koven and S. Michel. 1990. 'Womanly Duties: Maternalist Politics and the Origins of Welfare States in France, Germany, Great Britain, and the United States, 1880–1920', *American Historical Review* 95(4), 1076–108. See also the introduction to their co-edited volume, S. Koven and S. Michel (eds). 1993. *Mothers of a New World: Maternalist Politics and the Origins of Welfare States*, New York: Routledge, 1–42.

4. In exploring these developments, these scholars used the concept of maternalism in their own particular ways. Ladd-Taylor, who sought to delineate the term more precisely, distinguished between 'progressive maternalists', who focused on issues of social justice and often used maternalist rhetoric very strategically, and 'sentimental maternalists', typically clubwomen who tended to be more traditional and religiously oriented. A number of historians have embraced this typology. M. Ladd-Taylor. 1994. *Mother-Work: Women, Child Welfare, and the State, 1890–1930*, Urbana: University of Illinois Press. Gordon, who analysed the differences between white and black clubwomen and reformers, identified a 'black maternalism' that departed in critical ways from the white model. She argued that 'Black maternalism operated with less distance and condescension between helper and helped, and combined some romanticization of womanhood and motherliness with respect for women's economic independence'. L. Gordon. 1994. *Pitied But Not Entitled: Single Mothers and the History of Welfare, 1890–1935*, New York: Free Press, 141. And Theda Skocpol ambitiously – and controversially – claimed that, up until the late 1920s, the U.S. had been on the road to developing a 'maternalist' welfare state that differed in crucial ways from the 'paternalist' welfare states that emerged in Western Europe. T. Skocpol. 1992. *Protecting Soldiers and Mothers: The Political Origins of Social Policy in the United States*, Cambridge, MA: Harvard University Press. For a trenchant critique, along with Skocpol's response, see: L. Gordon. 1993. 'Gender, State and Society: A Debate with Theda Skocpol', *Contention* 2(3), 113–57; and T. Skocpol, 'Soldiers, Workers and Mothers: Gendered Identities in Early U.S. Social Policy', *Contention* 2(3), 157–83. See also R. Muncy. 1991. *Creating a Dominion in Ameri-*

can Female Reform, 1890–1935, New York: Oxford University Press; L. Curry. 1999. *Modern Mothers in the Heartland: Gender, Health and Progress in Illinois, 1990–1930,* Columbus: Ohio State University Press; and G. Mink. 1995. *The Wages of Motherhood: Inequality in the Welfare State, 1917–1942,* Ithaca, NY: Cornell University Press.

5. See, for example, Koven and Michel, *Mothers of a New World;* and S. Pedersen. 1993. *Family, Dependence, and the Origins of the Welfare State: Britain and France, 1914–1945,* Cambridge: Cambridge University Press.

6. There have been a number of illuminating review essays on maternalism and literature on gender and the welfare state. See, for example: L.Y. Weiner et al. 1993. 'Maternalism as Paradigm: Defining the Issues', *Journal of Women's History* 5(2), 96–130; K.K. Barker. 1997. 'Federal Maternal Policy and Gender Politics: Comparative Insights', *Journal of Women's History* 9(2), 183–91; L.D. Brush. 1996. 'Love, Toil, and Trouble: Motherhood and Feminist Politics', *Signs* 21, 429–54; F.A. Kornbluh. 1996. 'The New Literature on Gender and the Welfare State: The U.S. Case', *Feminist Studies* 22(1), 171–97; J. Lewis. 1994. 'Women's Agency, Maternalism and Welfare', *Gender and History* 6(1), 117–23; Robyn Muncy. 2000. 'The Citizenship of Mothers in the United States', *Journal of Women's History* 11(4), 157–65; and Ellen Ross. 1995. 'New Thoughts on "the Oldest Vocation": Mothers and Motherhood in Recent Feminist Scholarship', *Signs* 20(2), 397–413. For a highly critical discussion of the concept of maternalism, see Louise Toupin. 1996. 'Des "usages" de la maternité en histoire féminisme', *Recherches féministes* 9(2), 113–35.

7. E. Larsen. 1996. 'Gender and the Welfare State: Maternalism – a New Historical Concept?' (University of Bergen, Norway), http://www.ub.uib.no/elpub/1996/h/506002/eirinn/eirinn.html (accessed July 21, 2011). It should be noted, however, that Larsen is ultimately quite critical of maternalism as an analytical category. She compares it to an 'archaeological tool' that has allowed scholars to recover forgotten or unexplored components of early welfare states, but a tool that 'restricts our field of vision' by focusing on motherhood rather than the gendered character of the welfare state more broadly. E. Larsen. 1997. 'The American Introduction of "Maternalism" as a Historical Concept', *Nordic Journal of Feminist and Gender Research* 5(1), 14–25 (quotation, 23).

8. Historian J. Stanley Lemons used the term 'social feminism' to describe an agenda that later scholars have called 'progressive maternalism'. J.S. Lemons. 1973. *The Woman Citizen: Social Feminism in the 1920s,* Urbana: University of Illinois Press. Similarly, French historian Karen Offen introduced the widely adopted term 'relational feminism', which she distinguished from 'individualist feminism', in 1998. 'Defining Feminism: A Comparative Historical Approach', *Signs* 14(1), 119–57. N.F. Cott advocated a more narrow use of the 'feminism' in 1989. 'What's in a Name? The Limits of "Social Feminism;" or, Expanding the Vocabulary of Women's History', *Journal of American History* 76(3), 809–29.

9. Ruth Lister and a team of scholars have recently defined maternalism as 'an explicitly feminist offshoot of the civic republican tradition'. R. Lister et al. 2007. *Gendering Citizenship in Western Europe: New Challenges for Citizenship Research in a Cross-National Context,* Bristol: Policy Press

10. For instance, German historians Geoff Eley and Atina Grossmann, referring specifically to Weimar Germany, defined maternalism as 'forms of policy, institutional innovation and terms of popular political address that stressed naturalized constructions of women's difference and their societal subordination as the primary or the only legitimate basis for their admission to citizenship'. They view maternalism as inevitably antithetical to feminist attempts to open up new 'political space' for women. G. Eley and A. Grossman. 1997. 'The Gendered Politics of Welfare', *Central European History* 30(1), 67–75 (quotation, 72).

11. Historian Donna Guy has noted, 'As the literature on Latin America feminism grows, it appears to have a more positive view of maternalist feminist politics, particularly since the prospects of engaging in successful campaigns for female suffrage were far more difficult there'. D.J. Guy. 2000. *White Slavery and Mothers Alive or Dead: The Troubled Meaning of*

Sex, Gender, Public Health, and Progress in Latin America, Lincoln: University of Nebraska Press, 59. See also L.G. Luna. 2003. 'Los movimientos de mujeres en América Latina y la renovación de la historia política', Centro de Estudios de Género Mujer y Sociedad, Universidad del Valle, La Manzana de la Discordia, Cali, Colombia; and K. Mead. 2000. 'Beneficent Maternalism: Argentine Motherhood in Comparative Perspective, 1880–1920', *Journal of Women's History* 12(3), 120–45. Mead is by no means uncritical of maternalists' efforts; she argues that their promotion of professional expertise ultimately undercut their own authority. But she credits them with greatly expanding social assistance to women and children. For historiographical essays that address the politics of motherhood in Latin America, see S.A. Buck. 2008. 'Constructing a Historiography of Mexican Women and Gender', *Gender and History* 20(1), 152–60; J. Olcott. 2011. 'Introduction: Researching and Rethinking the Labors of Love', *Hispanic American Historical Review* 91(1), 1–27; and C.A. Rakowski. 2003. 'Women as Political Actors: The Move from Maternalism to Citizenship Rights and Power', *Latin American Research Review* 38(2), 180–94.

12. J. Rollins. 1985. *Between Women: Domestics and Their Employers*, Philadelphia: Temple University Press.

13. M. Romero. 1993. *Maid in the U.S.A.*, New York: Routledge; P. Hondagneu-Sotelo. 2006. *Doméstica: Immigrant Workers Cleaning and Caring in the Shadows of Affluence*, Berkeley: University of California Press; J.M. Armado. 2003. 'Mistress–Maid Relations: The Philippine Experience', *Journal of International Women's Studies* 4(3), 154–77; N. Moukarbel. 2009. *Sri Lankan Housemaids in Lebanon: A Case of 'Symbolic Violence' and 'Everyday Forms of Resistance'*, Amsterdam: Amsterdam University Press; A.J. King. 2007. *Domestic Service in Post-Apartheid South Africa*, Hampshire: Ashgate. King uses the term 'pseudo-maternalism', which she defines as 'a female relationship that is patterned along paternalistic lines that inverts characteristics of maternalism to enhance the power and image of self in relation to "the other"' (16). See also B. Anderson. 2000. *Doing the Dirty Work? The Global Politics of Domestic Labour*, London: Zed Books.

14. Moukarbel, *Sri Lankan Housemaids in Lebanon*, 129. Taking a slightly different view, Pierette Hondagneu-Sotela differentiates 'maternalism' – which she views as reinforcing the power imbalance between employers and employees – with 'personalism', which she defines as entailing 'the employer's recognition of the employee as a particular person – the recognition and *consideración* necessary for dignity and respect to be realized'. *Doméstica*, 207–8.

15. S.E. Howe. 2006. 'The Madres de La Playa Mayo: Asserting Motherhood; Rejecting Feminism?' *Journal of International Women's Studies* 7(3), 43–50. See also M.G. Bouvard. 1994. *Revolutionizing Motherhood: The Mothers of the Plaza de Mayo*, Lanham, MD: SR Books.

16. M. de Alwis. 2001. 'Ambivalent Maternalisms: Cursing as Public Protest in Sri Lanka', in M. Turshen, S. Meintjes and A. Pillay (eds), *The Aftermath: Women in Post-Conflict Transformation*, London: Zed Books, 210–24.

17. A. Swerdlow. 1993. *Women Strike for Peace: Traditional Motherhood and Radical Politics in the 1960s*, Chicago: University of Chicago Press; L.Y. Weiner. 1994. 'Reconstructing Motherhood: The La Leche League in Postwar America', *Journal of American History* 80(4), 1357–81; and E. Blum. 2008. *Love Canal Revisited: Race, Class, and Gender in Environmental Activism*, Lawrence: University of Kansas Press. For an astute critical assessment of the maternalist framing of the Million Mom March, see P. di Quinzio. 2005. 'Love and Reason in the Public Sphere: Maternalist Civic Engagement and the Dilemma of Difference', in S.M. Meagher and P. di Quinzio (eds), *Women and Children First: Feminism, Rhetoric, and Public Policy*, Albany: State University of New York Press, ch. 12.

18. L. Haney and L. Pollard (eds). 2003. *Families of a New World: Gender, Politics and State Development in a Global Context*, New York: Routledge.

19. Lewis, 'Women's Agency, Maternalism and Welfare'; and A. Kessler-Harris, review of Skocpol's 1990. *Protecting Soldiers and Mothers* in *Journal of American History* 80(3), 1035–7. Here, Kessler-Harris points out that the policies Skocpol designates as 'maternal-

ist' – meaning that they were designed to 'help adult American women as mothers or as potential mothers' – in fact sometimes benefited working men and their families, while hindering the aspirations of self-supporting women.

20. Christine Kimberly Erickson has defined 'patriotic maternalism' as a 'fusion between a militant patriotism that defended American values and institutions against subversive forces and a sense that motherhood provided women with the unique ability to safeguard American ideals' in C.K. Erickson. 1999. 'Conservative Women and Patriotic Maternalism: The Beginnings of a Gendered Conservative Tradition in the 1920s and 1930s', Ph.D. diss., University of California, Santa Barbara, viii.

21. P. Baldwin. 2005. 'Beyond Weak and Strong: Rethinking the State in Comparative Policy History', *Journal of Policy History* 17(1), 12–33. See, for example, S.G. Pedersen. 1993. *Family, Dependence, and the Origins of the Welfare State: Britain and France, 1914–1945*, Cambridge: Cambridge University Press.

22. G. Esping-Andersen. 1990. *Three Worlds of Welfare Capitalism*, Princeton, NJ: University of Princeton Press.

23. Today, scholars are producing works that compare not only Norway and Sweden, for example, but also Norway and Iran. S. Razavi. 2008 'Maternalist Politics in Norway and the Islamic Republic of Iran', in N. Kabeer, A. Stark and E. Magnus (eds), *Global Perspectives on Gender Equality: Reversing the Gaze*, Oxford: Routledge, 64–86.

24. D. Sainsbury. 2001. 'Gender and the Making of Welfare States: Norway and Sweden', *Social Politics* 8(1), 113–43.

25. The New Zealand Royal Plunket Society was founded in 1907 'to help the mothers and save the babies'. Like the better-known Sheppard-Towner programme in the U.S., the organization was maintained by women volunteers, sometimes with government support; unlike Sheppard-Towner, the programme survived the 1920s, persisting as an organization largely controlled by voluntary women until the 1970s. Bryder recounts how Julia Lathrop, head of the U.S. Children's Bureau, looked to the Plunket Society as 'an example of the system she hoped to establish in the United States'. L. Bryder. 2003. *A Voice for Mothers: The Plunket Society and Infant Welfare, 1907–2000*, Auckland, NZ: Auckland University Press.

26. B.N. Ramusack. 1990. 'Cultural Missionaries, Maternal Imperialists, Feminist Allies: British Women Activists in India, 1865–1945', *Women's Studies International Forum* 13(12), 295–308; and A.M. Burton. 1990. 'The White Woman's Burden: British Feminists and the Indian Woman, 1865–1915', *Women's Studies International Forum* 13(12), 295–308. See also A.M. Burton. 1994. *Burdens of History: British Feminists, Indian Women, and Imperial Culture*, Chapel Hill: University of North Carolina Press. For a discussion of 'missionary maternalism' and 'imperial maternalism', see N.C. Lutkehaus. 1999. 'Missionary Maternalism: Gendered Images of the Holy Spirit Sisters in Colonial New Guinea', in M. Taylor and N.C. Lutkehaus (eds), *Gendered Missions: Women and Men in Missionary Discourse and Practice*, Ann Arbor: University of Michigan Press, 207–35.

27. Pedersen describes maternalism – which she identifies as the 'main track into which women's imperial involvements were channeled during these years' – as the 'feminine component of the ideology of trusteeship'. S. Pedersen. 2001. 'The Maternalist Moment in British Colonial Policy: The Controversy Over "Child Slavery" in Hong Kong, 1917–1941', *Past and Present* 171(1), 161–202 (quotations, 165, 202).

28. N.J. Cooper. 2009. 'Gendering the Colonial Enterprise: La Mère-Patrie and Maternalism in France and French Indochina', in H. Fischer-Tiné and S. Gehrmann (eds), *Empires and Boundaries: Rethinking Race, Class, and Gender in Colonial Settings*, New York: Routledge, 129–45.

29. M.D. Jacobs. 2009. *White Mother to a Dark Race: Settler Colonialism, Maternalism, and the Removal of Indigenous Children in the American West and Australia, 1880–1940*. Lincoln: University of Nebraska Press, 2009.

30. For instance, in her analysis of attempts of British missionaries and teachers to reduce infant mortality in Asante (today Ghana), historian Jean Allman has shown how Asante women selectively accepted, rejected and transformed various aspects of the colonists' teachings. Thus many women eagerly sought out healthcare, while avoiding mothercraft lectures and neglecting to bring their babies to the clinic to be regularly weighed. J. Allman. 1994. 'Making Mothers: Missionaries, Medical Officers, and Women's Work in Colonial Asante, 1924–45', *History Workshop Journal* 38, 23–47.

31. S. Hodges. 2008. *Conception, Colonialism, and Commerce: Birth Control in South India, 1920–1940*, Hampshire: Ashgate. Hodges contrasts this 'maternalist mode' of contraceptive advocacy – which promoted respectability and valorized science and modernity – with the more radical approach advocated by the Self Respect movement, which advocated contraception as part of a broader quest for individual emancipation.

32. F. Kashani-Sabet. 2006. 'The Politics of Reproduction: Maternalism and Women's Hygiene in Iran, 1896–1941', *International Journal of Middle Eastern Studies* 38, 1–29. See also idem. 2011. *Conceiving Citizens: Women and the Politics of Motherhood in Iran*, New York: Oxford University Press.

33. Koven and Michel, *Mothers of a New World*, 6.

34. Lewis, 'Women's Agency, Maternalism and Welfare', 120.

35. The workshop was organized by Marian van der Klein and co-financed by the Royal Dutch Academy of Sciences (KNAW) and the Dutch Organization of Scientific Research (NWO).

CHAPTER 2

MATERNALISM AND BEYOND

Sonya Michel

Since the early 1990s, when the term first made its way on to the academic scene, the scholarship of 'maternalism' has burgeoned exponentially. Using 'maternalism' as a keyword on WorldCat recently, I came up with dozens of articles and books dealing with maternalism in a variety of contexts, both geographical and chronological, and ranging across many disciplines, including history, of course, but also sociology, political science, literature and even chemistry.[1]

Needless to say, this scholarship – along with the essays in this volume – is hardly of one mind when it comes to the subject of maternalism, whether as historical movement, historiographical or analytical approach, or contemporary political strategy. Over the years, scholars have refined the term, challenged it and sometimes dismissed it altogether. In this essay, I will begin by giving some definitions of maternalism and then turn to three problematics: maternalism as a theory of women's political activity, maternalism as a specific historical development and, finally, maternalism as a form of post-feminist politics. In the course of this discussion, I will point to some promising new directions in historical and social science scholarship, as well as some recent political developments, specifically in the United States, that may take us 'beyond maternalism'.

The task of defining maternalism is in itself a tricky business. The concept is highly context-dependent, and because the political stakes are high, it is still very much in flux. Nevertheless, I think we can extract enough commonalities from the various definitions currently circulating to feel confident that we are tracking more or less the same species over time – and

to know when we need to call it something else. I should note at the outset
that the terms 'maternalism' and 'maternalist' are heuristic, not appella-
tions that activists normally used for themselves or their movements.

In our 1990 article 'Womanly Duties: Maternalist Politics and the Origins of Welfare States in France, Germany, Great Britain, and the United
States, 1880–1920', Seth Koven and I defined as maternalist 'ideologies
that exalted women's capacity to mother and extended to society as a
whole the values they attached to that role: care, nurturance, and morality'. Our definition grew out of an analysis of women's political mobiliza-
tions from the late nineteenth to the early twentieth centuries in Western
Europe and North America. 'Maternalism', we argued, 'always operated
on two levels: it extolled the private virtues of domesticity while simultaneously legitimating women's public relationships to politics and the
state, to community, workplace, and marketplace.'[2] Several years later, in
a forum at the Social Science History Association (later published in the
Journal of Women's History), Lynn Weiner distilled our formulation into
the following: 'a kind of empowered motherhood or public expression
of those domestic values associated in some way with motherhood'.[3] For
Molly Ladd-Taylor, however, this definition was far too loose. In that
same forum, she criticized the practice of deploying the term maternalism 'to describe practically any woman activist who used the language
of motherhood to justify her political activities' and sought instead to
restrict application of the maternalist label to women who held the following beliefs:

> (1) that there was a uniquely feminine value system based on care and nur-
> turance; (2) that mothers performed a service to the state by raising citizen-
> workers; (3) that women were united across class, race, and nation by their
> common capacity for motherhood and therefore shared a responsibility for all
> the world's children; and (4) that ideally men should earn a family wage to
> support their 'dependent' wives and children at home.[4]

Having specified maternalism considerably, Ladd-Taylor went on to divide
it into two types, 'sentimental' and 'progressive', categories that more or
less succeeded one another chronologically, with some overlaps.[5]

While Ladd-Taylor attempted to periodize maternalism more precisely
as well as flesh out its content, Eileen Boris signalled her sharp criticism
of the *politics* of maternalism by defining it as 'a rhetoric that conflates
women with mothers; that suggests that all women are potential mothers
capable of nurturing children for whom they hold primary responsibility',
as well as the 'policies based on this set of assumptions'. In 'What About
the Working of the Working Mother?' Boris pointed out that because ma-

ternalist reformers were primarily concerned with women as 'childbearers and rearers' (and because, as Ladd-Taylor stipulated, they assumed uncritically mothers' dependence upon male wages), they tended to ignore the special needs mothers might have *as workers*.[6] These values, in turn, not only led maternalists to discourage women from working outside the home, but kept them from supporting the types of services and policies that might have assisted mothers in the workplace. Thus, they campaigned for state-supported mothers' pensions but not public child care, for pure milk stations but not equal treatment in the labour market. As Boris and others have shown, in the United States the separation of motherhood and employment was particularly harmful to African American and other women of colour, who were – and still are – much more likely to work outside the home than their white counterparts.[7]

Boris's critique rightly focuses our attention on the negative effects of maternalist discourses and movements on welfare clients or 'target' populations, but we must also bear in mind the ways in which this ideology simultaneously empowered maternalist activists. While these two aspects are, of course, often politically opposed, for analytical purposes they should not be separated, for, as historian Patrick Wilkinson explains, maternalists' success was premised at least in part upon the 'cultural work' that the poor performed.[8] As numerous scholars have pointed out, maternalism in practice was an ideology or political strategy most frequently deployed by middle-class women (*white* women, it is important to note in the American context, though race and ethnicity are often no less significant elsewhere) to justify their own political participation as well as the establishment of institutions, policies or legislation directed at poor or working-class women and children. This was often achieved at the expense of pathologizing, infantilizing, racializing or otherwise denigrating the poor, who were usually barred from representing themselves in public arenas. Maternalists effaced the culture of racial, ethnic and/or socio-economic 'others', silencing them as they (the maternalists) specified their needs through the lens of (white) middle-class values and romanticized visions of family life.

Despite their thoroughgoing effacement, Wilkinson nevertheless grants the poor a certain kind of agency in the policymaking process. While rarely seen as individuals, they were, he claims, nonetheless able to assert themselves by exerting '*collective* pressure' on the state through their demands and, however mutely and inadvertently, legitimating the efforts of female reformers through their representation (by others) as helpless, suffering victims.[9] Portraits of extreme abjection (whether created by maternalists or by male journalists, politicians or advocates) '*worked* within the political culture of the day in a way that other depictions of injustice did not'.[10] They not only 'created [an] opening through which impersonal or *structural* explanations of poverty could be advanced … [and] secured the legitimacy of the state's new forays into welfare work', but provided an excuse for activist women to enter the public sphere, in the guise of 'simply attending to … domestic duties' by coming to their aid.[11]

To gain a deeper understanding of this process, cultural analysis can be a useful tool. Take, for example, Rosemarie Thomson's suggestive readings of three nineteenth-century American novels by female authors in her article 'Benevolent Maternalism and Physically Disabled Figures: Dilemmas of Female Embodiment in Stowe, Davis, and Phelps'.[12] Thomson shows that each of these novels deploys triads in which maternalist characters gain stature and authority vis-à-vis stronger male characters by being positioned over disabled figures. In the famous abolitionist saga *Uncle Tom's Cabin*, for instance, Harriet Beecher Stowe endows the enslaved mother Eliza, whose child is sickly, with a maternal form of 'agency and self-determination' to create 'a figure that resembles the idealized liberal self … self-reliant, wilful, unimpeded by bodily limitation'.[13] Thomson's point dovetails nicely with Wilkinson's observation that 'journalists, judges, and politicians who were readily disposed to see poor women as *victims* were not, generally, quite as ready to see middle-class women as *agents*, like themselves, in the political arena'.[14]

To be sure, the chief figures in maternalist rhetoric during its heyday in the late nineteenth and early twentieth century were not the disabled but poor women and children. It is worth pondering for a moment why the rhetoric shifted in this way from the 1850s, when *Uncle Tom's Cabin* was published. While the disabled, like women and children, had commanded women reformers' attention and charity in the first half of the nineteenth century, by the latter decades their claims were being diverted elsewhere. Many categories of disability (deafness, blindness, infirmity, mental illness, etc.) had gained public recognition (often at women's behest), and care of the disabled was rapidly becoming institutionalized and professionalized, a trend that gained even greater momentum after the Great War.[15] As a result, both the discursive and political space disability had once afforded maternalist reformers was shrinking. At the same time, however, the plight of poor women and children was, if anything, becoming more urgent owing to immigration, industrialization and urbanization. When presented as abject, helpless dependents, these figures could continue to perform the 'cultural work' the ideology required. Moreover, maternalists regarded their condition as one that was amenable to their ministrations, which often comprised inculcation in middle-class values and domestic practices. Thus, the response most often evoked by the poor was not pity but condescension and moralism.

The emphasis on condescension is significant, because it distinguishes maternalism from other types of female reform (as I shall discuss below), while aligning it closely with paternalism. The two ideologies differ in terms of their implications for the gendered distribution of power, but they are similar when it comes to the spread of power along socioeconomic and racial-ethnic lines. As Lynn Weiner has pointed out, the term paternalism 'relies on assumptions about a specific authoritarian style of fatherhood'; according to the dictionary, it refers to 'the policy of governing or controlling people in a paternal way, providing for them by giving them no responsibility'.[16] To this we might add ignoring people's needs as *they* might define them, denying them a voice in shaping the forms of their own assistance and generally failing to treat them as equals, while empowering the authors or instigators of the policy.[17]

Specified in this way, it becomes easier to differentiate maternalism from other discourses of motherhood and sort them all out politically. Thus, although middle-class African American women reformers often invoked women's maternal duties, Boris and others argue that they were *not* maternalists precisely because they understood and accepted poor black women's needs – for example, the need to work outside the home – and their rhetoric gave little hint of condescension toward their clients, but rather a sense of righteous indignation at the injustices that caused their plight.[18] Boris wants to subsume African Americans' rhetoric under the rubric 'oppositional discourses of motherhood' and suggests using a term other than maternalist – perhaps Elsa Barkley Brown's 'womanist' – to describe them.[19]

Similarly, Dutch scholars Annemieke van Drenth and Francisca de Haan prefer to use another term – what they call 'caring power' – to refer to the work of prison reformer Elizabeth Fry, anti-prostitution campaigner Josephine Butler and their followers in the Netherlands and Britain in the nineteenth century. In many ways, caring power, as they define it, sounds quite similar to maternalism: it was associated primarily with elite women and helped them to develop 'new public identities' by making them primarily responsible 'for others not their own family members'.[20] Yet van Drenth and de Haan take pains to distinguish the two concepts. Rejecting Koven's and my notion of maternalism as too narrow, they argue:

> However important ideas about a spiritual or social motherhood may have been, they do not cover all women's social and reform work, nor all of their motives. A (religiously founded) responsibility for those of their own sex, friendship and sisterhood were just as much a part of nineteenth-century women's vocabulary and mental universe, and they inspired many of women's social and political activities on behalf of other women.[21]

On first reading, I must confess, I had trouble seeing the difference between maternalism and caring power. Maternalism, as deployed by numerous other scholars in addition to Koven and myself, has hardly excluded either the gendered or religious dimensions of women's reform; indeed, we argued that it was precisely the conjunction of the two, as embodied in evangelicalism and assumptions about female moral superiority, that provided essential political space as well as motivation for women's nineteenth-century reform efforts. But there *is* a distinction between maternalism and caring power. As noted above, in many accounts, the elements that made up maternalism co-existed easily (at least in the minds of elite women) with varying degrees of condescension toward the objects of reform or depended upon their cultural abjection. By contrast, van Drenth and de Haan contend, caring power broke down class barriers between groups of women; Butler in particular 'fought for the fundamental recognition of women as subjects', regardless of their social position. In this way, they argue, the movements engendered by caring power led more readily to the formation of modern feminism than did maternalism.[22]

The relationship between maternalism and feminism has, of course, vexed feminist scholars from the outset. Maternalism's tendency toward condescension, which impeded cross-class and cross-racial alliances, was not its only problem; its acceptance of the existing gender order, although strategically necessary, also hindered the expansion of women's roles and rights. While Koven and I, along with many others, emphasized the ways in which maternalism enabled women seeking power and authority in the public sphere, we were also keenly aware of the inescapable paradox that the ideology (at least in what Ladd-Taylor would call its 'sentimental' form) also endorsed an essentialized view of women that confined them to maternal and domestic roles. Ladd-Taylor claims that progressive maternalists avoided this paradox by deploying maternalism strategically. While adhering to the criteria mentioned above, they also worked actively for suffrage and 'combined their motherhood rhetoric with progressive appeals to justice and democracy, rather than morality and social order'. Further, they 'staked their claim to authority ... not on their feminine capacity to nurture but on their professional expertise'.[23] Thus they could more easily be regarded (and regard themselves) as feminists.

Surveying German women's history, Ann Taylor Allen also found a form of maternalism that she regards as compatible with feminism. Indeed, she defines maternalism as 'a feminism that takes women's experience as mother and nurturer as the basis for interpretations of women's history, for distinctively female approaches to ethical and social questions, and for improvements in women's status'.[24] (Allen's definition of maternalism bears close resemblance to what French historian Karen Offen has

called 'relational feminism'.)[25] Other historians, however, prefer to differentiate sharply between feminist activism, even when it involves maternal
and child welfare reform, and maternalism, with its connotations of condescension and essentialism. Instead, they label the former type of politics
'social justice feminism'. This is the approach taken by Kathryn Kish Sklar
in discussing the American reformer Florence Kelley and comparing Kelley and her colleagues with their German counterparts.[26]

Mapping the relationship between feminism and maternalism requires
teasing out the subtle differences among ideologies that appear, at least
superficially, to be quite similar. While Ladd-Taylor and Allen alert us to
the ways in which maternalist ideologies change over time and vary from
one national context to another, it is also useful to bear in mind Kathleen
Uno's stipulation that maternalism can gain political traction only when
'motherhood and mothering are very important not only to the home
but to the larger society'; in other words, in order to flourish, maternalism needs a national ideological platform.[27] As Allen argues, scholars must
study 'the relationship of women as speakers to the discourses of their
time. Such a theory would assert that speech is not just an individual but
a social act, the product of the interaction between individual creativity
and the intellectual paradigms and frameworks provided by a given culture and period'.[28] Thus, in charting what Alice Kessler-Harris would call
a 'gendered meaning system', scholars should consider the rhetorics of
contemporary male-dominated politics as well as those emanating from
women's groups and movements.[29]

Historians like Allen and Uno anticipated an approach to maternalism
sketched out more fully by two historical sociologists, Julia Adams and
Tasleem Padamsee, in their article 'Signs and Regimes: Rereading Feminist Work on Welfare States'.[30] According to these authors, 'discursive approaches can … illuminate the ways in which networks and groups of actors
are created and bounded by signifying processes, and how the manipulation of signs incorporates some subjects and includes or actively repels others. They also point up the political possibilities present in certain historical
moments and cultural conjunctures'. While this approach would work well
in studying any type of political ideology or rhetoric, Adams and Padamsee
offer an insight that is particularly relevant to the way in which scholars
have understood maternalism, namely, that 'the range and fate of those
possibilities are never dictated by the "essential" characteristics or experiences of those to whom politics appeals, but some may well be foreclosed
on a specific field of politics'.[31] That is, while historical actors may themselves base their claims on presumed essential characteristics or experiences,
it is the way those phenomena are constructed and understood in their own
moment that endows them with political valence.

Although Adams and Padamsee give pride of place to cultural factors (and, by extension, to what they and others call 'gender regimes') in determining the power of maternalist politics, they also seek to account for agency. Invoking Louis Althusser's concept of interpellation, they argue that certain groups of historical actors 'were invited to recognize themselves in [the rhetorical claims of maternalism] and to join in forwarding them', and that, once self-constituted or recruited as subjects, 'maternalist activists and their antagonists tried again and again to define and fix the field of political meanings ... and on that basis to mobilize actors, both individual and organizational, into effective political networks'.[32] Similarly, while Patrick Wilkinson acknowledges the importance of the 'arena of public discourse' in fostering maternalism, he also emphasizes what he calls the 'structure of opportunity' maternalists might exploit.[33] In our 1990 article, Koven and I also pointed to structural factors, drawing attention to what we called the 'political space' afforded women by strong and weak states. Wilkinson, by directing scholars to look at states, courts and the professions in the U.S., is operating at a deeper level of specificity, but one that is undoubtedly productive in explaining maternalists' successes or failures in cases that might appear to be culturally similar.[34]

Clearly, the proliferation of new scholarship on maternalism challenges us to reconsider and broaden our historical frame. Let me return briefly to our original attempt at explanation. In 'Womanly Duties', Koven and I identified as 'maternalist' women's movements arising simultaneously in four Western, more or less democratic, secular, urbanizing and industrializing societies: France, Germany, Great Britain and the United States. Our comparison revealed that these movements enjoyed varying degrees of success, which we attributed to a range of different factors, with the relative strength of the central state (by which we meant specifically its welfare bureaucracy) foremost among them.

Several scholars have taken issue with this explanation. For example, Theda Skocpol, in her important book, *Protecting Soldiers and Mothers: The Political Origins of Social Policy in the United States*, while generally accepting our definition of maternalism, criticized our measure of state strength for being 'too crude to get at the differences among national political systems that affected how likely women are to become politically active and ... in what ways women can have an impact on policy decisions'.[35] Her analysis of the differences between Britain and the U.S. – both of which we identified as 'weak' states – and the ways in which they produced political space for women is persuasive.[36]

Today, with the prompting of our critics as well as more recent scholarship, we would no doubt want to refine our explanation of why certain national contexts were more conducive to maternalism than others. In ad-

dition to looking at political systems, as Skocpol suggests, we would examine the specific nature of the *welfare state regimes* that were either in place
or in formation in each society. Using this more complex formulation, we
would be better able to identify and compare the structural entry points
available to women.[37] We would also give greater weight to culture – especially *political* culture – and its receptivity to maternalist arguments, as well
as to the ways in which male-dominated politics and women's movements
contributed to welfare state-building. In this light, the paradoxical success
of maternalist *policies* in societies with weak maternalist *movements* (France
and Germany vs Great Britain and the United States) may be attributed
not (or not only) to the relative strength of their central states, but to the
greater congruence between maternalist goals – however weakly expressed
– and the welfare visions upheld by male-dominated political structures.

Here, the impact not only of maternalism but also of feminism should
be taken into account. Sad to say, it may well be the case that the relative
strength of egalitarian feminism (as well as maternalism) in Britain and the
United States – for all of its failure to achieve its own goals – nevertheless
'interrupted' maternalist ideologies in those countries, squelching masculine
enthusiasm for maternalist goals.[38] Consider, for example, the rapid demise,
in the wake of female suffrage, of the federal maternal and child health programme established by the Sheppard-Towner Act in the United States after
its initial passage in 1921.[39] At the same time, in the U.S. at any rate, differences over the issue of state-building among 'motherhood reformers' (divided between social justice feminism and laissez-faire maternalism) blocked
the formation of a solid social democratic maternalist core, weakening the
push for all but the most gender-conservative policy initiatives.[40]

The conclusions to be drawn from this particular set of comparisons
may have varying relevance to other cases, as the essays in this volume
illustrate. What we need to extract from studies like 'Womanly Duties' is
not some kernel of comparative essence, but an approach that can help us
understand different maternalisms not only in and of themselves, but also
as a key to the entire spectrum of women's politics at specific historical
moments, over time and across societies. This approach must incorporate
theoretical and historiographical insights at varying levels of specificity,
some derived from – and germane to – studies of maternalism, others not.
We need to ask some general questions about periodization and about
the nature of political as well as cultural regimes that proved more or less
congenial to the rise of maternalism. How important were the emergence
of civil society and the presence of classical liberal values? Were certain
religions, e.g. Protestantism, more hospitable than others, e.g. Catholi-
cism? How did the modern European and North American maternalisms
of the late nineteenth and early twentieth centuries differ from those of

societies like mid-nineteenth-century Russia, where Adele Lindenmeyr has identified something she labels 'imperial maternalism', or early modern France, where Katherine Lynch has discovered the roots of what she calls 'a recognizable tradition of maternalism'? And was maternalism a uniquely Western phenomenon, or can we find similar discourses and movements in other parts of the world?[41]

Finally, going beyond maternalism – and feminism – what are we to make of movements concerned with the politics of family life that were neither initiated by female reformers nor exclusively concerned with mothers and children, but also with fathers and fatherhood? Surveying such instances, one group of scholars, led by Lynne Haney, a sociologist of Eastern Europe, and Lisa Pollard, a historian of modern Egypt, have called for another, more generic term – 'familialism'. Their concept extends well beyond maternalism to include regimes in which 'actual familial norms and principles constituted the political structure and elite', or in which 'the family, whether literal or figurative, was often a convenient vehicle for other agendas'.[42] This broader scope raises the question of the relationship between maternalism and familialism. Should maternalism be considered a subcategory of familialist ideologies, as Laura Lovett has suggested?[43]

A related but different set of questions arises when we turn to the discourses of motherhood being deployed nowadays. Should they be considered maternalist or neo-maternalist? Do such ideologies make political sense in today's post-feminist environment? Consideration of historical cases suggests that maternalist strategies are most likely to succeed when there is a cultural as well as a structural 'fit' between the ideology, its agents and its political context. The newer discourses have emerged in response to the crisis produced by the growing need for social provisions such as child care and elder care as female employment increases, on a collision course with neo-liberal efforts to reduce and restructure welfare states.[44] How well can we expect maternalist discourses to 'perform' under such conditions?

Not well, in the view of sociologist Ann Shola Orloff. In a provocative essay, Orloff argues that the current shift toward policies designed to encourage employment for all, including mothers, has affected gender politics as well:

> Notably, 'maternalist' arguments are on the decline among advocates of women's equality, and political claims based on mothering are meeting less popular and elite approval. This is not to say that 'motherhood' has lost its cultural support and resonances, simply that making claims on the state for resources and recognition on the basis of motherhood, or care, is more difficult, and in some cases, politically impossible.[45]

Orloff's bold assertions may not be entirely accurate. For one thing, political claims based on mothering seem to be proliferating, not declining, at present – at least in the United States. A recent article in *Time* noted the persistence of 'Ma Power', citing groups such as MomsRising ('working together to build a family-friendly America') and The Mothers Movement Online ('Resources and Reporting for mothers and others who think about social change').[46] Motherhood claims have also proliferated in electoral politics of late. On Mother's Day 2006, Senator Hillary Clinton announced that she would soon be launching a website called Moms for Hillary.[47] Such a step on the part of Clinton, who is well known for her finely tuned political instincts, indicated that she, for one, believed that maternalist arguments were not out of synch with the current climate. The results of the Democratic presidential primary revealed, however, that they were not sufficient to win her the nomination. But that did not deter Republican vice-presidential candidate Sarah Palin from picking up on the motherhood motif, comparing her fierceness to that of a 'mama grizzly' protecting her young.

While Palin's invocations of motherhood seem to be more or less rhetorical, the new progressive movements make concrete claims for two types of claims based on motherhood: those for reform in areas *other than motherhood* (such as improving the environment) and those for state resources *for motherhood*. It is important to distinguish between the two. The persistence of the first type affirms Orloff's assertion about the ongoing cultural resonance of motherhood. With regard to the second, Orloff may also be right: in the current political climate, such claims-making is 'difficult, and in some cases, politically impossible'. But this does not mean that discussion of these issues has abated. For at least a decade now, scholars and activists of all political stripes have been looking for ways to address the 'care deficit' produced by increased maternal employment in the face of neo-liberal inattention to social provision and policies. Feminists have focused on broadening the issue by de-coupling it from women alone. Thus, while acknowledging the historical association between women and motherhood, many prefer to use the more generic term 'caring' to refer to the *content* of motherhood without perpetuating the gendered link. Most call for some sort of public recognition of caring as work, but they differ on questions of how it should be structured and who should perform it. Conservative women, in contrast, have attempted to defend private motherhood from what they see as the triple onslaughts of feminism, the labour market and the state.

One feminist position was marked out by Nancy Fraser in her 1997 'postindustrial thought experiment', which calls for a 'caregiver parity model' in which caring and non-caring work are divided equitably among both women and men. Fraser's scheme is closely allied to Trudie Knijn's and Monique Kremer's proposal for state support for caring work in the form of 'time to care' – also gender-neutral.[48] Another stance was that of the Women's Committee of 100/Project 2002, a group of American feminist academics, activists and professionals who, in the face of what they perceived as draconian welfare reform measures, issued an 'Immodest Proposal: Rewarding Women's Work to End Poverty' that called for a state-funded 'caregivers' allowance', calculated along a sliding scale, for all those who provide care, whether for children, elders, the ill or the disabled. Under this policy, recipients could choose either to purchase services or provide the care themselves.[49]

Conservative women have taken the opposite tack. Through the contemporary 'mothers-at-home' movement, they have sought to gain recognition and (presumably non-public) support for women who choose to remain at home and care for their children and other family members full time.[50] While the rhetoric of this movement bears some resemblance to that of the 1970s Wages for Housework campaign, which was regarded as quite radical in its day, the current version is distinctly anti-feminist. It ignores both economic conditions as well as policies such as welfare reform that bar poor and low-income women from exercising a 'right to care'.[51]

Let us consider all of these positions from two perspectives, the historiographical and the political. Asking which, if any, of these initiatives should be considered maternalist or neo-maternalist not only helps us to understand their own dynamics but also sharpens our conceptualization of maternalisms of the past.

In contrast to earlier examples, contemporary discussions of the 'work–family dilemma' do not reflect the efforts of a disenfranchised female elite seeking to empower itself at the expense of a subordinate class of women. This is, of course, not surprising, given the advent of second-wave feminism and of left-wing identity politics in general, both of which have sharply criticized such hierarchies. With the exception of the 'Immodest Proposal', all have been self-generated by the 'client' group, and even in the case of the Women's Committee of 100, where advocates and client groups were not identical (the group worked in coalition with welfare rights groups), the elite's political rights were not at issue. Notably, however, an advertisement opposing welfare reform run by the group in 1996 that sought to invoke a cross-class, cross-race identification between elite women and welfare recipients stirred little response on the part of either group.

A second difference is the gender assignment of responsibility for care. Fraser as well as Knijn and Kremer argue for its more equitable distribution between the sexes. The Immodest Proposal was also intended to be gender-neutral, though it tended to be interpreted as implicitly aimed at women, and specifically at women of colour. It did, however, expose the inequity of assigning care work to women without simultaneously providing them with adequate support. Only the mothers-at-home movement fully accepts (and celebrates) women's more or less exclusive assignment to motherhood, often in an unquestioning manner that ignores ways in which race and class deprive many women of the option of caring.[52] Interestingly, none of these discourses claim that mothers performed a service to the state. Nevertheless, all except the mothers-at-home advocates assume that the state owes caregivers some sort of support.

While this quick comparison reveals certain similarities between more recent discussions of motherhood and those we might now call 'classical' or 'traditional' maternalisms, it is clear that there are also significant differences, such as the absence of the element of elite empowerment at the expense of 'others', insistence (except among the mothers-at-home) on a re-gendering or de-gendering of caring work, and an acceptance, albeit with reservations, of maternal employment. If we want to use the term 'neo-maternalist', then these would be its hallmarks. But given the significant overtones of feminism in such discourses, perhaps it would be more accurate to think of them as an updated form of social justice feminism.

Labels notwithstanding, it appears that neo-liberal policies and welfare state regimes, rather than discouraging a politics based on motherhood, as Orloff suggests, may have actually incited it. Debating ways to address the care deficit and the difficulties of 'reconciling work and family' has drawn attention to the critical condition of motherhood and served as a mobilizing point for a new generation of mothers. Moreover, though making claims on the neo-liberal state for resources to support motherhood may be futile, this has not undermined motherhood's cultural resonance, but, if anything, revalorized it, providing a rhetorical platform for other types of claims.[53]

If, as Lisa Brush has quipped, maternalism has often served as 'feminism for hard times', then perhaps advocacy for an equitable division of caring work can serve as 'maternalism for postfeminist times'.[54] But even with its gender sleight of hand, policies to support caring work face tough going in the current climate of neo-liberal restructuring. Until gender redistribution is accomplished and states establish generous programmes of public support and services, it appears that caring work will remain women's responsibility. Thus, even as they seek to reorganize caring work, today's advocates – whatever scholars call them or they choose to call themselves – share a core set of values with their maternalist predecessors.

Notes

My thanks to the anonymous readers of this manuscript for their challenging comments.

1. J. Aldrich et al. 1991. 'Chemistry vis à vis Maternalism in Lace Bugs (*Heteroptera Tingidae*): Alarm Pheromones and Exudate Defense in Corythucha and Gargaphia Species', *Journal of Chemical Ecology* 17(11), 2307–22.
2. S. Koven and S. Michel. 1990. 'Womanly Duties: Maternalist Politics and the Origins of Welfare States in France, Germany, Great Britain, and the United States, 1880–1920', *American Historical Review* 95(4), 1079. In the collection we subsequently edited, we added the cases of Sweden and Australia to those discussed in this article, but the time frame remained more or less the same. Idem (eds). 1993. *Mothers of a New World: Maternalist Politics and the Origins of Welfare States*, New York and London: Routledge.
3. L.Y. Weiner. 1993. 'Introduction and Comment' in 'Maternalism as a Paradigm: Defining the Issues', *Journal of Women's History* 5(2), 96.
4. M. Ladd-Taylor. 1993. 'Toward Defining Maternalism in U.S. History', ibid., 110.
5. Ibid.
6. E. Boris. 1993. 'What about the Working of the Working Mother?', *Journal of Women's History* 5(2), 104.
7. Ibid. See also, for example, G. Mink. 1995. *The Wages of Motherhood: Inequality in the Welfare State, 1917–1942*, Ithaca, NY: Cornell University Press; J.L. Goodwin. 1997. *Gender and the Politics of Welfare Reform: Mothers' Pensions in Chicago, 1911–1929*, Chicago: University of Chicago Press.
8. That is, the poor were portrayed in such as way that they came to symbolize a specific condition or state that, within the ideology of maternalism, necessitated middle-class women's ministrations and activism on their behalf. The term 'cultural work' is from J. Tompkins. 1986. *Sensational Designs: The Cultural Work of American Fiction, 1790–1860*, New York: Oxford University Press.
9. P. Wilkinson. 1999. 'The Selfless and the Helpless: Maternalist Origins of the U.S. Welfare State', *Feminist Studies* 25(3), 590; in this and the following quotation from Wilkinson, italics are in the original.
10. Ibid., 591. For a discussion of a similar process earlier in the nineteenth century, see S. Michel. 1994–95. 'Dorothea Dix, or the Voice of the Maniac', *Discourse* 17(2), 2.
11. Wilkinson, 'The Selfless and the Helpless', 592. For a somewhat different but also compelling interpretation of the relationship between maternalists and the poor, see Berteke Waaldijk's chapter in this volume.
12. R.G. Thomson. 1996. 'Benevolent Maternalism and Physically Disabled Figures: Dilemmas of Female Embodiment in Stowe, Davis and Phelps', *American Literature* 68(3), 555–86.
13. Ibid., 562.
14. Wilkinson, 'The Selfless and the Helpless', 592. Both Thomson's and Wilkinson's analyses raise another interesting point: whether the kind of agency being sought by maternalist activists fit the conception of the 'idealized liberal self' or, in its emphasis on collectivity, represented something different. My thanks to Robyn Muncy for raising this issue.
15. On women's role, see Michel, 'Dorothea Dix, or the Voice of the Maniac'. On changes in services for the disabled, see S. Koven. 1994. 'Remembering and Dismemberment: Crippled Children, Wounded Soldiers, and the Great War in Great Britain', *American Historical Review* 99(4), 1167–202; D. Cohen. 2001. *The War Come Home: Disabled Veterans in Britain and Germany, 1914–1939*, Berkeley: University of California Press; and S.F. Rose. 2008. 'No Right to Be Idle: The Invention of Disability, 1880–1930', Ph.D. diss., University of Illinois at Chicago.
16. *Oxford American Dictionary*, 1980, 489; quoted in Weiner, 'Introduction and Comment', 98.
17. For a different perspective on this point, see Berteke Waaldijk's chapter in this volume.

18. Boris, 'What about the Working of the Working Mother?' See also L. Gordon. 1991. 'Black and White Visions of Welfare: Women's Reform Activisms, 1890–1945', *Journal of American History* 78(2), 559–90; E.B. Higginbotham. 1993. *Righteous Discontent: The Women's Movement in the Black Baptist Church, 1880–1920*, Cambridge, MA: Harvard University Press. Deborah G. White suggests that, while class clearly divided black women reformers from their clients, all shared an understanding of black women's need for paid employment. D.G. White. 1999. *Too Heavy a Load: Black Women in Defense of Themselves, 1884–1994*, New York: W.W. Norton.

19. E. Boris and S.J. Kleinberg. 2003. 'Mothers and Other Workers: (Re)Conceiving Labour, Maternalism, and the State', *Journal of Women's History* 15(3), 90–117; E.B. Brown. 1989. 'Womanist Consciousness: Maggie Lena Walker and the Independent Order of St. Luke', *Signs* 14(3), 610–33.

20. A. van Drenth and F. de Haan. 1999. *The Rise of Caring Power: Elizabeth Fry and Josephine Butler in Britain and the Netherlands*, Amsterdam: Amsterdam University Press, 17–18.

21. Ibid., 19.

22. Ibid., 166. Compare this interpretation with that of Waaldijk in this volume.

23. Ladd-Taylor, 'Toward Defining Maternalism in U.S. History', 111.

24. A.T. Allen. 1993. 'Maternalism in German Feminist Movements', *Journal of Women's History* 5(2), 99.

25. K. Offen. 1988. 'Defining Feminism: A Comparative Historical Approach', *Signs* 14(1), 119–57.

26. K.K. Sklar. 1993. 'The Historical Foundations of Women's Power in the Creation of the American Welfare State, 1830–1930', in Koven and Michel, *Mothers of a New World*, 43–93; K.K. Sklar, A. Schüler and S. Strasser (eds). 1998. *Social Justice Feminists in the United States and Germany: A Dialogue in Documents, 1885–1933*, Ithaca, NY: Cornell University Press.

27. K. Uno. 1993. 'Maternalism in Modern Japan', *Journal of Women's History* 5(2), 126–30.

28. Allen, 'Maternalism in German Feminist Movements', 99–100.

29. A. Kessler-Harris. 1995. 'Designing Women and Old Fools: The Construction of the Social Security Amendments of 1939', in L.K. Kerber, A. Kessler-Harris and K.K. Sklar (eds), *U.S. History as Women's History*, Chapel Hill: University of North Carolina, 87–106.

30. J. Adams and T. Padamsee. 2001. 'Signs and Regimes: Rereading Feminist Work on Welfare States', *Social Politics* 8(1), 1–23.

31. Ibid., 14.

32. L. Althusser. 1972. 'Ideology and Ideological State Apparatuses', in idem, Ben Brewster (trans.), *Lenin and Philosophy and Other Essays*, New York and London: Monthly Press Review, 127–86; and Adams and Padamsee, 'Signs and Regimes', 13.

33. Wilkinson, 'The Selfless and the Helpless', 583.

34. See, for example, K. Mead. 2000. 'Beneficent Maternalism: Argentine Motherhood in Comparative Perspective, 1880–1920', *Journal of Women's History* 12(3), 120–45.

35. T. Skocpol. 1992. *Protecting Soldiers and Mothers: The Political Origins of Social Policy in the United States*, Cambridge, MA: Harvard University Press, 37.

36. For a critique of Skocpol's distinction between states, which is based on definitions of maternalism and paternalism, see van der Klein, this volume.

37. An excellent starting point for this effort would be G. Esping-Andersen. 1990. *The Three Worlds of Welfare Capitalism*, Princeton: University of Princeton Press. Though much criticized by feminists (for a cogent critique, see J. Lewis. 1992. 'Gender and the Development of Welfare Regimes', *Journal of European Social Policy* 2[3], 159–73), Esping-Andersen's discussion of how specific welfare state regimes develop and remain relatively coherent over time is essential to our understanding of the process. To a certain extent, he answers his critics in G. Esping-Andersen, with Duncan Gallie, Anton Hemerijck, and John Myles, 2002. *Why We Need a New Welfare State*, New York: Oxford University Press.

38. See S. Pedersen. 1993. *Family, Dependence, and the Origins of the Welfare State: Britain and France, 1914–1945*. Cambridge: Cambridge University Press.

39. See M. Ladd-Taylor. 1994. *Mother-Work: Women, Child Welfare, and the State, 1890–1930*, Urbana: University of Illinois Press; R. Muncy. 1991. *Creating a Female Dominion in American Reform, 1890–1935*, New York: Oxford University Press.

40. Sklar, Schüler and Strasser, *Social Justice Feminists in the United States and Germany*; and S. Michel and R. Rosen. 1992. 'The Paradox of Maternalism: Elizabeth Lowell Putnam and the American Welfare State', *Gender and History* 3(4), 364–86.

41. A. Lindenmeyr. 1993. 'Maternalism and Child Welfare in Late Imperial Russia', *Journal of Women's History* 5(2), 114–25; K.A. Lynch. 2003. *Individuals, Families, and Communities in Europe, 1200–1800: The Urban Foundations of Western Society*, New York: Cambridge University Press, 2003. For one non-Western example, see M. Pernau. 2008. 'Veiled Associations: The Muslim Middle Class and Colonial Power in India', in K. Hagemann, S. Michel and G. Budde (eds), *Civil Society and Gender Justice: Historical and Comparative Perspectives*, Oxford and New York: Berghahn Books, 2008.

42. L. Haney and L. Pollard. 2003. 'In a Family Way: Theorizing State and Familial Relations', in idem (eds), *Families of a New World: Gender, Politics, and State Development in a Global Context*, New York: Routledge, 4.

43. L. Lovett. 2000. 'Land Reclamation as Family Reclamation: The Family Ideal in George Maxwell's Reclamation and Resettlement Campaign', *Social Politics* 7(1), 80–100.

44. For an important discussion of the policies emerging from this conjuncture, see R. Mahon. 2002. 'Child Care: Toward What Kind of Social Europe?' *Social Politics* 3(9), 343–79.

45. A.S. Orloff. 2006. 'From Maternalism to "Employment for All": State Policies to Promote Women's Employment across the Affluent Democracies', in Jonah Levy (ed.), *The State After Statism: New State Activities in the Age of Liberalization*, Cambridge, MA: Harvard University Press.

46. H. Barovick. 'Ma Power', *Time*, 15 May 2006. Retrieved 29 January 2011 at http://www.time.com/time/archive/preview/0,10987,1191842,00.html. See also www.momsrising.org and www.mothersmovement.org.

47. E-mail message from Hillary Clinton to supporters, 12 May 2006.

48. N. Fraser. 1997. *Justice Interruptus: Critical Reflections on the 'Postsocialist' Condition*, New York: Routledge, 1997; T. Knijn and M. Kremer. 1997. 'Gender and the Caring Dimension of Welfare States: Toward Inclusive Citizenship', *Social Politics* 4(3), 328–61; S. Michel. 2000. 'Claiming the Right to Care', in M.H. Meyer (ed.), *Care Work: Gender, Labor, and the Welfare State*, New York: Routledge, 37–44; and Women's Committee of 100/Project 2002, 'An Immodest Proposal: Rewarding Women's Work to End Poverty'. Retrieved 29 January 2011 from http://www.wc100.org/displays.html.

49. Women's Committee of 100/Project 2002, 'An Immodest Proposal'.

50. Michel, 'Claiming the Right to Care'; and Mink, *The Wages of Motherhood*.

51. See M. dalla Costa and S. James. 1975. *The Power of Women and the Subversion of the Community*, Bristol: Falling Wall Press.

52. See, for example, Adams and Padamsee, 'Signs and Regimes'; and A.S. Orloff, 'From Maternalism to "Employment for All"'.

53. A notable exception to this pattern may be seen in certain former state socialist societies, where, in the name of giving women 'a choice', welfare state regimes supporting working motherhood have been largely dismantled, while neo-liberal political economies have slowed the creation of substitute policies to promote at-home motherhood. Surprisingly, these situations have rarely given rise to neo-maternalist movements on the part of women themselves, though the rhetoric of the new states certainly embraces maternalist values, constituting what might be called 'state maternalisms'. For a compelling study of one case, see: Tatyana Teplova. 2009. *Child Care, Labour Markets and Politics: The Transformation of the Russian Welfare State*, Saarbrücken: VDM Verlag.

54. L.D. Brush. 1996. 'Love, Toil, and Trouble: Motherhood and Feminist Politics', *Signs* 21(2), 431.

CHAPTER 3

THE STATE, THE WOMEN'S MOVEMENT AND MATERNITY INSURANCE, 1900–1930
A Dutch Maternalism?

Marian van der Klein

The Netherlands is internationally known as a country where the partici-pation of women in the labour market was rather low prior to 1970.[1] Un-til well into the twentieth century, roughly one-quarter of the registered workforce was female, and about one-quarter of all adult women were registered as performing paid labour. In the course of the twentieth cen-tury, Dutch society became increasingly geared to male breadwinners.[2] Both before and after World War II, confessional governments, Protes-tants and Catholics, whose breadwinner principles were supported by the Social Democrats, attempted to ban women from the labour market and to encourage them to serve as homemakers, yet without providing fi-nancial support for mothers.[3] The reigning tax system and social security arrangements implicitly discouraged married women's employment. In general, post-war society saw women as mothers.

In light of this history, it is understandable that the Dutch version of the so-called 'second feminist wave' was not very keen to put forward motherhood as a positive progressive social force. The company in which they would have found themselves was rather conservative. Any attempt to use motherhood to advance women's status appeared to reinforce an essentialized view that limited women to maternal and domestic roles.

Notes for this chapter begin on page 55.

Thus, economic independence, employment and changing gender roles seemed more appropriate vehicles for achieving women's liberation. Yet at the same time, the feminist project also sought to re-evaluate caring work: the work that mothers had been performing for centuries, feminists insisted, was valuable.[4]

This feminist ambivalence with regard to motherhood is not a particularly Dutch phenomenon. In the rest of Europe and the United States, too, the women's movements of the 1970s tended to combine a deeply rooted aversion to a deterministic, sociobiological discourse that defined women as mothers with fierce calls for greater recognition of the domestic labour that housewives and mothers performed. Western societies put mothers on a pedestal while at the same time treating them as second-class citizens. Paradoxically, all of this together served to restrict unbiased thinking on motherhood. It was only in the last decade of the twentieth century that historical and scientific interest in motherhood revived under the new rubric of 'maternalism'. American scholars who wrote about early U.S. welfare policies showed historians at least that motherhood could be a banner under which progressive change might be achieved. Foremost among these works was Theda Skocpol's *Protecting Mothers and Soldiers: The Political Origins of Social Policy in the United States*, a brilliant book that explores the lobby of the white American women's movement for social policies between 1910 and 1920.[5]

Skocpol and the Paradigm Shift

Skocpol shows how and why the women's movement in the United States managed to achieve so much more with its campaign for the interests of mothers and children than did the labour movement, which campaigned for social insurance for workers. The concerted efforts of the General Federation of Women's Clubs, the National Congress of Mothers and the Women's Christian Temperance Union – all middle-class women's organizations – resulted in the establishment of mothers' pensions in numerous states (1911–13), the founding of the Children's Bureau (1912) and the passage of the Sheppard-Towner Act (1921). The mothers' pensions were state-controlled, regular benefits for impoverished – often widowed – mothers with dependent children. The Children's Bureau was financed by the federal government. It registered as many births as possible, as well as the socioeconomic situation of the mother and child. The aim was to improve maternal and child health and to reduce infant mortality in the United States, which was quite high compared to other industrialized nations. The Bureau, run by well-educated and reform-minded women, in turn successfully lobbied for the Sheppard-Towner Infancy and Maternity Protection Act. This federal law required states to provide expectant mothers with health information and support from professionally trained nurses.

Skocpol states that the American women's movement in the early twentieth century was a maternalist movement, though she does not precisely define the term. This maternalist women's movement managed to capitalize on the opportunities that the middle-class doctrine of the separate spheres offered women at a time when they still lacked the right to vote. Women's responsibility for the domestic domain formed the basis of their success in obtaining social and political power in the public domain.

Skocpol was not the only one to research maternalism: Seth Koven, Sonya Michel, Kathryn Kish Sklar, Joanne Goodwin and Molly Ladd-Taylor were among those who also investigated the successful fight for mothers' pensions in the United States.[6] Internationally, they gathered a following: everywhere in the Western world, historians, political scientists and sociologists began to study so-called maternalist pressure groups. Although every scholar defines maternalism differently, the concept has become central to the interpretation of social politics.[7] In the process, assessments of maternalist politics, with its appreciation for motherhood in both the public and in the private sphere, have also undergone tremendous changes. Whereas second-wave feminism, with its outspoken critique of mandatory motherhood, tended to dismiss the maternalist women's movement as trapped in the assumptions of a patriarchal society, we can now look at this type of movement from a new perspective and describe and analyse it much more in terms of agency, reform and empowerment. Likewise, whereas state expenditures on women with children were previously viewed with deep scepticism – as providing a mere pittance to keep women slaving away at home while men went out to work – there is now room to interpret such expenditures differently. For example, it is possible to reassess such benefits in regard to population policy, or from the interests of those concerned, or in terms of the implications for women's role in the public sphere, and by extension their status as citizens. In other words, the American authors have made possible a paradigm shift in the field of the history of women and the welfare state. They have given us a new perspective on the development of welfare states and on women's movements.

In this article I apply this new perspective to the history of the Netherlands between 1900 and 1930. I concentrate on women's contributions to the public debate about *moederschapszorg* (maternity provisions and mothers' aid) that took place in roughly the same period at stake in the literature on the United States. In the Dutch discussion about care for mothers, the emphasis was on maternity insurance: the debate concerned a nationally organized, compulsory maternity provision. The first maternity benefit in the Netherlands was embedded in the Health Act of 1929, which provided insurance for workers and came into effect in 1930.[8] After briefly reviewing its significance, I discuss the new approach to welfare states that Skocpol and other scholars initiated and the complications involved in drawing international comparisons. I argue that attempts to label states 'maternalist' or 'paternalist' are highly problematic, and that it is more useful to think about maternalism as a historical manifestation of feminism that: (1) promoted progressive reform; (2) stood up for the interests of mothers; (3) held that mothers performed a service to the state by raising citizen-workers;[9] and (4) motivated the participation of women in the public debate through the doctrine of social motherhood. I then proceed with a study of the possibilities for maternalism in the Dutch context by surveying the involvement of various Dutch women's organizations that expressed competing views on mothers' interests and rights. In searching for a Dutch maternalism, I stress the importance of surrounding discourses.

Maternity Insurance in the Health Act: A Brief Overview

The maternity insurance of 1929 was the first form of financial *moederschapszorg* (maternity care) that the Dutch state offered to women. Articles 39.3 and 39.4 of the Health Act defined the benefits connected with delivery and lying-in. The beneficiaries were entitled to treatment by a midwife or a doctor and to 100 per cent of their previously earned income for twelve weeks. For the first time, the state compensated the compulsory but unpaid maternity leave of female industrial workers. With the Labour Act of 1889, the Dutch state had prohibited women from performing paid work during the four weeks prior to giving birth. In 1919 it expanded the period to four weeks following delivery as well. It took forty years before compensation was provided for this gendered loss of income, but from 1930 onwards, the state provided benefits to individual women for pay lost due to maternity.

Analysing the Health Act in terms of class, ethnicity, gender and marital status raises the following issues. The maternity benefit was paid only to married female workers with an income of under 3,000 guilders a year. Only some eight hundred women per year benefited from this arrangement. In a population of a little less than 8 million, including roughly 1,850,000 women of childbearing age, only an estimated 50,000 to 60,000 women were insured. These employed married women lived and, more importantly, worked mostly in the Netherlands. Nearly all were white. No Health Act applied to their counterparts in the overseas colonies (the Dutch Indies, Surinam and the Dutch Antilles). Within national borders in the narrowest sense, the colour, ethnicity and nationality of female workers did not affect their eligibility. But the few Surinamese or Indian women who received benefits from 1930 onwards were exceptions.[10]

There are many ways of analysing this arrangement. In terms of welfare history, it may be noted that within the Health Act, the maternity paragraph was anomalous in important respects. For example, it was the only paragraph that distinguished between married and unmarried insurance holders, and the only one that entitled beneficiaries to 100 instead of 80 per cent of their previous income. In terms of gender roles, it should be noted that this benefit was seen as maternity care; fatherhood apparently was not perceived as requiring any similar investment in care or time. One might attempt to assess the emancipatory effects of the maternity clause in the Health Act on women's economic independence, for example, or by comparing the result with the preceding situation. Did the Health Act improve or worsen the situation of (expectant) mothers in the Netherlands? One might attribute significance to the maternity benefit in the Health Act in regard to notions of the female body, reproduction, evolution and biology. Or one could try to characterize this arrangement as paternalist (because only married women were entitled) or maternalist (because it generated money for mothers) and compare the pros and cons of this analysis with arrangements in other countries. During the last decade it has been rather popular to compare different countries in terms of paternalist and maternalist regimes. This approach, however, leads to certain problems, as I will show by reviewing some recent literature.

American Maternalism vs European Paternalism?

Skocpol, Koven and Michel use the term 'maternalist' not only to describe a social movement, but also to characterize policies, politics and even states. Skocpol is of the opinion that not only the women's movement but also American social policies around 1920 can be characterized as maternalist. In *Protecting Soldiers and Mothers*, she developed a clear dichotomy for categorizing the emerging Western welfare states of the 1920s. On the one hand, Skocpol argues that the United States was well on its way to developing a maternalist welfare state. On the other hand, she claims that Australia, New Zealand and especially Europe paved the way for a paternalist model that aimed to secure the income of male workers. Skocpol states that the United States made more provisions for mothers and children than any other nation. She compares the American situation primarily to that which pertained in Britain – where, according to Jane Lewis, the strong male breadwinner system *par excellence* was under construction[11] – and, to a lesser extent, Germany. Thus in her book, the British situation becomes a template for all of Europe.

Skocpol states that in Europe, male policymakers aimed their social policies mainly at the wellbeing of male breadwinners, and that the central goal of the first European social insurance systems was to replace lost male wages. The state initiated social insurance primarily for the registered industrial workforce (which was predominantly male) and expected these male workers to pass any possible benefits, like wages, on to their families, which were assumed to be fully dependent on them. Skocpol terms this arrangement 'paternalist' – a word that I use without wishing to invoke its traditional patronising connotations. While I assume that every set of social insurances has a directive effect on people's lives, I do not maintain that paternalist systems are necessarily more patronising than maternalist ones.

More convincing than Skocpol's European–U.S. dichotomy is the comparative approach developed by Sonya Michel and Seth Koven. They found that, surprisingly, mothers and children were better off income-wise in Germany and France in around 1914 than their American (and British) counterparts.[12] Although Britain and the United States had strong women's movements, the maternalist demands and desires they voiced seem to have rallied more support on the continent.

From the Dutch context, I can add that there is very little evidence that the United States played a leading role in maternity issues between 1900 and 1930. Contemporary Dutch publications that inventory foreign examples in maternity arrangements mention Denmark, France, Germany and Norway as favourite models. Each of those states was seen as offering a facet of maternity care worthy of adoption in the Netherlands. The British, Swiss, Italian, Spanish, Greek, Romanian and Bulgarian solutions were also discussed. Even the Mexican state of Coahuila de Zaragoza, as well as Australia and Chile, were studied.[13]

Indeed, Dutch publications and archives reveal very little evidence of inspiration from the United States in regard to mothers' aid or maternity benefits. At various points, the Protestant women's movement, the feminists of the National Bureau for Women's Labour and social benefit specialist Jochum van Bruggen, to name the most visible participants in the debate, all stressed the fact that, in the United States, little to 'nothing has been done in this field'.[14] Even those few feminists who felt that women rendered a service to the state by bearing and rearing children– a service for which they should be paid – did not point to the United States as a model.[15] In other words, the maternalist policies that Skocpol presents as so groundbreaking and influential failed to make an impression on Dutch feminists and policymakers. Perhaps Skocpol somewhat overstates the provisions for mothers in the U.S. And perhaps, following from this, the dichotomy between European paternalism and American maternalism is something of a caricature. The Dutch enthusiasm for predominantly European examples confirms Koven and Michel's thesis: in so-called paternalist states, mothers were often financially better off than in maternalist America.

International Comparison of Early Welfare States: Slippery Ground

International comparison of early welfare states is a popular and challenging project with many drawbacks and pitfalls.[16] The characterization of national insurance systems often takes place based on stereotypical – rather *too* stereotypical – images of the countries and the welfare systems involved, and scholars often do not take the time to develop a versatile approach to international research. For the post-World War II period, a plethora of comparable research and source material is available, and international comparisons are often quite successful.[17] For the pre-1940 period, however, a different situation pertains. To study that time, most scholars concentrate on legislation, especially the wording of particular acts. They tend to note large contrasts between the United States and Europe, but these are often based on previously formed models. The significance of implementation, administration, jurisprudence and even governing coalitions are often neglected, not to mention related tax legislation and other more locally organized welfare provisions. The greater the geographical scope, the more contradictory the results. The apparently inevitable preference for Britain as representative of the 'European system' does not help the accuracy of these comparisons. Often, if one pursues historical research a little further, the whole construct becomes untenable.

Koven and Michel at least draw on sources that one can compare. Their notes refer back to one of the most relevant sources on funds for mothers worldwide: the International Labour Office Studies and Reports Series M. (Social Insurance). This survey shows that mothers' pensions in the United States, regardless of large variations among different states, were intended as 'social assistance' 'to provide care in their own homes for children *deprived of the support of the father*'.[18] In other words, the mothers' pensions were mainly paid out to mothers without a male breadwinner, which is why they were often called 'widows' pensions'. In this way, they generally resemble the fundamentally paternalist arrangements for surviving relatives (a little insurance and a lot of social assistance) in Europe, for example. On further consideration, one may ask whether the emerging maternalist welfare state that Skocpol discerns was really so fundamentally different from its European counterpart. Is it possible that these mothers' pensions supported the same basic goal as the provisions designed to support the male breadwinner model? Might one argue that the United States was attempting to solve similar problems as European governments, but by focusing attention on female caregivers rather than male breadwinners?

Here it is worth mentioning an inspiring article by Alice Kessler-Harris on how national self-image can influence social policy. In 'In the Nation's Image', the author's youth in post-war Britain figures as a kind of counterpoint for comparison with pre-war America.[19] Kessler-Harris maintains that, to 'the European mind', the funding of a relatively narrow social insurance scheme appears to be a constraint on the rights of the excluded rather than a benefit for the included. Yet when I look at the pre-war Netherlands, I observe an expanding system of selected workers' insurance that had no trouble excluding certain groups while depicting the inclusion of the chosen groups as a great good. And Kessler Harris's description of the American preoccupation with notions of individual dignity, which led to reluctance to mix assistance and insurance, does not look unfamiliar. Similar arguments surfaced in Dutch debates before 1940. Moreover, participants in the European debate on poor relief and social insurance also stressed the need to distinguish between the 'right' to 'insurance' and the 'need' for 'assistance'.[20]

Kessler-Harris argues that in the American system women were seen as mothers or 'co-earners', whereas men were seen as family breadwinners. Her work links up with interpretations of the emerging American welfare state as a two-channel system featuring an assistance channel for women and an insurance channel for men.[21] Thus, from Skocpol's perspective, Kessler-Harris's interpretation of the American welfare state as based on a male breadwinner model would paradoxically place it under the heading 'paternalist'. When the labels seem so malleable in different hands, maybe it is time to consider the idea that maternal and paternal welfare *regimes* could inform each other more than we have previously assumed.

Conflicting interpretations of a similar constellation can also be found within Europe, for example, with regard to prewar France, which both Susan Pedersen and Laura Frader have examined. But whereas Pedersen discerns a parental model, with direct 'child benefits' for both men and women,[22] Frader sees a male breadwinner-oriented welfare system arising.[23] The difference in opinion here possibly originates in the fact that one makes international comparisons (Pedersen), while the other (Frader) focuses on one country only. Furthermore, both scholars use different criteria to demonstrate the presence or absence of a male-breadwinner ideology. Again, this example shows how different premises and perspectives most certainly can lead to very different conclusions.

International comparisons often take place based on the end result of other researchers. It is not always easy to come by comparable material. As noted, Koven and Michel are much more meticulous than many others in this regard. But another problem regarding maternalism surfaces in their work. The distinction they make between 'limiting' and 'redistributive' maternalist states is understandable, but at the same time serves to weaken or confuse the concept of maternalism. As they define it, a limiting maternalist state keeps women locked in their traditional gender roles, whereas a redistributive one opens up new possibilities at an economic as well a discursive level. Koven and Michel characterize Great Britain before 1918 as an example of a very limiting maternalist state, which obstructed mothers from earning an income rather than providing them with opportunities. Recall that Skocpol has labelled this kind of limiting maternalism 'paternalism'. Here again, the line between a limiting maternalist and a paternalist state becomes blurred, and the power of maternalism as a concept – its paradigmatic revolutionary quality – quickly fades away.

In summary, I find the debate as to whether pre-1940 states are maternalist or not problematic. Maybe certain policies can be characterized as explicitly pro-maternal policies, and maybe certain Western states before World War II can be said to more or less favour a male breadwinner model, but that is as far as we can go on the basis of the current literature. In my opinion, the paternalist/maternalist dichotomy does not help to clarify the situation. What seems more promising is an enquiry into maternalism as a historical manifestation of feminism – a women's movement that tried, by waving the banner of motherhood, to claim and maintain a place in the public domain for women and which worked on behalf of the interests of mothers (and children). Did such a movement exist in the Netherlands?

Social Motherhood, Maternalism and Mothers' Interests

Over the past few years Dutch historians have traced several cases of what they have called the invoking of social motherhood (*sociaal* or *maatschappelijk moederschap*), collective motherhood (*collectief moederschap*, '*de grootere moederschap*') or spiritual motherhood (*geestelijk moederschap* or '*moederschap in grooten stijl*').[24] In order to gain suffrage, peace, (r)evolution, a voice in social work or anti-prostitution legislation, feminists expanded the mother-role into the public domain. As 'mothers of the new world',[25] they claimed power and authority in the public sphere, simultaneously accepting the existing gender order and seeking to broaden women's roles and rights. Certainly in the first half of the twentieth century, this kind of maternalism can be discerned in the Dutch women's movement. In this respect, it is telling that the Dutch historians Marjan Schwegman and Jolande Withuis in the Dutch edition of *A History of Women in the West* identified a shifting relationship between motherhood and the quest for citizenship. Their contribution to this prestigious publication is entitled 'Motherhood from Stepping Stone to Obstacle: Women, Nation and Citizenship in Twentieth-Century Netherlands'.[26]

But the intriguing thing is that the Dutch women's movement hardly ever used this maternalist discourse to demand social benefits for mothers. The discourse of social motherhood seems to have been more effective in addressing other interests than in meeting the needs of actual mothers. In 1907 the National Bureau for Women's Labour (NBV, *Nationaal Bureau voor Vrouwenarbeid*) – a non-governmental Bureau founded by the Dutch women's movement in 1901, using the proceeds of the 1898 National Exhibition on Women's Labour – researched Dutch welfare provisions for pregnant women and new mothers/workers. Bureau director Marie Jungius drew the following depressing conclusion:

> One wonders at the fact that women themselves so seldom make a stand for the mighty gift of motherhood, which does not seem to be sufficiently appreciated by women themselves nor by others. So far, for most women, from all walks of life, it is no more than a physical coincidence. But this lack of appreciation, among men and women both, even if in large part subconscious, does succeed in permeating the whole of our society with its adverse effects.[27]

This mindset does not seem to have changed during the subsequent two decades. Dutch women certainly busied themselves with the improvement of *moederschapszorg* (maternity provisions and mothers' aid), but they did not justify their claims to care and rights for mothers by emphasizing the 'compact doctrine'[28] of social motherhood. References to the 'mighty gift of motherhood' are remarkably absent in their contributions to the public debate about pro-maternal policies the first decades of the twentieth century. This is dramatically different from the situation that Skocpol describes in the U.S. Let us take a closer look at the Dutch situation.

Mutual Women's Assistance and the National Bureau for Women's Labour

In the Netherlands, several women's organizations concerned themselves with mothers' interests during these first decades of the twentieth century. Among the most important organizations prior to World War I were

Onderlinge Vrouwenbescherming (Mutual Women's Assistance, 1897) and the abovementioned National Bureau for Women's Labour (NBV, 1901). Mothers, especially single mothers, were also the target group for the feminist Mutual Women's Assistance (OV), which was styled after the French *Mutualité Maternelle* and sought to help single mothers without stigmatizing them. In reaction to the more condescending assistance that mostly Protestant women offered to 'fallen women' within institutions, the OV offered individual benefits. In addition, the Association formed a network to help single mothers find employment. The main principle emphasized by the OV was solidarity among all women in difficult and dangerous delivery times. With the employment and benefits, single mothers could sustain themselves and keep their children. If single mothers would be enabled to take care of themselves and their children, it would enhance their self-esteem and ameliorate their economic situation at the same time. Part and parcel of the project that the OV undertook was an attack on the double standards that Dutch society held in relation to single mothers, prostitution and sexual contact in general. Arguing that men should no longer be allowed to flee their responsibility for unwed pregnancies, the association also demanded the introduction of paternity suits. The OV combined practical assistance for women with a political struggle.[29]

The same combination can be found in the work of National Bureau for Women's Labour (NBV), although in a different area – that of women's employment and professional opportunities. The NBV organized career guidance, carried out research on the labour market, lobbied for equal opportunities and equal rights, and gathered information. They relied heavily on volunteers: only two women, the director and her assistant, were paid by the NBV. The newspaper and magazine clippings collected by the Bureau, housed at the International Information Centre and Archives for the Women's Movement in Amsterdam (IIAV, now called Aletta), are a treasure trove for anyone who wishes to know more about the women's movement in the Netherlands prior to World War II.[30]

This collection demonstrates that NBV volunteers did not concentrate on motherhood as a separate and distinct category. They did focus on delivery (which fell under the heading 'poor relief') and infant welfare (which came under 'domestic care'), but the documentation in these categories is comparatively sparse. The articles on motherhood that ended up in the NBV archives are there because of a link with labour: the Bureau's thoughts on motherhood were always related to work. Therefore, it comes as no surprise that the Bureau from early on addressed the dilemma of how to combine paid labour and care-giving. Director Jungius' text of 1907 mentions 'a double burden' on the mother/worker, which frequently 'weighs down heavily' on her and on her child.[31]

Incidentally, the only reference to mothers' pensions in the archives' inventory relates to the pension debate rather than to motherhood. In the 1920s, the NBV and a number of Members of Parliament wanted to enlarge the group of surviving relatives entitled to pensions of civil servants. Often, unmarried female civil servants provided for other family members, such as an unemployed sister who managed the housekeeping and cared for their parents. The NBV felt that such surviving relatives, like widows, should also be entitled to a pension.[32]

Between 1908 and 1936 Anna Polak, a politically liberal Jew, held sway over the Bureau. Prior to that, Marie Jungius was its managing director. In general, both women appeared more comfortable with a form of feminism that advocated equality than with the special recognition, stigmatization and separate identity on which American maternalism was based. To Polak and her supporters, a special status for women as opposed to men hindered women in their freedom of action and employment. In this respect they resembled the U.S. women to whom Linda Gordon refers in a contentious debate with Theda Skocpol. Gordon argues that Skocpol, in emphasizing maternalism, pays too little attention to equal rights feminism in the U.S.[33] Like other equal rights feminists, those in the NBV were rather flexible and pragmatic in using notions of equality and difference, as long as the aim was to improve the economic position of women.[34]

Neither the NBV nor the OV accepted the nineteenth-century gender order. In that respect they were not maternalists according to Skocpol's use of the term. Another feature that disqualifies these Dutch organizations from the label 'maternalist' as Skocpol employs it is that they did not use the discourse of social motherhood to obtain maternity care. However, they by no means avoided motherhood as a topic. For a consultancy bureau in women's employment, the NBV was rather active in the lobby for maternity care. Between 1905 and 1930 Jungius and Polak took part in the national and international debate. They conducted research and published their results and opinions in six large pieces for Dutch magazines and newspapers.[35] Although it was not the focus of their Bureau, the NBV women considered motherhood as the *condition humaine* of a large group of women. In the public arena, the NBV and the OV spoke on behalf of mothers and defended mothers' interests – each from their own perspective – in the political debate. Seen from that point of view, I might call them progressive maternalists, although NBV directors like Jungius and Polak probably would have raised their eyebrows at this characterization, given that their main concern was paid work.

In any case, in their publications about maternity care, one can clearly see a narrowing scope over the course of time. At first the NBV argued that maternity provisions should be made available to *all* expectant mothers of little means. Maternity provision in general was their aim. In 1907 Marie Jungius wrote that 'motherhood was a job like any other' and argued that a special Maternity Act should provide different groups of mothers what they needed to do their job. In 1921 Polak made a distinction between working mothers and housewife mothers. She argued that the former should receive premium-free compensation of the compulsory pregnancy leave and that the latter should be able to insure themselves voluntarily against 'the extra costs delivery, lying-in, nappy baskets and the lactation period entailed'. But by 1929 the Bureau ended up more and more on the defensive, trying to save what they thought of as a little piece of maternity care for a very small group of working women. This moderation of demands had to do with the development of dominant surrounding discourses. For the NBV, the bottom line was that the state had to remove the barrier it had put up for working mothers since 1889: the compulsory, but unpaid, pregnancy leave had to be compensated. But, as we will see, even this relatively modest goal was hard to achieve at the end of the 1920s.

Ann Taylor Allen, a specialist in German history, argues that we should stop judging maternalism in teleological or contemporary ways.[36] Instead, she favours studying women's movements within their own discursive contexts. The Dutch story seems to prove her case. In the second decade of the twentieth century, the call for maternity provisions had become increasingly embedded in a debate about social benefits and a political discourse concentrating on social insurance. The NBV was not the only organization that had to adapt to this change: all others concerned with maternity provision in the Netherlands remodelled their ideas as well. Frida Katz, the spokeswoman of the Protestant part of the Dutch women's movement, for example, abandoned her attempts to lobby for a maternity insurance for the wives of male workers.

Maternity Insurance for Working Women: The Importance of Surrounding Discourse

Between 1910 and 1930 the debate about welfare legislation in the Netherlands was dominated by the issue of the Health Act. In 1913 the Protestant Minister Talma had managed to formulate a programme concerning industrial workers' insurance. His Health Act included a maternity benefit for women workers. With contributions of employers and workers, the state would provide paid maternity leave and medical assistance for single and married new mothers. No provision was included for the wives of male workers. The Act was accepted by the States General, but the programme was not implemented because of conflicts about the nature of the implementing bodies. Socialists, Liberals, Protestants and Catholics endlessly discussed the role of the state, employers and trade unions in the making and managing of this and future social security arrangements.[37]

In this context, the attention was drawn from the content of the provisions to the moment of implementation. With Talma's programme, the package of measures had already been set, and it was only a matter of when the provisions would be adopted. For the Dutch women's movement, little discursive space remained for promoting a broader pro-maternal agenda. Some individual women made tentative suggestions, but compensation for wet nursing, mothers' wages or mothers' pensions were politically out of the question in the Netherlands.[38] The Dutch version of mothers' aid that emerged was one of social insurance for maternity leave designed for industrial women workers.

This focus on maternity care for women doing paid labour was strengthened in 1919 when the first International Labour Conference held in Washington adopted an important draft Convention concerning the employment of women before and after childbirth. Again the issue of *moederschapszorg* was discussed in the narrow terms of workers' interests. Besides an employment ban during pregnancy and delivery, this Convention also contained the clause that mothers should receive compensation for lost wages during the weeks that they were banned from working. This benefit had to be sufficient for the mother's own maintenance and that of the child under proper hygienic circumstances. Furthermore, women were entitled to treatment by a doctor or midwife, free of charge.[39]

On the eve of the Conference the Dutch National Bureau for Women's Labour had lobbied for 'a premium-free compensation from the State'.[40] In order to achieve this, the Bureau wrote to the preparatory Committee in London and to all delegates and female advisors, various trade union congresses and the domestic social-democratic women's organizations. But the efforts were in vain. As for the draft Convention adopted in Washington, each country that ratified it was free to determine the amount of compensation and also whether this compensation would be obtained from public funding or through an insurance system. In the Netherlands the question was already settled in favour of a contributory insurance system.

In the national discussion, Dutch politicians made frequent reference to the draft Convention. Socialists and some Liberals tried to put pressure on the confessional governments (Protestants and Catholics) to ratify the Convention. But the confessionals were in power (they held more than 50 of the 100 seats in parliament), so no progress was made. Catholic

delegation member Van Thienen had already stated in his ILO-Confer-
ence report in 1920 that he considered Washington a 'rather far-reaching'
agreement.[41] The Convention applied not only to industrial but also to
trade companies; it provided for a leave of absence for one half-hour twice
a day if a mother was nursing her baby; and it did not distinguish between
married and unmarried women and legitimate and illegitimate children.
This last provision in particular was hard for the Dutch confessional parties to stomach. In 1929, during the parliamentary debate about the revision of Talma's Health Act, they seized the opportunity to debate maternity benefits for single mothers and proposed an amendment to exclude
unmarried mothers from the motherhood paragraph. Again the scope of
the debate about mothers' aid was narrowed. Thus, what Dutch feminists
at first had intended as a premium-free compensation for all women was
limited to social insurance for industrial workers, and then further limited
to cover married industrial women workers only.

The Parliamentary Debate of 1929:
Dominance of Catholic and Protestant Voices

In his draft of the revision of the Health Act, the responsible Protestant
Minister Slotemaker de Bruïne did not exclude single mothers from the
benefits of the Health Act. Like their married sisters, they were to receive
100 per cent of their previously earned wages for twelve weeks around delivery. It was the Roman Catholic Member of Parliament Piet Aalberse who
introduced the particular amendment excluding unmarried women, while
at the same time proposing to reserve more money for the ecclesiastical and
philanthropic institutions that cared for single mothers up until then.[42]

The Catholic and Protestant women's movement fervently supported
Aalberse's idea. They believed that providing benefits to unmarried wom-
en was a 'violation of the deep moral and social significance of marriage'
that could result in a 'subversion of the moral awareness' of the Dutch
population. State and society could not tolerate immoral behaviour, they
argued, and parliament had to protect family life. In their letter to parliament, the women stressed that they were not merciless: they did not in-
tend to leave single mothers to their own devices, but rather to have them
cared for and looked after by established institutions with experience in
such matters. In other words, they argued that government funds would
be better spent on the philanthropic institutions of the parties signing the
letter than on individual single mothers themselves.[43]

If any group in the Dutch debate about mothers' aid and maternity
provisions can be called maternalist in the way that Sonya Michel defines

maternalism in this volume, it was this coalition of Protestant and Catholic women's organizations and institutions, which had traditionally provided moralistic and condescending help to young girls and single mothers. But in contrast to the U.S., this Dutch coalition was rather conservative and interested in marriage, family life and moral purity rather than in mothers themselves or in social motherhood.

The confessional women's movement had entered the public debate about maternity provisions around 1920, right after World War I and right after Dutch women acquired the vote (1917 passive; 1919 active). It certainly advocated pro-maternal policies. In particular, the role of juriste Frida Katz, founder of the *Nederlandsche Christen-Vrouwenbond* (the Dutch Christian Women's League), should be noted.[44] But such women promoted pro-maternal policies within the constraints of the existing gender order. Their intention, for example, was not to get more women in the administration and management of the hospitals and institutions where single mothers could receive help, and in the parliamentary debate Katz in no way presented herself as an expert because of the fact that she was a woman. Indeed, none of the seven female MPs at the time assumed such a stance. Most of them lined up with their party, which can be read as another indication that the debate about mothers' aid was highly politicized.

A Pragmatic Approach

Of course, Mutual Women's Assistance (OV) and the National Bureau for Women's Labour (NBV) objected to the exclusion of single mothers. Polak felt that the Health Act was a professional arrangement aiming to prevent 'a reduction in prosperity'. According to OV and the NBV, moral considerations should not enter into the picture. Moreover, they argued that a government that imposed an employment ban on expectant mothers should not be allowed to hit them when they were down.[45]

In parliament, such women had support of some social liberals (*Vrijzinnig Democratische Bond*) and the whole social democratic labour party (SDAP). The spokeswomen of these parties, Wilhelmina van Itallie-van Embden and Suze Groeneweg, did what they could, stressing the practical work of OV and citing the articles of the National Bureau (NBV).[46] But their efforts were in vain. The religious parties had too great a majority in parliament. Moreover, the rescue operation for the single mothers' benefit was complicated by the lobby of Dutch employers and a rather clumsy and isolated amendment of the liberal feminist Johanna Westerman.

Westerman thought that it was wrong to incorporate such a 'blessing' as pregnancy in the Health Act.[47] In Dutch, the Health Act was called the

'Illness Act', and Westerman objected to the notion of equating childbirth with illness. Almost all feminists – and not only feminists – had objected to the incorporation of maternity care in the Health Act. Indeed, that was one of the reasons why they would have preferred to have it placed under a special Maternity Act. But by 1929, the time for revisiting this issue had passed; it was time to be pragmatic, especially given that employers adopted Westerman's argument to lobby for a cheaper Health Act.[48] Maternity benefits were relatively expensive, and getting rid of the maternity paragraph altogether would have suited the employers very much.

But in the Dutch context this would have meant leaving all mothers, even the married ones, emptyhanded. As Polak noted at the end of her 1929 article, in the Netherlands it was unrealistic to hope that maternity insurance might be attained in any way except through the Health Act. Therefore, the NBV and all the other pro-maternal participants in the debate about the Health Act (except for Westerman) adopted a pragmatic approach: they agreed that 'this hard-won piece of maternity provisions'[49] should not be allowed to be withdrawn from the law. As MP Suze Groeneweg (SDAP) stated in a glowing speech, Dutch women had been waiting long enough for compensatory measures for the employment ban.[50] Research had shown that the Netherlands were providing far too little for workers who were new mothers. In this respect, the Netherlands were 'unfortunately!' among the most backward countries in Europe. Even though Minister Aalberse, a Roman Catholic, had claimed during the first International Labour Conference in Washington in 1919 that his country was in the vanguard of civilization with regard to labour legislation, Groeneweg, Van Itallie-van Embden and Polak knew better. 'With regard to the care for working mothers,' Polak wrote, 'the Netherlands shamefully brought up the rear.'[51]

Conclusion

The German historian Gisela Bock has suggested that in the Netherlands, as in the rest of Europe, the passing of a maternity provision in the Health Act can be attributed to feminist efforts.[52] In this article I have shown that to be a case of wishful thinking. Dutch women certainly did not dominate the public debate about provisions for mothers and children. Compared to what Skocpol tells us about the United States, the women's movement in the Netherlands was rather weak in this field. Neither before nor after they got the vote were they able to control the debate, though they did not remain silent. Dutch women representing different perspectives participated in the discussion about maternity care and mothers' aid, but others set the political agenda. The dominance of Catholic and Protestant, mostly male politicians eventually resulted in a social insurance programme that covered only married women workers. Only religious women's organizations could wholeheartedly endorse this arrangement. The more progressive branches of Dutch women's movement were disappointed, though they felt they had tried to make the most out of a difficult situation.

My search for a Dutch maternalism between 1900 and 1930 has a rather complicated outcome. Maternalists (both men and women, as far as I am concerned) tried to use motherhood to improve the political status of women. But in the Dutch context, a comprehensive maternalist movement did not materialize. In the Netherlands, there were women's organizations that expanded the mother-role to gain power and authority in the public sphere. But they did not lobby specifically for mothers' interests and mothers' rights. The organization most active in this effort, the National Bureau for Women's Labour, did not justify its efforts through the discourse of social motherhood. In the public arena the NBV spoke on behalf of mothers without being condescending. The coalition of Protestant and Catholic women's organizations that became active in the 1920s did tend to employ condescending, maternalist rhetoric, but they were more concerned with the protection of marriage and family life than with mothers themselves.

In this article, maternalism has helped to illuminate the complexities of the Dutch women's movement. With regards to the characterization of welfare states, however, it has proven less useful. Analysing recent literature has led me to conclude that attempts to distinguish between paternalist and maternalist welfare states are problematic. One might instead argue that the United States and Europe attempted to solve similar problems, but starting from different angles, the former trying to support female caregivers, the latter trying to support male breadwinners. Maybe it is time to consider the idea that maternal and paternal *regimes* of welfare could inform each other more than we assumed until now.

Notes

1. J. Plantenga. 1993. *Een afwijkend patroon: honderd jaar vrouwenarbeid in Nederland en (West-) Duitsland*, Amsterdam: SUA; and idem. 1998. 'Double Lives: Labour Market, Participation, Citizenship and Gender', in J. Bussemaker, R. Voet and M.C.B. Voet (eds), *Gender, Participation and Citizenship in the Netherlands*, Brookfield, Hampshire: Ashgate, 51–65; C. van Eijl. 1994. *Het werkzame verschil: vrouwen in de slag om arbeid 1898–1940*, Hilversum: Verloren, 416–20; and idem. 1997. *Maandag tolereren we niets meer: vrouwen, arbeid en vakbeweging 1945–1990*, Amsterdam: Stichting beheer IISG, 324.
2. T. Akkerman. 1998. 'Political Participation and Social Rights: The Triumph of the Breadwinner in the Netherlands', in Bussemaker, Voet and Voet, *Gender, Participation and Citizenship*, 38–51.

3. For a non-gendered overview of the development of the Dutch welfare state, see: R.H. Cox. 1993. *The Development of the Dutch Welfare State: From Workers' Insurance to Universal Entitlement*, Pittsburgh and London: University of Pittsburgh Press.

4. M. van der Klein. 1998. *Kranig en dwars: De Vrouwenbond NVV/FNV 1948–1998*, Amsterdam: Stichting beheer IISG, 92–3.

5. T. Skocpol. 1992. *Protecting Soldiers and Mothers: The Political Origins of Social Policy in the United States*, Cambridge, MA: Harvard University Press.

6. S. Koven and S. Michel (eds). 1993. *Mothers of a New World: Maternalist Politics and the Origins of Welfare States*, New York and London: Routledge; S. Michel and R. Rosen. 1992. 'The Paradox of Maternalism: Elizabeth Lowell Putnam and the American Welfare State', *Gender and History* 4(3), 364–86; S. Michel. 1999. *Children's Interests/Mothers' Rights: The Shaping of America's Child Care Policy*, New Haven: Yale University Press; J.L. Goodwin. 1992. 'An American Experiment in Paid Motherhood: The Implementation of Mothers' Pensions in Early Twentieth-Century Chicago', *Gender and History* 4(3), 323–42 and idem. 1997. *Gender and the Politics of Welfare Reform: Mothers' Pensions in Chicago, 1911–1929*, Chicago: University of Chicago Press; and M. Ladd-Taylor. 1994. *Mother-Work: Women, Child Welfare and the State, 1890–1930*, Urbana and Chicago: University of Illinois Press.

7. For example, a forum on maternalism from the early 1990s demonstrates the range of ways in which scholars have defined the term: several authors in 1993 'Maternalism as a Paradigm', *Journal of Women's History* 5(2), 95–131.

8. *Staatsblad*, no. 329. Wet van den 24sten Juni 1929, tot wijziging der Ziektewet. (Health Act.)

9. Unlike Molly Ladd-Taylor, I view maternalism as a historical form of feminism. Nevertheless, I have adopted this point of her definition. 'Maternalism as a Paradigm', 110.

10. I would like to thank Emile Schwidder (IISH, Amsterdam) and Albert Dekker (Van Vollenhove Institute, Faculty of Law, Leiden) for information on the social insurance situation in the colonies. Ethnicity was not an official criterion for exclusion in the Netherlands, I deduce, for instance, from an appeal by two Surinamese women running a boarding house in Amsterdam.

11. J. Lewis. 1994. 'Gender, the Family and Women's Agency in the Building of "Welfare States": The British Case', *Social History* 19(1), 37–56; and idem. 1992. 'Gender and the Development of Welfare Regimes', *Journal of European Social Policy* 2(3), 159–73.

12. S. Koven and S. Michel. 1990. 'Womanly Duties: Maternalist Politics and the Origins of Welfare States in France, Germany, Great Britain, and the United States, 1880–1920', *American Historical Review* 95(4), 1076–108.

13. M. Jungius. 1907. *Wat doet Nederland voor zijn arbeidsters-kraamvrouwen?* 24–31, Amsterdam: W. Versluys; A. Polak. 1921. '"Voorbarige" wenschen', *Sociale Voorzorg* 3, 114–23; idem, 'Moederschapszorg in draught convention en voorontwerp-ziektewet', *Bijvoegsel Algemeen Handelsblad*, 16 April 1927, 6.

14. Jungius, *Wat doet Nederland voor zijn arbeidsters-kraamvrouwen?*; J. van Bruggen. 1920. 'Het probleem der moederschapverzekering', *Sociale Voorzorg* 2, 187–201; and C.F. Katz. 1920. *Moederschapszorg*, Rotterdam: Libertas. See also H.S.S. Kuyper. 1921. *Tweede reis naar Amerika: Vier weken te Washington (rondom de eerste Internationale Arbeidsconferentie)*, Amsterdam: Ten Have. The cited text is from Katz, *Moederschapszorg*, 10.

15. Around 1920, some social democratic women, like Carrie Pothuis-Smit, Mathilde Wibaut-Berdenis van Berlekom, Willemijn Mansholt-Andreae and Henriette van der Meij, and some liberal women, like Mia Boissevain-Pijnappel and Welmoed Wijnaendts Francken-Dijserinck, flirted with the idea of a mothers' wage.

16. See K.K. Sklar. 1990. 'A Call for Comparisons: Comment', *American Historical Review* 95(4), 1109–15. For the drawbacks and pitfalls see: M. van der Klein, 'How to Identify a Male-Breadwinner-Ideology? The Origins of the Dutch Welfare State', unpublished paper for the European Social Science History Conference, Amsterdam, April 2000, IISH.

17. See for example G. Esping-Andersen. 1990. *The Three Worlds of Welfare Capitalism*, Princeton: Princeton University Press; idem. 1999. *Social Foundations of Postindustrial Economies*, Oxford: Oxford University Press; J.S. O'Connor, A.S. Orloff and S. Shaver. 1999. *States, Markets, Families: Gender, Liberalism, and Social Policy in Australia, Canada, Great Britain and the United States*, Cambridge: Cambridge University Press; and M. Kremer. 2002. 'The Illusion of Free Choice: Ideals of Care and Childcare Policy in the Flemish and Dutch Welfare State', in S. Michel and R. Mahon (eds), *Child Care Policy at the Crossroads: Gender and Welfare State Restructuring*, New York: Routledge, 113–42.
18. Emphasis added. *International Survey of Social Services* 1933, Geneva, 1936 (International Labour Office. Studies and reports Series M. [Social Insurance]) no. 13, 694.
19. A. Kessler-Harris. 1999. 'In the Nation's Image: The Gendered Limits of Social Citizenship in the Depression Era', *Journal of American History* 86(3), 1251–80.
20. M. van der Klein. 2003. 'The Widows of the Gasworks: Gendered Path Dependency and the Early Dutch Welfare State', *Social Politics* 10(1), 1–25. For this problem, but connected to American exceptionalism, see also: J.W. Kooijman. 1999. *... And the Pursuit of National Health: The Incremental Strategy toward National Health Insurance in the United States of America*, Amsterdam: Rodopi Bv Editions.
21. See B.J. Nelson. 1990. 'The Origins of the Two-Channel Welfare State: Workmen's Compensation and Mothers' Aid', in L. Gordon (ed.), *Women, the State, and Welfare*, Madison: University of Wisconsin Press, 1990, 123–57; A.S. Orloff. 1991. 'Gender in Early U.S. Social Policy', *Journal of Policy History* 3(3), 249–82; L. Gordon. 1992. 'Social Insurance and Public Assistance: The Influence of Gender in Welfare Thought in the United States, 1890–1935', *American Historical Review* 97(1), 19–54.
22. S. Pedersen. 1993. *Family, Dependence, and the Origins of the Welfare State: Britain and France, 1914–1945*. Cambridge: Cambridge University Press.
23. L. Frader. 2008. *Breadwinners and Citizens: Gender in the Making of the French Social Model*, Durham, NC: Duke University Press. See also: M. van der Klein. 2000. 'Conference Report on Women, Work and Breadwinner Ideology, from the Fifteenth to the Twentieth Century', *International Labour and Working Class History* 58, 318–21.
24. P. de Vries. 1984. 'Alle vrouwen zijn moeders: Feminisme en moederschap rond de eeuwwisseling', *Socialisties-Feministiese Teksten* 8, 126–48; M. Braun, *De prijs van de liefde: De eerste feministische golf, het huwelijksrecht en de vaderlandse geschiedenis*, Amsterdam: Het Spinhuis, 93–4, 259–62; L. Bervoets. 1994. *Opvoeden tot sociale verantwoordelijkheid: De verzoening van wetenschap, ethiek en sekse in het sociaal werk in Nederland rond de eeuwwisseling*, Amsterdam: Stichting Beheer IISG; M. Mossink. 1995. *De levenbrengsters: Over vrouwen, vrede, feminisme en politiek in Nederland 1914–1940*, Amsterdam: Stichting Beheer IISG, 81–3; B. Waaldijk. 1996. *Het Amerika der Vrouw: Sekse en geschiedenis van maatschappelijk werk in Nederland en de Verenigde Staten*, Groningen: Wolters-Noordhoff; P. de Vries. 1997. *Kuisheid voor mannen, vrijheid voor vrouwen: De reglementering en bestrijding van prostitutie in Nederland 1850–1911*, Hilversum: Verloren, 119–22; and M. Huisman. 1998. 'Moederschap als metafoor: evolutiedenken in de eerste feministische golf', *Lover* 25(2), 18–22. Annemieke van Drenth and Francisca de Haan prefer the term 'caring power'. See A. van Drenth and F. de Haan. 1999. *The Rise of Caring Power: Elisabeth Fry and Josephine Butler in Britain and the Netherlands*, Amsterdam: Amsterdam University Press.
25. Koven and Michel adopted the phrase, first used by the early twentieth-century American feminist Charlotte Perkins Gilman. Koven and Michel, *Mothers of a New World*, 1993.
26. M. Schwegman and J. Withuis. 1993. 'Moederschap: van springplank tot obstakel: Vrouwen, natie, burgerschap in twintigste-eeuws Nederland', in F. Thébaud (ed.), G. Duby and M. Perrot (series eds), *Geschiedenis van de vrouw: De twintigste eeuw*, Amsterdam: Agon, 557–84.
27. Jungius, *Wat doet Nederland voor zijn arbeidsters-kraamvrouwen?*, 32.
28. D. Riley. 1988. *'Am I That Name?' Feminism and the Category of 'Women' in History*, London: Macmillan.

29. Projekt Prostitutie. 1986. 'Heb je wel gehoord van de zeven, de zeven. Onderzoek naar de
     uitspraken van zeven vrouwen over betaald en onbetaalde seksuele contacten 1890–1914',
     unpublished paper, University of Utrecht, 1986, IIAV (http://www.aletta.nu/aletta/nl),
     7–16; and E. Hueting and R. Neij. 1990. *Ongehuwde moederzorg in Nederland*, Zutphen:
     Walburg Pers, 20–21. See also the speech of Van I.-van Embden in Dutch parliament in
     1929, *Handelingen Tweede Kamer der Staten Generaal 1928/1929*, 1726.
30. The very rich archives of the NBV are in the International Information Centre and Ar-
     chives for the Women's Movement (IIAV, Amsterdam; http://www.aletta.nu/aletta/nl).
     D. Groffen. 1989. *Inventaris van de archieven van het Nationaal Bureau voor Vrouwen-
     arbeid en de Nationale Vereniging voor Vrouwenarbeid (1863) 1901–1949 (1951)*. Amster-
     dam: IIAV.
31. Jungius, *Wat doet Nederland voor zijn arbeidsters-kraamvrouwen?* 32.
32. See NBV archives (IIAV, Amsterdam; http://www.aletta.nu/aletta/nl), 794 and 785.
33. L. Gordon. 1993. 'Gender, State and Society: A Debate with Theda Skocpol', *Contention*
     2(3), 131–57; and T. Skocpol. 1993. 'Soldiers, Workers and Mothers: Gendered Identities
     in Early U.S. Social Policy', *Contention* 2(3), 157–83. See also N. Cott. 1987. *The Ground-
     ing of Modern Feminism*, New Haven: Yale University Press.
34. According to Ulla Jansz, this flexibility is a constant in Dutch first-wave feminism. See U.
     Jansz. 2000. *Denken over sekse in de eerste feministische golf*, Amsterdam: Sara/Van Gennep.
35. M. Jungius. 1905. *Wenschelijkheid en Werkelijkheid: Eene bijdrage tot de kennis van het
     leven der arbeidster-moeder*, Amsterdam: W. Versluys; idem, *Wat doet Nederland voor zijn
     arbeidsters-kraamvrouwen?* Amsterdam: W. Versluys; A. Polak, 'Vergeten belangen', *De
     Telegraaf*, 27 November 1921, 10; idem, '"Voorbarige" wenschen'; idem, 'Moederschaps-
     zorg in draught-convention en voorontwerp-ziektewet', *Bijvoegsel Algemeen Handelsblad*,
     16 April 1927, 6; and idem, 'Het ontwerp-Ziektewet bekeken van vrouwenstandpunt',
     Bijvoegsel Algemeen Handelsblad, 2 maart 1929, 10.
36. Ann Taylor Allen considers maternalism a form of feminism. A.T. Allen. 1993. 'Maternal-
     ism in German Feminist Movements', *Journal of Women's History* 5(2), 99–103.
37. I. Kuijpers and P. Schrage. 1997. 'Squaring the Circle: Unemployment Insurance in the
     Netherlands from Wage Bargaining Instrument to Compulsory Legislation, 1861–1949',
     in A. Knotter, B. Altena and D. Damsma (eds), *Labour, Social Policy and the Welfare State*,
     Amsterdam: Aksant Academic Publishers, 83.
38. See Akkerman, 'Political Participation and Social Rights', and the speeches of Katz and
     Slotemaker de Bruïne in parliament, *Handelingen Tweede Kamer der Staten Generaal
     1928/1929*, 1731.
39. League of Nations. 1920. *International Labor Conference: First Annual Meeting October
     29, 1919 – November 29, 1919*, Washington, D.C., 259, 260. For a Dutch commentary on
     this convention, see: J. van Bruggen and A. F. van Lakerveld. 1930. *De ziektewet: Handlei-
     ding voor de Praktijk*, Deventer: Kluwer, 8.
40. *Mededeelingen* and *Jaarverslag* (Annual Report) of the NBV 1918/1919, 1919/1920.
41. G.J. van Thienen, 'Beknopt verslag van het verhandelde op de Internationale Arbeidscon-
     ferentie te Washington (samengesteld door den secretaris der Nederlandsche afvaardiging)
     benevens de Nederlandsche vertaling der aangenomen ontwerpverdragen en aanbevelin-
     gen' *Maandschrift van het Centraal Bureau voor de Statistiek*. Bijvoegsel Maart 1920.
42. *Handelingen Tweede Kamer der Staten Generaal 1928/1929*, 1715.
43. Archives of the Tweede Kamer der Staten Generaal 1815–1945, Den Haag Algemeen
     Rijksarchief (ARA), 1542.
44. Katz, *Moederschapszorg*.
45. Polak, 'Vergeten belangen'; A. Polak. 1929. Archives of the Tweede Kamer der Staten
     Generaal 1815–1945, Den Haag ARA, 1311: 13 maart 1929, request Vereeniging Onder-
     linge Vrouwenbescherming.

46. *Handelingen Tweede Kamer der Staten Generaal 1928/1929*, 1725–6.
47. *Handelingen Tweede Kamer der Staten Generaal 1928/1929*, 1713.
48. Archives of de Tweede Kamer der Staten Generaal 1815–1945, Den Haag ARA, 1309: Den Haag, 19 februari 1929.
49. Polak, 'Het ontwerp-Ziektewet bekeken...' *Bijvoegsel Algemeen Handelsblad* 2 maart 1929.
50. *Handelingen Tweede Kamer der Staten Generaal 1928/1929*, 1717. Groeneweg's speech was also published: *Een eereschuld aan de moeders: Kamerrede van Suze Groeneweg gehouden op 14 maart 1929*.
51. Ibid. See also V.I.-van Embden, *Handelingen Tweede Kamer der Staten Generaal 1928/1929*, 1725; and Polak, 'Vergeten belangen'.
52. For a discussion of Talma's Health Act of 1913, which was never implemented, see G. Bock. 1994. 'Poverty and Mothers' Rights in the Emerging Welfare States', in F. Thébaud (ed.), G. Duby and M. Perrot (series eds), A. Goldhammer (trans.), *A History of Women in the West: Toward a Cultural Identity in the Twentieth Century*, Cambridge, MA: Harvard University Press.

CHAPTER 4

MOBILIZING MOTHERS IN THE NATION'S SERVICE
Civic Culture in France's Familial Welfare State, 1890–1914

Lori R. Weintrob

Mutualists of France who hear me, give us back the army corps
that we lose every year through such guilty lack of foresight.
Engerand, *progressiste* deputy, 1908[1]

In his 1903 play *Maternité*, French socialist playwright Eugène Brieux mocked the politicians and businessmen who, despite their preoccupation with the national decline in fertility, ignored the economic problems of female citizens.[2] To curry political favour, the sub-prefect Brignac hastily pledges in one scene to enact the Minister's proposal 'to see the whole of France covered with associations having the increase of the population for their object'. Yet, as an embodiment of official and bourgeois hypocrisy, Brignac pitilessly drives from his home a pregnant servant and even his wife's younger sister, both seduced and abandoned because they had no dowry. Brieux's play proposed that the government's response to depopulation was inadequate to the needs of poor mothers. Yet even as his play denounced its limits, Brieux pinpointed the strategy of prominent politicians, industrialists and civic activists in the Third Republic – not only on the issue of maternal and infant health but also on accident insurance, pensions and hygiene – to forge a partnership between the public and private voluntary sectors and thus generate a new national commitment to social citizenship. France's Third Republic did not so much 'lag behind' Germany on social policies of health, insurance and old-age schemes. Rather, this chapter argues that French policymakers used a different strategy, which, like the American and British systems, relied more on private, voluntary associations and civil society.

To create an infrastructure and consensus on social welfare reform, the leading social reformers, moderate and radical republicans known as Solidarists mobilized civic associations, including unions (*syndicats*), cooperatives, mutual aid societies (*mutualités*), and feminist and other women's groups. Of these, mutual aid societies, known collectively as the Mutuality, boasted two million members in 1900, making it the largest social movement in France, with twice as many members as the trade unions. In particular, the *mutualités maternelles* (mutual insurance societies for maternity services and benefits) were 'destined to become one of the most popular maternal and child welfare institutions'.[3] Government leaders, businessmen and feminists contributed to the transformation of these private, voluntary networks of social insurance into partners of the state. The use of this private network to create social solidarity, and particularly to fight against depopulation, is one of the most essential yet largely overlooked elements in the republican consolidation of power during the Third Republic, both in France and in its overseas colonies.[4]

Private secular institutions like the Mutuality, with their female volunteers and administrators, helped popularize solidarist ideals and practices, not only towards pre- and post-natal care, but also in regard to citizenship and social welfare. To build national solidarity and attenuate class conflict, Solidarists promoted a vision of a nation of mutually dependent individuals with social duties and obligations towards those 'at risk', from infancy to old age. The term 'solidarity' gained widespread currency through the writings and work of radical Republican statesmen, political reformer and theoretician Léon Bourgeois. Solidarist strategies of social reform employed word, deed and image to mobilize the electorate and create a 'third path' between liberalism and socialism. The public alliance with the private sector in the implementation of public healthcare, education, accident insurance and maternal and infant programmes created a welfare state that was, to use Philip Nord's term, 'republican and familist in mold'.[5] Solidarists fostered a civic culture that placed motherhood, fertility and breastfeeding on stage and in the public eye. Indeed, '[R]epublican motherhood was to provide the cornerstone of a new secular national morality', as Karen Offen has argued.[6] Moreover, during this period of intense anti-clericalism, political leaders supported the development of private, secular and scientific agencies of social protection, most notably within the Mutuality, not least because they recruited, in unprecedented numbers, women of all classes previously associated only with Catholic charities. In generating administrative responsibilities, they mobilized maternalists as diverse as the fervently pro-Dreyfusard J. Desparmet-Ruello, one of France's first female high school principals, and social Catholic philanthropist and militant feminist Marie-Louise Bérot-Berger, among others.

The strong link between motherhood and citizenship in France challenges widely accepted views on the origins of the welfare state. Standard explanations of welfare state development focus on such factors as the pace of industrialization, the strength of unions, state formation and national values; only recently have studies shed light on the importance of gender and family policy to social reform and state development.[7] France boasted the highest percentage of women active in the labour force in the Western world, 59 per cent in 1906, including 20 per cent of married women, thus anticipating later developments in other countries.[8] Depopulation and the high rates of women in the workforce were important factors in the emergence of state regulation and the rise of a discourse of the citizen-producer (to use Jane Jensen's term), both of which addressed the needs of women workers. Further, political preoccupations in France generated both legitimacy and resources for a range of public and private organizations to benefit women and children, even if, as Seth Koven and Sonya Michel have suggested, state centralization could limit women's authority.[9] The development of maternity insurance was to profoundly impact local and national political culture.

Sociologists of the contemporary French welfare state argue that its two most distinctive and effective features are familial programmes and private mutual insurance coverage.[10] Both features developed at the turn of the century and became visible in debates on maternity policies. While earlier works on the origins of the welfare state in France, particularly in relation to old age pensions, represent the Mutuality as a factor that slowed state legislation, adding gender and civil society to the equation reveals a more progressive dynamic. The flourishing of private maternity insurance and healthcare networks confirms the role of employers in social policy, as revealed in groundbreaking work by Henri Hatzfeld and François Ewald and, most recently, Susan Pedersen and Paul Dutton, who have focused on the interwar years.[11] Yet the actions of wage-earning mutualists, their political supporters and middle-class women within these health networks had already critically affected debates and practices regarding social insurance before 1914. The goal of protecting its citizens from cradle to grave meant that the family and motherhood were central to social reform. In republican ideology since the French Revolution, as Elinor Accampo argues, 'the private act of mothering took on a public function' as a civic responsibility to educate and nourish future citizens.[12] In the Third Republic, that civic duty was institutionalized as social solidarity using both public and private networks.

Many republican feminists became allies with the Solidarists in this battle, often accepting their discursive framework and the goal of alliance with civic associations as an opening wedge for more ambitious policies. Feminist Louise Koppe, for example, called upon individual initiative and public authority to work jointly to establish maternity homes; she relied upon the support of Léon Bourgeois in 1891 to found the first *Maison Maternelle* in Paris to prevent child abandonment.[13] According to Anna Cova, in France 'the strategy of the feminist movement as a whole was to utilize the apparent demographic danger and the glorification of motherhood as a weapon in the struggle for the rights of mothers'.[14] While many European feminists demanded recognition of maternity as a 'social function', which merited paid leave, 'the French version', Gisela Bock has argued, 'seems to have come to the fore earliest and in the most pronounced and diversified ways'.[15] French solutions were adapted to meet the needs of women in and beyond Europe, in Latin America, North Africa, Russia and the Middle East.[16] For example, the *mutualité maternelle* in Paris, a private initiative, became the model for the first maternity assistance fund in Italy.[17] Maternalist politics, defined as state policies regarding mothers' and childrens' rights and women's role in their conception and/or implementation, became a 'distinctive feature' of feminist campaigns in France and throughout the French empire.[18]

In the era before the Great War, at a moment when France's stature as a great nation was challenged by imperialist crises, the recruitment of women to national defence through their maternal services was often described in yet more urgent 'solidarist' terms, as comparable to the call of men to military duty. The maternal embrace and breastfeeding became poignant symbols of national solidarity and regeneration in an age of anxiety and heightened nationalism. Through words, deeds and actions intended to mobilize public opinion, solidarist reforms attempted a complete revamping of civic culture in a manner comparable to the nationalist, patriarchal and anti-clerical ambitions of the French revolutionaries of 1793.[19] 'Maternity', as the dramatist Alexandre Dumas fils wrote, 'is woman's brand of patriotism'.[20] This particular conception of motherhood and citizenship, mediated through public and private channels, was central to the identity and social policies of the modern French state and society.

Private Maternity Insurance: Origins

After France's crushing defeat to Germany in the 1870 Franco-Prussian war, concern with the military, industrial and demographic strength of France burgeoned. To combat the risk of depopulation and infant mortality, many doctors and social reformers advocated post-partum rest and particularly breastfeeding. In 1874, the Roussel law took the first steps toward regulating wet nursing, an industry where infant death rates were documented as at their highest. For the next quarter-century, this was the only law in France protecting infants and maternity. However, the medical and political attention to infant mortality led to the establishment of the first non-Catholic charity by feminist Léon Béquet of Vienne to encourage breastfeeding, primarily among poor mothers.[21] Significantly, between 1886 to 1892, national debates on labour legislation for women raised the issue of maternity leaves and stimulated further medical inquiries into the benefits of rest periods and of breastfeeding. The 1892 law banned night work for women, but concern over state interference in women's private or 'intimate' lives, as well as resistance to compensation, stalled action on maternity leaves. Feminist Louise Koppe protested, arguing that just as a Ministry of War intervened in family life to enlist soldiers, a child welfare bureau was needed to enlist mothers and to prepare for life. Comparison of motherhood to military service would soon dominate the debate on maternity leaves.[22] Yet despite the best efforts of feminists and reformers, by the early twentieth century, France was the only nation in Europe, along with Russia and Turkey, to have no law mandating post-partum rest for industrial workers.[23]

The creation of the first private maternity insurance programme to provide compensation to female workers was a direct response to renewed concerns over depopulation and national defence. At a public lecture in 1891, the liberal politician Jules Simon argued that France lost a battalion a year because it 'lets the infants of the poor die ... We let 180,000 infants perish each year. Does France have 180,000 too many that we can allow such assassinations?'[24] He pointed with alarm to the census of 1891, which showed that the German population had increased at rate more than four times that of France. Simon's nationalist rhetoric, and the menace represented by Germany's increasing strength, convinced Felix Poussineau, a Parisian clothing manufacturer, to heed Simon's warning. With several other leaders of employers' groups in the sewing, embroidery and trimming industries – trades with predominantly female employees – he established a system of maternity leaves funded with mutual insurance benefits and jointly administered by six employers and six employees.[25] This programme was modelled on the *Association des Femmes en Couches de Mulhouse*, founded in 1862 by the Protestant industrialist Jean Dollfus, which funded a required six-week maternity leave for female workers in Alsace; his grandson Mathieu Brylinski served as the first president of the new maternity insurance programme. Female workers contributed modest dues of 6 francs a year; in exchange, they received 12 francs a week for maternity leaves and 20 francs for breastfeeding, more than double what Public Assistance paid its mothers.[26] The programme's financing increasingly drew on municipal, regional (*Conseil general de la Seine*) and national subsidies and honorary contributions, often from employers' unions. By 1906, external sources accounted for 80 per cent of its income, making political patronage essential.[27]

At its inception, city councillor Paul Strauss, Radical Republican Solidarist and an ardent child welfare activist, suggested the name *mutualité maternelle* – a politically astute but highly unlikely choice.[28] He intended to link the new maternity insurance programme with a well-established and fast-growing mutualist movement with over one million members, and to thus ensure it both political and popular support. Strauss, in fact, was vice-president of the *groupe mutualiste* in the Senate, with an astonishingly strong membership of 110 Senators.[29] Yet the Mutuality was rather inhospitable terrain for a maternity programme. Organized by trade, neighbourhood or among war veterans, these predominantly male associations provided wage earners support in case of illness and old age and funds for burials. Many mutual aid societies (like friendly societies in England and the U.S.) had long excluded women due to the allegedly higher costs of women's illnesses, particularly those related to childbirth. During the Second Empire, Napoleon III introduced state subsidies for their pension programmes to reduce class tensions and to tie these workers to the state. Sickness insurance did not cover maternity benefits, however, since, as one society regretted, 'workers' wives take a long time to recover'.[30]

Considered as the 'godfather' of the new institution, the *mutualité maternelle*, Strauss took on a militant role in the crusade against, in his own words, 'the 'national peril of depopulation', in which the Mutuality was destined to play a critical role.[31] In 1892, while spearheading the drive to increase government subsidies to the Mutuality, he supported the proposition of Doctor Pierre Budin, one of the leading advocates of breastfeeding and post-partum rest, to establish in the capital the first free post-natal clinics in France. As vice-president of the *mutualist* group in the Senate, Strauss assured the passage of an 1898 law to allow societies to combine forces in regional federations (seen as a dangerous precedent for unionized workers) on the grounds that it would permit the creation of maternal and infant welfare programmes, including clinics, pre- and post-natal consultations and *gouttes de lait* (milk sterilization programmes).

These maternal health services had not figured previously as part of the mutualist agenda. Finally, in 1899, Strauss introduced a law on paid maternity leaves, financed by either the Mutuality or public assistance (the 1893 law). Both private associations and the state could provide the ammunition for the 'battle for national defence' against infant mortality.[32]

The Mutuality began to adapt its services to second the state in its mission to protect infant health, but disagreements persisted as to the form of this engagement. In the 1890s only two textile industrialists opened *mutualités maternelles*, in Vienne (Isère), where feminist Béquet had opened the first secular maternity programme in the 1870s, and in Lille. Senator Lourties, president of the *Ligue de la Prévoyance et de la Mutualité*, urged employers in all branches of industry to accept their responsibility and offer maternity insurance for their female workers as an act of 'social peace … solidarity and patriotism'.[33] The rival *Union des Presidents des Sociétés de Secours Mutuels* recruited benefactors, on the other hand, among the popular classes by reminding workers and employees of their patriotic and 'brotherly' duties to the women working alongside them. The president of the Union, Joseph Barbaret, an employee in the Minister of the Interior and a former labour leader, also founded *mutualités militaries maternelles* to aid wives of soldiers, a growing number given the new law mandating three years of military service for every Frenchmen in response to the rising international tensions and crises. Like military duty, the maternity benefits were needed, according to Barbaret, to fight the 'danger of depopulation which menaces the security of our country'.[34] Even so, in 1903, the *Conseil supérieur de la mutualité*, a para-parliamentary committee regrouping congressmen, senators and leading mutualists, voted against the proposition of a law to mandate that every Frenchwomen belong to a *mutualité maternelle*, mooted by industrialist Eugène Roche of Rouen and supported by Poussineau. For the other mutualist leaders, still attached to liberalism, such an intervention into domestic life by the state was unacceptable. In their eyes, such a law would only reinforce state bureaucracy and increase public charges.[35] Above all, they perceived it as a dangerous step toward the *Etat Providence* (welfare state) at precisely the moment when state-funded pensions were being voted on in the Senate.

Maternity protection became a political battlefield. The growing contribution of the Mutuality to both working and non-working mothers attracted the attention of the first extra-parliamentary commission against depopulation. Established by René Waldeck-Rousseau, it constituted, according to Catherine Rollet-Echalier, 'on the one hand a response to the aggravated demographic conjecture and, on the other hand, a political operation to undermine the Conservatives' in the *Alliance nationale pour l'accroissement de la population française*, founded in 1896. In a report to the commission, Dr Budin, ardent Solidarist, emphasized the remarkable and unexpectedly high rates of breastfeeding among women enrolled in *mutualités maternelles* – 80 per cent![36] In addition, the rates of infant mortality fell to 7 per cent versus a national average of almost 20 per cent. For Budin, the *mutualités maternelles* were an excellent way to spread scientific caretaking practices to children of all classes and an ideal testing ground for more far-reaching state reforms. In 1902, in accordance with the wishes of many Solidarists, Strauss, Budin and Roussel created the League against Infant Mortality (*Ligue contre la Mortalité Infantile*) in order to promote *both* public and private remedies to combat infant mortality.[37] Spurred on, the *mutualités maternelles* of Paris and Vienne, imitating the regional federations of Lyon and St Etienne, opened their doors to all women, not only working women. In these large urban centres, mutualist leaders congratulated themselves on reducing the rates of infant mortality, on offering new opportunities for insurance not assistance and, not least, uniting all social classes.[38] Finally, the establishment of Mutualism in the colonies after 1904 spread these benefits beyond the hexagon to French territories overseas.[39] Using the Mutualist infrastructure, republican officials implemented maternal and infant health initiatives as an alternative to more conservative pronatalist campaigns.

The promotion of social solidarity by 'Republican motherhood' was the central ingredient of the *mutualités maternelles*. Through their actions, the traditional membership of the Mutuality expanded to women of all classes. Poussineau defined the *mutualité maternelle* as 'an association of well-to-do mothers and working-class mothers in order to provide for the latter sufficient benefits ... to stop working for four weeks and to breastfeed'.[40] Volunteer dames patronesses, recruited among the wives of civil servants, doctors and engineers, or female school teachers, distributed layettes, money and clean clothes and laundry. In contrast to the older *sociétés de charité maternelles* (of Catholic inspiration), they promoted a secular and scientific morality. Further, the *mutualités* extended resources and aid to unmarried mothers, a group championed by feminists and Solidarists but excluded from the *sociétés de charité maternelles*. Mutualist *visiteuses* also played an important role in directing women to apply for aid from other philanthropic organizations or from the state. One seven-and-a-half-month pregnant, newlywed woman, for example, sadly beaten by her husband after telling him she could no longer work, was sent to the refuge run by feminist Madame Béquet of Vienne.[41]

By expressing their motherhood outside their own homes, in actions designed to ameliorate public welfare, these middle-class and upper-class republican women began to assume new responsibilities, including even administrative functions. Among these early maternalists, the principal of Lyon's first public high school Madame J. Desparmet-Ruello, a vocal proponent of girls' scientific education and a staunch Dreyfusard, presided over the *Union des Femmes Lyonnaises* and the *mutualité maternelle* in France's second city. The Protestant Léonie Toureille, married to the secretary of the *Union des Sociétés de secours mutuels du Gard*, acceded to a position in that organization after she created *La Prévoyante féminine* (1905) and *la Mutualité maternelle du Gard* (1908). Their engagement was an important innovation in the mutualist movement.[42]

What was the feminist position on maternity leaves and benefits, and how did that impact policy? According to Anna Cova, although the feminist impact is difficult to evaluate, 'it is equally difficult to imagine that this legislation would have come about without the continuous pressure feminists put on Parliament even without the benefit of the vote'. Beginning in 1892, the first women's conference to call itself 'feminist' stressed the need for 'social protection for all mothers'. In 1896, delegates at the Fifth International Feminist Congress in Paris appealed to parliament for a law that would provide for maternity welfare during two months before and two months after childbirth. Léonie Rouzade, socialist militant of *La Solidarité des Femmes*, declared at the Congress that maternity ought to be recognized as work, considered a 'social function' and subsidized by the state, as was military service. This terminology of maternity as a 'social function', first used by Rouzade in the 1880s, was picked up by *La Fronde*, the most important forum for feminist debate the following decade. *La Fronde* was founded by Margarite Durand, an advocate of equal pay for equal work, including housework, as well as a proponent of maternity insurance.[43] When Durand organized women workers in unions, these included mutual aid funds.[44] Interestingly, even ardent suffragette Hubertine Auclert supported mutualism over socialist unions at the 1880 worker congress in Le Havre.[45] In 1899, Auclert advocated maternity endowments to be financed by a paternal tax on men which would serve as a remedy for depopulation. Some years later she proposed 'payments for indispensable service to the state' for mothers.[46] In 1900, Julie Siegfried and Sarah Monod, Protestants married to Solidarists politicians (active in the Mutuality), presided at a republican feminist Congress which, after hearing from Poussineau, voiced their support for a law under debate on maternity leaves and to increase subsidies to *mutualités maternelles*. Although some feminists indicated a preference for more direct state-fund insurance programmes, the Congress even endorsed the teaching of the Mutuality in girls' schools. Most notably, a year later, the *Conseil National des Femmes Françaises* was founded, with Sarah Monod as president and Julie Seigfried as vice president, explicitly to address concerns about maternal and child welfare. The CNFF became the largest feminist organization in France, with 75,000 members in 1909.[47]

In short, feminists supported maternity leaves as well as broader political reform for mothers of the range envisioned in Brieux's play *Maternité*, discussed above. This included revision of the civil code, especially article 340 on paternity suits, a constant demand of both liberal and Catholic feminist groups. Further, French women were frustrated that political decision-making was still dominated by men. As Léon Béquet argued, male policymakers were unwilling to recognize paternal irresponsibility and women's poverty as causes of depopulation, and female juries would understand why single mothers resorted to abortion.[48] Many feminists envisioned that recognition of the values of motherhood would lead to more rights for women, including the vote. Finally, by insisting that motherhood was a social function, not just a private one, feminists challenged the traditional cultural dichotomy between political and personal which was critical to the development of family and welfare policies.

One particularly interesting feminist maternalist operated at the confluence of these two movements and on the border of public and private aid. Mme Marie-Louise Bérot-Berger created the *mutualité maternelle* in Saint-Quentin, an industrial city of Aisne, with the aid of its Préfect in 1908. Two years later it enrolled two hundred members, served by thirty volunteer *visiteuses* and administered by a council of middle-class women and doctors. Bérot-Berger equally presided over two departmental feminist groups, the *Union Fraternelle des Femmes in Aisne* (with close ties to *Le Fronde* and the solidarist *Alliance d'hygiène sociale*) and the *Union française pour le suffrage des femmes*, both of which fought for political, civil and economic rights for women. In 1907, she founded a journal which brought together her multiple commitments: '*le journal des travailleuses*' was to be 'the echo of social works in France and abroad of the feminist and mutualist movements'.[49]

A social Catholic and member of the LePlaysian *Société d'économie sociale*, Bérot-Berger co-authored a monograph about a working-class mother, using her case to demonstrate the importance of the 1907 law allowing married women control of their salaries. Her work also called for a '*mutualité paternelle*' a tax on all men ages twenty-five to fifty, which, not unlike Auclert's paternal tax, would support all children under age thirteen. Close to Léon Bourgeois and Léon Mirman, director of Public Assistance and Hygiene in the Ministry of the Interior, Bérot-Berger represented the Ministry at diverse international congresses. At her request, natalist Jacques Bertillon visited the *mutualité maternelle* in 1907; he facilitated her appointment to the *Conseil Supérieur de la Natalité* after World War I. In 1911, when she spoke in Roubaix at the second annual congress of the *mutualités maternelles*, she was likely the first feminist to do so. In 1913, she and Léonie Toureille served as vice-presidents at the ninth National Mutualist Congress in Montpellier as advocates of expanding infant and child welfare services.

Indeed, while playing an important role in hygiene, education and class solidarity, the *mutualité maternelle* also attempted to institute new social rights. Working women, many in the textile trades or homeworkers, who received these services, came from the lowest classes: many had large families (up to ten living children), little furniture ('only beds but clean', one *visiteuse* wrote), or debts from back rent (for which, in some cases, extra money was given). Case records, collected by female visitors, also indicate some of the women were beaten or abandoned. Others had premature deliveries due to a physically arduous workload. Others still had husbands with tuberculosis or rheumatism or who were victims of work accidents. Using such concrete evidence, Poussineau affirmed that the 'misery' in the working classes was caused by social risks, illness and unemployment, for example. He challenged those who wrote off the genuine economic problems of poor women in moral terms and argued that even alcoholism was often the result of 'social risks'. In his eyes, their situation justified social solidarity by more fortunate citizens as in the Mutuality, which offered a form of mutual assistance superior to public assistance or *Sociétés de Charité maternelles*. Poussineau, pioneer employer for maternity benefits, argued that maternity protection was not alms or charity but a 'right'.[50] The *mutualité maternelle* contributed to the construction of republican social solidarity and to the ideological justification of Solidarism.

Publicizing Breastfeeding: The Secular Madonna

In their struggle against depopulation, Solidarists relied on the mutualist network not only to spread maternal education and hygiene but also to transform national civic culture through a publicity campaign highlighting particular images of maternity. Most notably, to display its commitment to care for its members from cradle to grave, the National Mutualist Federation (*Fédération nationale de la mutualité française*), created in 1902, offered a diploma to thousands of its members. Marked with the seal and signature of the Minister of the Interior, it symbolized the quasi-official role of the Mutuality and the recognition of its services by the state. The contribution of women to this cycle of insurance figured prominently but was limited to the theme of republican motherhood. While men are shown as workers and peasants, women are exalted for their role as 'scientific' educators of the family: a concerned wife, receiving instructions from the doctor, at her husband's bedside; volunteer *dames patronesses* weighing infants in baby clinics; and most notably, a young mother nursing her child. Significantly, an image of motherhood as secular, republican and scientific replaced an image of nuns acting as nurses on the mutualist certificate issued by Napoleon III. In another image from 1906, the allegorical Republic, breasts exposed, symbolically nurtures national unity and solidarity amidst male workers and peasants. Yet another example, from the letterhead of the *Union Mutualiste de Rhône*, highlights the mother-citizen breastfeeding her baby. All these images, which associate women uniquely with mothering (whether in her home or in a limited public venture), ignored a daily reality for female workers and employees, over 20 per cent of the mutualist membership and over one-third of the active population in France. The mother-citizen, not the mother-producer, dominated in mutualist publicity. While men provided labour for the Republic, the mother-citizen only seemed to provide nourishment for healthy children, future workers and soldiers.[51]

Similar images exalting motherhood and breastfeeding, which reflect both demographic fears and anti-clerical tendencies, proliferated in the art and literature of the Third Republic. Anne Cova has suggested that Emile Zola's novel *Fecondité* (1899), written during his exile in London for his republican and anti-clerical writings in support of Alfred Dreyfus, was not only 'a call to procreate but a glorification of breastfeeding'.[52] For Zola, Marianne, the fertile mother, symbolized an organic and natural source of life, 'truer than the cult of the virgin'. Her breasts were 'a living temple', 'a great river of nurturing milk ... younger and healthier with each spring'.[53] In an interview for Marguerite Durand's feminist newspaper *le Fronde*, Zola argued 'Maternal breastfeeding is an obligation so natural it seems unnecessary to comment on it ... it is useful for the entire race'. Further, the artist Eugène Carrière, also a *dreyfusard* closely connected to Solidarist circles, was recognized by the public and the state as 'the painter of modern maternity'. He received his first government commission for his 1885 painting *L'Enfant Malade* (*The Sick Child*). This moving image expressed not only France's concerns with infant health but also his own tragic loss of a son that year. Viewers like Edmond de Goncourt emphasized that Carrière's work represented the modern bourgeois heiresses of 'divine maternity'. Unlike the pietas of 'epochs of faith', however, these captured 'the mother's black thoughts, always anxious, and in which the troubled grip of the arms around the body of her infant seem perpetually in defence against sickness and death'.[54] Carrière's tragic experience spoke to the urgency of Solidarist goals to protect those 'at risk', of the interdependent body politic and the need to protect the nation from infant mortality. In later works like *Le Baiser du Soir* (*Good Night Kiss*), breastfeeding was at the centre of a tender but disquieting image of fertility. Critics paid tribute to 'the harmonious beauty of instinctual gestures'. The secular vision of maternity reached a climax in another painting, 'Nativité' (1905), painted the year after the separation of church and state in France. In his nativity scene, however, Carrière focused on the breastfeeding mother rather than the sacred theme of the Virgin Birth to Christ.

These hymns to 'the cult of motherhood' secularized the traditional iconography of breastfeeding by the Madonna, which frequently symbolized Charity, as seen in Ingres (*Charité*, 1842) and de Bougereau (*Charité*, 1878). In glorifying the nursing mother as a secular Madonna, the Solidarists not only provided an incentive to breastfeed, but also suggested that the church and its charitable associations were no longer adequate and that their functions had been replaced by secular institutions and the state. Indeed, Solidarists aspired through social assistance and insurance to replace the traditional functions of the church and more generally to undercut the political right as guardians of the family and the nation. The ideal of the Republic educating and nurturing its children had arisen in Daumier's 1848 sketch of *The Republic*, but Carrière and the mutualists seemed to make this not only the state's but every woman's duty.[55]

The transformation of breastfeeding into a secular and patriotic duty situates the Solidarists as heirs to the more radical phase of the French Revolution. In 1793 the National Convention decreed that only nursing mothers would be eligible for state support.[56] At Revolutionary festivals, mothers were encouraged to breastfeed so that 'military and generous virtues could flow, with maternal milk, into the heart of all the nurslings in France!'[57] At the source of this enthusiasm for breastfeeding were the doctors who denounced the elite practice of wet nursing in the eighteenth century. Above all, it reflected the influence of philosopher and educator Jean-Jacques Rousseau, who first promoted Republican motherhood and breastfeeding as a natural and national duty, as part of a 'social contract'. In his novel *Emile*, Rousseau wrote, 'Let mothers deign to nurse their babies, morals will reform themselves, feelings of nature will reawaken in all hearts, the state will be repopulated'.[58]

Preoccupied, as were the Jacobins, by national defence and territorial expansion, depopulation, social and political conflicts and women's roles, Solidarists in the early twentieth century turned to the 'Cult of Republican Motherhood'. Gender, expressed in patriarchal nationalism, lay at the heart of the continuity between the social vision of Rousseau and Léon Bourgeois, for whom solidarity was 'nothing else but the social contract retroactively adhered to'.[59] In his crusade against infant mortality, Paul Strauss repeated a maxim of 1793: 'All French citizens have a right to existence ... public assistance is a sacred debt'.[60] And while Solidarists did not actually banish women from the public sphere, as in 1793, their electoral platform did not advocate the vote for women but rather limited their support to assistance for poor mothers and maternity leaves.[61] Like the Revolutionaries in 1793, this new generation of republicans sought to solidify the nation by promoting a vision of unity and 'fraternity' through culture as well as law, one which encouraged women as citizen-mothers to perform their patriotic duties.

La Mutualité Maternelle: Partner in the 'Nationalist Revival'

In 1906, the *progressiste* deputy Engerand energetically defended the idea that repopulation was an act of national defence that justified sacrifices of the collectivity. Yet when he proposed a law of voluntary eight-week maternity leaves, he envisioned that compensation would come from private sources, with a significant increase in government subsidies to the Mutuality and other private institutions. To overcome resistance to this compromise bill for greater state intervention, he argued that pregnant women and new mothers should have the same rights to job protection as men 'called to accomplish their period of military service' under the 1901 law. The mother, like the soldier, had 'a patriotic duty'.[62] The founder of the first *mutualité maternelle* in the provinces, the textile magnate Bonnier, orchestrated a barrage of Chamber of Commerce petitions in favour of the eight-week break.[63] Delegates to the 1907 National Mutualist Congress in Nice voted to support Engerand's legislation, although only 5 per cent of mutual aid societies offered such services.[64] Even before the law was adopted, the Minister of the Interior expanded subsidies to the *mutualités maternelles*, which had grown to 41 institutions aiding 15,000 women in France. The state thus strengthened its links in response to the growing contribution of the Mutuality to a domain until then associated with charity and public assistance.

The public support for the Mutuality developed rapidly in the face of growing concerns for national strength. Under the presidency of Léon Bourgeois, spokesperson for Solidarity, the congress of the *Alliance pour l'hygiene social* in 1907 not only endorsed Engerand's bill but also recommended the obligatory enrolment of all French women in a *mutualité maternelle*, as well as provisions for work breaks while nursing. The following year, Barbaret organized the First National Congress of *mutualités maternelles*, presided by Paul Strauss and with a notable presence of other politicians as well as women. Although all the organizing committee and honorary presidents were men, over a hundred women participated and four members of the commission were female presidents of local sections.[65] On this occasion, Engerand thanked the mutualists for 'having eased the way to' (*fait passer dans les moeurs*) proper infant care practices, thanks to their action in the popular classes. He called upon his audience to continue their efforts: '*Mutualistes de France,* give us back the army unit that each year we lose with such guilty lack of foresight [*imprévoyance*]'.[66]

By 1909, with the passage of Engerand's bill, the state was linked more than ever to the Mutuality and intensified its participation in the publicity of its new maternity programmes. In several large cities, Lyon and Angers, for example, information on the *mutualités maternelles* was distributed along with marriage certificates. Despite the hesitation of the *Conseil supérieur de la Mutualité,* which petitioned to increase state support for pension services by the Mutuality, the government augmented its subsidies to societies that offered maternity programmes. From 41 in 1907, the number of *mutualités maternelles* grew to 127 in 1911, a 300-per cent growth. That year, they received 104,000 francs in state subsidies, or one-fifth of the state budget for private maternity programmes, only slightly less that the far older *Sociétés de Charité maternelles.*[67] In early 1913, the municipal council of Paris gave 80,000 francs to the *mutualité maternelle,* which had a network of twenty sections in the capital and forty-one in the suburbs; this was the largest public subsidy to any other private maternal and child welfare agency in the country. As a result, the Mutuality took over the administration of much of the city's maternal welfare programme, extending its services to the poorest women.[68] The mobilization of the popular classes in the battle against depopulation was well underway. The coverage of maternity benefits and clinics had become an integral part of the mutualist agenda.

With the passage of the Strauss law in 1913, the state made the *mutualités maternelles* partners in the patriotic mission to fight depopulation. Feminists, in close cooperation with the few members of parliament who supported their cause, deserve partial credit for this more ambitious programme.[69] Under the law, the state finally paid maternity benefits to female employees, domestic servants and factory workers for a mandatory four-week post-natal break and, when medically necessary, an optional four-week pre-natal break. Article 10 empowered women trained by the Mutuality to manage and distribute the public funds, just as mutualists did for state-financed pensions since 1910. To better guide these efforts of collaboration with the state, Strauss, Poussineau and Leopold Mabilleau, president of the National Mutualist Federation, created the *Union Française des mutualités maternelles.*

Those mutualists who protested against becoming an 'executor of Public Assistance' to help women who were '*imprévoyante*' were reminded that motherhood was a 'national service'. Mothers who gave up their salaries for maternity leave were in exactly the same situation as the nation's soldiers, affirmed the doctor Commandeur, head of Lyon's *mutualité maternelle*, at their Third National Congress in 1914, under the presidency of Paul Strauss. In addition, the revolutionary socialist deputy Jean Allemane pointed out, to 'our honor as mutualists', that they would now be 'loyal, if critical, collaborators' of the government in the battle to protect infants. Allemane suggested asking for even more subsidies for these maternity programmes since they operated beyond the provisions of the Strauss law in helping not only working women but all women (including wives of members) for the entire nine months of their pregnancy and during two years afterwards.[70] In just over a decade, through an ingenious combination of subsidies and political support, the public authorities had enlisted in the fight against infant mortality the mutualist movement – a network of five million Frenchmen and women – reshaped to serve not only their members but their country.

Allied with the state, mutualist leaders male and female embraced the politicized discourse that promoted the mother-citizen as an agent of social solidarity and nationalism. In her guidebook destined for *dames patronesses* working within the confines of the Strauss law, Marie-Louise Bérot-Berger urged French women to respond to the 'sinister call' of their legislators: 'the Patrie is in danger because of depopulation'.[71] Her book opened with a quote from Rousseau as a precursor of the solidarist axiom, 'he who receives, owes', and demanded that more fortunate French women remember their duties to the nation. French women must not, she demanded, force state bureaucrats to do a mother's job of educating other mothers. And she reminded readers that, in the words of the French Medical Academy, the infant has the 'right' to its mother's breast. On the eve of World War I, mutualist publicity could not have been clearer in espousing nationalist goals. 'The *mutualité maternelle*, in aiding young women, prepares the defenders of our country.' Solidarists had succeeded in mobilizing private groups and volunteers of both sexes to promote motherhood and breastfeeding to save the nation, if not the race.

The popular response to the Strauss law demonstrated the success of the Solidarists' political and cultural strategy to promote a cult of maternity without overburdening the state treasury. Among the Frenchwomen who demanded maternity benefits in 1914, 68 per cent of the women took the bonus for breastfeeding while only 11 per cent asked for benefits for maternity leave. Two years after the First World War, in 1920, the figures had grown to 78 per cent and 40 per cent respectively. Four years later, the proportion of women who received indemnities for breastfeeding reached 88 per cent. That year, 242 *mutualités maternelles* supervised the delivery and nursing of over 28,000 babies and boasted of performing 200,000 weighings in mutualist clinics. The effective propaganda for 'republican

maternity' and state indemnities contributed to the success of the legislators in the campaign to fight infant mortality through breastfeeding.

However, tensions remained between the protection of women as
mothers and the realities of working-class life. The glorification of solidarity between rich and poor mothers did not address the low salaries of
female workers, nor other political and social aspects of women's lives,
whether working or not. Moreover, the exaltation of the mother in the
battle against infant mortality could as easily lead to pronatalism as provisions for family allowances.[72] Brieux's play, itself part of an active civic
culture debating maternity, rightly called attention to the limits of the
alliance between public associations and the state and of the danger of
defining women exclusively in terms of pronatalism. And yet the relative
failure of pronatalism compared to the more successful battle against infant mortality and for health insurance is noteworthy.

Faced with social conflicts and the threat of war, maternity protection offered
a means to combat infant mortality and at the same time promote social solidarity and nationalism. Maternity protection became a right as well as a duty to
defend the nation comparable to that of the (male) soldier. Maternity insurance
by the Mutuality and other private institutions offered a secular network of social services to French women of all classes, a network that the state called upon
to treat its most urgent problems. Moreover, *mutualités maternelles* generated
leadership opportunities for middle-class Republican women in organizations
that only a few decades earlier had been almost exclusively male. Through the
Mutuality, the Republican mother replaced Charity in actions and images as
the cement of civil society in an age of anxiety. Private associations in France,
as in England and the United States, became agents of maternity protection
and pressure groups on lawmakers. As the Solidarists had intended, the protection of French male and female citizens from cradle to grave was increasingly
accepted as a civic responsibility. In the Third Republic, the alliance between
public and private efforts led to a limited but significant social reform and to
the construction of a 'republican and familial' welfare state.

Notes

1. Funding for research and conference travel was provided by Social Science Research Council, Rotary International and Wagner College. I would like to thank Rachel Fuchs, Cheryl
   Koos, Laura Morowitz, my co-editor Rebecca Jo Plant and the other participants at the
   IISH maternalism conference for their suggestions. The citation by Engerand, discussed
   below, is from *Premier Congrès National de la Mutualité Maternelle*, 1908, 170.
2. E. Brieux. 1904. *Maternité*, Paris: P.V. Stock.: On Brieux, see J.E. Pederson. 2003. *Legislating the French Family: Feminism, Theater, and Republican Politics, 1870–1920*, New
   Brunswick: Rutgers University Press.

3. A. Klaus. 1993. *Every Child a Lion: The Origins of Maternal and Infant Health Policy in the U.S. and France, 1890–1920*, Ithaca, NY: Cornell University Press, 186.
4. Philip Nord argues for the critical role of civil society in the consolidation of republican power before the Third Republic in P. Nord. 1995. *The Republican Moment: Struggles for Democracy in Nineteenth Century France*, Cambridge, MA: Harvard University Press. Maurice Agulhon demonstrates the importance of mutual aid and other popular associations in the circulation of Republican ideas between 1789 and 1848 in M. Agulhon. 1970. *La République au Village: Les populations du Var de la Révolution à la IIe République*, Paris: Plon. On social reformers in the colonies, with explicit reference to mutualist groups, see J. Horne. 1998. 'In Pursuit of Greater France: Visions of Empire among Musée Social Reformers, 1894–1931', in J. Clancy-Smith and F. Gourda (eds), *Domesticating the Empire: Race, Gender and Family Life in French and Dutch Colonialism*, Charlottesville: University of Virginia Press.
5. For a brief discussion of mutual aid groups, see P. Nord. 1994. 'The Welfare State in France, 1870–1914', *French Historical Studies* 18(3), 838. See also S.M. Beaudoin. 1996. 'A Neutral Terrain: Public Assistance, Private Charity and the State in Third Republic Bordeaux, 1870–1914', Ph.D. diss., Carnegie Mellon University.
6. K. Offen. 2000. 'Feminism, Anti-Feminism and National Family Politics in Third Republic France', in M.J. Boxer and J.H. Quartaert (eds), *Connecting Spheres: European Women in a Globalizing World*, New York: Oxford University Press, 209; and idem. 1984. 'Depopulation, Nationalism and Feminism in Fin-de-Siècle France', *American Historical Review* 89(3), 648–76.
7. G. Bock and P. Thane (eds). 1994. *Maternity and Gender Policies: Women and the Rise of the European Welfare States, 1880s–1950s*, London and New York: Routledge; and S. Koven and S. Michel (eds). 1993. *Mothers of a New World: Maternalist Politics and the Origins of Welfare States*, New York and London: Routledge. See also G. Bock. 1994. 'Poverty and Mothers' Rights in the Emerging Welfare States', in F. Thébaud (ed.), G. Duby and M. Perrot (series eds), A. Goldhammer (trans.), *A History of Women in the West: Toward a Cultural Identity in the Twentieth Century*, Cambridge, MA: Harvard University Press, 4402–32. On comparisons of France to the U.S. and Britain, see J. Jensen. 1990. 'Representations of Gender: Policies to "Protect" Women Workers and Infants in France and the United States before 1914', in L. Gordon (ed.), *Women, the State and Welfare*, Madison: University of Wisconsin Press; and S. Pedersen. 1993. *Family, Dependence and the Origins of the Welfare State: Britain and France, 1914–1945*, Cambridge: Cambridge University Press. For a groundbreaking work that introduces an emphasis on civil society to polity-centred explanations of the welfare state, see T. Skocpol. 1993. *Protecting Soldiers and Mothers: The Political Origins of Social Policy in the United States*, Cambridge, MA: Harvard University Press.
8. Klaus, *Every Child a Lion*, 184.
9. Jensen, 'Representations of Gender', 158; S. Koven and S. Michel. 1990. 'Womanly Duties: Maternalist Politics and the Origins of Welfare States in France, Germany, Great Britain, and the United States, 1880–1920', *American Historical Review* 95(4), 1089. See also L.L. Clark. 2000. 'Feminist Maternalists and the French State: Two Inspectresses-General in the pre-World War I Third Republic', *Journal of Women's History* 12(1), 32–61. On the continuity of the citizen-producer ideology in post-World War II France, see J. Jensen. 1987. 'Both Friend and Foe: Women and State Welfare', in R. Bridenthal (ed.), *Becoming Visible: Women in European History*, 2nd edn, New York: Houghton Mifflin. For a fascinating look at the politics of fertility debates in the 1980s, see L. King. 1998. 'France Needs Children: Pronatalism, Nationalism and Women's Equity', *Sociological Quarterly* 39(1), 33–52.
10. D. Ashford. 1991. 'Advantages of Complexity: Social Insurance in France', in J.S. Ambler (ed.), *The French Welfare State: Surviving Social and Ideological Change*, New York: New York University Press. On private sector initiatives, particularly those of employers in the interwar era, see L.L. Downs. 1992. 'Between Taylorism and *Denatalité*: Women, Welfare

Supervisors and the Boundaries of Difference in French Metal Working Factories, 1917–35', in D. Healy and S. Reverby (eds), *Gendered Domains: Rethinking Public and Private in Women's History*, Ithaca, NY: University of Cornell Press, 289–302; and Pedersen, *Family, Dependence and the Origins of the Welfare State*.

11. H. Hatzfeld. 1971. *Du Pauperisme à la Securité Sociale*, Paris: Armand Colin; F. Ewald. 1986. *L'Etat Providence*, Paris: Bernard Grasset; A. Gueslin. 1987. *L'invention de l'économie sociale: le XIXe siècle français*, Paris: Économica; B. Gibaud. 1986. *De la mutualité à la securité sociale: Conflits et convergences*, Paris: Éditions ouvrieres; idem. 1998. *Mutualité, Assurances (1850–1914): Les Enjeux*, Paris: Économica; and P. Dutton. 2002. *Origins of the French Welfare State: The Struggle for Social Reform in France, 1914–1947*, Cambridge, MA: Harvard University Press. Closest to my methodology in studying para-political networks and interest groups is B. Dumons and G. Pollet. 1994. *L'Etat et les retraites: Genèse d'une politique*, Paris: Belin.

12. E.A. Accampo, R.G. Fuchs and M.L. Stewart (eds). 1995. *Gender and the Politics of Social Reform in France, 1870–1914*, Baltimore: Johns Hopkins University Press. See also J. Cole. 1996. '"There are Only Good Mothers": The Ideological Work of Women's Fertility in France before World War I', *French Historical Studies* 19(3), 639–72.

13. A. Cova. 1994. 'French Feminism and Maternity Theories and Policies', in Bock and Thane *Maternity and Gender Policies*, 121.

14. Ibid. Further, the largest feminist group, the *Conseil National des Femmes Françaises*, recruited from associations 'that concerned themselves with the lot of women or of children', according to S. Hause with A.R. Kenney. 1984. *Women's Suffrage and Social Policy in Third Republic France*, Princeton: Princeton University Press, 38.

15. Bock, 'Poverty and Mothers' Rights', 407.

16. K. Offen, 'National Family Politics', 206. For a contemporary example, see B.R. Bergmann. 1996. *Saving our Children from Poverty: What the United States Can Learn from France*, New York: Russell Sage Foundation.

17. A. Buttafuco. 1991. 'Motherhood as a Political Strategy: The Role of the Italian Women's Movement in the Creation of the *Cassa Nazionale di Maternità*', in Bock and Thane, *Maternity and Gender Policies*, 183–84.

18. Cova, 'French Feminism and Maternity', 119–20. The coincidence of the rise of feminism, the welfare state and 'new' imperialism is striking, as is the use of terms like 'child' to describe colonized groups and 'mother' to describe the colonizer. For preliminary work on this dynamic in the French empire, see R.D.E. Burton. 1993. 'Maman-France Doudo: Family Images in French Colonial Discourse', *Diacritics* 23(3), 69–90; A. Conklin. 1998. 'Redefining Frenchness: Citizenship, Race Regeneration and Imperial Motherhood in France and West Africa, 1920–1940', in Clancy-Smith and Gourda, *Domesticating the Empire*, 65–82; and E. Camiscioli, 'Reproducing the French Race: Immigration and Pronatalism in early 20th Century France', in T. Ballantyne and A.M Burton (eds), *Bodies in Contact: Rethinking Colonial Encounters in World History*, Durham, NC: Duke University Press, 219–33. On the ideology and practice of motherhood in the British Empire, the starting point is A. Davin. 1978. 'Imperialism and Motherhood', *History Workshop Journal* 5(1), 9–66. See also A.M. Burton. 1994. *Burdens of History: British Feminists, Indian Women, and Imperial Culture, 1865–1915*, Chapel Hill: University of North Carolina Press. Although focused on Canadian feminism, international implications of discourse on degeneration are considered in M. Valverde. 1992. '"When the Mother of the Race is Free": Race, Reproduction and Sexuality in First-Wave Feminism', in F. Iacovetta and M. Valverde (eds), *Gender Conflicts: New Essays in Women's History*, Toronto: University of Toronto Press, 3–26. For Germany, see L. Wildenthal. 1998. '"When Men are Weak": The Imperial Feminism of Frieda von Bulow', *Gender and History* 10(1), 53–77.

19. M.L. Stewart (McDougall). 1983. 'Protecting Infants: The French Campaign for Maternity Leaves, 1890–1913', *French Historical Studies* 13, 99; and J. Stone, 'The Republican

Brotherhood: Gender and Ideology', in Accampo, Fuchs and Stewart, *Gender and the Politics of Social Reform*, 54.

20. Cited in Offen, 'National Family Politics', 209.
21. C. Rollet-Echalier. 1990. *La Politique à l'égard de la Petit Enfance Sous la IIIe République*, Paris: IEUD/Presses Universitaires de France.
22. Cova, 'French Feminism and Maternity', 121.
23. Stewart (McDougall), 'Protecting Infants', 79–105; and ibid. 1989. *Women, Work and the French State: Labour Protection and Social Patriarchy, 1879–1919*, Ontario: McGill-Queen's University Press.
24. R. Fuchs. 1992. *Poor and Pregnant in Paris: Strategies for Survival in the Nineteenth Century*, New Brunswick: Rutgers University Press, 60–61. On Simon, see A. Gueslin. 1992. *L'Etat, l'économie et la société française au XIX-Xxe siècle*, Paris: Hachette, 36.
25. Dr J. Mornet. 1910. *Les Mutualités Maternelles*, Paris: Blaud, 8.
26. Fuchs, *Poor and Pregnant*, 149. To receive full benefits, women had to be members of the society for at least nine months. However, often workers who had not joined previously received 'extra-statuary benefits' of 15 francs indemnity and a 10 franc bonus for breastfeeding. This likely reflected the reality that low salaries prevented poor working women from joining in advance of their delivery. See also, A. Vallin, *La Femme salarié et la maternité*, Paris, 1911.
27. Stewart (McDougall), 'Protecting Infants', 83.
28. *Ier congrès national de la mutualité maternelle*, Paris, 1908, 178. On Strauss' maternalism, see R. Fuchs, 'The Right to Life: Paul Strauss and the Politics of Motherhood', in Accampo, Fuchs and Stewart, *Gender and the Politics of Social Reform*, 88.
29. R. Samuel and G. Bonét-Maury. 1914. *Les Parlementaires français, 1900–1914: Dictionnaire*, Paris: Rouston, 478.
30. O. Faure. 1989. 'La médicalisation de la société dans la région lyonnaise au XIXe siècle (1800–1914)', thèse d'état, University of Lyon II, 556–7.
31. Fuchs, 'The Right to Life', 88.
32. Dr E. Bonnaire. 1910. 'La Mutualité Maternelle', *Revue Philanthropique* 27, 252.
33. Speech by Lourties, 'La Mutualité Maternelle', *Revue de la Prévoyance et de la Mutualité*, 1900, 414–19.
34. L. Mabilleau. 1904. *La Mutualité Française: doctrine et applications*, Bordeaux: Delmas, 99–100.
35. Archives Nationales, C7279/258–61, Assemblé Nationale, Législateur, *Procès Verbaux du Conseil Supérieur des sociétés de secours mutuels*, May 1903, 98–103.
36. P. Budin. 1904. 'La Mortalité Infantile', in L. Bourgeois (ed.), *Les Applications sociales de la solidarité sociale: leçons professées à lécole des hautes études sociales*, Paris: Ecole des Hautes Etudes Sociales, 1902, 32; and Rollet-Echalier, *La Petit Enfance*, 228.
37. Stewart (McDougall), 'Protecting Infants', 93.
38. *Quatrième Congrès de l'Alliance d'Hygiène Sociale tenu à Lyon*, presided by Léon Bourgeois, 1907, 29–30.
39. Horne, 'In Pursuit of Greater France', 31–2.
40. F. Poussineau. 1911. *La Maternité chez l'ouvrière en 1910*, Paris: Mutualité Maternelle, 3.
41. Poussineau's, *La Maternité* sadly offers a detailed list of such cases, indicating the husband's (and less often the wife's) profession and salary, the number of children, and brief notes on their home, indemnities requested and the status of the most recent infant. Husbands' professions ranged from civil servants to small shopkeeper to painters, delivery men and day labourers. It is not clear why so few of these women seemed to work or whether that was not of interest to the caseworkers. Jean-Pierre Chaline argues for using the term 'maternalist' to describe philanthropic women with close ties to local government functions, as in Angers since the 1840s: J.-P. Chaline. 1997. 'Sociabilité féminine et "maternalisme": les Sociétés de Charité Maternelle au XIXème siècle', in A. Corbin, J. Lalouette and M. Riot-

Sarcey (eds), *Femmes dans la cite, 1815–1871*, Paris: Creaphis, 69–78. See also C. Adams. 2010. *Poverty, Charity and Motherhood: Maternal Societies in Nineteenth-Century France*, Urbana-Champaign: University of Illinois Press.

42. Archives Départementales du Rhône, Officiers de l'Academie, 1M 285–303, on Desparmet-Ruello and other examples. On Toureille, see M. Dreyfus. 2006. *Les Femmes et la Mutualité: De la Révolution française à nos jours*, Paris: Éditions Pascal, 54–5. In 1893, a female delegate of the *Sociétés Méres de Famille (Saint-Louis)* served on the departmental council in the Gironde, an earlier example of regional maternalist leadership: see Archives Départementales de la Gironde, *Statuts du Syndicat Girondin des Institutions de Prévoyance et de Mutualité* (1893) and L. Weintrob. 2000. 'Burns, Burials and Benefits: Women Workers in Mutual Aid Societies', in panel on Women's Activism in Modern France, Society for French Historical Studies, Arizona; Cova, 'French Feminism and Maternity', 124; and Bock, 'Poverty and Mothers' Rights', 406; Cova, 'French Feminism and Maternity', 124.

43. Bock, 'Poverty and Mothers' Rights', 406.

44. M.-H. Zylberberg-Hocquard, *Féminisme et Syndicalisme en France*, Paris: Éditions Anthropos, 213–26.

45. Claire Moses describes the 1880 split as follows: 'Although it is ironic that feminists allied with the mutualists, whose socialism derived from the anti-feminist Proudhon, and opposed the collectivists, whose socialism drew upon the feminists Marx and Engels, the mutualist (and later the "gradualist") feminists were harkening back to their utopian roots. They particularly resisted the Guesdists ideology of class struggle.' Yet, as she points out in her conclusion, bourgeois women had taken over the leadership of the feminist movement after the 1870s, and their allies were republicans, not socialists. See C.G. Moses. 1984. *French Feminism in the Nineteenth Century*, Albany: State University of New York, 224, 234, 277 (n. 57).

46. Bock, 'Poverty and Mothers' Rights'.

47. Cova, 'French Feminism and Maternity', 124–7.

48. General Meeting of the *Oeuvre de l'allaitment maternel*, 1909, as cited in A. Klaus, '*Depopulation and Race Suicide*: Maternalism and Pronatalist Ideologies in France and the United States', in Koven and Michel, eds, *Mothers of a New World*, 199.

49. Information on Bérot-Berger is drawn from the valuable study by F. Battagliola. 2003. 'Philanthrope et féministe: Itinéraire d'une bourgeoise picarde et vision de la famille ouvrière', *Sociétés contemporaines* 53, 123–40.

50. Poussineau, *La Maternité*, 3. In 1933, George Grau, president of the *Union nationale des mutualités maternelles*, still insisted on the fact that this was not charity (like the *Sociétés de charité maternelles*) but a right, as cited in Rollet-Echalier, *La Petite Enfance*, 234, n. 53.

51. On the political implications of images of maternity, see, for example, L. Schiebinger. 1993. *Nature's Body: Gender in the Making of Modern Science*, Boston: Beacon Press; L. Hunt (ed.). 1991. *Eroticism and the Body Politic*, Baltimore: Johns Hopkins University Press; and M. Yalom. 1997. *A History of the Breast*, New York: Ballatine Books.

52. Cova, *Maternité et Droits de Femme*, 41.

53. Cited in C. Toubin-Malinas. 1986. *Heurs et Malheurs de la femme au XIXe siècle: Fecondité de Emile Zola*, Paris: Méridiens Klincksieck, 130.

54. Cited in P. Desjardins. 1907. 'Eugène Carrière', *Gazette des Beaux Arts* 37, 265–38 and 38, 12–26, 131–46.

55. M. Agulhon. 1981. *Marianne into Battle: Republican Imagery and Symbolism in France, 1789–1880*, Cambridge: Cambridge University Press, 82–84. Henri de Man described the cult of Marianne as a 'direct descendent of the cult of the Madonna'. See Agulhon's later work, *Marianne au Pouvoir: l'imagerie et la symbolique républicaine de 1880 à 1914*, 1989, 300–307. Comparisons with the imagery in Britain is striking: eugenicist Caleb Saleeby in 1908 wrote, 'There is no State womb, there are no State breasts, there is no real substitute for the beauty of individual motherhood', arguing against municipal milk depots. See

Davin, 'Imperialism and Motherhood', 29. For continuity during World War I, see M.-M. Huss, 'Paternalism and the Popular Ideology of the Child in Wartime France: the Evidence of the Picture Postcard', in R. Wall and J. Winter (eds), *The Upheaval of War: Family, Work and Welfare in Europe, 1914–18,* Cambridge: Cambridge University Press, 1988.

56.   Yalom, *A History of the Breast,* 115.

57.   Cited in ibid., 117.

58.   Cited in C. Blum. 1988. *Rousseau and the Republic of Virtue: The Language of Politics in the French Revolution,* Ithaca, NY: Cornell University Press, 47.

59.   Léon Bourgeois, *Solidarité,* 7th edn, Paris, 1912, 61.

60.   Stone, 'The Republican Brotherhood', 30.

61.   Ibid., 54

62.   Stewart (McDougall), 'Protecting Infants', 99; Rollet-Echalier, *La Petite Enfance,* 232.

63.   Stewart (McDougall), 'Protecting Infants', 101.

64.   Réné Viviani, *Rapport sur les S.S.M. au Président de la République,* 1907, xlvi.

65.   *Premier Congrès National de la Mutualité maternelle,* 1908, 4–5, also cited in Klaus, *Every Child a Lion,* 187–88. Klaus interprets this more pessimistically: 'Despite the key role of women in maintaining these organizations, men and employers dominated the movement'. While this is certainly true, the presence of so many female delegates at a mutualist congress is remarkable given the history of the movement and, as she notes, suggests their critical role at the local level.

66.   *Premier Congrès National de la Mutualité maternelle,* 1908, 170.

67.   Klaus, *Every Child a Lion,* 116.

68.   *Bulletin Trimestrielle de la Ligue contre la mortalité infantile,* 2nd ser., 1913, 5, cited in Klaus, *Every Child a Lion,* 188.

69.   Bock, 'Poverty and Mothers' Rights', 416.

70.   *Troisième Congrès Nationale de la Mutualité maternelle,* 86–8.

71.   M.-L. Bérot-Berger. 1914. *La Dame Visiteuse dans la Bienfaisance publique ou privé,* Paris: Giard, 3, 14.

72.   Rollet-Echalier, *La Petite Enfance,* 228.

CHAPTER 5

SPEAKING ON BEHALF OF OTHERS
Dutch Social Workers and the Problem of Maternalist Condescension

Berteke Waaldijk

This essay analyses the origins of professional social work in the Netherlands in the late nineteenth and early twentieth centuries. My main argument is that the concept of maternalism is a useful category for understanding the ambiguities within the connected histories of the origins of social policies and of women's struggles for full citizenship. I will use the distinction between social, political and civil rights to analyse some of the ambivalence contained in the new professional discourse. Social workers tried to speak on behalf of others and, in so doing, combined condescension and respect in a way that deserves the critical attention of gender historians.[1]

Civil, Political and Social Rights

In 1950 the British sociologist T.H. Marshall introduced the distinction between the 'civil', 'political' and 'social' rights of citizenship. He defines civil rights as freedom of speech and organization and the protection of the citizen against unlawful intrusion by the government. In time these rights were supplemented with political rights, the right to exercise political power and to be represented in government. Social rights are defined by Marshall – who was defending the policies of the post-war British

Labour Party – as covering the basic social security that a state should provide for citizens: employment, education and insurance against illness, accidents and old age. According to Marshall, social rights make citizenship complete.[2] Feminist revisions of Marshall's chronology of rights, most recently by Alice Kessler-Harris, Eileen Boris and Sonya Michel, have convincingly shown that women did not share in the successive acquisition of these rights.[3] These revisions have mostly focused on political and social rights, with civil rights receiving little attention. The concept of maternalism has been used effectively to examine the connections between the role that women played in defining social rights and their battle for political rights as female citizens. Thus, the maternalist paradigm has made it possible to write new gendered histories of citizenship.

In what follows, I argue that the notion of 'civil rights' as defined by Marshall should be included in these histories. I will describe how women social workers involved in early social policies and their implementation in the Netherlands defined not only the 'social' rights of their clients, but also addressed their 'civil' rights.[4] The focus on civil rights suggests new ways of understanding the gendered history of the welfare state, while also allowing me to address – and to refute – some of the criticism directed against the concept of maternalism.

Maternalism has often been criticized as a form of feminism that served only its advocates.[5] Maternalists have generally been identified as educated women from the upper-middle classes who found rewarding careers as architects of new social policies that helped lower-class women survive as homemakers. Especially in the U.S. historiography, the case has been made that the two-channel welfare state that distinguishes between the needs of women (administered by social workers) and the rights of men (guaranteed by federal legislation) can be attributed to ambitious maternalist activists. According to this view, the 'New Woman' who discovered a niche in the political culture of the early twentieth century, where she could build a Children's Bureau, support the Sheppard-Towner Act or start her training as a social worker, served primarily her own interests. The main result was that middle-class women found fulfilling careers in social policies – careers for women who worked on behalf of other women. Condescension lay at the heart of their project: they believed that they could and should act on behalf of the disadvantaged women whom they wanted to help, support or rescue. Racist, classist and even sexist assumptions often lay at the heart of maternalist ideology; the women who themselves wanted to be 'housekeepers of the nation' urged working-class mothers to focus on caring for husbands, children and homes.[6] These presuppositions have been rightly denounced. And indeed, the last thing I would want to do is to suggest that these attitudes should be excused. The implicit condescension of these policies is not only visible with hindsight, but was criticized by contemporaries, especially clients, who objected to the ways in which they were treated by social workers and government officials.[7]

Does this mean that the concept of maternalism should be rejected and that it should not have a place in either our research on gender and welfare policies or the historiography of women's struggles for citizenship? On the contrary, precisely because the concept confronts us with the problematic relationship between women who speak on behalf of other women, precisely because it reveals the way the needs of one group of women could be a basis of rights for another group of women, I want to retain the concept as a useful methodological tool. The problematic of maternalism allows us study the process of redefining citizenship, the connections between the history of women gaining citizenship and the development of social policies by Western states at the beginning of the twentieth century.

As has been noted, maternalism is a term that encompasses multiple components: it is a practice of social policy and legislation, an ideology that mobilizes women who want to be active citizens and shape social policy, and an ideology that prescribes motherhood for women as objects of social policy.[8] It is therefore useful to distinguish between maternalist legislation aimed at mothers, maternalism as an ideology that legitimized women's role as homemakers and maternalism as a political strategy that legitimized women's role as policymakers and stakeholders in the new socially defined state.[9] The three are distinct, but it is imperative to study the ways in which they have been historically interconnected. This will supply us with a historical example that will help illuminate the paradoxes of contemporary social policies that – although explicitly aimed at supporting women – have seriously hampered women's emancipation.[10] There is, in addition, something else that close scrutiny of the connections between social policy, women's political participation in national policymaking and maternalist ideology can help us to achieve. That is to understand the new definitions of citizenship that were being articulated when the first women entered the public sphere to exercise their political rights as citizens. In the Netherlands, the entrance of women into the new domain of professional social work resulted in the expansion of women's political rights, allowing them for the first time a share in decision-making in a public sphere. At the same time, as these social workers began to grapple with delicate issues, such as their clients' needs for privacy and confidentiality, they introduced new ways of thinking about civil rights for women.

Social Work as a 'Counterpublic'

My use of the concept of a public sphere relies on the vocabulary of Jürgen Habermas. I invoke his concept because it allows me to draw on Nancy Fraser's criticism of it.[11] Fraser maintains that the idea of public spheres (she uses the plural, where Habermas identifies a single public sphere) should not be limited to the Habermasian notion of a disinterested conversation among disembodied men about a nationally defined common good. 'Public sphere' in her view might be used to describe communities that aspire – in order to reach full democracy – to create a public domain where opinion is connected with accountability. For Fraser, the concept of democracy is empty when public opinion limits itself to voicing opinions. Thus she includes parliamentary debates in the public sphere, even though they are bound up with the authority of lawmaking and the maintenance of the state. The new public spheres, or 'counterpublics' as Fraser calls them, can be 'weak' (lacking political power) or 'strong' (being able to exercise political or legislative power). To use Marshall's terms, one might say that for Fraser, in a strong public sphere, civil rights must be accompanied by political rights.

The creation of counterpublics involves difficult dilemmas: it brings us to the distinction between civil rights (freedom to express an opinion) and political rights (the entitlement to make a decision that involves others). It is easy to have a disinterested discussion when no decisions are being made. Political rights, however, necessarily involve representational structures. A parliamentary decision or a regulation will affect all members of a community. This implies that certain citizens should be allowed to represent others and to speak and decide on behalf of those others. Joan Landes (following Michael Warner) calls this the 'fraud' that lies at the heart of bourgeois power. She argues that the act of representation produces the people on whose behalf power is exercised.[12] I think it is unwise to denounce all representative democracy as fraudulent, but I agree that representation constructs the object that it represents.[13]

I propose to look at the construction of professional social work as an attempt to create a counterpublic, 'strong' in the sense that it involved not only the exchange of opinions, but also the exercise of power and authority. This will allow me to study the interconnections between the construction of the client and the construction of the social worker who could speak on her (and sometimes his) behalf. I will thus take a closer look at the way in which new self-proclaimed authorities formulated the conditions under which they could speak and decide on behalf of others (thus formulating political rights) and the way in which the objects of their interventions were constructed as subjects in the field of social work (and thus granted civil rights).

From Philanthropy to Social Work

Social work as a field that required special training and involved professional standards evolved in the Netherlands, as it did in most European
countries, from the reorganization of philanthropy at the end of the nineteenth century.[14] Dutch women involved in this process were relatively
early in creating a school for social work. In Amsterdam the first full programme started in September 1899 with twenty-three female students.[15]
The preceding years had witnessed rising interest in schooling for charity
visitors. Connections to the movement for women's emancipation played
an important role in this growing concern. Consider, for example, Helene
Mercier, a prolific writer who published many popular articles on both the
'Woman's Question' and 'social problems' in the 1880s and 1890s.[16] She
wrote about the problems of the working classes and how women from
the middle classes needed fulfilling ways to participate in social life. One
of the women inspired by her called the fact that there was simultaneously
a 'social problem' and a 'woman's problem' a 'happy coincidence': now
women could contribute to the solution of social issues.[17]

As in other countries, a lobby to reorganize philanthropy began to
gain influence in the last decades of the nineteenth century. Since the
revised Constitution of 1853, public and private poor relief in the Netherlands had been strictly separated.[18] Private relief was divided among
church-run charities, while non-religious private organizations focused
on specific forms of support, such as housing, clothing or fuel, and special
groups of people, such as the elderly, orphans or prostitutes. Public poor
relief by local government – no national relief system existed – was by law
required to limit itself to the bare minimum required to keep a person
alive. Moreover, such relief was only to be given after it was convincingly
demonstrated that churches and private charity would not help the people involved. This system had functioned relatively well in the predominantly agrarian country that the Netherlands had been for most of the
nineteenth century, when the majority of people lived in villages. But in
the 1880s and 1890s industrialization – which occurred later in the Netherlands than in neighbouring Belgium and Germany – began to change
the nation's demographics. The population of big cities like Amsterdam
and Rotterdam increased rapidly, as did problems of structural poverty in
working-class neighbourhoods.

Especially for the private organizations in big cities that dealt with increasing numbers of working-class families that were not integrated into
churches, the limitations of traditional poor relief became evermore clear.
The call for better coordination between different forms of poor-relief
– for the institution of a system of registration and closer checks on re-

ligious charity – spread rapidly.[19] A growing number of people active in private charity advocated an expanded role for government in providing social welfare. They wanted local public poor relief to be able to dispense more than the bare necessities. The local government, they argued, should be allowed to help people become economically independent again, for instance by providing them with some extra funds to set up an income-generating activity. For the advocates of an increased role for the government, the main source of inspiration was Germany. Here a successful Eberfelder system was developed in which private volunteers worked with paid civil servants to provide poor relief while advising and helping the poor to regain independence through an individualized approach.[20]

At the time – from the 1880s to the 1910s – the movement to reform poor relief was associated with the advance of progressive liberal ideas that advocated an expanded role for government in guaranteeing social welfare. Due to the late industrialization in the Netherlands, a social democratic mass movement did not have a strong impact on the early discussions about social policies. Only after 1900 did the Social Democrats become a power to be reckoned with in political and social respects. In the progressive liberal circles that debated solutions to what was called the 'Social Question', a clear gendered division is detectable. The men in this political movement were representatives in parliament, often scholars who published academic works on social issues. They focused mostly on legislation that would set limits to the exploitation of the working classes. They initiated parliamentary investigations into the working conditions in factories and proposed the legislation of 1889, which limited the working hours of children and women in factories.[21] In contrast, the women who belonged to this group of reformers were excluded from political representation (female suffrage was introduced in 1919) and from academic study (the first woman to defend a dissertation at a Dutch university was Aletta Jacobs in 1879, and she remained an exception until after 1900). Women were predominantly active in the field where their authority was respected: charity and poor relief.

The role of women in private philanthropy and religious charity had long been established in the Netherlands. On the whole, women did not create a separate domain of women-led organizations, but they played an integral role in the practical organization of charity, especially that directed towards children and women.[22] Although they did not generally serve on the boards of private and religious charitable institutions, they were very active within those organizations. Marie Muller-Lulofs, for example, had in 1890 established an 'Association for the Improvement of Charity in Utrecht', one of the new private associations for poor relief that advocated reform. While she was the brains and the inspiration for this association, she asked her husband to serve as chair, fearing that it would harm the cause for a woman to take the lead.[23] The Association that she founded was one of the first to provide official training for charity workers.

For progressive male liberals, a larger social role for government was logically connected to the expansion of the political rights for men of the lower income strata of Dutch society. In the last decades of the nineteenth century, the property requirements for the right to vote had been reduced in different legislative acts. Socialists did not yet form a strong mass movement, as they did in Germany; however, by the 1890s the Dutch parliament no longer exclusively represented the aristocracy and wealthy propertied classes. The advocates of this expansion of the male vote were the progressive liberals in parliament. General male suffrage would wait until 1917, but as the lower middle classes of male shopkeepers and artisans received the right to vote, new political parties gained influence: the Reformed Protestants claimed to represent the 'small man'; Socialists represented labour; Catholics represented a group that had long been treated as second-class citizens in the Dutch Protestant nation. All shared the belief of the progressive liberals that citizenship should not be based on extensive property, but on what was called 'productive virtue', a concept that could include everyone whose labour contributed to the national wealth and who through the work of his hands could take care of himself.[24] For these groups the expansion of political rights to 'new' citizens went hand-in-hand with new conceptions about the responsibility of the state.

But men were not the only ones who redefined citizenship. The attitude exemplified by Muller-Lulofs, who in 1890 refused to chair the association that she had created, began to change; women began to take formal public responsibility for the organization of charity. At first this happened only in organizations that dealt exclusively with women, but increasingly women showed their willingness to be accountable in areas where they had to deal with men as well.[25] Some of these women became advocates of female suffrage; the increasing support in the 1890s for women's suffrage organizations testifies to that. But many women who were active in the movement for the modernization of charity were not suffragists. Does this mean they were not interested in political rights for women? That would only be the case if we limit our understanding of political rights to the right to vote for the national government. When we follow Nancy Fraser in her attention to the construction of other public spaces, we are in a better position to evaluate how women in the field of charity tried to expand their right to exercise power, to become accountable, to have a say in decision-making. Their activities can then be described as the struggle for the expansion of their political rights within the field of social work. They tried to transform charity into a 'strong public', an institution that voiced opinions and that exercised authority. The boards of private agencies that decided on the amount and form of poor relief, the councils within churches that determined the allocation of charity and the directors who decided how to help a family in need were all part of a public domain that was, in Fraser's words, a 'strong public'. Here decisions were being made, actions undertaken. Women's increased participation in these boards, councils and directorships not only signified their participation in formulating opinions, but also the exercise of political power.

After 1900 this expansion of women's public authority became explicitly connected to the struggle for suffrage. If private organizations and churches admitted women as specialists of poor relief, the argument went, then local and national government should accept their authority in the field as well. A booklet published in 1909 entitled *Women's Role in Social Work* (*Het aandeel der vrouw in het maatschappelijk werk ten onzent verricht*) clearly illustrates how women perceived their participation on the boards of relief organizations as directly relating to the aspiration for female suffrage. In the introduction, the feminist director of the Bureau for Women's Labour, Anna Polak, pointed out that the city council was the governing board of the public charity in a given city; thus women's exclusion from voting meant that public poor relief for women was provided by women (who did most of the individual visiting) but regulated by men.[26] This connection between the struggle for the vote and the growing role of women in social work did not mean that all social workers were feminists. The women who tried to strengthen their position in the domain of social work did not always do so on the basis of a supposed female or feminist solidarity. The representational rights these women demanded on boards of charity and within relief organizations were limited to those women who worked for the agencies: they were not asking for the rights of clients to be represented on the boards.

However, there was a connection between the clients and the social workers who worked on their behalf. This connection was created in the elaboration of the professional discourse about social work. The struggle for positions of authority and the right to influence policy in an agency overlapped with the quest for more knowledge and professional standards in the field of charity and poor relief. The concept of 'social work' began to replace 'charity' and 'friendly visitors' evolved into 'social workers'. The new jargon indicated a modern approach of the problem of poverty and pauperism in which professional training was deemed crucial. Social workers were to acquire knowledge based on the direct experience of visiting the poor, learning about their problems and finding effective ways to assist them. The women who had been advocating this practice in philanthropic organizations began to talk publicly and to write about training for social work. International contacts played a critical role in shaping their views. Some were in contact with German women who professed the idea of social work training for women (Alice Salomon and others in Berlin); others went to London and learned about settlement houses. 'Toynbee-work' (work in settlements and community centres) became a familiar expression in circles of Dutch social workers. In 1898, at several of the conferences organized by the 'National Exhibition of Women's Labour' held in The Hague, the first public discussions about the need for training schools for social work were held. A woman who had visited London mentioned the Women's University Settlement in London, while others spoke about social work in the field of social housing and the training that it required.[27]

The idea that women should and could be trained for social work was based on the notion that they were particularly knowledgeable about the problems that recipients of charity and poor relief faced. Women in general were supposed to know about housekeeping, raising children, making ends meet and dealing with irresponsible husbands. It was argued that female social workers therefore might connect better with poor women who needed relief, support or advice. However, even if women were seen as 'naturally' adept at social work, professional training was also viewed as essential. In particular, professional instructors could provide the knowledge that would allow social workers to more readily identify their clients, to imagine what it meant to be dependent on others. Marie Muller-Lulofs, for example, in an article designed to instruct prospective charity visitors, reproduced a budget of a working-class family. She hoped that this type of concrete information would help her readers to share the perspective of the client, to understand what hard choices a poor mother had to make. The financial situation of a friendly visitor and that of her clients might be so different that the former would be unable to provide useful advice or assistance. Early social work educators also stressed shared female experiences such as motherhood and housekeeping to strengthen bonds of empathy. Marie Muller-Lulofs, for example, often referred to common interests like love and anxieties about children, the responsibility for other members of the family and the need for self-esteem. Empathy – the ability to imagine oneself in the position of the other – was part of the professional attitude; it was thought to follow from and to complement a 'scientific' understanding of poverty.

These ideas lay at the heart of the first school for social work, which opened its doors in the winter of 1899 in Amsterdam. One of the innovative elements in the curriculum in the first years was an internship as a household assistant to a poor family, helping an overburdened mother with cleaning, cooking and child care. The experience must have been a shock for some of the students, who all came from rather affluent backgrounds. The other part of the curriculum stressed serious study of social and economic conditions. Lecturers from Amsterdam University taught prospective social workers to analyse social and economic structures with scientific rigour.

Thus the early professional identity of social workers was conceived as a combination of empathy and distance. This conclusion is not new; many histories of professional social work describe the coming together of these two approaches. What I want to argue here is that the invention of professional social work can also be seen as a chapter in the history of citizenship. Social workers elaborated a new form of representational citizenship: they argued that they could speak on behalf of the poor because they could simultaneously identify with their clients and distance themselves in order to see the larger picture. To gain authority for themselves, social workers stressed the fact that clients were human beings with their own responsibilities and rights. A social worker could only be a translator of the needs of the poor if the needs of the poor were to be taken seriously.

This approach served the first social workers in their efforts to have a larger say in the organization of poor relief. They based their claim to influence and power in the field of social work on a professed representational authority. They argued that, as trained social workers, they knew more about the culture of poverty, the dilemmas of single mothers and the needs of poor families than did the men who served on the boards of relief agencies. Their partial identification with poor women resulted in detailed attention to the rights of the clients. In the early twentieth century, texts that instructed prospective social workers about how to behave emphasized the paramount importance of respecting clients and safeguarding their right to privacy.[28] Social workers were urged to see the world from the position of the client.[29] Encouraging social workers to think in this manner led to the first efforts to describe the 'rights' of clients – to privacy, to confidentiality, to a minimum of intervention and interference by agencies and to knowledge about what information was being used in decisions about them (such as, for example, whether to reduce the amount of relief or to send children to a foster home).

It is important to note that these newly invented clients' rights were, in Marshall's words, civil rights, not political rights. They did not involve the right of the clients to influence the policies to which they were subjected, but only set limits to the interventions by the authorities. Two points should concern us here. First is the fact that a discourse about the rights of the poor and needy emerged before general male suffrage was instituted. Second, these civil rights were formulated by women whose own citizenship (civil and political) had not yet been realized. The shared exclusion from white, male, upper- and middle-class citizenship may have stimulated female social workers to be more sensitive to their clients' need for civil rights. It did not, however, make social workers and their clients equals. On the contrary, the careful mixture of distance and identification that middle-class women displayed when they addressed clients reinforced class difference more often than not.

Distance and Identification

The persistence of class differences in the domain of social work is illustrated by examining the 1898 National Exhibition of Women's Labour. This exhibition was organized by women who wanted to celebrate the inauguration of Queen Wilhelmina with an event that would demonstrate that all women could contribute to the national well-being. The room devoted to 'Social Work' was the main venue designed to confront middle-class women who visited this huge exhibition with the social problems of their time. While the Hall of Industry celebrated women's participation in paid labour as responsible factory workers, the room devoted to social work showed the disastrous effects of sweatshops, home industries and low wages in agriculture. The texts and images that confronted visitors with representations of 'how the other half lives' were combined to produce both a sense of distance and immediate identification.[30] Visitors were invited to peep almost literally into the worlds of working-class women: through a hole in a black screen they could see an image of heartbreaking working conditions; they could also look inside a model of a hut made out of peat, where families who worked in this industry lived, with several men, women and children often sharing a room or even a bed.

The exposition did not merely seek to invoke feelings of pity and compassion. The personal responsibility of consumers who bought clothing that had been produced in sweatshops was also addressed. Mimicking a shop display, a table exhibited pieces of clothing, but with price tags that indicated not the selling price, but the pitiful amount that had been earned by the woman who had stitched or embroidered the dress or shirt. Here the connection between compassion and personal responsibility was constructed. The implicit argument was that the middle-class woman who bought clothes had the duty to know about the life of her less fortunate sisters. Being a consumer brought with it social responsibilities.

The texts that accompanied these representations not only urged women who visited the exhibition to be conscientious consumers, but also addressed them as potential citizens who needed to reflect on solutions to the 'social issue'. The female organizers of this exhibit were Protestant, Catholic and Jewish women, most of who were involved in the movement for the reorganization of poor relief and charity. They wanted the audience to move beyond what they dismissed as 'easy emotions'. To be shocked by the living conditions of poor women was not enough. The middle-class women interested in social work should see it as their duty to acquire knowledge and to understand social relations. This knowledge and understanding should be based partly on the ability to identify with women who experienced poverty and pauperism. But the identification had to be balanced by analytical insight and scientific understanding of social relations. Women social workers thus defended their authority with a two-part argument. They argued, in essence, 'We can identify with these women and can therefore describe their problems better than any male social scientist, and we have the knowledge that allows us to behave like dispassionate, responsible citizens or politicians'.

By staking their authority on these two claims, female social workers based their demands for political rights in the domain of poor relief on their ability to defend the interests of others. Representing the interests of poor women who needed social support, social workers claimed that they knew what was best for their clients. They articulated a form of citizenship that I want to call custodial. The clients were implicitly turned into 'wards' – dependent protégés entitled to protection and limited civil rights. The description of clients as dependent went hand-in-hand with the construction of the aspiring woman-citizen as independent and self-reliant. The identification with the other was as necessary as the distance created by specialized knowledge and insight. Institutionalized condescension was integral to this conception of women's emancipation through careers in social work, but so was a keen awareness that, in the past, many forms of charity had not really done justice to women who needed help. The early social workers used many of the same arguments that feminist critics of condescending welfare practices still voice: pity is not enough; solving social problems requires more than sentimental responses or harsh moral judgements; people who profit from the poverty of others should be held accountable.

It is important to note that these early social workers were the first to address explicitly the ambivalence inherent in all relationships in which one person cares for another. They were the first to see how such relations can be at the same time empowering and disabling, limiting and liberating. Muller-Lulofs urged prospective social workers to be aware of their own deeper emotions and of their own dependency upon the helping relationships that they created. She spoke about women who treaded the 'holy ground of charity' with 'worn dancing shoes'. This image refers to the fact that many social workers were women who had, in the eyes of contemporaries, 'failed' to find a husband and have children. Muller-Lulofs argued that in itself this 'fact' was not a problem as long as social workers were aware of the importance of the task they took upon themselves. Social workers had to accept that they themselves profited from their profession.

This conception of citizenship as based on responsibility for others was not new. It resonates with older conceptions of eighteenth-century civic republicanism: the idea that only those men who can take care of themselves and others (in a financial and military sense) could be citizens.[31] The progressive liberal and socialist conceptions of equality as the basis for citizenship reduced the impact of this older ideal at the end of the nineteenth century, but the idea of the citizen as the custodian of other, weaker, 'not-yet-citizens' was being re-invented and celebrated in the context of colonial imperialism. While male equality was celebrated at home, European imperialists reproduced the idea of the citizen as someone who takes care of 'others' who are weaker, or not yet 'adult' enough to rule themselves. In both official and popular colonialist discourse, the image emerged of the Western citizen shouldering the weighty responsibility of ruling over an indigenous population. Whether a civil servant governing colonial society or an employer running a plantation or a mine, the white European male in the colonies was seen as the custodian for the indigenous population whom he protected 'against themselves'. It has often been noted that, for middle-class women at the turn of twentieth century, a visit to the slums of London or Paris resembled the adventures of young men who travelled to the colonies, and it seems worthwhile to investigate how these images of a journey into the unknown have shaped the expectations of citizenship.[32] It is striking to see how the same notion of citizenship, based on the idea that one could speak on behalf of others, was formulated in the both the social domain and in the arena of imperialism. Furthermore, it permeated the language of both the conservative and progressive social workers, just as it can be detected in the language of both the defenders and the critics of imperialism.[33]

By introducing the phrase 'custodial citizenship' I have, for a moment, suspended the gender of the citizenship the early social workers were advocating. While only women can be mothers and only men can be fathers, both sexes can – in theory – be custodians. This allowed me to reveal the similarities between the ways in which female social workers and male colonial employees envisaged their roles. Now let me reintroduce gender by returning to the concept of 'maternalism'. The concept of maternalism as developed by Sonya Michel and Seth Koven invokes the metaphor and the reality of motherhood in late nineteenth and early twentieth century.

It is a notion that is inherently ambiguous. While the mother is endowed with power over her children, her authority is limited by her husband's power as the head of the household. The power of fathers – especially within the middle-class families that women social workers came from – is far less ambiguous; inside the household his power is more or less absolute. A father can afford to be entirely condescending towards his children. In contrast, a mother is in position where she must find a balance between being in charge and being powerless. She cannot afford to be entirely patronising; her condescension is always part of a larger picture, one in which she may find herself the object of condescension.

For me the ambiguity of powerful and powerless motherhood that is invoked by the concept of 'maternalism' is extremely fruitful. It allows me to think about the histories of women and social policy in a manner that goes beyond the simple opposition of 'good' social workers who respected clients and 'bad' ones who patronized them. I hope to have shown that – at least in the case of early Dutch social workers and their clients – the history is more complex. In order to present themselves as suitable participants in the discussions about poverty, charity and social work, female middle-class social workers claimed that they represented the poor. These ambitious middle-class women argued that a new professional language was needed in the field of poor relief. They defined this language in such a way that it could only be developed successfully if women were admitted to centres of decision-making in the field. In so doing they constructed the client as someone who should be represented as a subject in her (or his) own right. Just as political representation creates the people who are being represented, so the discourse of professional social work creates the clients whose interests are being served.

Female social workers could not have successfully based their claims to power on the interests of clients without actually listening to those clients; they could not have emancipated themselves if they had been entirely deaf and blind to their clients' subjectivity. They needed the idea that clients were authorized to speak for themselves to strengthen their own position. United in their status as not-yet-citizens, middle-class women and working-class clients together created a nascent language that allowed welfare providers and welfare recipients to criticize condescension, reject abuses of power by relief agencies and condemn unlimited intervention in the lives of the poor. One might deplore the fact that we still need that discourse today, but this was the first attempt to see the poor and dependent as people with legitimate claims to civil rights. It created the client and the professional social worker at the same time. That is why it remains necessary to study the twin histories of the invention of the client and the invention of the social workers as a single story full of ambiguities.

Notes

1. The connection between middle-class women's ambitions to exercise political rights on the one hand and their efforts to define social rights for poor women and children on the other may be obvious now, but when first developed in the early 1990s, it was dramatically new and necessary. In this respect the contributions of Seth Koven, Sonya Michel and Theda Skocpol to the histories of welfare state and to the histories of feminism cannot be overstated. S. Koven and S. Michel (eds). 1993. *Mothers of a New World: Maternalist Politics and the Origins of Welfare States*, London and New York: Routledge; idem. 1990. 'Womanly Duties: Maternalist Politics and the Origins of the Welfare States in France, Germany, Great Britain, and the United States, 1880–1920', *American Historical Review* 95(4), 1076–108; and T. Skocpol. 1992. *Protecting Soldiers and Mothers: The Political Origins of Social Policy in the United States*, Cambridge, MA: Harvard University Press.
2. T.H. Marshall. 1992 (orig. 1950). *Citizenship and Social Class*, London: Verso, 1992.
3. A. Kessler-Harris. 2001. *In Pursuit of Equity: Women, Men, and the Quest for Economic Citizenship in 20th-Century America*, New York: Oxford University Press; E. Boris and S. Michel. 2001. 'Social Citizenship and Women's Right to Work in Postwar America', in P. Grimshaw, K. Holmes and M. Lake (eds), *Women's Rights and Human Rights: International Historical Perspectives*, Basingstoke and New York: Palgrave Macmillan, 199–219.
4. A. de Swaan. 1998. *In Care of the State: Health Care, Education and Welfare in Europe and the USA in the Modern Era*, New York: Oxford University Press introduced the concept of 'welfare arrangements'.
5. L. Gordon. 1991. 'Black and White Visions of Welfare: Women's Welfare Activism, 1890–1945', *Journal of American History* 78(2), 559–90; E. Boris. 1993. 'What about the Working of the Working Mother?', *Journal of Women's History* 5(2), 104–7; and M. Ladd-Taylor. 1994. *Mother-Work: Women Child Welfare and the State, 1880–1930*, Urbana: University of Illinois Press.
6. The metaphor 'housekeepers of the nation' is discussed in K.K. Sklar. 1995. *Florence Kelley and the Nation's Work: The Rise of Women's Political Culture, 1830–1930*, New Haven: Yale University Press.
7. On the protests of the poor, see: F.F. Piven and R.A. Cloward. 1993 (orig. 1972). *Regulating the Poor: The Functions of Public Welfare*, rev. ed. New York: Vintage Press; and B. Stadum. 1992. *Poor Women and Their Families: Hard Working Charity Cases, 1900–1930*, Albany: State University of New York Press.
8. See Sonya Michel, 'Maternalism and Beyond' in this volume.
9. Skocpol, *Protecting Soldiers and Mothers* and de Swaan, *In Care of the State* stress legislation, whereas Koven and Michel (eds), *Mothers of a New World*, pay more attention to the importance of ideology in legitimizing specific roles for women.
10. R. Muncy. 1991. *Creating a Female Dominion in American Reform, 1890–1935*, New York: Oxford University Press; and L.R.Y. Storrs. 1998. 'Gender and the Development of the Regulatory State: The Controversy over Restricting Women's Night Work in the Depression-Era South', *Journal of Policy History* 10(2), 179–206. Kessler-Harris refers to these works when she writes: 'This recent work suggests that women's networks promoted legislation that in the end hindered women's economic citizenship': *In Pursuit of Equity*, 299. See also: Boris and Michel, 'Social Citizenship'; and S. Michel. 1999. *Children's Interests/Mothers' Rights: The Shaping of America's Child Care Policy*, New Haven: Yale University Press. For European examples, see G. Bock and P. Thane (eds). 1991. *Maternity and Gender Policies: Women and the Rise of the European Welfare States, 1880–1950s*, London and New York: Routledge.
11. N. Fraser. 1996 (orig. 1992). 'Rethinking the Public Sphere: A Contribution to the Critique of Actually Existing Democracy', in C. Calhoun (ed.), *Habermas and the Public Sphere*, Cambridge, MA: Harvard University Press, 109–42.

12. J. Landes. 1995. 'The Public and the Private Sphere: A Feminist Reconsideration', in J. Meehan (ed.), *Feminists Read Habermas: Gendering the Subject of Discourse*, New York: Routledge, 90–116.
13. For a particularly insightful description of how this process takes place when social welfare is directed at the 'empowerment' of clients, see B. Cruikshank. 1999. *The Will to Empower: Democratic Citizens and Other Subjects*, Ithaca, NY: Cornell University Press.
14. For a comparative study of the origins of social work in different countries in Western, Central and Eastern Europe, see S. Hering and B. Waaldijk (eds). 2003. *History of Social Work in Europe (1900–1960): Female Pioneers and Their Influence on the Development of International Social Organizations*, Opladen: Lesk + Budrich.
15. L. Bervoets. 1994. *Opvoeden tot Sociale Verantwoordelijkheid: De verzoening van weten- schap, ethiek en sekse in het sociaal werk in Nederland rond de de eeuwwisseling (Education for Social Responsibility: The Conciliation of Science, Ethics and Gender in Social Work in the Netherlands around 1900)*, Wageningen (published dissertation); B. Waaldijk. 1996. *Het Amerika der Vrouw: Sekse en geschiedenis van maatschappelijk werk in Nederland en de Verenigde Staten (A New World for Women: Gender and the History of Social Work in the Netherlands and the United States)*, Groningen (published dissertation).
16. Helene Mercier (1839–1910) published several books about social issues and the role of women in Dutch society, including H. Mercier. 1897. *Verbonden Schakels*, Haarlem: H.D. Tjeenk Willink, 1889; and idem. 1897. *Sociale Schetsen*, Haarlem: H.D. Tjeenk Willink.
17. M. Muller-Lulofs referred to the 'happy coincidence' in M. Muller-Lulofs. 1916. *Van Men- sch tot Mensch (From One Human Being to Another)*, Haarlem: H.D. Tjeenk Willink, 92. For an analysis of Helene Mercier, see S. Dudink. 1997. *Deugdzaam Liberalisme (Virtuous Liberalism)*, Amsterdam: Stichting beheer IISG, 1997.
18. For background on the history of social welfare in the Netherlands before 1954, see F. Gouda. 1995. *Poverty and Political Culture: The Rhetoric of Social Welfare in the Nether- lands and France, 1815–1954*, Boston: Rowman and Littlefield.
19. Calls for a system that would allow for greater oversight and accountability resembled those of British and American Charity Organization Societies. K. Woodroofe. 1962. *From Char- ity Organization to Social Work in England and the United States*, London: Routledge and Kegan Paul.
20. For a recent overview of the development of social work in Germany, see S. Hering and R. Münchmeier. 2000. *Geschichte der sozialen Arbeit (History of Social Work)*, Weinheim und München: Juventa Verlag.
21. U. Jansz. 1991. 'Sociale kwestie en sekse in de politieke geschiedenis: De Arbeidswet van 1889', *Jaarboek voor Vrouwengeschiedenis* 12, 70–90; S. Stuurman.1989. 'John Bright and Samuel van Houten: Radical Liberalism and the Working Classes in Britain and The Neth- erlands 1860–1880', *History of European Ideas* 11, 593–604; and S. Stuurman. 1997. 'The Discourse of Productive Virtue: Early Liberalism in Europe and the Netherlands', in S. Groenveld and M.J. Wintle (eds), *Under the Sign of Liberalism: Varities of Liberalism Past and Present*, Zutphen: Walburg Pers, 33–45.
22. T. de Bie en W. Fritschy. 1985. 'De "wereld" van Reveilvrouwen, hun liefdadige activitei- ten en het ontstaan van het feminisme in Nederland', *De eerste feministische golf. Jaarboek voor Vrouwengeschiedenis* 6, 30–58.
23. See Bervoets, *Opvoeden*.
24. Stuurman, 'The Discourse'.
25. The first women's organizations in the Netherlands, *Arbeid Adelt* and *Tesselschade* (found- ed in 1871 and 1872 respectively), supported middle-class women who attempted to make a living through selling their needlework. They have often been called the origin of the Dutch women's movement.
26. A. Polak. 1909. *Het aandeel der vrouw in het maatschappelijk werk ten onzent verricht*, Gravenhage: Nationaal Bureau voor Vrouwenarbeid.

27. For discussions of the National Exhibition of Women's Labour in 1898, see M. Grever and
     B. Waaldijk, intro. A. Burton. 2004. *Transforming the Public Sphere: The Dutch National
     Exhibition of Women's Labour in 1898*, Durham, NC: Duke University Press.
28. M. Muller-Lulofs. 1916. *Van Mensch tot Mensch*, Haarlem: Tjeenk Willink. This is a col-
     lection of articles that the author had published about the social work in the preceding
     twenty years in different journals. All of them addressed issues pertinent to a social worker
     or friendly visitor. The second major Dutch publication with instructions for social workers
     was: J.H. Adriani. 1923. *Voorlezingen over Armenzorg en Maatschappelijk Werk (Lectures
     about Social Work)*, Utrecht: Ruys. In the introduction he thanked Muller-Lulofs for her
     teachings, a rare instance of gender reversal in training and education of the times.
29. In this approach we can now easily recognize the more recent concepts used in social case-
     work that stress empowerment and respect, as illustrated by the principle 'Start where the
     client is'. M.L. Waaldijk and A. Boet. 2003. '"Start Where the Client Is": Marie Kamphuis
     and the Professionalization of Dutch Social Work', in Hering and Waaldijk, *History of So-
     cial Work in Europe*, 45–52.
30. J.A. Riis. 1962 (orig. 1895). *How the Other Half Lives: Studies among the Tenements of New
     York*, New York: Hill and Wang.
31. B. Siim. 2000. *Gender and Citizenship: Politics and Agency in France, Britain and Den-
     mark*, Cambridge: Cambridge University Press, 2000, traces different definitions of citi-
     zenship, including civic republicanism.
32. P.J. Keating (ed.). 1976. *Into Unknown England 1866–1913: Selections from the Social Ex-
     plorers*, Manchester: Rowman and Littlefield; M. Perrot. 1994. 'Outside the Circle', in F.
     Thébaud (ed.), G. Duby and M. Perrot (series eds). A. Goldhammer (trans), *A History
     of Women in the West: Toward a Cultural Identity in the Twentieth Century*, Cambridge,
     MA: Harvard University Press; and A.L. Stoler. 1995. *Race and the Education of Desire:
     Foucault's* History of Sexuality *and the Colonial Order of Things*, Durham, NC: Duke Uni-
     versity Press.
33. The first and most famous anti-colonial Dutch novel, the pseudonymous Multatuli's *Max
     Havelaar*, was written by a colonial civil servant who spoke from a position of Dutch
     responsibility for the interests of the population in the colonies. Multatuli, W. Siebanhaar
     (trans), intro. D.H. Lawrence. 1927 (orig. 1860). *Max Havelaar; or The Coffee Sales of
     the Netherlands Trading Company*, New York and London: A.A. Knopf. See also the anti-
     imperialist writings by Leonard Woolf, who had served as a civil servant in India. L. Woolf,
     E.F.C. Ludowyk (ed.). 1981 (orig. 1913). *The Village in the Jungle*, Oxford: Oxford Uni-
     versity Press; and L. Woolf, intro. P. Cain. 1998 (orig. 1920). *Empire and Commerce in
     Africa: A Study in Economic Imperialism*, London: George Allen and Unwin.

CHAPTER 6

'RESPECTABLE CITIZENS OF CANADA'
Gender, Maternalism and the Welfare State in the Great Depression

Lara Campbell

> Mr. Bennett, we women of Canada are not going to let our children starve for you or any other government in Canada ... I'm not here speaking for myself ... but for other women all over Canada. This can't go on ... If we are bitter, it is you have made us bitter. We women can't go on bringing kids in this world just for them to starve.[1]

This speech gained Mrs William Wilkinson of North York, Ontario, some notoriety during a meeting with Canadian Prime Minister R.B. Bennett in August 1932. The only female delegate at the communist-sponsored Workers' Economic Conference, Wilkinson reportedly criticized Bennett's employment policy and pounded his desk when he disagreed with her. One Toronto newspaper, the *Daily Star*, sympathetically portrayed her as a strong, working-class woman, whose militancy was an extension of her maternal role. 'It's a far cry from a little home in North York to the chambers of the highest executive in the land,' claimed the newspaper. 'But foremost in her mind and back of that was the thought of her family of five and of her anxious husband in their little home.'[2]

Mrs Wilkinson was one of many women who used the language of maternalism to protest the economic conditions of the Great Depression. This paper studies the discourse of maternalism from the grassroots perspective of mainly Anglo-Canadian, working-class women in Ontario who

Notes for this chapter begin on page 115.

were the wives and mothers of unemployed men and children. Rather than looking at the ways in which maternalism was used by middle-class women's groups to expand their role in the welfare state or to regulate the lives of poor women, it explores how working-class women and wives of unemployed men demanded economic security as part of their full citizenship rights. They did so by emphasizing their gendered roles of wife and mother, their patriotic loyalty to the nation and their status as respectable Anglo-Canadian mothers.

This paper will first examine letters of protest written to local and provincial politicians and explore how women articulated their sense of entitlement as mothers and as citizens. I will argue that conceptions of Anglo-Canadian identity drew together wives of unemployed men, widows on Mothers' Allowance and wives of unemployed World War I veterans, and that women played a crucial role in welfare state formation that they could rarely achieve at the formal political level.[3] Then, using records relating to the grassroots protests of unemployed unions, I will explore how domestic issues were central to relief protest and how women themselves participated in local politics. This section will also look extensively at men, who were motivated to radical protest not simply by their identity and concerns as workers, but as fathers and breadwinners.

Women's claims on the state during the Depression extended beyond the earlier fight for political citizenship to embrace economic and social citizenship based on material security and the elimination of charity. Though the gendered roles of breadwinning and domesticity were set in opposition, married men understood the importance of women's domestic labour to working-class family survival. Men's willingness to protest on behalf of domestic issues and to embrace the language of domesticity illustrates that both men and women embraced familial and maternal rhetoric for political purposes and for collective protest. Though women's maternal claims on the state rarely challenged men's breadwinning status, their demands for entitlement in the 1930s helped to reshape the postwar Canadian liberal welfare state.

The Great Depression was a crucial turning point in the notion of welfare state entitlement and citizenship. Canada had only minimal welfare programmes in place by the 1930s. Like Britain, Australia and New Zealand, Canada had nineteenth-century labour regulations in place for both men and women and introduced an old age pension (1927).[4] Canadian provinces, like many American states, gradually introduced Mothers' Allowance legislation and Workmen's Compensation. But the country lacked a comprehensive, state-sponsored programme to deal with unemployment levels that, by 1933, had risen as high as 30 per cent. In some Ontario communities, relief recipients totalled 35 per cent of the population.[5] Citing the federal-provincial division of powers under the British North America Act, the federal government initially refused to take responsibility for the unemployed. By 1930, however, Prime Minister R.B. Bennett's Conservative government initiated a series of emergency Relief Acts that gave money for public works and relief, though eligibility rules and rates continued to be determined by the municipalities. Therefore, regulations differed widely across the country.[6] Relief was administered in a hierarchical fashion based on gender and marital status. Married men were expected to claim relief on behalf of their wives and children. If they refused, women had few options, though they could use the family court system to press charges of desertion or non-support.[7] However, women were not invisible in relief politics. In their individual and collective protests as 'militant mothers', women and maternalist rhetoric were central to relief protest and policy in the Depression era.[8]

Definitions of Maternalism

Maternalism has been defined by Sonya Michel and Seth Koven as an exaltation of women's 'natural' capacity to mother applied to state policies concerned with the interests of women and children.[9] It was one way for middle-class women to play a wider role in the public sphere and to help create social policy. This concept of maternalism has informed Canadian and international literature that explores how middle-class women embraced the glorification of motherhood and applied it to the political sphere, carving out a public and often powerful place for themselves in campaigns for suffrage and social reform.[10] Also central to Michel's definition of maternalism is the notion that middle-class women spoke on behalf of their poorer 'sisters' and claimed the right to 'instruct and regulate' the lives of non-white, poor or immigrant women.[11] Historians have often argued that middle-class reformers helped to create policies that punished women who did not conform to the normative standards of white womanhood. Thus, there is considerable debate over the conservative nature of maternalist arguments and how these were entwined with notions of respectable white middle-class womanhood.[12] Some scholars contend that the term itself is too limiting and embrace the concept of familialism in order to emphasize how government policies were designed to uphold, strengthen and support concepts of normative family life.[13] Indeed, there are striking similarities across geographical boundaries – as the articles in this collection demonstrate – in the way that governments sought to incorporate images of the family in both welfare policy and nation-building.

But what happens to our understanding of the concept of maternalism when we explore instances in which maternalist rhetoric was employed from the ground up, to critique government policy, to demand rights or to fight against unemployment? Looking at the development of the welfare state from a grassroots perspective, I believe, adds an important component to this debate. Most historical and political studies of the welfare state, even those that incorporate a gendered analysis, tend to focus on policymakers or reformers rather than on clients themselves.[14] Some historical literature now encourages an examination of how welfare policies were received and interpreted by clients, especially as historians increasingly utilize welfare or courtroom case files.[15] But I would like to take this one step further and argue that it is also important to look at the role that the unemployed and poor played in shaping, creating or inspiring new policy initiatives. This is particularly relevant to Canada, since the height of state expansion in social welfare came in the aftermath of World War II. Therefore, massive unemployment and political and cultural upheavals across Canada in the 1930s had a profound impact on the nature and extent of post-war reconstruction. It was the disruption of the Great Depression and high male unemployment, Canadian historian Nancy Christie has argued, that led to the post-war consolidation of the welfare state around the male breadwinner wage, established fatherhood as a basis for increased social and economic rights and linked employment status to the best-paying social insurance programmes, such as Unemployment Insurance.[16] As Rebecca Jo Plant's article on anti-maternalism in the United States demonstrates, by the 1950s, women were less able to make claims based on their special status as mothers. While women's demands on the state for themselves and their families did help to restructure the post-war welfare state, the increased bureaucratization and formalization around rights to work, welfare and economic security served to at least partially erode women's moral claims to the special status of motherhood.[17]

This paper examines maternalism as a discourse embedded in the language of protest and as a motivator of political action. Maternalist language and action was used by wives and mothers suffering the effects of high unemployment in 1930s Canada. This language could also be described as familialist, because it was embedded in a value system based on the male breadwinner family model. But such rhetoric can still be described as maternalist, because women claimed the right to a public voice on behalf of their families' right to economic security. Women used maternalist rhetoric to fight against unemployment, to argue for better welfare policy and to inform and legitimate direct action when necessary. The language that upheld motherhood and domesticity was not sentimental, but was rather shaped by the experiences of women in working-class families. These women knew that unemployment made it difficult, if not impossible, to meet the demands and expectations of respectable motherhood. They employed a language of maternalism that reflected their own particular needs for adequate wages, less-humiliating methods of welfare provision and government provision of social welfare to support, nurture and protect the role of motherhood and familial life.

A central factor differentiating the use of maternalist rhetoric by middle- and working-class women was the language of moral guidance employed by social reformers well into the twentieth century. As numerous scholars have argued, middle-class maternalists were concerned both with maintaining their own class and ethnic positions of power in a rapidly urbanizing and industrializing Canada and with attempting to draw women into public life by politicizing the role of motherhood. Part of the project of maintaining power rested on the desire to guide and reform poor women, children and families by supporting welfare policies that emphasized supervision and regulation of the poor, even those considered most deserving of aid, such as widows.[18] In contrast, working-class women embraced a material politics of motherhood by emphasizing the economic value of women's domestic labour, the centrality of women to working-class family survival and the material necessity of adequate relief provision. These mothers rejected the view of the poor and unemployed as moral failures and instead argued that state intervention was necessary to support themselves and their families.

Still, it is important to remember that the citizenship ideals embraced by women were not completely inclusive. Though increasingly rights-oriented, the residual approach to welfare provision that differentiated between the 'deserving' and 'non-deserving' remained.[19] Thus, the claims of those who presented themselves as hard-working, respectable women were predicated on the category of the non-deserving. There were also few non-white and non-Anglo women making public welfare demands on the state in Canada. This does not imply that non-white women in Canada failed to protest or voice concerns throughout the Depression. We know that many Eastern European immigrant women were active in Communist Party politics, for example, and future research on women in unemployed unions in particular should lead to a more in-depth analysis on the connections between race, ethnicity and protest. Clearly, however, the definition of most deserving citizen was rooted in connection to 'Britishness'. Even though the category of Anglo-Celtic identity remained distinct from that of Anglo-Saxon, during this time of economic distress, those who could draw on any tenuous links to the greater myth of Britishness could make the most powerful demands for economic security.

Women's Maternal Claims on the State

During the Depression, thousands of Ontario citizens, both male and female, wrote letters of concern, anger and protest to Premier George Henry (1930–34) and Premier Mitchell Hepburn (1934–43). These letters upheld the concept of a reciprocal relationship between citizen and state, insisting that the government had the moral responsibility to nurture and protect its citizens. While men referred to their status as rightful workers and breadwinners, however, married women tended to make indirect claims on the state, rooted in their position as wives, mothers and dependents. The male breadwinner ideal remained strong in most public and private discourse in the 1930s, and male unemployment was consistently viewed as a threat to men's gender identities. In contrast, women's unemployment was barely recognized as a social issue and was not depicted in public discourse as undermining their gendered identities as wives and mothers.[20]

In their letters, women clearly upheld the association between men and work, arguing that their husbands needed work to fulfil their obligations as men. 'It is awful,' noted Mrs A. McKenna regarding her husband, an unemployed moulder, 'when a man is willing to work and can't get work at anything.'[21] When Mrs Alice Boulton wrote to Premier Henry for the second time to criticize government unemployment policy, she asked 'for work to keep us human', meaning a job for her husband that would allow him to support her and their ten dependent children.[22] Women consistently asked for jobs for husbands and aid for children. '[M]y husband feels terrible, he loves his family, is willing to work hard,' wrote a mother of seven, whose university-educated husband had lost his job as a salesman. Her husband and many other men, she claimed, were 'people who have always paid their way ... [P]eople unaccustomed to hardship are losing everything they ever worked for through no fault of theirs'.[23]

Though the idea of the family wage excluded women from paid employment, women drew on the rights associated with it to criticize government unemployment policy and the lack of adequate relief. As one woman wrote, 'It is almost winter and our men have had no work for ages and we have no winter clothes and no prospects of any my own children have no clothes ... It's work we want not relief. We don't our living [sic] for nothing we want work and lots of it'.[24] Women repeatedly insisted on adequate food, clothing, schoolbooks and medicine for their children, reminding politicians that their husbands required jobs to obtain these necessities. Mrs Wallace Gow wrote to Premier Henry on behalf of all mothers of Sturgeon Falls to demand jobs for their husbands and sons. The 'situation we mothers are up against', she told Henry, was unbearable. Unemployment, she wrote, had led to kitchens with 'barren cupboards' and men with empty 'lunch pales [sic]'.[25] Using the rhetoric of 'militant mothering' to protest on behalf of husbands and children was one way that women could subvert assumptions of female domesticity to make claims on the state.[26] In their letters, women opposed the government's handling of unemployment, threatened to withhold their votes in the next election and demanded political accountability. As one woman admonished Henry after writing to him three times in vain to request a farm loan and schoolbooks for her daughter, there was 'one vote here the last time and will be three this time if I get no help I give none'.[27] As historian Linda Gordon points out, when women made demands for relief, they were rejecting charity, 'inventing rights' and claiming the status of rightful citizen.[28]

Women who were deserted, separated, widowed or never married could also draw on the language of entitlement to claim the right to Mothers' Allowance (MA). While MA often acted as a form of moral regulation, many recipients understood it as a right, not charity, and used a discourse of entitlement to legitimate their requests for financial aid. By 1935, Charlotte Whitton, director of the Canadian Council on Child and Family Welfare, worried that '[t]here are a great number of people who do not hesitate to apply for a Mothers' Allowance ... there is a real problem of an increasing tendency to look upon a public grant as a right just by virtue of widowhood'.[29]

Female recipients attempted to define their needs as rights that were inextricably tied to the female roles of marriage and motherhood. '[T]o raise a future Canadian in the way he should be raised', claimed one widow, 'is an important and full time job, enough responsibility for any woman however strong without the added burden of trying to find a job'.[30] Women were able to draw on the gendered expectations of womanhood to legitimate their requests and to demand recognition, frequently asserting that the state owed them economic support in return for fulfilling their proper roles as mothers. A deserted wife whose remarriage disqualified her from a veterans' pension protested by stressing her status as a mother, claiming, 'at the same time after I have struggled to raise my boys up to manhood the Government would expect my boys to step out and do their share to protect the country would a war break out; that go to show how much respect the Government has for the citizens of the country'.[31] Surviving case files indicate the various ways that women responded when allowances were cut off or denied. They contacted local Mothers' Allowance Boards, wrote to politicians and continually insisted upon explanations for cutbacks or the denial of allowances. These actions were sometimes, though not often immediately, successful, and aid given to single mothers has remained one of the most stigmatizing, highly regulated forms of social assistance.[32]

In letters of complaint about the intrusiveness of investigators, inadequate benefits or eligibility restrictions that resulted in being cut off, recipients resisted being cast as grateful and passive recipients. Women claimed they were deserving mothers raising 'honest and respectable' children. As one women claimed, the Allowance 'belongs to my kids'.[33] As another woman wrote in her successful appeal, 'I am a Canadian girl born and raised in Toronto and I am a Mother. I think I am deserving of that allowance'.[34] Martina Barton fought with the local Mothers' Allowance investigator who was attempting to control where she bought her groceries. In July 1932, the investigator reported that Mrs Barton was telling people that 'the check belongs to her. That she can do as she likes with it. She stated that I have nothing to say about what she does'.[35] Similarly, Anna Boucher, a deserted mother who supplemented her Mothers' Allowance with domestic work to support her six children, resented the intrusions of the MA investigator, who reported that she was a 'very aggressive type'. In a letter to Judge J.P. Balharrie of the Ottawa juvenile court in October 1934, Boucher asked for his help, saying that the social worker 'has taken too much authority in my home', and claiming, 'I'm giving all the good in me to save my children and I'm constantly under nervous strain from effects ... is there anything that can be done to get justice from these female social workers, not all of them, mind you, one or two of them'.[36] As women and mothers, these women believed that they were entitled to economic security for themselves and their children, as did most women who wrote to the premiers asking for help.

That sense of entitlement was rooted in a particular ethnic and national identity. These particular notions of ethnicity were embedded in the language of women's protest. In letters written to the Ontario premiers, women created an 'imagined community' that placed themselves, along with the politicians they were addressing, within a collective yet narrowly defined Canadian identity.[37] Anyone who was white and of British heritage was a true Canadian and therefore most worthy of financial aid and economic justice. Notions of Britishness drew together such disparate groups as mothers, veterans and unemployed Anglo-Canadian men into a collective national identity that marked their claims for government intervention as particularly deserving. Yet this restrictive definition of citizenship narrowed the image of the proper citizen and obscured the particular problems of non-Anglo families. Historians have shown how race and ethnic-based politics could effectively unify the unemployed and the working class, even as they proved to be profoundly exclusive and limiting.[38]

To many letter writers, the United Empire Loyalists and the early pioneers symbolized the belief in an organic community in which generations of Canadians were linked together in the creation of the Canadian nation. Canadian historians have pointed out that late nineteenth- and early twentieth-century intellectuals and amateur historians used the Loyalist myth to emphasize the imperial tie between Canada and Great Britain and to symbolize the Canadian nation-state as one of civilization, progress and Anglo conquest over aboriginal peoples and French Canadians.[39] One woman explicitly linked the Hepburn government with 'pioneer British stock' from 'the Stirring days of Alexander McKenzie'.[40] Amateur female historians in particular celebrated female Loyalists and pioneers as a way to connect women to the creation of the modern Canadian nation.[41] While these discussions took place at elite and middle-class levels of culture, it is clear that some of these ideas had filtered down to the popular level. An unemployed man on the verge of foreclosure wrote to Henry to ask for help in saving his home by claiming, 'My wife is a Canadian of three generations back and myself I am forty-five years in Canada a British subject at that'.[42] A woman's status as a member of the Anglo-Canadian community could be used to argue for greater recognition, entitlement to aid and a place within the national narrative.[43] The native-born, according to female letter writers, helped to build the nation and should therefore receive recognition from the state. 'I am no foreigner,' wrote a widow who was facing foreclosure. 'I was born in Ontario from parents that [were] also born in Ontario. My grandfather was a U.E.L [United Empire Loyalist]. My grandparents on my mother's side were Irish. My husband was also a good Canadian born in Canada from English blood.'[44] Another woman queried, 'are we not true, loyal Canadians from the same descent as your wife Mrs. Henry[?]. Her ancestry [sic] Laura Secord was mine also as well as Sir Allen McNab and the other faithful early settlers'.[45] Even single mothers could call on Canadian nationality to assert more forcefully their status of respectability. A woman who was turned down for Mothers' Allowance wrote to say 'We are respectable citizens of Canada and have been for generations back. I am bringing up my family descent and respectabel [sic] and educating them the best I can ... I feel I have been dealt out of my rights by some-one who thinks it there [sic] duty to save government money'.[46]

At the popular level in the 1930s, Britishness, loyalty and sacrifice were still crucial signifiers of national belonging and were used as markers of full citizenship rights for those who could claim some connection to British ancestry. This notion of citizenship based on shared ethnic background was particularly appealing for women in this period. The liberal construction of citizenship, with its emphasis on the political and economic independence of the male worker and citizen, was essentially masculine in nature. Thus, a notion of citizenship linking ethnicity and the shared experience of motherhood could enhance women's citizenship status and ultimately serve as an effective political tool of protest.[47]

Wives of World War I veterans were able to make even more powerful claims of entitlement on the state, because veterans argued that they had made crucial sacrifices in the name of nation and empire and had acted with courage, honour and duty. Canada's Vimy Ridge and, interestingly, Australia's Gallipoli were symbolic flashpoints in each country's historical myth of the journey from colony to nation, and both linked wartime sacrifice to greater rights of social citizenship.[48] Letters written by veterans and their families to Ontario politicians and the records of veterans' organizations, particularly the Royal Canadian Legion, indicate that ex-servicemen and their families attempted to influence government policy by using arguments based on male entitlement to employment as well as asserting British rights.

This tendency to use ethnicity and Britishness as a claim for entitlement was one way for the poor and the unemployed to claim respectability and to make demands for economic and political justice. But the narrow definition of who constituted a true Canadian excluded those 'foreigners' who were not of British background. Those excluded from claiming Canadian identity were therefore unable to demand these rights with the same degree of power and were not considered full members of the Canadian state.[49] Writers bitterly complained about foreigners claiming Canadian jobs and stealing potential opportunities. 'Is there a chance', asked one unemployed man, 'for a good honest Canadian Citizen to make an honest living for himself and Family[?]' The government, he complained, allowed 'our own Canadians to be shut out all classes of foreigners placed in their positions'.[50] Veterans also blamed foreigners for stealing jobs. Anti-immigrant sentiment abounded among Legion leaders and members, who consistently claimed that foreigners had stolen their jobs and union seniority while they served overseas.[51] Yet while veterans' version of 'British justice' was xenophobic and exclusionary, it also critiqued unemployment and class-based inequality and supported unemployment insurance, subsidized healthcare and affordable housing.[52]

Wives and mothers of veterans were also able to draw on these demands of economic security and British justice. Veterans and their families continually pointed out that the government's past and future security rested on the willingness of *mothers* to send young men to war. Women argued that economic security and the ability to support a home and family were expressly linked to loyalty to the state. One mother reminded Premier Henry, 'If this country ever has to fight again it can call on my eight boys to protect it well[.] You cannot expect them to protect homes they haven't got'.[53] Veterans and their wives also protested against evictions in some working-class communities, drawing on the symbolic notion of British rights, patriotism and security of homes. In East York in 1932, for example, a group of two hundred veterans and their families draped a Union Jack over the door of a house and blocked the bailiff, while their wives sang 'God Save the Queen'.[54] Their sons, mothers argued, could only be expected to sacrifice their lives for the state if they could enjoy economic security on the homefront.

Breadwinning, Domesticity and Unemployed and Relief Workers' Unions

Canadian labour historians have tended to focus on the development of union organization and politics. As a result, one prominent labour historian has dismissed the 1930s as a time of quiescence, when unions cut back on organizing drives and strikes and waited for better times.[55] Clearly, traditional union tactics and organizing did not work well in a period of massive unemployment. In response to high unemployment and municipal regulations requiring men to work for relief payments, however, new unemployed organizations and relief worker unions developed across the province of Ontario. The Communist Party had some success in organizing unemployed workers across the country. The first unemployed workers' union was founded in September 1929 in Vancouver; by fall of 1931, there were six in Saskatoon alone.

While women's political activism in relief politics is not well documented, some historians have noted their support for relief camp strikes, as well as the consumer activism of housewives in groups organized by Communist leaders. As Joan Sangster points out, both the Communist Party and the Co-operative Commonwealth Federation organized women around consumer issues, such as the prices of milk and meat, although the radicalization of domestic issues was not used to 'emancipate' women from hierarchical gender roles. The Jewish Communist movement led a kosher meat boycott in Toronto in 1933 that involved protests, rallies, mass meetings and pickets. Such forms of housewife activism were also common in the United States, as in the 1935 meat boycotts in Chicago, New York and Detroit.[56]

Even in those unemployed organizations founded and led by the Communist Party, however, most members were not socialists, but rather drawn from parties across the political spectrum.[57] Records of relief strikes held by the Department of Labour indicate that a number of associations in Ontario municipalities became known as radical and effective organizations, particularly those in East York and other urban Toronto suburbs, such as North York, Etobicoke, Mimico and Longbranch. These organizations were not only comprised of unemployed men and relief workers, but usually included their wives and children as well. Women's protest embraced traditional 'female' concerns, such as rising food prices, children's health and welfare, and budgeting for household needs. Women also demonstrated, spoke to crowds and meetings, met with premiers and politicians and occasionally participated in taking welfare officials or town politicians hostage. As Lynne Taylor notes in her examination of food riots in Europe and North America, 'furious mothers and housewives' had a long tradition of grassroots protests based on their presumed 'right' as women and mothers to feed their families. While rooted in pressing material concerns, women also vocalized a powerful belief in the right to demand that local businesses and the state provide an affordable standard of living, economic security and adequate food, clothing and shelter for their families.[58] Thus, women's Depression-era protest was grounded in two powerful notions of entitlement, one derived from eighteenth-century notions of 'moral economy' and the other from twentieth-century views of citizenship rights and state obligations for welfare. Both men and women made demands and arguments based on the recognition of the importance of women's domestic roles, illustrating the close connection between home and work to working-class family survival.

Women played an important role in unemployed organizations, both as active participants and as auxiliaries of support. Women in unemployed organizations clearly expected and encouraged their husbands to protest inadequate wage and relief rates, framing these actions within the proper duties and responsibilities of manhood. After the arrest of Stratford relief strikers in 1936, one wife wrote a series of letters to the Attorney General and Premier Hepburn. She asked, '[w]hy should our children and I be denied having a good husband and father in our home just because he protested against the low standard of relief?'[59] In Longbranch in December 1935, the Workers' Association led relief strikers in protest against low food, fuel and clothing allowances, and requested 'useful works' and cash wages. Fifteen women, along with a hundred men, picketed relief projects and surrounded the men still working. 'The women noisily exhorted the strikers to "be men" and "stand by their families", while the men at a distance, alternately jeered and cheered.'[60]

Women did not simply organize around their husbands' right to work, however. They participated in relief strikes by forming mothers' committees and organizing around domestic interests and consumer issues. In Oshawa, wives of unemployed men organized a Mothers' Association in order to protest relief conditions, the relief store system and inadequate relief food. Newly elected president Mrs Gardner criticized the relief officers and the mayor for 'telling me what to fed my family and preparing my budget ... [w]e can go and ask for what we want nicely first, but if we don't get what we want then we can try something else'. At the inaugural meeting, Mrs C. Smoker, a nurse, proclaimed that the health of unemployed families was being jeopardized by rickets and tuberculosis, and that the relief system degraded families with low-quality provisions, prying interviews, insults by the relief officer and having to line up in public to receive rations.[61] In York Township, the second relief strike of the summer began in July 1932 over the issue of cash vs voucher relief. Women found it difficult to cook and prepare nutritious meals for their families on the relief given by vouchers. On 22 July 1932, women picketed a number of relief projects, urging all the men to quit work. When, as the *Toronto Star* reported, a woman called one of the workers 'yellow', he retorted, 'Go home and wash your dishes'. 'We haven't any dishes to wash,' she snapped. 'We never eat.'[62]

Women voted on strike actions, attended demonstrations, mass meetings and parades, and lobbied all levels of government. It was three female members of the Toronto Township General Workers' Union, for example, who ended a relief strike in October 1936 when they negotiated an agreement between the union and Minister of Public Welfare David Croll. The government promised to investigate relief grievances and to renew relief vouchers immediately.[63] Women were therefore a visible presence in local protest, both to their husbands and strike organizers, who took their concerns seriously, and to state officials and local authorities, who often received them in deputations. The York Township strike executive, for example, consisted of five men and two women.[64] During a day-long strike in Oshawa over inadequate relief store food, 250 male strikers were addressed by Mrs Lillian Williams and Mrs A. Vipond, who both criticized the poor quality of food given to families on relief.[65] At the York Township relief strike, one woman told a crowd of over a thousand people that she took exception to Premier Henry's statement that 'no one would starve', declaring, 'I have four children ... and not one of them has gained a pound since Christmas'.[66] Women in York Township held mass meetings for women during the June 1936 relief strike. Mrs McGregor told the crowd, 'If we stick together we will be able to do things for this strike that even men can't do'.[67] Women achieved a level of leadership and visibility in relief organizations and protests that they rarely enjoyed in political parties or the labour movement.

Women also took a prominent role in direct action, challenging presumptions of women as passive dependents by participating in physical retaliations against relief officials and municipal politicians. There are numerous cases of women occupying relief offices until local governments restored relief cuts. For example, fifty-three women 'mobbed' the office of the relief officer in Blind River in 1936 after a 10 per cent reduction in relief; afterwards, 100 relief strikers met with local MPP W.L. Miller and were promised a restoration of the cut.[68] In Lakeview in October 1936, during a two-week relief strike, forty women 'besieged' Relief Officer R.S. Moore in his own office, demanding food vouchers for themselves and their children. The women agreed to leave only after the provincial police arranged a meeting between women's representatives and the Minister of Public Welfare.[69] In a London relief strike in the spring of 1935, wives of relief strikers twice tried to break down the police barricade outside the township offices. In the resulting fracas, 'Mrs. Cleverly was struck on the face by Police Constable Snell. Mrs. Patterson's foot was badly jammed on by police' and Councillor Hardue 'was set upon by a striker's wife and forced to flee for shelter'.[70] During an Oshawa relief strike in March 1936, ten to twelve female members of the Unemployed Association tried to get city salvage workers to quit in solidarity by resorting 'to physical force to remove the men from their jobs'.[71]

Children, home and family were central symbols in strikes and protests, connecting women and children to union tactics. School strikes were a popular tactic, for example, and relied on mothers keeping children home from school in support of a strike or protest.[72] For example, when the Etobicoke Workers' Association called a relief work strike in October 1933, demanding a 50 per cent increase in relief, cash payments and the creation of public works, over 500 children were kept home from school.[73] In an East York strike of 1935, schoolchildren and their mothers picketed the local public school, wearing sandwich boards with such slogans as 'No cash relief/no school' and 'We need warm winter clothing/support our strike'.[74] Images of innocent children were often used in parades and rallies to protest against relief cuts. Popular banners and sandwich boards held such captions as: 'We protest the Liberal government starving our children on relief' and 'Liberal government called Henry government baby starvers – then gave us a cut in relief'[75] or 'Give us This Day Our Daily Bread'.[76] Similar symbols were used by the East York Workers' Association in their November 1935 strike, when, during a school strike, children picketed with sandwich boards reading: 'We need warm winter clothing/support out strike' and 'Can you think?'[77]

During the Depression, the tensions between the themes of charity and entitlement were central to the actions and rhetoric of men's protest. Men were expected, by other men as well as women, to fight against unemployment and to protest the conditions of relief. In examining the many relief strikes in the 1930s, it becomes clear that the shame associated with being dependent on relief collided with the development of a sense of entitlement to economic and family security, motivating many men to make claims on the state. The traditional notion of the shame-filled and quiescent 'reliefee' simply cannot explain the actions of men who refused to play the role of the grateful charity recipient.

Men sought not only to protest labour concerns, such as wages, hours and working conditions, but domestic issues as well, such as adequate and nutritious food or proper clothing for their children. Men deeply believed in their right to a living wage, which conferred respectable status on themselves and their families. The family wage argument was clearly embedded in the masculine right to paid employment. The ideal, however, also encompassed demands for adequate wages and a dignified standard of living.[78] As the primary male identity of worker and provider was destabilized by economic insecurity, Depression-era protests attempted to reinforce the association between masculinity and work. The demand for work rather than charity was not simply an economic argument; it was tied to a working-class notion of respectability rooted in the ability to support a wife and children, hard work and independence.[79]

As historian Ava Baron suggests, to men, work and family were deeply interconnected, and their pride and sense of manly family respectability were 'significant for class action' and integral parts of the language of their protests and demands.[80] While the rhetoric of maternalism was predicated on the oppositional categories of breadwinner and homemaker, the two often overlapped in public rhetoric and in practice, because the 'private' sphere of the family and the 'public' sphere of paid employment were not always oppositional categories.[81] One woman from Welland observed, 'there are millions of men driven to being red. A man can stand a good deal but when his wife and children suffer if *he is a man* [sic] he becomes desperate'.[82]

Department of Labour records reveal that men were moved to protests, petitions, parades and strikes not just by poor working conditions but by anger over such 'domestic' concerns as food, clothing, bedding, nutrition and health. These material concerns were important to working-class family survival, to housewives' ability to maintain households and to men's sense of responsibility as providers. Of the approximately seventy-seven relief strikes and protests recorded in these files, almost half involved issues of adequate food, clothing or housing along with disputes over wages and methods of relief distribution.[83] Fourteen (or 18 per cent) of these Ontario relief strikes were motivated primarily by domestic concerns.[84] The rhetoric of unemployed protestors connected demands for work and wages with concerns over the health, comfort and dignity of children and women. Therefore, maternal roles and domestic life could motivate both working-class men and women to protest and to claim a voice in the creation and critique of public policy.

Concern over adequacy and quantity of food was a central preoccupation of unemployed men. Food vouchers or relief given in kind were problems for families, and many unemployed men protested the difficulty their wives faced shopping, budgeting and cooking with limited food supplies or poor quality goods. In the fourteen strikes precipitated by primarily domestic concerns, eight revolved around the cost, quality and choice of food. In Kitchener, for example, a strike was precipitated over bread tickets. A relief strike erupted when the Unemployed Workers' Association protested against the city's system of granting restricted bread tickets, but the men returned to work once the relief board guaranteed they could redeem them 'wherever they chose'.[85] Food concerns were also central to many other strikes. In Oshawa in 1932, 250 men demanded that the civic relief store provide more nutritious food. Their wives, they claimed, found the food to be of poor quality and taste.[86] Men motivated by lack of food for their families could be a threat to the social order, but could also elicit a degree of sympathy. In York Township, several hundred men gathered in front of council offices, claiming that 'unless food was provided, there would be nothing left but to loot grocery stores'. Noted the *Globe* with some sympathy, '[T]he spectacle of hundreds of men asking only for food for themselves and their weak dependents when their last dollar of savings has been spent, is one that a civilized community cannot witness unmoved'.[87]

While food was an immediate concern to poor families, inadequate relief compromised family survival in other ways. Authorities did not budget for such 'extras' as adequate clothing, shoes, mattresses, cooking utensils or children's schoolbooks. Fifty Mimico relief workers went on strike in November 1934 for stoves, bedding, kitchen utensils and free schoolbooks for their children.[88] In Kitchener, the main complaint of striking relief workers was the situation of Paul Ferret and his family, who had been denied a cooking stove by the relief board. As a result, Ferret had been badly burned while cooking food in his furnace.[89] Relief workers in Longbranch went on strike in February and May 1934 when the council refused to turn on the water for families who could not pay water bills, and again in November 1934 when at least six families on relief were discovered sleeping on the floor without mattresses or blankets. Workers throughout Northern Ontario went on strike over inadequate clothing allowances for their families.[90] Clearly, when women's ability to manage the household was compromised, domestic issues were important enough to compel men to protest. Whether or not these men can be called 'maternalists', the larger point is that husbands and fathers, and wives and mothers, shared similar concerns that motivated protest based on men's right to work and women's right to run a household properly. While theoretically and analytically these roles can be pulled apart, the historical record suggests that the boundaries between mothers and fathers were often blurred and deeply entwined.

The decade of the Great Depression embodied an uneasy tension between social welfare benefits based on rights and entitlement and older notions of charitable aid based on the distinction between the deserving and undeserving poor. Women and men framed demands for aid in the economic discourse of 'commercial exchange' and linked their demands to the classical liberal language of rights and entitlement. While this language was more inclusive than that of charity and did help to expand government responsibility for social welfare provision, it did not ultimately challenge a definition of citizenship that based the reward of social provision on service and duty to the state.[91] Part of that service to the state was, in the 1930s, based on the intertwined roles of maternalism and breadwinning. In a society where full participation in state and society was predicated on employment and economic independence, the highest form of citizenship was gendered masculine, and, as a result, employment policy and post-war social welfare was concerned to uphold the status of the male breadwinner role.[92]

The protest of women in this decade should be understood as a form of maternalist political action, rooted in the realities and experiences of poor women and unemployed families. The term maternalism retains the historicity of motherhood as a politicizing category, with its potential for creating social change. Speaking for themselves, their children and their husbands, and lacking a sentimental conception of motherhood, these maternalists could also be considered 'militant mothers'. In the mid twentieth century, women's maternal claims to entitlement, however restrictive, helped to frame post-war concerns for family economic stability, and thus their individual and collective protests were a powerful force in shaping the future liberal welfare state.

Notes

1. *Toronto Daily Star*, 2 August 1932, 1; and *Toronto Daily Star*, 3 August 1932, 3.
2. *Toronto Daily Star*, 3 August 1932, 18.
3. In the United States, progressive female reformers played an important role in shaping federal New Deal policies, but in Canada, unemployment policy focused on large public works projects, then on direct relief. The Conservative government of R.B. Bennett also opened relief camps for single men in 1933. See L. Brown. 1987. *When Freedom Was Lost: The Un-*

employed, the Agitator and the State, Montreal-Buffalo: Black Rose Books; and J. Struthers. 1983. *No Fault of Their Own: Unemployment and the Canadian Welfare State, 1914–41*, Toronto: University of Toronto Press, 95–103. The National Employment Commission, established in 1936, had a Women's Employment Committee that emphasized domestic service as a solution to female unemployment. See W. Atkin. 1988. 'The Women's Employment Committee, 1936–1938: Changing Attitudes Towards Women's Work in Canada', M.A., Queen's University.

4. See T. Skocpol. 1992. *Protecting Soldiers and Mothers: The Political Origins of Social Policy in the United States*, Cambridge, MA: Harvard University Press, 9, Table One. Canada introduced Factory Acts during the 1880s, Workmen's Compensation beginning in 1914, Mothers' Allowances beginning in 1916, Unemployment Insurance in 1940 and Family Allowances in 1944. D. Guest. 1985. *The Emergence of Social Security in Canada*, Vancouver: University of British Columbia Press.

5. B. Palmer. 1992. *Working-Class Experience: Rethinking the History of Canadian Labour, 1880–1991*, Toronto: McClelland and Stewart, 241; and M. Horn. 1988. 'The Great Depression: Past and Present', in M. Horn (ed.), *The Depression in Canada: Responses to Economic Crisis*, Toronto: Copp Clark Pittman, 276.

6. Struthers, *No Fault of Their Own*, 47–8.

7. D. Chunn. 1992. *From Punishment to Doing Good: Family Courts and Socialized Justice in Ontario, 1880–1940*, Toronto: University of Toronto Press.

8. J. Sangster. 1989. *Dreams of Equality: Women on the Canadian Left, 1920–1950*, Toronto: McClelland and Stewart, 91–164.

9. S. Michel. 2000. 'Introduction', *Social Politics* 7(1), 1; and S. Michel and S. Koven (eds). 1993. 'Introduction', *Mothers of a New World: Maternalist Politics and the Origins of the Welfare State*, New York: Routledge, 6.

10. For just a few Canadian examples, see L. Kealey (ed.). 1979. *A Not Unreasonable Claim: Women and Reform in Canada, 1880s–1920s*, Toronto: The Women's Press; E.G. Muir and M.F. Whiteley (eds). 1995. *Changing Roles of Women Within the Christian Church in Canada*, Toronto: University of Toronto Press; and V. Strong-Boag. 1979. '"Wages for Housework": Mothers' Allowances and the Beginning of Social Security in Canada', *Journal of Canadian Studies* 14(1), 24–34.

11. Koven and Michel, 'Introduction', *Mothers of a New World*, 17.

12. M. Valverde. 1992. '"When the Mother of the Race is Free": Race, Reproduction, and Sexuality in First-Wave Feminism', in F. Iacovetta and M. Valverde (eds), *Gender Conflicts: New Essays in Women's History*, Toronto: University of Toronto Press, 3–26; M. Little. 1998. *'No Car, No Radio, No Liquor Permit': The Moral Regulation of Single Mothers in Ontario, 1920–1997*, Toronto and New York: Oxford University Press; C. Bacchi. 1983. *Liberation Deferred? The Ideas of the English-Canadian Suffragists, 1877–1918*, Toronto: University of Toronto Press; and J. Fiamengo. 2002. 'A Legacy of Ambivalence: Responses to Nellie McClung', in V. Strong-Boag, M. Gleason and A. Perry (eds), *Rethinking Canada: The Promise of Women's History*, 4th edn, Toronto: Oxford University Press, 149–63.

13. See the articles in *Social Politics* 7(1), 2000.

14. N. Christie. 2000. *Engendering the State: Family, Work and Welfare in Canada*, Toronto: University of Toronto Press; P.M. Evans and G.R. Wekerle (eds). 1997. *Women and the Canadian Welfare State: Challenges and Change*, Toronto: University of Toronto Press; R.R. Pierson. 1990. 'Gender and the Unemployment Insurance Debates in Canada, 1934–1940', *Labour/Le Travail* 25, 77–103; and J. Struthers. 1994. *The Limits of Affluence: Welfare in Ontario, 1920–1970*, Toronto: University of Toronto Press.

15. The most well-known work is L. Gordon. 1988. *Heroes of their Own Lives: The Politics and History of Family Violence*, New York: Penguin Books. See also F. Iacovetta and W. Mitchinson (eds). 1998. *On The Case: Explorations in Social History*, Toronto: University of Toronto.

16. Christie, *Engendering the State*.
17. For a similar phenomenon in nineteenth-century Canadian politics, see R. Bitterman. 2002. 'Women and the Escheat Movement: The Politics of Everyday Life on Prince Edward Island', in Strong-Boag et al., *Rethinking Canada*, 47–58.
18. Little, *No Car, No Radio, No Liquor Permit*. See also articles in L. Gordon (ed.). 1990. *Women, the State and Welfare*, Madison: University of Wisconsin Press.
19. Guest, *The Emergence of Social Security in Canada*.
20. P.M. Evans. 1997. 'Divided Citizenship? Gender, Income Security, and the Welfare State', in Evans and Wekerle, *Women and the Canadian Welfare State*, 91, 95; M. Hobbs. 1993. 'Equality and Difference: Feminism and the Defense of Women Workers During the Great Depression', *Labour/Le Travail* 32, 201–23; A. Kessler-Harris. 1989. 'Gender Ideology in Historical Reconstruction: A Case Study from the 1930s', *Gender and History* 1(1), 31–49; and M. Klee. 1998. 'Between the Scylla and Charybdis of Anarchy and Despotism: The State, Capital and Working Class in the Great Depression, Toronto, 1929–40', Ph.D. diss., Queen's University.
21. Archives of Ontario (AO), RG 3, Series 9, Hepburn Papers, #180, file: Unemployment relief #1, Mrs A. McKenna to Hepburn, 16 July 1934.
22. AO, RG 3–8, Henry Papers, MS 1744, file: Positions, general, June 1931–June 1932, Mrs Alice Boulton to Henry, 27 June 1931.
23. AO, RG 3–8, Henry Papers, MS 1745, file: Relief, asked for, Mrs W.A. Rowland to Henry, 1 October 1931.
24. AO, RG 3, Series 9, Hepburn Papers, #180, file: Unemployment Relief, Mrs W.H. to Hepburn, 1934.
25. AO, RG 3–8, Henry Papers, MS 1747, file: Unemployment Relief #3, Mrs W. Gow to Henry, 29 September 1931.
26. See Sangster, *Dreams of Equality*, I. Howard. 1988. 'The Mothers' Council of Vancouver: Holding the Fort for the Unemployed, 1935–38', *BC Studies* 69–70, 249–87; and A. Orleck. 1993. '"We Are that Mythical Thing Called the Public": Militant Housewives during the Great Depression', *Feminist Studies* 19(1), 147–72.
27. AO, RG 3–8, Henry Papers, MS 1736, file: Agricultural Development Board, Mrs A.S. to Henry, 26 August 1931.
28. L. Gordon. 1994. *Pitied But Not Entitled: Single Mothers and the History of Welfare, 1890–1935*, New York: Free Press, 627.
29. Quoted in Little, *'No Car, No Radio, No Liquor Permit'*, 81. Margaret Little notes that lobbyists and recipients in British Columbia saw Mothers' Pensions as payment for a service performed. M. Little. 2002. 'Claiming a Unique Place: The Introduction of Mothers' Pensions in British Columbia', in Strong-Boag et al., *Rethinking Canada*, 285–303. See also Struthers, *Limits of Affluence*, 48.
30. AO, RG 3–10, Hepburn Papers, #190, file: Public Welfare Department, Mothers' Allowance, Mrs R.H. to Hepburn, 21 February 1935. Quoted in Struthers, *Limits of Affluence*, 99.
31. AO, RG 3 Series 9, Hepburn Papers, #180, file: Unemployment Relief #2, Mrs J.W. to Hepburn, 6 September 1934.
32. M. Little. 1999. 'The Limits of Canadian Democracy: The Citizenship Rights of Poor Women', *Canadian Review of Social Policy* 43, 59–76.
33. AO, RG 29–35, Mothers' Allowances Case Files, Box 2, 1923–39; Box 3, 1931–8.
34. Ibid., MS 1757, file: Mothers' Allowances Commission, Mrs R.C. to Henry, 5 March 1933.
35. AO, RG 29–35, Mothers' Allowance Case Files, Box 2, 1931–7. All names in Mothers' Allowance Case Files and in Adult Case Files have been changed in compliance with terms of the Freedom of Information Act.
36. AO, RG 22–1333, Carleton County Adult Case Files, 1922–63, Box 7, 1934.

37. For historical work that examines elite conceptions of nationality, see: M. Vipond. 1982. 'Nationalism and Nativism: The Native Sons of Canada in the 1930s', *Canadian Review of Studies in Nationalism* 9(1), 81–95; and C. Berger. 1986. *The Writing of Canadian History: Aspects of English Canadian Historical Writing Since 1900*, Toronto: University of Toronto Press. See also B. Anderson. 1983. *Imagined Communities: Reflections on the Origins and Spread of Nationalism*, London: Verso.

38. For the United States, see D. Roediger. 1991. *The Wages of Whiteness: The Making of the American Working Class*, London: Verso; N. Ignatiev and J. Garvey. 1996. *Race Traitor*, New York: Routledge; R. Dyer. 1997. *White*, London: Routledge; and P.A. Kramer. 2002. 'Empires, Exceptions, and Anglo-Saxons: Race and Rule between the British and the U.S. Empires, 1880–1910', *Journal of American History* 88(4), 1313–53.

39. C. Berger. 1970. *The Sense of Power: Studies in the Ideas of Canadian Imperialism*, Toronto: University of Toronto Press; and C. Morgan. 2001. 'History, Nation, and Empire: Gender and Southern Ontario Historical Societies, 1890–1920s', *Canadian Historical Review* 82(3), 491–528.

40. AO, RG 3–10, Hepburn Papers, #225, file: M.F. Hepburn, private #3, Miss M.E. M. to Hepburn, 3 July 1934.

41. Morgan, 'History, Nation and Empire', 495.

42. AO, RG 3–8, Henry Papers, MS 1762, file: Unemployment Relief, Mr T.H. to Henry, 14 January 1933.

43. See A.M. Burton. 1994. *Burdens of History: British Feminists, Indian Women, and Imperial Culture, 1865–1915*, Chapel Hill: University of North Carolina Press; and A. Curthoys. 1993. 'Identity Crisis: Colonialism, Nation, and Gender in Australian History', *Gender and History* 5(2), 165–76.

44. AO, RG 3–8, Henry Papers, MS 1750, file: Mothers' Allowances Commission, Mrs S.B.S. to Henry, 24 February 1932.

45. Ibid., MS 1760, file: Relief, asked for, Mrs C.R.C. to Henry, 2 August 1933.

46. Ibid., MS 1745, file: Relief, asked for, Mrs A.H.M. to Henry, 29 December 1931.

47. See T.H. Marshall. 1950. *Citizenship and Social Class*, Cambridge: University Press; and N. Fraser and L. Gordon. 1992. 'Contract vs. Charity: Why is there No Social Citizenship in the United States?' *Socialist Review* 22(3), 52–6.

48. See Pierson, 'Gender and the Unemployment Insurance Debates'; J. Vance. 1997. *Death So Noble: Memory, Meaning and the First World War*, Vancouver: University of British Columbia Press; P. Neary and J.L. Granatstein (eds). 1988. *The Veterans Charter and Post World-War II Canada*, Montreal: McGill-Queen's University Press; and D. Morton and G. Wright. 1987. *Winning the Second Battle: Canadian Veterans and the Return to Civilian Life, 1915–1930*, Toronto: University of British Columbia Press. See also Skocpol, *Protecting Soldiers and Mothers*; M. Lake, 'A Revolution in the Family: The Challenge and Contradictions of Maternal Citizenship in Australia', in Koven and Michel, *Mothers of a New World*, 378–95; D. Morton. 1991. '"Noblest and Best": Retraining Canada's War Disabled, 1915–23', *Journal of Canadian Studies* 16(3/4), 75–85; and Jeffrey Keshen. 1996. *Propaganda and Citizenship during Canada's Great War*, Edmonton: University of Alberta Press.

49. See Roediger, *The Wages of Whiteness*. Although it is difficult to assess the exact ethnic background of letter writers, a careful study of the letters reveals few non-Anglo names.

50. AO, RG 3–8, Henry Papers, MS 1744, file: Positions, general, Mr B.C. to Henry, 19 November 1931.

51. See, for example, 1932. *The Legionary* 6(12), 7; 1935. *The Legionary* 11(1), 20.

52. See L. Campbell. 2000. '"We Who Wallowed in the Mud of Flanders": First World War Veterans, Unemployment, and the Development of Social Welfare in Canada', *Journal of the Canadian Historical Association*, 11, 125–49; and idem. 2009. *Respectable Citizens: Gender, Family, and Unemployment in Ontario's Great Depression*. Toronto: University of Toronto Press.

53. AO, RG 3–8, Henry Papers, MS 1744, file: Positions, general, Mrs A.B. to Henry, 27 June 1931.
54. P. Schulz. 1975. *The East York Workers' Association: A Response to the Great Depression*, Toronto: New Hogtown Press, 34.
55. D. Morton. 1990. *Working People: An Illustrated History of the Canadian Labour Movement*, Toronto: Summerhill Press.
56. Sangster, *Dreams of Equality*; R. Frager. 1992. *Sweatshop Strife: Class, Ethnicity, and Gender in the Jewish Labour Movement of Toronto*, Toronto: University of Toronto, 163; and Orleck, '"We Are that Mythical Thing Called the Public"'.
57. Brown, *When Freedom Was Lost*, 25; and J. Manley. 1998. '"Starve, Be Damned!": Communists and Canada's Urban Unemployed, 1929–1939', *Canadian Historical Review* 79(3), 471–3.
58. L. Taylor. 1996. 'Food Riots Revisited', *Journal of Social History* 30(2), 492; Bitterman, 'Women and the Escheat Movement', 47–58; N.Z. Davis. 1975. *Society and Culture in Early Modern France*, Stanford: Stanford University Press, 124–87.
59. AO, RG 3–10, Hepburn Papers, #203, file: Provinicial Secretary's Department, Mrs L.M. to Hepburn, 10 May 1936.
60. National Archives of Canada (NAC), RG 27, Department of Labour, Strikes and Lockout Files, v. 375, #57, 1935.
61. *Oshawa Daily Times*, 29 October, 1932, 1.
62. NAC, v. 351, #86, 1932.
63. Ibid., v. 380, #40, 1936.
64. Ibid., v. 380, #25, 1936.
65. Ibid., v. 351, #66, 1932.
66. Ibid., v. 351 #86, 1932.
67. Ibid., v. 380, #25, 1936.
68. Ibid., v. 380, #17, 1936.
69. Ibid., v. 380, #40, 1936.
70. Ibid., v. 374, #30, 1935.
71. Ibid., v. 380, #11, 1936.
72. Patricia Schulz argues that the EYWA found the school strike to be an effective form of protest because it had an impact on provincial education grants, which were based on daily attendance figures. Schulz, *East York Workers' Association*, 28.
73. RG 49–63, MS 755, #6336, October 1933.
74. NAC, v. 375, #56, 1935.
75. Ibid., v. 374, #14, 1935.
76. Ibid., v. 358A, #64, 1933.
77. Ibid., v. 375, #56, 1935.
78. M. May. 1985. 'Bread Before Roses: American Workingmen, Labor Unions and the Family Wage', in R. Milkman (ed.), *Women, Work and Protest: A Century of U.S. Women's Labor History*, New York and London: Routledge and Kegan Paul, 1–21. For another view, see R. Rothbart. 1989. '"Homes are What Any Strike is About": Immigrant Labor and the Family Wage', *Journal of Social History* 23(2), 267–84.
79. See J. Sangster. 1995. *Earning Respect: The Lives of Working Women in Small-Town Ontario, 1920–1960*, Toronto: University of Toronto Press, 126.
80. A. Baron. 1994. 'On Looking at Men: Masculinity and the Making of a Gendered Working-Class History', in Ann-Louise Shapiro (ed.), *Feminists Revision History*, New Brunswick: Rutgers University Press, 158. Labour protest was 'about home and family', not only working conditions and wages. Rothbart, 'Immigrant Labour', 278. Nineteenth-century craft values of respectability and work were remarkably elastic concepts used by labourers and the unemployed well into the 1930s. See articles in A. Baron (ed.). 1991. *Work Engendered: Toward a New History of American Labor*, Ithaca, NY: Cornell University Press.

For Canada, see B. Palmer. 1979. *A Culture in Conflict: Skilled Workers and Industrial Capitalism in Hamilton, Ontario, 1860–1914,* Montreal: McGill-Queen's University Press; and Palmer, *Working-Class Experience,* 58–9.

81. Koven and Michel argue that 'maternalist ideologies … implicitly challenged the boundaries between public and private, women and men, state and civil society'. Koven and Michel, 'Introduction: Mother Worlds', 6.

82. AO, RG 3–10, Hepburn Papers, #250, file: Comments on unemployment relief, 29 July 1935.

83. The seventy-seven cases include seventy-three strikes, three strike threats or votes by unemployed councils that were averted by concessions, and one case of sole direct action without the context of a strike. Relief camp protests were not included in this sample. Of the strikes, 49 per cent were motivated either completely by or partly by domestic concerns such as food, clothing, housing, evictions, light and water, while 48 per cent were motivated by issues of wages or work-related concerns. Of the thirty-seven cases focused on work and wages, however, nine (24 per cent) involved rhetoric or symbolism of gender, home and family, such as women leading parades, women and children as barricades, or male relief workers demanding a family wage.

84. Fourteen strikes, or 18 per cent of these Ontario relief strikes, were motivated by primarily domestic concerns.

85. NAC, RG 27, v. 358A, #54, 1933.

86. Ibid., v. 351, #66, 1932.

87. AO, RG 49–63, Records of the Legislative Assembly, Press Clippings, MS 755, #592, from *Toronto Globe,* 16 May 1932, 'Relief Troubles Acute'.

88. NAC, v. 366, #65, 1934.

89. Ibid., v. 394, #21, 1937.

90. As did workers in Kitchener and Oshawa in 1933 and Longbranch in February, May and November 1934.

91. See Fraser and Gordon, 'Contract vs. Charity'; and Pierson. 'Gender and the Unemployment Insurance Debates', 77–103.

92. Christie, *Engendering the State.*

CHAPTER 7

THE GOLD STAR MOTHERS PILGRIMAGES

Patriotic Maternalists and Their Critics in Interwar America

Rebecca Jo Plant

Scholars typically view the late 1920s as marking the decline of maternalist politics in the United States, but this interpretation obscures both the persistence of maternalism in the interwar period and the various reasons why different groups of Americans came to revile it.[1] In fact, maternalism – loosely defined as the belief that motherhood represented a civic role that entitled women to make claims upon the state – remained a powerful force in American political culture, but one that was increasingly appropriated by patriotic and right-wing women's groups. As progressive women struggled to reposition themselves within a post-suffrage context and politically conservative climate, many moderated or abandoned sentimental appeals to motherhood and female moral superiority. At the same time, a growing number of conservative and patriotic women unhesitatingly employed such rhetoric, even as they adopted overtly political lobbying tactics and strategies.[2] In part because of these women's highly visible and often controversial activities, a growing number of Americans began to view maternalist appeals as an illegitimate form of political discourse that masked anti-democratic attitudes. By the time the nation entered World War II, maternalism had been significantly discredited as a basis for women's political activism.

Notes for this chapter begin on page 141.

This essay attempts to demonstrate the continued viability of maternalism in the late 1920s and to enumerate the reasons for its subsequent decline by analysing a largely forgotten episode in American history: the gold star mothers pilgrimages of 1930 to 1933.[3] Enacted in March 1929, during an era noted for its fiscal conservatism and limited conception of government, the legislation that provided for these government-run pilgrimages stands out as a remarkable departure.[4] During the worst years of the Depression, it allowed more than 6,600 women to travel to Europe to witness the graves of loved ones who had perished in the Great War.[5] Housed in first-class hotels, the pilgrims spent a full two weeks in Europe, shepherded though detailed itineraries that included sightseeing and shopping excursions, as well as visits to cemeteries and battlefields. Although unmarried widows also took part in the programme, mothers constituted the overwhelming majority of the pilgrims, and policymakers justified the trips almost exclusively in maternalist terms.[6] Yet while the campaign for pilgrimages, and the government's conduct of them, reveal the enduring potency of a highly sentimental and nationalistic conception of motherhood, the programme also drew criticism as it progressed over time, and indeed long after its conclusion. Because the pilgrimages so dramatically exemplified a certain strain of maternalism, they provoked some Americans to question the beliefs and assumptions that lent motherhood its political and symbolic capital. To that extent, the programme also served as an agent of change, helping to discredit the very ideas and images it sought to reaffirm.

The success of the pilgrimage legislation suggests that the 1920s did not witness the demise of maternalism per se, but rather that 'progressive maternalism' came to be challenged, and to some extent supplanted, by 'patriotic maternalism'.[7] In June 1929, less than three months after passing the pilgrimage bill, Congress effectively killed the Maternity and Infancy Protection Act (otherwise known as the Sheppard-Towner Act), the first federal programme designed to improve maternal and infant health. Passed by a wide margin in 1921, the legislation had initially enjoyed the support of nearly all women's groups, including the Daughters of the American Revolution. Yet by 1926, in a shift that reflected the growing polarization of organized womanhood, the D.A.R. and other conservative women had joined the American Medical Association in calling for its termination. Women's historians have therefore rightly linked the Sheppard-Towner's repeal to the splintering of the broad-based coalition of women's groups that had previously lent support to maternalist initiatives.[8] Yet they have not discussed the near-simultaneous passage of the pilgrimage bill, which established a federal programme, designed explicitly for mothers, that required roughly the same level of annual expenditure over a period of four years.[9] Even as progressive maternalists encountered bitter defeats, conservative women succeeded in shaping public policy by emphasizing the civic dimensions of motherhood.

Although historians have generally defined the term 'maternalism' more narrowly, there are compelling reasons for considering the activities of women like those who campaigned for the pilgrimages under its rubric. Like progressive reformers, the organized war mothers who lobbied for the pilgrimages held that motherhood was not simply a private, familial role: mothers who raised soldier-sons, they claimed, fulfilled a civic duty as crucial as soldiering itself. And like their progressive counterparts, they cast the state in the role of a benevolent caretaker, insisting that war mothers deserved consolation (in the form of pilgrimages), and, if needed, material compensation (in the form of pensions).[10] The two constituencies differed fundamentally, however, in their use of motherhood as a political platform. Whereas progressive maternalists argued that all mothers made a civic contribution by rearing *citizens,* organized war mothers based their claims on the fact that they had reared and sacrificed *soldier-sons.* And whereas progressive maternalists strove to improve material conditions for poor, working-class and rural mothers, patriotic maternalists stressed the emotional and symbolic aspects of motherhood by privileging a select group of elderly women no longer actively engaged in maternal work. In 1929, when Congress passed the pilgrimage legislation and yet refused to renew funding for the Sheppard-Towner Act, it signalled that the psychological needs of bereaved war mothers had gained precedence over the material needs of practising mothers.

When 'maternalism' is defined to encompass its appropriation by conservative and patriotic women, its downfall must be dated later and attributed in part to its growing association with a host of controversial political positions. As criticism of the pilgrimage programme reveals, in the minds of many politically liberal Americans, paeans to American motherhood came to connote not only retrograde gender roles, but also narrow-minded bigotry, disregard for social and economic inequality, and lockstep patriotism and militarism.[11] Commentators wary of the type of nationalism that had prevailed during World War I began to denounce maternalist rhetoric as incompatible with modern democracy – a notion that appeared borne out in 1939, when a sprawling coalition of reactionary mothers' groups, some overtly fascist, emerged to protest U.S. intervention in World War II.[12] To be sure, the history of maternalist politics cannot be viewed as simple story of its appropriation by the far right, for some progressive women, most notably peace activists, continued to employ maternalist arguments and rhetoric in the interwar period and beyond.[13] But to a significant extent, patriotic and conservative women's groups usurped maternalism, making it more difficult to employ for progressive aims.

The story of the gold star mothers pilgrimages also illustrates how an assault on sentimental ideals of motherhood helped to erode the cultural foundation of maternalist politics. Increasingly after World War I, psychological experts, writers, filmmakers and other cultural producers derided the Victorian notion of 'mother love' as a selfless and benevolent force, insisting that women's attachments to their children could be narcissistic and potentially pathological.[14] Historians of maternalism have not fully contended with these attacks on moral motherhood, perhaps because social welfare history and cultural history tend to be conceptualized as separate enterprises. But anti-maternalist cultural criticism played a crucial role in shaping the larger climate within which policymaking occurred. Unlike equal rights feminists, who rejected maternalism as inimical to women's quest for equality, popular writers and others who debunked American mothers did not advance a politically coherent critique of maternalist ideology. Yet whether they rejected the self-sacrificing mother as a worthy ideal, or simply lashed out at modern mothers for falling short of it, cultural producers and critics railed tirelessly against the image of mothers as morally superior and politically disinterested. In the process, they helped to deflate the longstanding ideal of motherhood that lay at the heart of maternalist politics.

This study of the gold star mothers pilgrimages highlights a transitional moment, allowing us to explore how the long-standing tradition of Republican motherhood, inflected by Victorian sentimentalism and Progressive Era maternalism, played out in the post-suffrage era. Whereas some proponents justified the pilgrimages as a gift bestowed by a benevolent and paternal government, others portrayed them as compensation due to citizen-mothers. But by the time the next cohort of American women found their sons called up for service, both arguments had begun to wear thin. Although war mothers would again be venerated during World War II, they would never recapture the privileged status they held during World War I and its aftermath.

* * *

The archetypical war mother embodies the enduring conflict between the individual and the state; between personal desire and public duty. Her plight is an agonizing one: she must overcome her maternal impulse to nurture and protect, relinquishing her child for the greater good of the whole. The impossibility of this charge renders the war mother a potential subversive, for what mother would willingly consent to such a sacrifice?

At the same time, the ardently patriotic war mother – like the legendary Spartan mother who exhorted her son to return with his shield or upon it – evokes even deeper ambivalence. Publicly lauded, her patriotism is privately dreaded. For if she becomes the enforcer of the patriarchal law – if the mother and the state close ranks – then there is no private realm, no respite for a man seeking relief from the hard demands of the public world. The image of the ever-loyal war mother, anxiously awaiting her son's return, is thus shadowed by a counter-image: the punitive war mother who willingly surrenders her son to the state.

Yet if the war mother is an inherently fraught figure, cultural representations of war mothers and the political influence accorded to them have varied according to time and place. Prior to World War I, the term 'war mother' was not widely used in the United States, nor did American women claim the identity as grounds for mobilization. The Mother celebrated in Civil War literature, poetry and songs bore her suffering in solitude and silence, never calling attention to her sacrifices and pain.[15] She appeared less frequently as a subject in her own right than as the focus of contemplation, as in the famous letter that Abraham Lincoln allegedly wrote to Lydia Bixby, a woman believed to have lost five sons in battle:

> I have been shown in the files of the War Department that you are the mother of five sons who have died gloriously on the field of battle. I feel how weak and fruitless must be any words of mine which should attempt to beguile you from the grief of a loss so overwhelming. But I cannot refrain from tendering to you the consolation that may be found in the thanks of the Republic they died to save. I pray heavenly Father may assuage the anguish of your bereavement, and leave you only the cherished memory of the loved and lost, and the solemn pride that must be yours to have laid so costly a sacrifice upon the altar of freedom.[16]

Here, the bereaved mother appears only in a dim outline, as the object of Lincoln's tender feelings and noble sentiments. She did not come forward to proclaim her losses or demand compensation; a third party brought her tragic case to Lincoln's attention. Such self-effacing passivity was no minor detail, but rather part of what made her worthy of presidential consolation.

The organized war mothers of the interwar period present a striking contrast to this image of the solitary and apolitical war mother. While their rhetoric resembled that of their Victorian predecessors, they politicized the ideal of sentimental motherhood by appropriating the Progressive Era notion of motherhood as a form of civic service. During World War I, as historian Susan Zeiger has shown, government officials and producers of popular cul-

ture, alarmed by the flourishing women's peace movement and worried that
mothers might oppose conscription, promoted an ideal of patriotic motherhood that deemed a woman's willingness to 'sacrifice' her son as the ultimate
expression of female fealty.[17] Self-identified war mothers carried this ideal forward into the post-war period, eventually establishing two main national associations, the American War Mothers, founded in 1919, and the American
Gold Star Mothers, founded in 1928. The former, open to any mother with
a son who had served in the war, had a predominantly Anglo-Saxon constituency but included a small number of Jewish and African American members.
The latter, composed of women whose sons had perished in the war, admitted only women of the 'Caucasian race'.[18] (It should be noted, however,
that the terms 'war mother' and 'gold star mother' were already in general
use and thus did not necessarily imply an organizational affiliation.) Whereas
American women had long engaged in voluntary activities to support servicemen and memorialize wartime sacrifices, these groups represented a new
departure: never before had the mothers of veterans and deceased servicemen formed their own, separate organizations and collectively asserted their
right to influence U.S. policymaking.

Though ostensibly non-partisan, war mothers' organizations advocated military preparedness and consistently aligned with the forces of
anti-radicalism, as historian G. Kurt Piehler has shown.[19] Their emergence should be viewed as part of a larger trend, the rise of the nation's
first broad-based conservative women's movement. Historians have been
slow to appreciate the scale and import of this movement, but it played
a crucial role in fracturing the coalition that had supported maternalist
initiatives prior to the war, as Kirstin Delegard and Christine Erickson
have demonstrated.[20] Fuelling the polarization of organized womanhood
were sharply divergent views on questions concerning militarism and international relations. In 1925, a group of right-wing women, determined
to counter the influence of the Women's League for International Peace
and Freedom, established the Women's Patriotic Conference for National
Defense, an umbrella organization that aimed to coordinate the activities
of conservative and patriotic women. By the late 1920s, as many as one
million women, associated with some forty organizations, had coalesced
under the WPCND's rubric.[21] Such women challenged maternalist peace
advocates by depicting a commitment to military preparedness as a maternal duty. 'As the mother of an only child who lies under a white cross
in France', demanded one gold star mother who protested cuts to the
Navy's budget in 1928, 'have I not the right to demand that the Nation
shall provide every mechanical device possible to protect the living bodies
of other sons who volunteer for service?'[22] Conservative women thus both
drew upon and departed from Victorian gender ideology: although they

jettisoned the idea of 'separate spheres' by addressing 'masculine' issues like defence allocations, they held tight to a belief in female moral superiority and a highly sentimental conception of motherhood.

The history of the pilgrimage legislation, which unfolded over a ten-year period beginning in 1919, reflects the growing influence of conservative and patriotic women's groups in general and war mothers' organizations in particular. The idea of government-funded pilgrimages to European gravesites did not, in fact, originate with war mothers, nor did the initial proposal privilege maternal grief. In 1919, the decorated war veteran and congressman Fiorello LaGuardia devised a bill that would have subsidized trips for fathers, mothers or widows, so long as the family consented to having the body interred in one of the eight American military cemeteries scheduled to be built in Europe. But the bill failed to receive a hearing. As LaGuardia subsequently explained, 'Everything was concentrated on getting those bodies back'.[23] Organized war mothers subsequently began to call upon the government to provide trips for mothers who had allowed the bodies of their sons to remain in Europe and could not afford to travel there to witness the site. In 1924, Congress held hearings on such a bill, but it floundered due to disagreements over logistical issues. The third bill, introduced in September 1927 and enacted in March 1929, succeeded primarily because organized war mothers had persistently lobbied Congress, supported after October 1928 by the powerful American Legion.[24] By restricting eligibility to those who had not previously visited their loved one's grave, the legislation retained the basic idea of a needs-based programme, but government officials waived this provision once the pilgrimages got underway.[25] As will become clear, what began as a proposal to serve poor war mothers ultimately evolved into a programme that showcased the American wealth and governmental munificence.

Although the pilgrimage bill owed its eventual passage to their exertions, the war mothers who provided congressional testimony tended to downplay, even obscure, their political influence. They declined to speak as representatives of a newly enfranchised constituency; in fact, at no point during the hearings did they even implicitly acknowledge the recent change in women's political status. Instead, they spoke as bereaved mothers and benevolent ladies, repeatedly differentiating themselves from both special interest pleaders and the poor women whom they hoped to assist. 'We have no paid lobbyists', the National Representative of the Gold Star Mothers, Mathilda Burling, declared in 1928. 'We have but ourselves and our hearts to crave a favor our country should grant.'[26] The fact that nearly all those who testified had already visited their sons' graves, some on multiple occasions, was repeatedly noted by congressmen and the women themselves, for it attested to the selflessness of their motives. As Mrs Frederick C. Guderbrod explained in 1924, 'I do not have to go over there; I have been. But I do hope we can send the other mothers over that can not go. There is nothing that would comfort them so much'.[27] Situating themselves within the longstanding tradition of female benevolence, and appealing to the congressmen as honourable gentlemen who held the power to grant them a special favour, the war mothers appeared to deny that they were even engaged in a political process.

Yet as they appealed for benevolence, the war mothers also claimed entitlement. Fluctuating between these two modes, they articulated a gendered conception of citizenship that historian Linda Kerber has done much to illuminate. Long after suffrage, Kerber has shown, white women's rights as citizens continued to be subordinated to, or even defined as, the 'right' to enjoy special *privileges* (especially exemption from onerous civic duties).[28] In other words, for white women, the denial of rights has historically been linked to the granting of exemptions and privileges, which could in turn come to be misconstrued as 'rights'. This helps to explain why leading war mothers often used the terms 'privilege' and 'right' interchangeably, and how they could shift so quickly from a stance of supplication to one of reproach. 'May I ask you gentlemen why all of this discussion is here to-day or at any time in the House or Senate on this bill?' Burling demanded at the end of one hearing in which some objections to the pilgrimages had been raised. 'It is something that we mothers should not be pleading for ... The Government should have considered this long ago ... Please, I beg of you ... console these mothers.'[29] The war mothers felt at liberty to press their case in large part because their status as respectable ladies, combined with their willingness to accept hierarchical gender relations, produced a strong sense of entitlement. They had fulfilled their prescribed civic role, even at its most cruelly demanding. They had not challenged male authority. From their perspective, the government simply could not refuse them.

Such feelings of entitlement also derived from a particular conception of the maternal role. The women who testified at the hearings viewed motherhood as an experience of unparalleled emotional intensity, rooted in physical suffering and self-sacrifice. Men could never understand the pain of maternal loss, they argued, because men never experienced such strong feelings of identification and attachment to another human being. 'I want to begin by telling you that you are all men and you have not and cannot feel the way a mother feels,' Effie Vedder stated at the outset of her testimony in 1924. 'It is part of her body that is lying over there. She spent 20 years, anyway, in bringing up that boy; she gave her time, both day and night, and none of you can realize what a mother's loss is.'[30] Emphasizing the pain that they had endured in childbirth and the care that they had expended in raising their sons to adulthood, the mothers presented their losses in a highly possessive manner: the bodies that fell in Europe were *their* bodies – the bodies that they had produced and sustained. 'It was the mothers who suffered to bring these boys into the world, who cared for them in sickness and health,' Mathilda Burling stressed, 'and it was our flesh and blood that enriched the foreign soil.'[31] Such rhetoric not only privileged maternal suffering almost to the exclusion of fathers and wives, but effectively blurred the boundary between mother and son, thereby equating the mother's sacrifice with that of her fallen son.

A few women, who viewed the love between mother and son as more pure and enduring than that between husband and wife, felt that widows should not be allowed to participate in the programme. The final bill ensured that the pilgrimages would honour women's undying devotion by barring widows who had remarried, even if the subsequent marriage had ended due to death or divorce. Yet these parameters did not satisfy Ethel Nock, who warned that including the widows might transform the sacred pilgrimage into a 'junket' or 'pleasure trip'. 'You must remember,' she testified, 'that many of these widows are girls whom the boys would never have met had it not been for the contingency of camp life ... Many of these widows are not worthy.' When pressed by a senator, she turned the question back to him, asking if he knew of any wife to whom the words of Kipling's poem 'Mother o' Mine' could apply. (The senator conceded that he did not.) No wife, Nock insisted, could love a man as much as his mother did:

> I think that mother love is greater than anything in the world. The widows, those who have not remarried, perhaps it is the result of circumstance and not wish. The mother lets no one take the place of that boy, and we mothers are carrying on, but there are times in the night when it is hard, when we think we ought to have him back.[32]

According to Nock, the mother alone should be entitled to make the pilgrimage, because she alone could be trusted to remain true to 'her boy'.

As for fathers, the legislation excluded them entirely.[33] Because fatherhood lacked the civic meaning and emotional intensity attributed to motherhood, paternal claims carried less weight.[34] Fathers did not usually speak of 'giving' their sons to the nation, in part because men did not define their relationship to the state through their paternal role, and in part because cultural norms barred fathers from adopting such a possessive stance toward their sons. During the hearings, several people testified on behalf of gold star fathers, but even those who argued for their inclusion readily acknowledged the superiority of maternal claims. For example, the Veterans of Foreign Wars proposed an amendment that would have allowed gold star fathers to make the journey if no mother or wife survived. The father 'probably feels not quite, but almost as keenly the situation as the mother', the VFW representative noted, hastening to add that his organization would not press for the amendment if it in any way imperilled the legislation for the mothers.[35] Similarly, a Connecticut resident argued for fathers' inclusion on the grounds that their presence would facilitate the trips for mothers, since most women were 'not used to travel alone'. Only then did he assert his claim as a father, recounting how he had encouraged his younger son to enlist after his firstborn had been killed. 'It seems that gold star fathers deserve some consideration', he ventured.[36] Even in their grief, men tended to speak and behave in accordance with the assumption that their wives had suffered a still greater loss.

In contrast to their more reticent husbands, gold star mothers who testified at the hearings openly proclaimed their anguish, justifying the pilgrimages as a salve for their mental and physical distress. In their testimony, they drew on both medical and religious language to convey the healing effects of their own personal pilgrimages. Jennie Walsh explained that the news of her son's death had left her 'struck deaf', like a shell-shocked soldier; she believed that her trip to Europe, taken on her doctor's advice, had 'saved' her 'reason'.[37] Relating a similar story in 1929, Ethel Nock concluded, 'I have tried to show you, through my own experience, how greatly a mother may be improved mentally and physically by the pilgrimage'.[38] Nock urged the congressmen to act with haste, noting that statistics gathered by the American War Mothers indicated that gold star mothers were dying at twice the rate of women whose sons had returned home uninjured.[39] Only the experience of witnessing the actual gravesite, she argued, would help to restore these mothers' debilitated bodies and minds.

In the face of these emotional appeals, the pilgrimage bill proved, in Piehler's words, 'impossible to resist politically': the House of Representatives paid homage to the mothers by passing the bill without debate, and without a single dissenting vote.[40] Maternalist claims not only served as the pilgrimages' primary justification, but also stood essentially unchallenged, even by those who opposed the bill's passage. Indeed, the only notable group of dissenters were those who believed that the funds would be better spent caring for living, disabled veterans – or *their* mothers and wives. 'What's the idea of giving the gold-star mothers a trip to Paris and doing absolutely nothing for the mothers of the disabled soldier ...?' demanded one woman who wrote to Senator Hiram Bingham to protest the proposed legislation. 'They had to witness those promising lads, the fruit of their life's work, returned wrecks'.[41] But in the flush economic times that still prevailed in 1928, most Americans, and virtually all politicians, seemed disinclined to weigh the mothers' claims of worthiness against those of others who had suffered because of the war.

This seeming unanimity, however, masked significant differences of opinion as to the fundamental meaning of the pilgrimage programme and the form that it ought to assume. Most leading war mothers viewed the pilgrimages as a social provision designed to meet the special needs of a uniquely deserving group of citizens. But some of the women, along with a number of congressmen, also imagined the pilgrimages as a grand commemorative gesture, akin to the 1921 entombing of the Unknown Soldier.[42] Although pilgrimage advocates rarely perceived these two visions as incompatible, they in fact entailed strikingly divergent conceptions of the programme and the pilgrims themselves.[43] Defined as a form of compensation, the pilgrimages cast each war mother as an individual beneficiary, and the emphasis fell on the emotional catharsis that she would presumably experience at her son's gravesite. Defined as an act of commemoration, the pilgrimages cast the war mothers as American icons, and the emphasis fell on the reactions they were designed to evoke in a national and international audience. In the end, the pilgrimage programme reflected elements of both models, never resolving the contradictions between them. Yet whereas an emphasis on compensation predominated during the congressional hearings, the idea of a grand patriotic gesture ultimately proved more crucial in determining how the pilgrimages unfolded. In particular, three important decisions – to have the War Department oversee the pilgrimages, to portray the programme as an unprecedented and exceptional form of social spending and to segregate the black gold star mothers – all reflected and furthered the government's nationalist aims.

The War Department's oversight of the programme represented a significant victory for those who believed that the pilgrimages should affirm an alliance between the military and the nation's mothers. Reflecting the pervasive antimilitarist sentiments of the 1920s and 1930s, a number of congressmen had promoted a very different vision of the pilgrimage programme, construing it as an internationalist gesture that would promote the cause of world peace. Representative Thomas Butler, who introduced the 1927 bill, proposed that the American Red Cross should run the programme, since such 'missions of mercy can be better attended by keeping the soldiery out of it'. The pilgrims, he added emphatically, 'are not to be taken on a parade'.[44] But leading war mothers opposed Butler's proposal, no doubt because it threatened to associate them with women peace activists who had framed some of their own initiatives as 'pilgrimages'.[45] In keeping with the war mothers' wishes, responsibility for the programme ultimately fell to the Quartermaster Corps, which conducted the pilgrimages as quasi-military ventures, steeped in patriotic ritual. For instance, at the ceremony marking the first group's departure, brass bands played old wartime favourites like 'Over There' and dozens of Navy fighting planes roared overhead when the ship disembarked.[46] Just as Butler had feared, the gold star mothers found themselves in the spotlight of a highly choreographed nationalist spectacle.

The pilgrimage programme also came to be represented as an incomparable and sacred undertaking that ought to be exempt from standard political vetting and fiscal concerns. Again, this particular conception of the programme was by no means inevitable, and in fact represented a significant departure from ideas articulated in the 1924 hearings. When Representative Samuel Dickstein introduced his bill, he compared it to measures on behalf of disabled veterans and to the World War Adjusted Compensation Act (the Soldiers' Bonus Act), enacted by Congress that same year.[47] The mothers who testified requested brief, no-frills 'tours' for women who could not afford to pay their own way; the language of 'pilgrimage' had yet to be adopted. Effie Vedder stated that the women would need only four nights in France, explaining that they did not 'care about the fine things of Europe'. And Mathilda Burling suggested that the government could use one of its own ships, assuring the congressmen, 'We are not asking to be sent across as a pleasure trip'.[48] But this emphasis on economising appeared more muted in the 1928–9 hearings and wholly vanished in the publicity leading up to the first pilgrimage. Instead, congressmen and journalists extolled the lavish accommodations that the pilgrims would enjoy. An article in the Quartermaster Corps' official publication promised that each pilgrim would feel 'as though some "influential" friend, with "means," had invited her to take a trip to Europe, which is exactly the case'.[49] Letters from the pilgrims bear out this prediction – many appear to have been quite stunned by unanticipated courtesies extended to them. 'It was a trip so far beyond my expectations that my gratitude can hardly be expressed in words', wrote one woman, 'I can only say that my heart swells with pride at the consideration shown me by my government'. Another pilgrim, who had fallen ill during the trip, wrote to President Hoover, 'had I been a queen no better attention could have been given me'.[50] Yet another woman, whose doctor had judged her health 'much improved' by the pilgrimage, attributed the change to the 'millionair [sic] treatment' she had received on what she described as 'the most wonderfull tripp [sic] I ever had in my life'. Rather than running the pilgrimages like a social programme for poor women, the government instead went to great lengths to treat the gold star pilgrims in a grand style – unless, that is, the women were black.

Although the pilgrimages had been championed as a manifestation of the nation's democratic spirit, in which poor and rich alike would be accorded equal honours, in March 1930 the War Department announced that African American women would be required to travel separately.[51] This decision reflected the institutionalized racism of the day, but it also manifested the conflict that inhered in the pilgrimage programme's dual justification. When viewed as an act of commemoration, what seems remarkable about the programme is that it included black women at all, considering the extent to which they were either excluded or demeaned in the national iconography of the time. Only a few years before enacting the pilgrimage legislation, the Senate had passed a bill that would have resulted in the construction of a national monument, on the Washington mall, commemorating the 'faithful colored mammies of the South'.[52] Although the legislation ultimately stalled in the House, its popularity in Congress provides some indication of how resistant many whites would have been to the idea of honouring black women as American war mothers. Yet when the pilgrimages are viewed as a form of compensation, the black pilgrims' inclusion appears less surprising, for in the realm of social provision, there was at least some precedent for recognizing black women's civic status. Despite intense opposition from southern elites, black servicemen's wives received allotments during World War I, which many had used to free themselves, at least temporarily, from the very jobs that the mythical mammy so contentedly performed.[53] By providing for segregated pilgrimages, the government tried to compensate black mothers while simultaneously upholding the racial construction of the all-American war mother – an utterly contradictory undertaking.

African Americans responded with predictable outrage, viewing the decision as one of a series of instances in which the government had egregiously betrayed wartime ideals and reneged on wartime promises. Throughout the spring and summer of 1930, black journalists and civil rights leaders devoted much attention to the issue.[54] In May 1930, the NAACP sent President Hoover a petition signed by fifty-five African American gold star mothers and wives declaring that they would boycott the programme if forced to travel in segregated groups. But Hoover refused to address the matter, and the War Department simply released a statement asserting that segregation was in 'the interests of the pilgrims themselves' and promising that all would receive 'equal accommodations, care and consideration'.[55] In fact, arrangements for the 280 black women who participated in the programme would differ significantly, at least prior to their arrival in France: whereas the white pilgrims stayed at Manhattan hotels, and the largest parties sailed on luxury liners, the black pilgrims stayed at the Harlem YWCA or black-owned hotels, and all parties sailed on second-tier passenger ships.[56]

Many black journalists and activists criticized the pilgrims in strikingly harsh terms, portraying their decision to participate in the programme as a maternal failure – a betrayal of their sons and the ideals for which they had sacrificed their lives. The charges they levelled reflected African Americans' distinctive appropriations of maternalism, which held mothers responsible for instilling and cultivating racial pride, as well as the rising influence of black nationalism.[57] 'Surely the dead will rise up to undo the wrongs of these mothers who accepted the morsel of the honor due a mother of one who died for his country', the Chicago *Defender* thundered when the first group of pilgrims sailed in July 1930. The paper went so far as to print the pilgrims' names and hometowns, prefaced with the stinging rebuke: 'Their Sons Died for Segregation'.[58] In the same issue, the celebrated sportswriter Frank A. Young accused the pilgrims of having 'set back' the entire race.[59] Another leading black paper, the Baltimore *Afro-American*, captioned a photograph: 'War Mothers Waving the Flag which allows them to be Jim crowed'.[60] Having failed to measure up to the ideal of the proud 'race mother', the pilgrims found themselves accused of complicity with a racist state and all but blamed for segregation.[61]

White liberals also denounced the segregation of the black pilgrims, but their critiques at times seemed inspired less by outrage over institutionalized racism than by antagonism toward the American Gold Star Mothers and other patriotic women's groups. Thus, whereas African American critics focused their attacks on those who had the power to reverse the decision – President Hoover and the War Department – their white counterparts appeared equally intent on deriding organized war mothers as hypocritical and self-righteous prigs. An editorial in the *Nation*, for example, argued that those women 'so delicately constituted that they could not endure to travel on the same ship with a black woman whose son or husband were killed in France' should have cancelled their passages.[62] This tendency to depict racism as a form of feminine snobbery gained strength over the course of the decade, as evidenced by the uproar that ensued in 1939, when the D.A.R. barred Marian Anderson, the famous African American contralto, from performing in Constitution Hall. According to a Gallup poll, most Americans supported Eleanor Roosevelt's decision to rebuke the organization by resigning her membership, but this result probably revealed more about populist scorn for the D.A.R. than it did about white Americans' commitment to ending segregation.[63] Similarly, although the controversy surrounding the black pilgrims reinforced negative perceptions of organized war mothers as small-minded and elitist, such sentiments did not reliably translate into a principled stance on racial issues.

If relatively few whites criticized the pilgrimages for perpetuating racism, however, a growing number did denounce the programme as an unjustifiable use of federal resources. The idea of sending gold star mothers on 'first-class' European pilgrimages initially attracted little dissent, but by the early 1930s, many viewed such a display of governmental largesse as insupportable. The fact that the programme tended to efface the class status of the white pilgrims only exacerbated matters. Elderly women in truth suffered disproportionately high rates of poverty, and many, if not most, of the pilgrims were poor: as one eye-witness observed, the trips afforded the majority of women, both black and white, 'their first real taste of luxury, and perhaps their last'.[64] But when crafting the pilgrimage legislation, congressmen had been reluctant to acknowledge this economic reality. For instance, they refused to consider a separate bill that would have granted cash bonuses of comparable worth to those impoverished gold star mothers who were too frail to travel.[65] By privileging emotional over material needs, the pilgrimage programme refashioned the gold star mothers as 'ladies' worthy of 'first-class' treatment, making them easy targets of resentment once the Depression took hold.

As economic conditions worsened, impoverished veterans and their advocates emerged as some of the most outspoken critics of the pilgrimage programme. In the late nineteenth and early twentieth centuries, veterans had been deemed particularly deserving recipients in U.S. political culture, as historian Theda Skocpol has shown.[66] But negative perceptions of the bloated and graft-ridden Civil War pension programme led many policymakers to resist the demands of the Great War's veterans. Though Congress did pass the World War Adjusted Compensation Act, or Soldiers' Bonus Act, to compensate veterans for lost wages, the law stipulated that no monies could be disbursed until 1945. Thus, it did nothing to lessen the impact of the Depression, which hit veterans with particular severity.[67] Underfunded programmes for disabled veterans also aroused resentment; critics accused government officials of treating veterans in a callous, 'hard-boiled' manner.[68] The wife of one such veteran, exhausted from pounding the pavement in search of work, exploded with fury in June 1932 after reading about the pilgrimages in the *Los Angeles Record*. 'I can hardly hold myself – just feel like shouldering a gun and going on the war path', she wrote to the editor. 'Think what all that money could have done for the men who were disabled for life and who cannot, even on their knees, get the sum of $50 a month for all the horror they went through overseas.' Vehemently repudiating the role of the patriotic war mother, she pledged that she would 'kill a son of mine with my own hands rather than let the government ruin him for life, then turn him loose like a whipped cur to beg, steal or commit murder in order to live'.[69] To many who believed that the government had failed to meet its obligations to the nation's veterans, the pilgrimage programme was an indefensible use of federal funds.

Anger over the government's treatment of veterans boiled over during the spring and summer of 1932, when thousands of destitute 'bonus marchers', some accompanied by family members, converged on Washington, D.C. The bonus marchers demanded immediate payment of the adjusted compensation that they were scheduled to receive in 1945. Although the amount due to each veteran differed according to the particularities of his service, the certificates' average value would have been around $1,000 in 1945; by way of comparison, the government was spending an average of $850 on each gold star pilgrim.[70] Tensions mounted following the defeat of the so-called Bonus Bill on June 17, when some 8,000 men refused to leave their shantytown in Anacostia Flats. On July 28, the stand-off erupted in violence, as U.S. troops commanded by Douglas MacArthur routed the veterans and destroyed their makeshift dwellings – a shameful display of force that epitomized the government's imperviousness to the prevailing desperation.[71] That very same day, members of the Quartermaster Corps ferried a contingent of gold star pilgrims about on sightseeing excursions outside of Paris.[72]

Given the striking contrast, it is easy to understand why the pilgrimage programme, which proponents had championed as above all financial consideration, aroused resentment. Still, the fact that many critics directed their anger toward the pilgrims themselves, rather than the congressmen who had enacted the legislation, suggests that they were not critiquing government policy alone – they were also levelling charges of maternal failure and betrayal. One woman who wrote to the *New York Times* in April 1932 professed amazement that gold star mothers could even 'think of accepting a trip abroad, increasing the expense from an already depleted Treasury' and 'lessening their sons' sacrifice'. 'Cannot they see,' she wondered, 'that giving them the trip abroad was simply a gesture of politicians who were not at all patriotic but simply thought a scheme like that would draw votes for them at the next election?'[73] In January 1933, another *Times* reader complained, 'Many of us are actually hungry, and insufficiently clothed; yet, through taxes, we are compelled to pay for these expensive trips to European countries. It does not seem human, or even possible, that these "War Mothers" would expect or could enjoy this visit to the graves of their loved ones which would add to the burden of suffering in the country for which their boys gave their all'.[74] These Americans believed that a truly patriotic war mother would never have allowed herself to be used as a pawn by craven politicians; she would have considered the nation's plight and selflessly declined the offer.

Similar arguments were advanced by peace advocates, who tended to view the pilgrimage programme as a publicity stunt designed to silence criticism of the government's wartime activities. The pilgrims served as targets for mounting anti-militarist sentiment as numerous Americans, outraged by revelations concerning the munitions industry, retrospectively questioned the nation's participation in the war. The publisher George Palmer Putnam, for instance, claimed that the War Department employed the ruse of 'protecting' gold star mothers in order to censor materials that would expose the true nature of modern warfare. He quoted an official who, upon denying his request for graphic wartime images, had instructed him to 'Think of the Gold Star mothers' who 'carried home in their minds beautiful pictures of ... well-kept resting places'.[75] Other commentators portrayed the gold star pilgrims as unwittingly complicit in the government's attempts to whitewash the war. The *San Francisco Examiner*, for instance, ran an anti-interventionist editorial in 1938 that derisively characterized the pilgrims as 'a pathetic little band of American mothers' who had 'shed futile tears ... over little white crosses'.[76] Although such critics stopped short of denouncing the gold star pilgrims, they strongly implied that the women had been duped, and that the government had cynically used them as props and decoys in order to pursue its militarist agenda.

The reaction to one renegade student group in the mid-1930s illustrates the public's tendency to associate criticism of the gold star pilgrims with support for the broad-based peace movement. In 1936, after Congress finally passed a Bonus Bill (over President Roosevelt's veto), some cheeky Princeton undergraduates expressed their dissent by founding an organization called the Veterans of *Future* Wars.[77] Students at Vassar College joined the hoax by establishing a women's auxiliary, the Association of Gold Star Mothers of the Veterans of Future Wars.[78] Striking a pose of dead seriousness, the students demanded $1,000 bonuses for every man under 36 who expected to be drafted, along with government-financed trips to Europe for every woman in the same age bracket. The soldiers of the next war, they reasoned, ought to be given money *before* they met their 'sudden and complete demise', just as future war mothers should be granted the opportunity to visit their sons' future burial sites *before* war ravaged the landscape. Staunch fiscal conservatives, the founders of the Veterans of Future Wars intended to ridicule Americans who used lofty patriotic rhetoric to pursue self-interested ends. But to their chagrin, critics and supporters alike interpreted their gesture as an anti-war statement.[79] Apparently, in an era notable for its pacifist sentiments, irreverent attacks on veterans and war mothers appeared to most observers synonymous with critiques of war and militarism.

Thus, by the mid-1930s, the pilgrimage programme had been criticized by disgruntled citizens on numerous grounds – for its discriminatory practices, consumption of scarce national resources and uncritical patriotism. The most hostile attacks on gold star mothers, however, appeared not in political discourse but in popular culture, and they attempted to expose not only those who betrayed the ideal of maternal self-sacrifice but the spurious nature of the ideal itself. Echoing leading childrearing experts of the era, these authors expressed a profound suspicion of sentimental or domineering mother love and intense anxiety about male autonomy. For instance, the 1933 John Ford film *The Pilgrimage* features an overbearing mother, Hannah, who sends her son Jim to war – and ultimately to death – simply because she disapproves of the girl he hopes to marry. 'I know her kind,' she carps in an early scene. 'She'd take you away from me. She'd poison your mind against me.' When the young lovers refuse to part, she instructs the local recruiter to draft Jim, who is soon thereafter killed overseas. On her pilgrimage, Hannah repents her actions and mourns her loss, returning home to embrace Jim's former girlfriend and illegitimate child. But the sentimental narrative of intergenerational reconciliation fails to efface the disturbing image of a mother bent on either possessing or banishing her son.[80]

Even more monstrous images of gold star pilgrims appeared in satirical works that conflated fears of maternal aggression, masculine vulnerability and the power of the modern state. In 1935 the new men's magazine *Esquire* published a particularly biting piece, subtitled a 'monologue in the true spirit of sacrifice by one who proudly gave her sons to the slaughter' and written in the voice of a pilgrim recounting her experiences to a women's group. To underscore their dimwitted nature, the women are literally portrayed as sacred cows – Mrs Holstein, Mrs Jersey, etc. The speaker is both ignorant (she makes many grammatical errors) and bigoted (she disdains the 'great black cow', Mrs Guernsey). But above all, she is bloodthirsty, mouthing platitudes about the 'Spirit of Sacrifice' while exalting in the mechanized killing of 'Our Dear Boys': 'They never stopped, but only whimpered a little for their mothers, and marched straight head of them, their eyes open, to make the Supreme Sacrifice before their Maker. And when the twenty-pound sledge fell and their front legs collapsed and the blood spurted I thought: How morvelous [sic]!' Clearly, elements of this dark satire – its debunking of racial bigotry and antimilitarist sentiment – echo earlier critiques of the gold star pilgrims, but the piece ultimately devolves into something far less rational. Appealing to the deepest of human fears – the fear the mother will fail to nurture and protect – it evoked a new and nightmarish vision: that of organized war mothers who enthusiastically applauded the state's attempts to sanitize the deaths of their own sons.[81]

A similarly hostile and satiric view of gold star pilgrims appeared as late as 1942, even as a new generation of American mothers confronted heartbreaking losses. In *Generation of Vipers*, the popular writer Philip Wylie introduced the term 'momism' to denote what he regarded as the distinctly American tendency to grant middle-aged, middle-class mothers excessive influence in both public and private life.[82] Women's historians have often referred to Wylie's book and quoted its many outrageous passages, but they have typically described the momism critique as an anti-feminist screed, failing to note that Wylie focused much of his wrath on conservative women's organizations, including those that represented war mothers.[83] In fact, the very image that inspired Wylie to coin his provocative neologism – an aerial shot of an infantry division of soldiers forming a giant 'MOM' in honour of Mother's Day – suggests that anxiety over Americans' reverence for war mothers played a major role in fuelling his critique.[84] The gold star pilgrimages must have made a similarly powerful impression, for nearly a decade after the fact, Wylie referred to them with undiminished outrage:

I have seen the unmistakable evidence in a blue star mom of envy of a gold star mom: and I have a firsthand account by a woman of unimpeachable integrity, of the doings of a shipload of these supermoms-of-the-gold-star, en route at government expense to France to visit the graves of their sons, which I forbear to set down here, because it is a document of such naked awfulness that, by publishing it, I would be inciting to riot, and the printed thing might even rouse the dead soldiers and set them tramping like Dunsany's idol all the way from Flanders to hunt and haunt their archenemy progenitrices – who loved them – to death.[85]

In hyperbolic fashion, Wylie portrayed the pilgrims as revelling in the accolades and prestige that their sons' deaths afforded them; beyond this, he went so far as to imply that they had somehow murdered their own sons. No longer the self-sacrificing figure whom soldiers fought to defend, the American war mother had become the self-aggrandising figure from whom they needed defending.

Of course, Wylie's views were hardly representative; probably no large-circulation magazine would have printed such a slur against war mothers during World War II. But letters from Wylie's fans suggest that his sensationalist attack struck a chord with readers who had already come to view self-identified war mothers with deep scepticism. In 1943, an 'ex-soldier' declared that he was 'most grateful to see a capable writer … fan the hell out of the self-pitying gratification found in the current momism of the blue and gold star cult'.[86] Another reader reported that she had been 'ranting for years ... against Gold Star mothers who "give" their sons to their country'.[87] Even a correspondent who took issue with Wylie's momism critique seemed prepared to make an exception in the case of gold star mothers: 'I don't know about the gold star mothers. I can't understand anyone ever claiming to be one.'[88]

War mothers' claims had not rankled so much during World War I, when issued within a cultural context that still assumed a harmonious mutuality between mothers and sons, and a political context in which women's exclusion from power remained more formal and complete. But by the 1940s, the rhetoric of patriotic maternalism had begun to resonate differently. The assault on mother love in popular culture and psychological literature gradually made Americans less comfortable with effusive rhetoric that valorized maternal sacrifice. This was reflected in the declining role of the middle-aged mother within popular culture and patriotic iconography: during World War II, the glamorous pin-up girl usurped the mother as the primary representative of American femininity, and romantic and sexual yearning surpassed mother love as the primary affective tie linking men to the homefront.[89] Increasingly, women defined their civic and political identities in ways that complicated or challenged the old separate spheres model. And once women could vote and even serve in the military, war mothers who defined their civic identities and wartime contributions in exclusively derivative and relational terms began to strike some Americans as anachronistic, even parasitic.

At the same time, political developments in the 1930s and 1940s contributed to a growing wariness of maternalist politics. By the time the U.S. entered World War II, events had demonstrated the ease with which maternalism could be retooled to serve anti-democratic purposes. In Germany and Italy, fascists constructed a special cult around the middle-aged war mother as the nation's officially recognized mourner.[90] And within the U.S., an anti-interventionist mothers' movement staged sensational and well-publicized protests in 1941, merging maternalist appeals with nativism and fundamentalist Christianity.[91] Although this movement waned following Pearl Harbor, popular magazines ran articles about 'The Menace of "Mothers"' as late as 1944 and respected commentators warned of the dangers of mixing motherhood and politics.[92] To be sure, maternalism never disappeared from the political landscape. Indeed, in the second half of the twentieth century, a variety of women's groups, from both sides of the political spectrum, would embrace a maternalist orientation.[93] But broadly speaking, American women who came of age in the 1940s and thereafter would be far less likely than their predecessors to view their maternal and civic roles as inextricably intertwined.

Conclusion

American women continued to join war mothers' organizations during and after World War II and many local communities continued to revere them, but the mothers of the war dead would not be honoured on a national scale in a manner comparable to that of their predecessors. During the 1920s, organized war mothers had succeeded in promoting the pilgrimage programme in part because they could still draw upon a sentimental and Victorian ideal of motherhood, and in part because many Americans had become receptive to the notion that mothers performed a civic duty that should be duly recognized by the state. But by the end of World War II, the assault on sentimental mother love in popular culture and the discrediting of patriotic maternalism in political discourse had rendered a gesture like the pilgrimage programme virtually inconceivable. Too closely associated with a possessive maternal stance now deemed pathological, with ethnocentric and racist views increasingly attacked as anti-democratic and with ritualized forms of patriotism that struck many as foolish or even sinister, the American war mother had been diminished as a symbol of national unity. Americans would continue to praise women for rearing citizen-soldiers, but most ceased to believe that the war mother who 'gave' her son to the nation made a unique and unparalleled sacrifice, entitling her to special compensation and acclaim.

Notes

For their helpful comments on earlier drafts of this essay, I am indebted to Frances Clarke, Andrew Wender Cohen, Nancy Cott, Carolyn Eastman, Lynn Gorchov, Rachel Klein, Marian van der Klein, Kathy Peiss and the participants of the Johns Hopkins History Seminar. Special thanks also to Sarah Heyward and the Radcliffe Institute of Advanced Study.

1. The concept of 'maternalism' was introduced in: S. Koven and S. Michel. 1990. 'Womanly Duties: Maternalist Politics and the Origins of Welfare States in France, Germany, Great Britain, and the United States, 1880–1920', *American Historical Review* 95(4), 1076–108; and S. Koven and S. Michel (eds). 1993. *Mothers of a New World: Maternalist Politics and the Origins of Welfare States*, New York and London: Routledge. Works that focus on maternalist politics in the U.S. include: M. Ladd-Taylor. 1994. *Mother-Work: Women, Child Welfare and the State, 1890–1930*, Urbana: University of Illinois Press; T. Skocpol. 1992. *Protecting Soldiers and Mothers: The Political Origins of Social Policy in the United States*, Cambridge, MA: Harvard University Press; L. Curry. 1999. *Modern Mothers in the Heartland: Gender, Health and Progress in Illinois, 1990–1930*, Columbus: Ohio State University Press; L. Gordon. 1994. *Pitied But Not Entitled: Single Mothers and the History of Welfare, 1890–1935*, New York: Free Press; and G. Mink. 1995. *The Wages of Motherhood: Inequality in the Welfare State, 1917–1942*, Ithaca, NY: Cornell University Press.
2. For discussions of conservative women's activism in the interwar period, see: N.F. Cott. 1987. *The Grounding of Modern Feminism*, New Haven: Yale University Press, ch. 8; K.

Delegard. 1999. 'Women Patriots: Female Activism and the Politics of American Anti-Radicalism, 1919–1935', Ph.D. diss., Duke University; Christine Kimberly Erickson. 1999. 'Conservative Women and Patriotic Maternalism: The Beginnings of a Gendered Conservative Tradition in the 1920s and 1930s', Ph.D. diss., University of California, Santa Barbara; and idem. 2004. '"So Much for Men": Conservative Women and National Defense in the 1920 and 1930s', *American Studies* 45(1), 85–102; F. Morgan. 2005. *Women and Patriotism in Jim Crow America*, Chapel Hill: University of North Carolina Press; and K. Nielson. 2001. *Un-American Womanhood: Antiradicalism, Antifeminism and the First Red Scare*, Columbus: Ohio State University Press.

3.   Prior scholarship on the gold star mothers pilgrimages has tended to focus on their significance in regard to the memory and commemoration of World War I. See G.K. Piehler. 1994. 'The War Dead and the Gold Star: American Commemoration of the First World War', in J. Gillis (ed.), *Commemorations: The Politics of National Identity*, Princeton: Princeton University Press, 168–85; idem, 1995. *Remembering War the American Way*, Washington, D.C.: Smithsonian Instituion Press, ch. 3; L.M. Budreau. 2008. 'The Politics of Remembrance: The Gold Star Mothers' Pilgrimages and America's Fading Memory of the Great War', *Journal of Military History* 72(2), 371-411; idem. 2009. *Bodies of War: World War I and the Politics of Commemoration in America, 1919–1933*, New York: New York University Press; J.W. Graham. 2005. *The Gold Star Mother Pilgrimages of the 1930s*, Jefferson, NC: McFarland; and L.L. Meyer. 2003. 'Mourning in a Distant Land: Gold Star Pilgrimages to American Military Cemeteries in Europe, 1930–33', *Markers* 20, 31–75.

4.   Private organizations in Europe, Canada and Australia also arranged for pilgrimages to battlefields and cemeteries in the 1920s and 1930s, but in no other instance did a government assume responsibility for organizing and financing such a venture. D.W. Lloyd. 1998. *Battlefield Tourism: Pilgrimage and the Commemoration of the Great War in Britain, Australia and Canada, 1919–1939*, Oxford: Berg.

5.   According to John Graham, 6,654 women made the pilgrimage, while 9,812 declined the government's offer, many no doubt because of advanced age or ill health. Graham, *The Gold Star Mother Pilgrimages of the 1930s*, 11–12.

6.   According to Lotte Larsen Meyer, more than 95 per cent of the pilgrims were gold star mothers. 'Mourning in a Distant Land', 34.

7.   Molly Ladd-Taylor has distinguished between 'progressive' and 'sentimental' maternalists, or mainstream clubwomen. She argues that the former supported women's participation in the public world, stressed 'justice and democracy' over 'morality and social order' and embraced science and professionalism. Ladd-Taylor, *Mother-Work*, 75. Christine Kimberly Erickson has defined 'patriotic maternalism' as a 'fusion between a militant patriotism that defended American values and institutions against subversive forces and a sense that motherhood provided women with the unique ability to safeguard American ideals'. Erickson, 'Conservative Women and Patriotic Maternalism', viii.

8.   The Sheppard-Towner Act focused on improving maternal and child health by providing matching federal grants to the states to disseminate educational materials and to establish clinics and visiting nurse programmes. Works that discuss the Sheppard-Towner and its downfall include: Ladd-Taylor, *Mother-Work*, ch. 6; Skocpol, *Protecting Soldiers and Mothers*, ch. 9; Delegard, 'Women Patriots', 262–84; J.S. Lemons. 1973. *The Woman Citizen: Social Feminism in the 1920s*, Urbana: University of Illinois Press, ch. 6; and R. Muncy. 1991. *Creating a Female Dominion in American Reform, 1890–1935*, New York: Oxford University Press, chs 4 and 5.

9.   Congress appropriated $5.38 million for the four-year pilgrimage programme, whereas allocations for the first four years of the Sheppard-Towner Act (1921-5) totaled $5.23 million. For funding of the Sheppard-Towner Act, see Ladd-Taylor, *Mother-Work*, 175. For details of the pilgrimage programme's budget, see Graham, *The Gold Star Mother Pilgrimages of the 1930s*, 66-8.

10. In 1936 and 1937, the American Gold Star Mothers campaigned for the passage of a bill popularly known as the 'Gold Star Mothers Bill', which extended and increased monthly payments to dependent mothers and fathers of deceased veterans. 'House Passes Gold Star Mothers Bill', *Washington Post*, 5 August 1937, 1.

11. For an illuminating discussion of the relationship between mother-blaming and the rise of racial liberalism, see R. Feldstein. 2000. *Motherhood in Black and White: Race and Sex in American Liberalism, 1930–1965*, Ithaca, NY: Cornell University Press.

12. For background on the right-wing mothers' movement, see L. McEnaney. 1994. 'He-Men and Christian Mothers: The America First Movement and the Gendered Meanings of Patriotism and Isolationism', *Diplomatic History* 189(1), 47–57; K. Frederickson. 1996. 'Catherine Curtis and Conservative Isolationist Women, 1939–1941', *Historian* 58(4), 825–39; G. Jeansonne. 1996. *Women of the Far Right: The Mothers' Movement and World War II*, Chicago: University of Chicago Press; and J.M. Benowitz. 2002. *Days of Discontent: American Women and Right-Wing Politics, 1933–1945*, DeKalb, IL: Northeastern University Press.

13. Works on women's contributions to the interwar peace movement include: H.H. Alonso. 1993. *Peace as a Women's Issue: A History of the U.S. Movement for World Peace and Women's Rights*, New York: Syracuse University Press; idem. 1989. *The Women's Peace Union and the Outlawry of War, 1921–1942*, New York: Syracuse University Press; C.A. Foster. 1995. *The Women and the Warriors: The U.S. Section of the Women's International League for Peace and Freedom, 1914–1940*, New York: Syracuse University Press; N. Berkovitch. 1999. *From Motherhood to Citizenship: Women's Rights and International Organizations*, Baltimore: Johns Hopkins University Press, 58–74; L.K. Schott. 1997. *Reconstructing Women's Thoughts: The Women's International League for Peace and Freedom before World War II*, Stanford: Stanford University Press; and S. Zeiger, 1990. 'Finding a Cure for War: Women's Politics and the Peace Movement in the 1920s', *Journal of Social History* 24(1), 69–86.

14. For an evocative portrait of the 1920s assault on the 'late Victorian matriarch', see A. Douglas. 1995. *Terrible Honesty: Mongrel Manhattan in the 1920s*, New York: Farrar, Strauss and Giroux. Works that discuss mother-blaming in psychological and social scientific literature and popular culture include: M.J. Buhle. 1998. *Feminism and its Discontents: A Century of Struggle with Psychoanalysis*, Cambridge, MA: Harvard University Press, ch. 4; Feldstein, *Motherhood in Black and White*, chs 1–2; and M.L. Margolis. 1984. *Mothers and Such: Views of American Women and Why They Changed*, Berkeley: University of California Press, ch. 2. See also M. Ladd-Taylor and L. Umansky (eds). 1998. *'Bad' Mothers: The Politics of Blame in Twentieth-Century America*, New York: New York University Press.

15. For discussions of sentimental representations of mothers in the Civil War North, see: F.M. Clarke. 2011. *War Stories: Suffering and Redemption in the Civil War North*, Chicago: University of Chicago Press; and Alice Fahs. 2000. 'The Sentimental Soldier in Popular Civil War Literature, 1861–65', *Civil War History* 46(2), 107–31.

16. In point of fact, two (rather than five) of Bixby's sons died in the war, and she herself sympathized with the Confederate cause. Moreover, most scholars now believe that Lincoln's personal secretary, John Hay, actually wrote the Bixby letter. M. Burlingame. 1999. 'The Trouble with the Bixby Letter', *American Heritage* 50(4), 64–7.

17. S. Zeiger. 1996. 'She Didn't Raise Her Boy to Be a Slacker: Motherhood, Conscription, and the Culture of the First World War', *Feminist Studies* 22(1), 6–39. The cultural construction of motherhood during World War I is also analysed in M.T. Coventry. 2004. '"God, Country, Home and Mother": Soldiers, Gender and Nationalism in Great War America', Ph.D. diss., Georgetown University; and K. Kennedy. 1999. *Disloyal Mothers and Scurrilous Citizens: Women and Subversion during World War I*, Bloomington: University of Indiana Press.

18. Piehler, 'The War Dead and the Gold Star', 175–7.

19. Ibid. Among the pilgrimage programme's enthusiasts was Lucia Ramsey Maxwell, author of the infamous 'Spider Web' chart, which accused numerous women reformers and women's organizations of alliance with an international socialist movement. Lucia Ramsey Maxwell to George Akerson, n.d. President's Subject Files, Box 165, Gold Star Mothers, Herbert Hoover Presidential Library, West Branch, IA (hereafter HHPL).

20. Delegard, 'Women Patriots'; and Erickson, 'Conservative Women and Patriotic Maternalism'.

21. Delegard, 'Women Patriots', ch. 2. Thanks to Christine Erickson for sharing information about the American Gold Star Mothers' participation in the WPCND's annual conventions.

22. 'From a Gold Star Mother', *Washington Post*, 22 December 1928, 6.

23. House Committee on Military Affairs, *To Authorize Mothers and Unmarried Widows of Deceased World War Veterans Buried in Europe to Visit the Graves: Hearing before the Committee on Military Affairs*, 70th Cong., 1st sess., 27 January 1928, 27. The U.S. government urged servicemen's next-of-kin to grant permission to have the bodies interred in American cemeteries in Europe, but it covered the expense of repatriating for those who refused. The Graves Registration Service returned 45,588 bodies to the United States, whereas some 30,000 remained buried in Europe. Mark Meigs. 1997. *Optimism at Armageddon: Voices of American Participants in the First World War*, New York: New York University Press, ch. 5. See also Piehler, 'The War Dead and the Gold Star', 171–4.

24. Lisa Budreau has argued that the passage of the final bill also owed much to timing, for by then work on the American military cemeteries in Europe was nearly complete. Budreau, *Bodies of War*, 198.

25. Graham, *The Gold Star Mother Pilgrimages of the 1930s*, 69. Graham provides a detailed discussion of the pilgrimage programme's legislative history.

26. Senate Subcommittee on Military Affairs, *To Authorize Mothers and Unmarried Widows of Deceased World War Veterans Buried in Europe to Visit the Graves: Hearing before a Subcommittee of the Committee on Military Affairs*, 70th Cong., 1st sess., 14 May 1928, 3.

27. House Committee on Military Affairs, *To Authorize Mothers of Deceased World War Veterans Buried in Europe to Visit the Graves: Hearings before the Committee on Military Affairs*, 68th Cong., 1st sess., 19 February 1924, 21.

28. L.K. Kerber. 1998. *No Constitutional Right to be Ladies: Women and the Obligations of Citizenship*, New York: Hill and Wang.

29. Senate Subcommittee on Military Affairs, *To Authorize Mothers and Unmarried Widows of Deceased World War Veterans Buried in Europe to Visit the Graves: Hearing before a Subcommittee of the Committee on Military Affairs*, 70th Cong., 1st sess., 14 May 1928, 29.

30. 1924 House Hearings, 15.

31. 1928 House Hearing, 22. See also 1928 Senate Hearing, 4.

32. 1928 Senate Hearing, 10. Mrs Charles Haas, New York State President of the War Mother's Association, seconded Nock's position, claiming: 'We have also a great many mothers who object very much to the widows going over ... We have in our own city a great many wives of soldiers who are divorced, and a great many of those who have remarried a short time after the boy was gone'. Ibid., 27.

33. In February 1930, Sen. Henry Allen introduced a bill that would have provided funds for fathers to make pilgrimages, but nothing came of the measure. 'Asks Trips for Fathers', *New York Times*, 14 February 1930, 15.

34. For histories of fatherhood that cover the interwar period, see: R. Griswold. 1993. *Fatherhood in America: A History*, New York: Basic Books; and R. LaRossa. 1997. *The Modernization of Fatherhood: A Social and Political History*, Chicago: University of Chicago Press.

35. 1928 Senate Hearing, 21–2. Likewise, one newspaper story reported on fathers who attempted to change the law by asserting they 'certainly' had 'as much claim to such a trip as a woman who was merely a guardian for a soldier killed in France'. (The law permitted

a woman who had acted *in loco parentis* to the deceased to make the pilgrimage.) The men did not, however, argue that a father had as much right to a pilgrimage as a biological mother. Unidentified newspaper clipping, Newspaper Clippings, Box New York, 1930–33, American Pilgrimage of Gold Star Mothers and Wives, Record Group 92, Office of the Quartermaster General, National Archives and Records Administration II, College Park, MD [hereafter RG 92, NARA].

36. Ibid., 18.
37. 1924 House Hearings, 20; see also 1928 Senate Hearing, 5–6.
38. 1929 Senate Hearing, 7.
39. 1929 House Hearing, 18.
40. Piehler, 'The War Dead and the Gold Star', 377.
41. 1928 Senate Hearing, 19.
42. The Tomb of the Unknown Soldier became associated with gold star mothers in 1925, when they began to make annual Mother's Day pilgrimages to the site. For background, see: Piehler, *Remembering War the American Way*, 116–25.
43. A report prepared for the Senate on the constitutionality of the proposed legislation clarified these dual justifications by pointing to two types of precedents for the pilgrimage programme – those which established the government's power to 'grant relief to soldiers and their dependents' and those which recognized the government's power to enact legislation that would 'further patriotic sentiment'. 'Memorandum Upon Constitutionality of Use of Federal Funds for Gold Star Mothers' Pilgrimages', 1929 Senate Hearing, 11–15.
44. 1928 House Hearing, 2. Long associated with the relief of suffering caused by war, the American Red Cross relied heavily on maternal imagery during World War I and the interwar period, representing itself as 'The Greatest Mother on Earth' in its fundraising campaigns. Foster Rhea Dulles, *The American Red Cross: A History*, New York: Harper & Brothers, 1950, 150.
45. For instance, in 1926, the Women's International League for Peace and Freedom led a 'Peace Pilgrimage' to London, calling for a World Disarmament Conference and urging the British government to sign the Optional Clause of the International Court of Justice.
46. 'Gold Star Ship Sails with 235 on Pilgrimage', *Chicago Daily Tribune*, 8 May 1930, 5; 'Gold Star Mothers Honored at Sailing', *New York Times*, 8 May 1930, 3; 'New York Pays Its Homage as Gold Star Mothers Sail', *Washington Post*, 8 May 1930, 3.
47. 1924 House Hearings, 4.
48. 1924 House Hearings, 16, 19.
49. Maj. L.C. Wilson, 'The War Mother Goes "Over There"', *Quartermaster Review* May–June 1930, 21–25. See also: William A. Du Puy, 'Pilgrimages of Mothers to Europe's War Graves', *New York Times*, 23 February 1930, sec. IX, 8.
50. Mrs C. Durkin to Pres. Herbert Hoover, 23 September 1930, President's Subject Files, Box 165, Gold Star Mothers, HHPL.
51. 'Capital Rebuffs Gold Star Negroes', *New York Times*, 30 May 1930, 12; and 'Gold Star Mothers Balk at Jim Crow Move', *Chicago Defender*, 7 June 1930, 2.
52. M.P. McElya. 2007. *Clinging to Mammy: The Faithful Slave in Twentieth-Century America*, Cambridge, MA: Harvard University Press.
53. K.W. Hickel. 2000. 'War, Region, and Social Welfare: Federal Aid to Servicemen's Dependents in the South, 1917–1921', *Journal of American History* 87(4), 1363–91.
54. R.A. Serrano, 'Poignant Protest', *Los Angeles Times Magazine*, 15 September 2002, I.16.
55. 'Capital Rebuffs Gold Star Negroes', 12.
56. The most complete account of the African American pilgrimages appears in: Graham, *The Gold Star Mother Pilgrimages of the 1930s*, ch. 6. See also Budreau, *Bodies of War*, ch. 22.
57. Linda Gordan discusses a type of 'black maternalism' that differed in significant respects from that promoted by white welfare reformers. See Gordon, *Pitied But Not Entitled*, ch. 5. Eileen Boris argues that 'womanist' is a more apt term for describing the politics of

motherhood that black women advocated. E. Boris. 1993. 'The Power of Motherhood: Black and White Activist Women Redefine the "Political"', in Michel and Koven (eds), *Mothers of a New World*, 213–45.

58. 'Gold Star Mothers Sail for France on Freight Steamer', *Chicago Defender*, 19 July 1930, 1.
59. 'The Gold Star Turns to Be One of Brass', *Chicago Defender*, 19 July 1930, 13.
60. 'Many Gold Star Mothers Cancel Jim Crow Trip', *Afro-American*, 19 July 1930, 1, 19.
61. Many black journalists and activists, however, softened their tone after witnessing the attentive care that the black pilgrims received during their journeys, and the overwhelmingly positive reception that the women received in Paris. See, for example: 'Paris Fetes War Mothers: France Seeks to Make up for U.S. Jim Crow', *Afro-American*, 26 July 1930, 1; 'Gold Star Mothers Wildly Greeted on Arrival in Paris', *Chicago Defender*, 26 July 1930, 4; 'Gold Star War Mothers Talk for the *Afro*', *Afro-American*, 9 August 1930, 1, 17.
62. Black and Gold Stars', *Nation* 131, 23 July 1930, 86.
63. On the Anderson episode, see: Morgan, *Women and Patriotism in Jim Crow America*, 153–5; and S.A. Sandage. 1993. 'A Marble House Divided: The Lincoln Memorial, the Civil Rights Movement, and the Politics of Memory', *Journal of American History* 80(1), 143–51.
64. J.A. Rogers, 'War Mothers in France Got First Taste of Liberty', *Afro-American*, 23 August 1930, 5.
65. Graham, *The Gold Star Mother Pilgrimages of the 1930s*, 52–6.
66. Skocpol, *Protecting Soldiers and Mothers*.
67. For a discussion of the Depression's impact on veterans, see J.D. Keene. 2001. *Doughboys, the Great War, and the Remaking of America*, Baltimore: Johns Hopkins University Press, 180–84.
68. For background on disabled veterans, see S. Gelber. 2005. 'A "Hard Boiled Order": The Reeducation of Disabled World War I Veterans in New York City', *Journal of Social History* 39(1), 161–80; and K.W. Hickel. 2001. 'Medicine, Bureaucracy, and Social Welfare: The Politics of Disability Compensation for American Veterans of World War I', in P. Longmore and L. Umansky (eds), *The New Disability History: American Perspectives*, New York: New York University Press, 236–67.
69. 'The Other War Mothers', *Los Angeles Record*, 24 June 1930, sent to Pres. Herbert Hoover by Richard P. Yockisch, 25 June 1930, President's Subject Files, Box 165, Gold Star Mothers, HHPL.
70. The average cost of a pilgrimage is cited in Graham, *The Gold Star Mother Pilgrimages of the 1930s*, 55. For historian Jennifer Keene's computation of the average bonus, see http://www.worldwar1.com/dbc/bonusm.htm.
71. For accounts of the Bonus March, see R. Daniels. 1971. *The Bonus March: An Episode of the Great Depression*, Westport, CT: Greenwood, 1971; P. Dickson and T.B. Allen. 2004. *The Bonus Army: An American Epic*, New York: Walker and Co.; and Keene, *Doughboys, the Great War, and the Remaking of America*, ch. 8.
72. Graham, *The Gold Star Mother Pilgrimages of the 1930s*, 140.
73. Letter to the Editor, 'War Mothers Pilgrimage', *New York Times*, 17 January 1933, 18.
73. L.F. Henry, 'Letters to the Editor', *New York Times*, 15 April 1932, 18.
74. Quoted in 'Editorial Paragraphs', *The Nation* 134, 23 March 1932, 327.
75. Scrapbook, Box 7, American Gold Star Mothers Collection, Library of Congress, Washington, D.C.
76. '"Future Veterans" Seek a Bonus Now', *New York Times*, 17 March 1936, 24; and 'Future Veterans', *Time* 27(13), 30 March 1936, 38.
77. Vassar president Henry N. MacCracken rebutted claims that a Future Gold Star Mothers chapter existed at Vassar, insisting that the college had not chartered the organization. 'Vassar Head Protests', *New York Times*, 27 March 1936, 46. By the time he issued his disclaimer, the Princeton students had already bowed to pressure from the American Gold

Star Mothers and renamed the women's auxiliary the 'Home Fires Division'. 'Future Veterans Bow to Criticism', *New York Times*, 21 March 1936, 19. See also: Lewis Gorin to Marys Austin Converse, 21 March 1936, Box 6, Folder 'Gold Star Mothers/Home Fires Division', Veterans of Future Wars Collection, Seeley G. Mudd Manuscript Library, Princeton University, Princeton, NJ.

78. D.W. Whisenhunt. 1994. 'The Veterans of Future Wars in the Pacific Northwest', *Pacific Northwest Quarterly* 85(4), 134–6; and J.P. Lash and J.A. Wechsler. 1936. *War Our Heritage*, New York: International Publishers, 135–42. See also the group's manifesto: L.J. Gorin, Jr, *Patriotism Prepaid*, Philadelphia: J.B. Lippincott.

79. For instance, the left-wing pacifist Oswald Garrison Villard rushed to the students' defence, enquiring acidly, 'Do the Gold Star Mothers wish to reserve for themselves the precious patriotic experience that is theirs of having given their sons at their country's behest in the most futile of wars, or are they willing to have others ennobled by this experience?' O.G. Villard, 'Issues and Men', *Nation* 142, 8 April 1936, 450.

80. The film is based on a short story that portrays the conflict between mother and son in more ambiguous terms – the son is more culpable and the mother less blameworthy. I.R.A. Wylie, 'Pilgrimage: A Story', *American Magazine* 114, November 1932, 44–7, 90–96.

81. P. Stevenson, 'Gold Star Mother', *Esquire* 3, December 1935, 205.

82. P. Wylie. 1942. *Generation of Vipers*, New York: Farrar & Rinehart.

83. On Wylie's momism critique, see: Buhle, *Feminism and its Discontents*, ch. 4; Feldstein, *Motherhood in Black and White*; and Rebecca Jo Plant. 2010. *Mom: The Transformation of Motherhood in Modern America*, Chicago: University of Chicago Press.

84. P. Wylie, 'More Musings on Mom', *The Saturday Review* 29, 7 December 1946, 21.

85. Wylie, *Generation of Vipers*, 192–3.

86. [N.p.], 5 June 1943, Scrapbook, box 285, Philip Wylie Papers, Firestone Library, Princeton University, Princeton, NJ [hereafter PWP].

87. [Layfette, IN], 29 June 1943, folder 4, box 232, PWP.

88. [Akron, OH, no date], folder 4, box 235, PWP.

89. R.B. Westbrook. 1990. '"I Want a Girl, Just Like the Girl That Married Harry James": American Women and the Problem of Political Obligation in World War II', *American Quarterly* 42, 587–614.

90. E. Heineman. 2001. 'Whose Mothers?: Generational Difference, War, and the Nazi Cult of Motherhood', *Journal of Women's History* 12(4), 139–64; and A.M. Wingenter. 2003. '*Le Veterane del Dolore*: Mothers and Widows of the "Fallen" in Fascist Italy', Ph.D. diss., Loyola University of Chicago.

91. McEnaney, 'He-Men and Christian Mothers'.

92. R. Whelan and T.M. Johnson, 'The Menace of the "Mothers"', *Liberty* 137, 24 July 1944, 18–19, 72–3; P. Lochridge, 'The Mother Racket', *Woman's Home Companion* 71, July 1944, 20–21, 71–4; and H.M. Jones, 'Mother Love Is Not Enough', *Saturday Review of Literature* 27, 28 October 1944, 16.

93. See, for example, A. Swerdlow. 1993. *Women Strike for Peace: Traditional Motherhood and Radical Politics in the 1960s*, Chicago: University of Chicago Press; and M.M. Nickerson. 2011. *Mothers of Conservatism: Women and Postwar Right*, Princeton: Princeton University Press.

CHAPTER 8

PROTECTING MOTHERS IN ORDER TO PROTECT CHILDREN

Maternalism and the 1935 Pan-American Child Congress

Nichole Sanders

In 1935 the president of the Public Welfare Directorate, Dr Enrique Hernández Alvarez, dedicated Romulo Velasco Ceballos' work *The Mexican Child Before Charity and the State* to the Pan-American Child Congress, convened that year in Mexico City.[1] This was a proud moment for Mexican reformers like Velasco and Hernández, who hoped that Mexican programmes could serve as a model for other countries. According to U.S. reformer Katherine Lenroot, Mexico was selected to host the Congress because it was a country 'that has done so much to protect children, that has conserved its Spanish heritage while overcoming its indigenous roots' and because it served as 'a point of contact between the Latin civilization and the Anglo-Saxon civilization'.[2] The Congress allowed Mexicans to showcase their post-revolutionary welfare reforms, helping to create a distinct Latin American maternal-child welfare discourse – a discourse that emphasized a strong role for the state and for women, working in partnership to 'uplift' Latin American populations.

In October 1935 representatives from twenty-two countries in North and South America met for the seventh Pan-American Child Congress. Delegates from Latin American nations eagerly embraced the opportunity to reform their populations, keenly aware of the differences in economic

---

Notes for this chapter begin on page 164.

and social development between Latin American countries and the so-called 'civilized' societies of North America and Europe. To 'overcome their indigenous roots' became Latin American reformers' 'civilizing mission'. This mission charged the state with the responsibility of bringing Latin America up to the economic, social and racial standards of the United States and Western Europe through policies focusing on children. Children needed to be trained to be future workers and to improve the racial stock of the nation. Policymakers attending the Congress contended that Latin America could civilize itself and become like Europe and their northern neighbours if this resource could be properly harnessed.[3] They believed that the state's 'civilizing mission' would be successful because it would work in partnership with women. Women, either professionally as social workers or through their 'natural' role as mothers, would aid the state in its drive to 'civilize' their societies. It was this new emphasis on the state that differentiated the Latin American welfare discourse from earlier discussions of poverty, charity and philanthropy.

The concern for public health and welfare reform was in part a response to a rapid population growth in the cities at the turn of the century. In Brazil and the southern cone nations, immigration from Europe spurred urban growth, while in other countries internal migration to the cities caused growth and concern. This rapid urbanization came with costs. Cities needed to control living and working conditions in order to avoid health problems. As Asunción Lavrin points out, 'Desirable as this growth was, it was plagued by alarming health problems that reflected badly on nations wishing to join the mainstream of Western "progress". One way of demonstrating "civilization" was to control the embarrassing social and medical problems affecting their cities'.[4] By the 1930s, these problems were exacerbated by the economic downturn of the Great Depression. As the older, export-led model of economic growth faltered, Latin American governments turned to state-sponsored industrialization in an effort to stimulate their economies. These governments had relatively large urban populations that needed to be trained to work in factories during a period of economic hardship. Part of the 'civilizing mission' was to turn this population into a stable workforce that would allow Latin American countries to 'catch up' economically with other Western nations.

The policymakers who dominated the Pan-American maternal-child welfare movement were primarily reformers of a middle-class or elite background. Papers and agreements forged through these Congresses, such as the *Actas Finales*, show a remarkable amount of homogeneity in attitudes towards gender, race and the role of the state in development. In large part, the ideologies and desires on the part of the reform movement to re-make gender roles within a reconstituted family and to improve 'the race' reflected Latin American middle-class aspirations, especially for increased social and political power. The ability to call oneself 'professional' and to have access to the education and training it took to be 'professional' allowed the middle class an important way to differentiate itself from the working and lower classes.

It also allowed this group to position itself as distinct from and superior to the traditional elite, aligned with the Catholic Church and conservative values. Alma Idiart's discussion in Chapter 12 of the shift in Argentina away from the *Sociedad de Beneficencia* to state control of welfare is an example of the middle-class professionals' aspiration to distinguish themselves from Catholic charity. The desire to frame one's work within the discourse of professionalism, and scientific professionalism in particular, created a dialogue within the professional community unmarred by rancorous debate.

The Pan-American Child Congress was influential in the construction of Latin American welfare states and expressed dominant Latin American views on development and modernization. In attendance were prominent physicians, politicians, educators, social workers and other professionals involved in health and welfare policymaking. These were the men and women who either implemented or designed policy at the national and local level in their own countries.[5] These Congresses influenced the way welfare states and discourses surrounding modernity developed in Latin America.[6]

The Pan-American Child Congress began in 1916 as part of a global movement that had its roots in the late nineteenth-century European and North American efforts to protect children and address racial and pronatalist concerns – movements discussed in several chapters in this volume. Because of these roots, and because of the active participation of many Latin American reformers in international discussions, the echoes of U.S. and European concerns can be heard in the Pan-American discussions. The Pan-American Child Congress offered a vision of maternal-child welfare that was similar to policies implemented in Europe, and in particular the United States, where concern for maternal child welfare not only was a result of increased poverty associated with industrialization and urbanization but also came out of late nineteenth-century religious movements such as Catholic social action and Protestant evangelicalism. Women actively participated in religious clubs and societies to establish a public presence for themselves and used their social role as mothers to justify their involvement. This was no less true in Latin America, where groups such as the *Unión de Damas Católicas* in Mexico, the *Sociedad de Beneficencia* in Argentina or the *Sociedad 'La Bonne Garde'* in Uruguay organized to provide welfare services for poor women and children. In places such as Argentina, much like Britain and the United States, the network of philanthropic agencies established by women's organizations became the basis for later state welfare efforts.[7]

What the delegates at the Pan-American Child Congress offered, however, was a distinct vision of welfare linked firmly to the state, rather than to religious or private groups. Governments in Latin America used state-sponsored programmes as a hedge against the social power of the Catholic Church.[8] The strong emphasis on the state also diverged from countries such as France, where, as Lori Weintrob demonstrates in Chapter 4 of this volume, a partnership between the private sector and the state emerged during the Third Republic. Latin American reformers also placed a far stronger emphasis on eugenics as a means through which to improve and 'civilize' their countries.

Social reformers capitalized on the momentum created by the Child Congresses to implement welfare policies in their home countries. As Donna Guy notes:

> Often, these formal, highly public and erudite ceremonies served as a legitimating function for intellectuals and politicians endeavoring to create political consensus on social topics ... both before and after the Congresses – advocates used professional authority to pressure political systems for reform.[9]

This was no less true in Mexico. Mexico's Revolution of 1911–17 resulted by the 1930s in calls for a renewed commitment to social justice. Mexican welfare workers used the 1935 Congress to showcase the revolutionary reforms they had implemented. Indeed, since the majority of the attendees at the Congress were Mexican reformers, they were poised to make an impact on the recommendations of the meeting. Mexican reformers, like other delegates, were also able to use the prestige of the Congress to push for an even greater state commitment to welfare. An examination of the talks given shows the importance of women and children to Mexican and Latin American welfare advocates.

The 1935 Pan-American Child Congress

Latin American delegates, influenced by eugenics, focused their attention on the young and demanded public health projects dedicated to racial improvement and economic development. Eugenic thought was popular in Europe and North America as well at this time, but in Latin America eugenics took a different form in the 1930s. Latin Americans embraced a neo-Lamarckian version of eugenics, which stressed the primacy of environmental factors, arguing that changes in environment could improve 'the race'. This was in contrast to the Mendelian form of eugenic thought popular in the United States, England and Germany, which argued for a more deterministic theory of genetics. Therefore, public health became central to Latin American eugenists, because it represented a positive way for their societies to improve racially and become 'civilized'.[10] Through this discourse, the poor as a class also became associated with racial inferiority. As Nancy Leys Stepan contends, 'These professionals assumed that social ills accumulated at the bottom of the racial-social hierarchy – that the poor were poor because they were unhygienic, dirty, ignorant, and hereditarily unfit'.[11] Any attempts to combat poverty during this period revealed not only class bias on the part of the reformers but a racial bias as well.

Reformers believed children had to be taught proper hygiene and be treated medically by trained doctors to ensure the future racial health of the nation. Policymakers saw mothers as crucial to the success of this mission, as mothers played such a central role in the early years of a child's upbringing. Mothers had to be specially trained in order to assure that children were properly raised to participate in these new societies. And, because someone had to train mothers, social workers became integral to the success of the 'mission' as well.

Professional Social Workers, the State and Social Transformation

Public health and welfare came to be accepted by the beginning of the twentieth century when women lacked suffrage as legitimate arenas through which they could enter the public sphere in Latin America. Women's participation in programmes that targeted children was viewed as a natural extension of their proper role as mothers. Indeed, policymakers considered women to be ideally suited for social work – they were kinder, more caring and more moral. One social worker highlighted these characteristics, declaring that:

> The country needs a woman, a woman that is above all an optimist who knows how to overcome the most difficult activities that present themselves, who has a strong character, a firm will, and who knows how to win the hearts and confidence of the poor, who is sweet and caring, energetic and firm as the circumstances dictate.[12]

Because the task could be so daunting, policymakers and social workers alike maintained that women who entered into the profession had to have very special characteristics, characteristics that were inherently feminine. Another social worker commented, 'The social worker should be an observer, be prudent, serene, discreet, altruistic, dynamic and impartial, intelligent ... she should be serious and happy'.[13] The social worker would serve as an investigator, educator, counsellor and social engineer. She would be perfect for working with other women and children, since, welfare advocates argued, women naturally possessed the qualities of understanding and tact necessary to enter people's homes, to be heard and to morally guide poor families.[14]

Ironically, while women in one sense were considered to be 'naturally' fit for work in the public health and welfare field, they nonetheless now had to be properly educated and trained to perform this role. With a new emphasis on an increased role for the state in social transformation came an increasing emphasis on social workers' professional training. By the 1920s several countries in Latin America had set up professional schools of social work, leading to the emergence of a professional cadre of female social workers by the 1930s. Social workers would help the state achieve its goal of becoming modern and civilized.[15]

One part of this civilizing mission was economic development. Latin American policymakers decried the difference in economic development between their countries and North America and Europe. Marisabel Simons, a Mexican teacher, explained that this gap in standards of living could in part be explained by North Americans' commitment to social service. Simons lamented the fact that, although workers' wages were just as low in the United States as in Latin America, the American working class and poor nevertheless enjoyed a much higher standard of living. While her claims about income may not have been true, they nevertheless allowed Simons to blame Latin American poverty on a lack of scientific training, rather than structural economic dependencies. Simons pointed to the transformational nature of social work as the explanation, arguing that social work and social workers in particular had trained poor and working-class Americans to improve themselves and work harder. She explained, 'Social work there [in the United States] has realized its main goal, it has transformed the masses, made them civilized, and has made their daily fight for life that much easier'.[16] Social work in the United States had created model workers; it could do the same in Latin America. Simons went on to call for the creation of more schools for social work in Latin America, noting that many of the schools in existence were located in Europe and North America.[17] Thus, educators like Simons linked economic growth with a need for social transformation. They believed that, through social work, their populations could be trained to be the kinds of workers needed to civilize their countries and fulfil their economic goals. But first, older notions of philanthropy had to be challenged.

In particular, welfare advocates objected to previous notions of charity, arguing that almsgiving hurt more than helped the poor: 'Many times alms are given, being moved by a feeling called charity, but the task of the social worker is to battle against charity. Once a pauper has spent what was given, and usually spent poorly, his labour, which should be constructive, is harder.'[18] Reformers maintained that simply giving handouts to the poor did not teach them how to work for their living, it merely rewarded them for begging. In addition, they maintained, the poor were poor in part because they could not manage their money. Once given money, no one could guarantee that it would be spent on necessities like food or shelter and not on vices such as alcohol. Social workers had to teach the poor to work:

> One should prepare the poor (*los miserables*) not to live off of handouts, but through their own efforts. We know that almsgiving does absolutely nothing to ameliorate the causes of misery. Rather, it temporarily hides the symptoms of the social maladjustment of the individual and contributes to the slow but sure transformation of that individual into someone without shame, without their own initiative, who lives materially and morally at the expense of the rest of us.[19]

Handouts would create a permanent class of the poor, who would rather beg than work. A nation would not be able to progress economically if it could not train its citizens to be good workers. Government officials and welfare advocates alike believed that well-trained workers would ensure the demographic health of the nation, enhance industrial productivity and contribute to national development.[20] Workers had to show discipline and initiative in order to improve themselves and their country. This was especially important as these nations shifted from an economic model that exported raw materials to an industrial economy.

Reformers' attitudes towards the poor reflect a complex set of social changes. Many earlier nineteenth-century elite believed that the poor would always exist. Poverty was a reflection of the moral failures of the unfortunate. Good Catholics could improve the moral state of their own souls through almsgiving and other good deeds. They believed that the poor had to be controlled, and that any aid granted to the underprivileged was best done through private charities or the church.

Reformers in the late nineteenth and early twentieth century, however, saw the poor as redeemable, through properly applied scientific methods. Welfare professionals critiqued older Catholic charity as inefficient and problematic. But while reformers in the 1930s saw poverty as something that could be ameliorated scientifically, it is clear that some of the older

attitudes towards the poor remained. Although the poor could be redeemed, middle-class welfare workers did not view the poor as equals.
Not only were they socially different, but eugenic thought confirmed
that the poor were racially distinct and inferior. In order to be redeemed,
the poor would have to submit to tutelage, much like children. New discourses of science and modernity mixed with older attitudes disdaining
the poor. An example is Simons' reference to the poor as *los miserables*.
Literally meaning the miserable or despicable ones, or the ones living in
unhappiness or misery, she (and other reformers) nevertheless used the
term as a synonym for the poor, reflecting their middle-class bias.

By the 1930s the increased role of the state and the professionalization
of social work reflected the new scientific emphasis. Child welfare specialists argued that 'social service was the scientific and modern form of
altruism'.[21] It was clear that traditional forms of charity had done nothing
to eradicate poverty. Social workers, therefore, would scientifically tailor
treatment to each individual case. Only after discovering the root causes
of poverty and recommending individualized treatments could the material and moral standards of living rise.[22] Almsgiving was at best a temporary solution. *Congresistas* contended that modern scientific programmes
would combat poverty at its source: the home. Social workers believed
that a visit to the home was a necessary first step in recommending a solution to the cause of a poor family's economic and social condition.

This was not an easy task. Welfare workers had to combat not only resistance from sectors of society that supported the older notions of charity, but the poor often resisted professional recommendations as well.
One teacher wrote:

> Generally social work is not well understood, a social worker is viewed as hav-
> ing bad intentions. She is seen as a propagator of dissolute ideas, as one who
> is encourages children against their parents. Finally, they feel her investigation
> is intrusive. Almost always her labour is poorly received.[23]

Many poor resisted the incursion of the state into their homes and resented professional advice. The majority of these social workers came from
middle-class backgrounds and did not always understand the reality of
life in a poor neighbourhood. For example, mothers in one working-class
Mexico City neighbourhood complained that the teachers in the *Casa
Amiga de la Obrera*, a vocational school run by the Secretary of Public
Assistance for the children of working mothers, often punished children
for infractions by suspending them from school for the day. Mothers
wondered where their children were supposed to go if they themselves
were working and could not be at home with them.[24] Child welfare ad-

vocates often recommended solutions to the poor's problems that could be difficult to achieve.

The social worker's primary task was to enter into the home of her clients and offer professional diagnoses and treatment for the socio-economic challenges the family faced. Delegates to the Congress viewed these specialists as a crucial link between the home, teachers and doctors:

> She ensures that mothers receive proper pre- and postnatal treatment. It is she, who with an intuition all social workers should possess, guides the mothers to avoid infant mortality … it is necessary that the social worker prepare mothers, showing them how to care for their children so that a strong, healthy, prepared and active generation can be created for the betterment of the country.[25]

The social worker worked with doctors to make sure that children were treated for illnesses and that mothers received pre- and post-natal care. They also taught mothers not to fear doctors. This was especially important in populations that had not been accustomed to visiting a medical doctor, relying instead on folk cures, or, during childbirth, a midwife. One of a professional's primary tasks was to make sure that mothers and children received 'appropriate', that is 'modern and scientific', medical care – although ironically the social worker was to use her intuition to guide poor mothers, suggesting, perhaps, that a middle-class intuition was superior to the poor's reliance on 'superstition'. Policymakers viewed infant mortality in particular as a failure on the part of the state to protect future generations. By 1930, delegates noted with alarm that most Latin American countries had child mortality rates that still compared unfavourably with Europe. Eugenists feared that failure to protect infants would weaken the nation, since without healthy children the nation could not fulfil its economic and social potential.[26]

Welfare specialists would also teach mothers and their children to avoid vices and instruct all on the benefits of a proper and healthy marriage.[27] Neo-Lamarckian eugenic thought claimed that vices such as alcoholism, drug use or syphilis damaged a country's racial stock. Not only could the foetus itself be damaged by a mother's addiction or disease, but eugenists also believed that these defects could be subsequently passed on to future generations. According to reformers, it was of utmost importance therefore that mothers avoid vice. As we will see, delegates also maintained that the nuclear family was the foundation of the nation, and as such sought to convince mothers that they should be in stable, state-sanctioned marriages. Mothers became the target for child welfare policies.

Training Mothers

Participants in the Congress – who influenced the way welfare reform would be instituted in their home countries – viewed the mother as the key to the creation of a healthy generation of children. As Judith Rivera de Rangel, a Mexican teacher, commented, 'Of course, everyone, prudent men and women alike are interested in the lives of children; but it is in the first seven years of life that the little one is exclusively in the hands of women'.[28] Training poor mothers to raise children with modern scientific techniques became the primary goal. Welfare advocates, many influenced by eugenic theories, considered the poor to be racially and morally inferior and the poor as a whole were especially vice-ridden. Therefore poor mothers had to be taught not only proper childrearing techniques, but, as mentioned, they had to be taught to avoid vices in order to give birth to healthy children. Welfare advocates gave working women in particular special attention, since they believed that a mother's physical working conditions would create unhealthy offspring. These policies reflect participants' class and racial biases; none of these programmes targeted middle- or upper-class women. Poor and working-class women, however, needed to be taught how to be 'modern' and 'civilized' mothers.

Educators argued that it was no longer appropriate to allow mothers to raise children using traditional methods. Enelda Fox, a prominent Mexican social worker who went on to be the Director of Social Action in the Mexican Secretary of Health and Welfare in the 1940s and 1950s, wrote:

> It is necessary to prepare mothers for the correct protection of their children. Our civilization has arrived at a state where it is necessary to recognize that the animal instincts humans possess are not enough to give confidence in the mother – she cannot depend on these instincts to guide her in raising, protecting and educating her children. The maternal instincts a mother has in common with animals are not sufficient as a preparation for a civilized life.[29]

It was no longer enough for women to rely on characteristics that were 'natural'. Indeed, Fox's prejudice is clear: the poor were not much better than animals, animals that had to be trained and domesticated to participate in modernity. Likewise, modern mothers had to be trained to realize their social role. Fox suggested that schools teach young women these skills, since without proper knowledge of how to raise them, children were in danger of physical and mental defects.

Fox continued, condemning these defects. She argued that these problems not only affected the child him or herself, but future generations as well. Defects that arose from exposure to vices were especially troublesome. She maintained that all vices and defects had to be eradicated in order to improve the country racially.[30] Fox contended that in order to facilitate this work, specialists should keep statistics and records on children in order to know what would work best to resolve the country's problems. She commented, 'From an economic point of view, modern societies consider that this continued vigilance of the child constitutes the most economical programme for the health of the country'.[31] Once again, racial health and economic growth were explicitly linked. The state would employ scientific techniques – statistics and record keeping (requiring an increased bureaucracy and more active state role) – to facilitate this transformation. Modern record keeping also privileged a certain kind of knowledge: that of scientific statistics over local female knowledge of a mother. For the civilizing mission to work, educators had to teach poor mothers to care for their children scientifically.

Most policymakers advocated training in both high schools and in Mother-Child Centres.[32] Future mothers needed to be taught not only how to physically care for babies, but also how to create clean and hygienic homes. If the mothers did not learn these skills in high school, social workers agreed that they should be encouraged to take puericulture (child care) classes at Mother-Child Centres, where many took their babies and received medical care anyway. In this manner, professionals could assure themselves that mothers were receiving the proper modern training necessary. Elena Torres, a Mexican professor and feminist organizer,[33] even suggested creating Youth Brigades to train mothers. She argued that once women were taught these new skills, within a generation the country would have a suitable generation of children who would positively contribute to a country's economic and social development.[34]

Social reformers not only were concerned that poor women avoid vices and learn to care properly for their children. They were also concerned that working women would inadvertently harm their babies because of the nature of their work. One social worker wrote, 'The decrease of the birth rate is, in general, a fact in countries that have achieved a state of advanced civilization. In our country the birth rate is decreasing and depends, not on the infecundity of the race but on the nefarious influence of modern civilization and its inconveniences'.[35] Thus, although civilization brought many advantages, modern industry came with its disadvantages as well.

Policymakers believed that women's work in factories was one particularly dangerous effect of modern civilization. This was especially true for pregnant workers. Pregnancies were imperilled due to the repetitive, physical nature of factory work or from exposure to toxic chemicals. Social workers also cited fatigue as another danger. They asserted that fatigue, from both the job and having to cope with the home as well, caused accidents and allowed women to become more predisposed to illness. Studies suggested that working women regularly delivered unhealthy babies with low birth weights. Working women were also more prone to abandon their babies when they returned to work. Delegates in particular were disturbed that the disease and death rates of working-class children were higher than any other social class.[36]

In order to combat these problems, social workers advocated several measures. In particular, they believed that pregnant workers should not be allowed to work during the last three months of pregnancy and for a month after delivering the baby. But they also argued that a woman should be paid for this maternity leave, even if complications in the pregnancy forced her to leave work before the last trimester. Special doctors should be scientifically trained to help working mothers. Centres for working mothers should be provided for healthy recreation and nursing centres should be set up in all factories with over fifty female workers so that mothers could nurse their own children the first year. If a mother worked in a factory with fewer than fifty women, she should receive extra pay because she herself could not nurse.[37]

Most policymakers agreed that if it was at all possible, a mother should stay at home and care for her children herself. But congress participants recognized the fact that many mothers had to work. Since working mothers were particularly at risk of illness and premature death, many argued that these mothers had to be regulated for the health of the nation. Modern science would have to combat the ills of modern civilization – or, put another way, modern science would be used to combat the social problems modern industry created.

Congress attendees saw education as the key to disseminating the scientific method and to creating future healthy generations of children. Policymakers viewed the health of these future generations as central to their own country's economic and social development. The Seventh Pan-American Child Congress therefore proposed the following:

> 1) A child's education should start in the cradle and it is therefore indispensable that mothers have the necessary preparation, 2) It is necessary to procure through as many means as necessary the security and training of the family in order to fulfill its corresponding social functions, 3) The education imparted in the home should correspond to the that of the schools, and the parents of the family should cooperate with the teachers whenever necessary, 4) Secondary schools need to teach children how to become good future parents, directing the education of their own children and efficiently and rationally cooperating with the schools, 5) It is desirable also that women's schools organize special classes for current and future mothers. Also – radio stations should organize conferences to illustrate to the women what her possibilities and responsibilities with respect to the education of her children and the well-being and progress of her family.[38]

Over and over again, doctors, teachers and social workers exhorted women to take special classes in order to learn these new techniques. Policymakers also argued for special classes in high schools to teach future parents. While the mother was considered to be the most influential person in a young child's life, welfare workers also recognized the importance of the father. Children should be raised in a two-parent family, they argued, because in the nuclear family all the benefits of education and support could be maximized. Therefore, educators focused not only on training mothers, but in educating children to get married and form their own families. Policymakers denounced men who abandoned their families and who did not live up to their responsibilities.

(Re)constructing the Family

Congresistas cited the mother as the most important figure in the child's life, arguing that 'the protection of the child is rooted in the protection of the mother. The two cannot be separated because this endangers their health and life'.[39] However, they also contended that a mother could do her job properly only if the father of her children adequately supported her. Many social workers, doctors and educators argued that the father's abandonment of his children represented the gravest threat to the health and welfare of children, maintaining that 'this is particularly true in the case of the single mother, who frequently, with good reason, is poor and unprotected'.[40] Single mothers and their illegitimate children had to be supported. Some advocated legislation to force fathers to take economic responsibility; others advocated education to teach young men the dangers of child abandonment. Many policymakers also argued that if the father could not be forced to support his family, the state should then take over his role and protect and support his children.

A. Sainz Trejo, a doctor from Veracruz, Mexico, conducted a study in which he discovered that almost half of all children born in Veracruz were illegitimate. He decried this situation, arguing that although single mothers tried their best, illegitimate children simply did not have the same advantages as other children. He explicitly linked this crisis to the nation's future, arguing that a failure to support these children would lead to race degeneration, thus endangering Mexico's potential.[41] According to Sainz Trejo, all children should have the right to equal support. 'What should this support be?' he asked, proceeding to explain:

> According to the Civil Code, not only food, clothing, assistance in the case of illness, but also the necessary financial support for a primary education and for

the child to learn a job skill or profession: this is what a legitimate child has a right to. The illegitimate child should have a right to this support as well.[42]

Others argued that courts needed to be created to protect single mothers – and to force men to complete their obligations and duties. Policymakers argued that a child had a right to his or her paternal surname and that single mothers had a right to the moral and financial support of the father.[43]

Reformers maintained that once men faced their responsibilities, proper families could be created and children would be healthier and happier. Some looked to the Soviet Union as an example of the effectiveness of legally forcing men to recognize all of their children. They argued that once laws forced men to support their children, women would be liberated, since they would no longer have to bear sole responsibility. This law would also combat child poverty and result in healthier children, since they would have the necessary resources.[44]

Thus, changes in legislation were needed. Policymakers argued that the distinction between illegitimate and legitimate offspring had to be erased and that children had a right to know who their parents were. Cuban lawyer and feminist organizer Ofelia Domínguez Navarro[45] proposed reformation of the legal codes to allow for the investigation of paternity, so that the legal status of legitimate and illegitimate children would be the same.[46] Forcing fathers to support all of their children would, according to Domínguez, go a long way towards alleviating childhood poverty, which threatened the strength of the nation.

This position put reformers at odds not only with the poor, who tended not to marry formally. Socially prominent men also tended to have affairs and blocked reformers' attempts to establish paternity laws. Enforcing paternity would mean that many men would have to admit to marital infidelities and meant that illegitimate children would have the right of support and inheritance. In fact, the issue had been raised at the Mexican 1917 Constitutional Convention, and voted down. Men feared that public naming of paternity would tarnish their honour and embarrass them in front of their wives and families. Reformers challenged middle- and upper-class men's unfettered sexual access to women.[47]

While policymakers urged that men be held legally accountable for their children, they also advocated educational projects to teach men to be good fathers. They argued that children, especially young girls, needed to be taught child care and hygiene. Boys needed to be taught to respect women, so that as future fathers they would know not to abandon their responsibilities. But policymakers did not limit these projects to just the school. Taking into account the large illiterate population in Latin America, they also urged that other methods of education be employed.

Suggestions included travelling expositions, primers, flyers, conferences, practical demonstrations and movies.[48]

Finally, many realized that even with legislation and education, a large number of illegitimate children would still exist. These children still needed to be fed and protected. Policymakers therefore concluded that it was the obligation of the state to care for these children. One doctor wrote:

> The state has the unavoidable obligation to protect illegitimate children. First, the state should, by any means possible, attempt to determine paternity. The state should also modify laws to assure that illegitimate and legitimate children have the same right to support. If it is impossible to determine paternity, the state should therefore be in charge of the protection and care of illegitimate children, as well as their education. Their education can be provided through foundling homes, orphanages etc. The state should put all of its resources to study these circumstances, being always a guide for the resolution of these problems.[49]

If fathers would not accept their responsibility, then the state would step in to assure children their protection, care and education.

Latin American policymakers articulated a clear vision of a 'civilising mission' that sought to uplift 'backward' and racially unfit populations to Western European and North American standards of social progress and economic development. Latin Americans advocated an increased state role on social planning and transformation, which in essence was an argument for the state to play a surrogate father role.[50] If poor women could be redeemed through training to be proper mothers, poor men would have to disciplined to accept their responsibilities as fathers and providers.

The participants in the 1935 Congress crystallized a view of child welfare that allowed women, either as mothers or social workers, to have a central responsibility. Latin American social reformers, concerned about their populations' perceived racial and economic inferiorities, championed the role of the state in 'civilizing' these 'backwards' peoples. These concerns continued throughout the late 1930s and 1940s, although the outbreak of World War II changed the geopolitical reality of the region and allowed Latin American policymakers to reshape the discourse to suit their own wartime contingencies.

Conclusion

Much literature has discussed the role of maternalism and the creation of the welfare state. Maternalism has been variously defined as policies that improve the well-being of mothers and children, policies for women by women, and as a feminist strategy whereby women demand civil rights based on their societal role as mothers or potential mothers. This chapter sees maternalism broadly, as policies that improve the well-being of mothers and children. As Idiart also shows, many welfare professionals were men. And while some Latin American feminists used maternalism strategically to demand civil rights, this was not what interested the reformers, male and female alike, at the 1935 Pan-American Child Congress.[51]

Seth Koven and Sonya Michel have posited a model for understanding the role of maternalism vis-à-vis the state. They argue that:

> the strength and range of women's private-sector welfare activities often varied inversely with the strength of the state. 'Strong states', defined as those with well-developed domestic-welfare bureaucracies and long traditions of government intervention, such as France and Germany, allowed women less political space in which to develop than 'weak states' like the United States and, to a lesser extent, Great Britain, which allowed women's voluntary associations to flourish.

While this provides an interesting model for the comparative analysis of welfare states in developed countries, it is less useful for understanding the creation of welfare policies in Latin America. It is difficult to characterize Latin American states as 'strong' or 'weak', based on Koven and Michel's definition, and the Pan-American vision of maternal and child welfare had significant differences from North American and Western European ideologies.[52]

I argue in this chapter that the vision of the welfare state espoused by the Seventh Pan-American Child Congress was that of a 'civilizing mission', a mission in which women explicitly were made partners of the state. Latin American policymakers keenly felt the economic, social and racial disparities between their countries and North America and Western Europe. Their conception of welfare therefore had to take into account this perceived disparity. Maternal and child welfare policies focused on modernising and civilising their populations. Welfare policymakers argued that these policies had to improve the conditions of children, the future wealth of their countries. Children not only had to be educated to be good workers, but also, in 1930s Latin America, they had to be educated to improve the racial stock of their nations. Through economic and racial improvement, congress delegates reasoned that Latin America could, one day, become modern and enter into the 'civilized' world.

Nanneke Redclift has argued that 'class, gender and race ... are not merely connected, they do not simply intersect ... they *are/stand* for each other'.[53] This is particularly pertinent for understanding the Pan-American vision of maternal and child welfare. Through eugenics, poverty was racialized in Latin America: reformers believed the poor to be racially unfit. Eugenic thought blamed Latin American countries' lack of progress on an inherent 'racial backwardness'. The weight placed on mothers also assured that poverty was feminized. Children were poor in many cases, policymakers contended, because single mothers had to raise children on their own. Public health and education programmes therefore emphasized policies designed to improve racial hygiene and convince men that they needed to support their children.

The Seventh Pan-American Child Congress promoted a maternalism that focused on policies to enhance the well-being of mothers and children. This conference is significant because it was the most important Pan-American congress convened in the 1930s that specifically dealt with child and maternal welfare. Hosted by Mexico, it also allowed Mexican reformers the opportunity to highlight the contributions their post-revolutionary government had made to international discourses on child-maternal welfare. It offered a vision of maternalism that differed from U.S. and European models – a vision that sought to 'civilize' their 'backward' countries and become more like the 'developed' world.

Notes

I would like to thank Donna Guy, Amelia Lyons, Rebecca Jo Plant, Steven Topik and Marian van der Klein for reading and commenting on various drafts of this essay.

1. R.V. Ceballos. 1935. *El Niño Mexicano ante la caridad y el estado*, México: Editorial Cultura.
2. *Memoria del VII Congreso Panmaericano del Niño*, México, 1937, 5. Katherine Lenroot had been an active participant in the U.S. Children's Bureau, serving as its director during the 1930s. For a discussion of Lenroot's activities in the United States, see L. Gordon. 1994. *Pitied But Not Entitled: Single Mothers and the History of Welfare, 1890–1935*, New York: Free Press. For Lenroot's activities in Latin America, see D.J. Guy. 2000. *White Slavery and Mothers Alive and Dead: The Troubled Meeting of Sex, Gender, Public Health and Progress in Latin America*, Lincoln: University of Nebraska Press, 52–69.
3. Unlike 'civilizing missions' imposed on other regions by colonial powers, this was a 'civilising mission' created by Latin American elites and imposed on their own populations. Scholars have discussed the role U.S. companies played in attempting to 'civilize' Latin American working classes. See, for example: T. Klubock. 1998. *Contested Communities: Class, Gender and Politics in Chile's El Teniente Copper Mine, 1904–1951*, Durham, NC: Duke University Press; T. O'Brien. 1996. *The Revolutionary Mission: American Enterprise in Latin America, 1900–1945*, New York: Cambridge University Press. I argue that there was a more important attempt to transform Latin American societies promulgated by Latin American, rather than U.S., elites.
4. A. Lavrin. 1995. *Women, Feminism, and Social Change in Argentina, Chile, and Uruguay*, Lincoln: University of Nebraska Press, 97. Efforts to combat poverty in Latin America took on added significance because most Latin American nations at this time had a very small middle class, if they had one at all. The majority of the Latin American population lived

in poverty. Latin American policymakers recognized the fact that the 'civilized' countries had poor as well. What concerned these delegates, however, was the scale of the problem in Latin America. Efforts to 'uplift' and 'civilize' the poor in Latin America have to be understood as efforts to transform a majority of the population.

5. The lines between the various professions, particularly for female professionals, tended to be fuzzy during this period. With the exception of medical doctors, other professions often overlapped. Thus, a teacher may have also been trained as a social worker, and many nurses performed functions that we would associate with social work. All delegates to these congresses held some sort of professional position, and most were in a position to influence, if not actually dictate, policy. All considered themselves to be aligned with social reform movements that advocated the health and welfare of children. Therefore, this chapter refers to *congresistas* interchangeably as reformers, policymakers, delegates, social workers and welfare advocates because they themselves would not have recognized a sharp delineation between these terms.

6. Guy, *White Slavery*, 34.

7. K. Mead. 2000. 'Beneficent Maternalism: Argentine Motherhood in Comparative Perspective, 1880–1920', *Journal of Women's History* 12(3), 120–45.

8. This chapter loosely defines maternalism as policies that aimed to improve maternal and child welfare. The Congresses were part of a larger Pan-American movement that sought to stimulate and encourage greater regional cooperation. Women were active in many of these conferences, in an effort to promote not only women's rights issues, but social concerns as well, such as maternal-child welfare. For a discussion of women's participation in inter-American conferences such as the Pan-American Scientific Congresses and the International Conferences of American States, see F. Miller. 1990. 'Latin American Feminism and the Transnational Arena', in E. Bergmann (ed.), *Women, Culture and Politics in Latin America*, Los Angeles: University of California Press. As Donna Guy points out, 'The child congresses are a part of Pan-Americanism that arose first among the Latin American nations, one that always reached out to the United States as an equal participant, never a primary force'. Guy, *White Slavery*, 40.

9. Guy, *White Slavery*, 36–7.

10. N.L. Stepan. 1991. *The Hour of Eugenics: Race, Gender and Nation in Latin America*, Ithaca, NY: Cornell University Press, 44–5.

11. Ibid., 37.

12. M.C. Simons, 'El trabajo social como redentor en la sociedad', in *Memoria del VII Congreso Pan-Americano del Niño*, 838.

13. Ibid., 840.

14. J.V. Vásquez and G. Loyo, 'Programa mínima de preparación de las enfermeras visitadoras y de las trabajadores sociales', in *Memoria del VII Congreso Pan-Americano del Niño*, 849–50.

15. Lavrin, *Women, Feminism, and Social Change*, 97, 118–19.

16. Simons, 'El trabajo social', 839.

17. Ibid., 839–40.

18. Ibid., 841.

19. Ibid.

20. See also K.A. Rosemblatt. 2000. *Gendered Compromises: Political Cultures and the State in Chile, 1920–1950*, Chapel Hill: University of North Carolina Press, 4.

21. Simons, 'El trabajo social', 841.

22. Ibid.

23. Ibid., 840.

24. AHSSA Fondo: Beneficencia Pública, Sección: Asistencia LG 3, Exp 4.

25. Simons, 'El trabajo social', 843.

26. Lavrin, *Women, Feminism, and Social Change*, 100–102.

27. Simons, 'El trabajo social', 843.
28. J.R. de Rangel, 'Coloboración de la familia y de la escuela en beneficio de los niños', in *Memoria del VII Congreso Pan-Americano del Niño*, tomo 2, 322.
29. E.G. de Fox, 'La Coordinación y desarrollo de los trabajos encaminados a preparar a las madres para la debida protección de sus hijos', in *Memoria del VII Congreso Pan-Americano del Niño*, 891.
30. Ibid.
31. Ibid.
32. Mother-Child Centres were sites where poor mothers could receive medical care for themselves and their children and participate in programmes designed to teach them child care and other domestic skills.
33. Torres was active in both the Mexican and the Pan-American women's movement. She served as the Vice-President for the Pan-American Association for the Advancement of Women in 1922; she was the chief of Mexico's Bureau for Cultural Missions in the 1920s and also helped to found the National Council of Mexican Women in 1918. See Miller, *Latin American Women*, 87, 92–3.
34. E. Torres, 'Servicio social infantil y de higiene doméstica', in *Memoria del VII Congreso Pan-Americano del Niño*, 867.
35. N. Hernández, 'La Coordinación y desarrollo de los trabajos encaminados a preparar a las madres para la debida protección de sus hijos: protección de madres obreras', in *Memoria del VII Congreso Pan-Americano del Niño*, 897.
36. Ibid., 898–9, 902.
37. Ibid., 903.
38. 'Congresos Pan-Americanos del Niño: Ordenación Sistemática de sus recomendaciones: 1916–1963', Montevideo, Uruguay, 83.
39. V.F. Quevedo L., 'Protección de la madre soltera', in *Memoria del VII Congreso Pan-Americano del Niño*, tomo 2, 103.
40. A.S. Trejo, 'Protección a los hijos ilegítimos', in *Memoria del VII Congreso Pan-Americano del Niño*, tomo 2, 135.
41. Ibid., 103.
42. Ibid.
43. Quevedo, 'Protección de la madre soltera', 106.
44. O.D. Navarro, 'La investigación de la paternidad como medida de protección al niño', in *Memoria del VII Congreso Pan-Americano del Niño*, tomo 2, 127.
45. Domínguez had been working on this issue since the 1920s in Cuba. See K.L. Stoner. 1987. 'Ofelia Domínguez Navarro: The Making of a Cuban Socialist', in W. Beezley and J. Ewell (eds), *The Human Tradition in Latin America: The Twentieth Century*, Wilmington, DE: Scholarly Resources, 119–40.
46. Ibid., 128.
47. A. Blum. 2009. *Domestic Economies: Family, Work, and Welfare in Mexico City, 1884–1943*, Lincoln: University of Nebraska Press, 117.
48. Quevedo, 'Protección de la madre soltera', 104.
49. Sainz Trejo, 'Protección a los hijos ilegítimos', 137.
50. Lavrin, *Women, Feminism, and Social Change*, 124.
51. For discussions of Latin American feminists' use of maternalism as a political strategy, see S. Buck, 'Activists and Mothers: Feminist and Maternalist Politics in Mexico, 1923–1953', Ph.D. diss., Rutgers University, 2002; A. Macias. 1982. *Against All Odds: The Feminist Movement in Mexico to 1940*, Westport, CT: Greenwood; J. Olcott. 2002. '"Worthy Wives and Mothers": State-Sponsored Women's Organizing in Postrevolutionary Mexico', *Journal of Women's History* 13(4), 106–31; idem. 2005. *Revolutionary Women in Postrevolutionary Mexico*, Durham, NC: Duke University Press; and E.T. Pablos. 1992. *Mujeres que se organizan: El Frente Unico Pro Derechos de la Mujer, 1935–1938*, Mexico: M.A. Porrua.

52. S. Koven and S. Michel (eds). 1993. *Mothers of a New World: Maternalist Politics and the Origins of Welfare States*, New York and London: Routledge, 24–5.
53. N. Redclift. 1997. 'Post Binary Bliss: Towards a New Materialist Synthesis?', in Elizabeth Dore (ed.), *Gender Politics in Latin America: Debates in Theory and Practice*, New York: 227.

CHAPTER 9

MATERNAL AND CHILD WELFARE, STATE POLICY AND WOMEN'S PHILANTHROPIC ACTIVITIES IN BRAZIL, 1930–45

Maria Lúcia Mott

During the past three decades, Brazilian and North American authors have produced more than a dozen historical works on the political participation of women in Brazil between the end of the nineteenth century and the beginning of the twentieth century. The majority of these studies use feminist or modernization theory as a lens to understand women's political participation. Unfortunately, these approaches have resulted in a biased view of women's activities, especially in regard to their participation in philanthropic organizations. This bias is also seen in studies of women's involvement in the Brazilian feminist and labour movements.

Historians have acknowledged middle-class and elite women's participation in philanthropic entities during the first decades of the twentieth century as a kind of step towards more public activities. But they have paid little attention to the issue, or dismissed it as unimportant. In general, philanthropic work is viewed as an antidote for a tedious and useless existence, one that allowed elite women an outlet for their talents or energy, or simply a pretext for assuming responsibilities outside their homes. The historiography of the period suggests that female contributions to such organizations were of secondary importance, limited primarily to raising funds at mundane parties. It regards the creation and management of philanthropic organizations, as well as the guiding proposals, as dictated by class and male interests. It even por-

---

Notes for this chapter begin on page 186.

trays married women's participation in philanthropic and charitable activities as a means of enhancing their husbands' professional and social status.[1]

The feminist movement that emerged in the early twentieth century has been viewed in a similar manner. The historiography is critical due to the fact that the movement was led by middle-class and urban elites who brought together women from different organizations, even from philanthropic associations, and because these women failed to question patriarchal social structures and women's roles as mothers and housewives. The historiography considers the struggles of that period as having a relatively conservative and reactionary character. Historical scholarship has tended to be more favourable toward some feminist forerunners who acted outside the organized movement, namely Ercilia Cobra and Maria Lacerda de Moura. Because these women published critical works as early as the 1920s that discussed the role of women in relation to the family, sexual freedom and reproductive rights, their thinking was more aligned with what was considered politically correct by most feminist scholars writing in the 1970s, 1980s and 1990s.[2]

Proposals for organizing labour and social legislation in Brazil were first credited to men's involvement and then to women's participation in different types of workers' movements (anarchists, socialists, communists, etc.). Women's contributions to the elaboration of proposals and the establishment of social welfare policies by means of feminist and philanthropic associations still need to be studied and evaluated more fully. The objectives of this study are: to review the proposals of philanthropic entities, organized and managed by women in the first half of the twentieth century; to rethink the role that women played in elaborating social welfare programmes and establishing public policies; and to call attention to the need for reassessing the Brazilian feminist movement. These topics will be approached through an analysis of the maternalist discourse espoused by middle- and upper-class women in the first decades of the twentieth century.[3] This discourse claimed that women, due to their inherently maternal nature, were especially well suited to defend the poor and to engage in welfare activities that targeted women and children.[4] Only recently, however, have scholars of Brazil begun to incorporate maternalism into their analyses of gender history and the history of the early welfare state.[5] This article therefore has a fourth objective: to alert historians to the importance of including maternalism in their analyses.

The research is based on documents from the archives of the *Cruzada Pró Infância* (Pro-Childhood Crusade), an organization founded in the city of São Paulo in 1930. The focus is on the proposals for maternity protection elaborated by Pérola Byington, managing director from 1930–45, the period known as Vargas Era (after President Getúlio Vargas).[6]

Social Conditions and Welfare Legislation

The timing of Brazilian social welfare programmes and policies differs from that of France, Britain, Germany and the United States.[7] During the late nineteenth century, Brazil passed through several changes in political and labour regimes. In 1888 slavery was abolished, and the following year armed forces and representatives of the elite and the urban middle class proclaimed the Republic. The new constitution established federalism, the separation of the Catholic Church from the state and universal suffrage, excluding minors (under 21 years old), illiterates, beggars, soldiers and monastic order clergymen. Although women's exclusion was not specifically mentioned, only men were considered to be full citizens.

In the mid-nineteenth century, coffee – mainly grown in the state of São Paulo in south-east Brazil – became the country's largest commodity. The new government turned its attention towards the expansion of agriculture and trade, promoting the interests of the coffee oligarchy. The government adopted measures favouring coffee production and trade, such as maintaining prices, building railways, subsidizing immigration, establishing tax policies, obtaining funds from abroad, controlling the port, combating epidemics and repressing social movements that represented obstacles to those interests. The country's population during this period consisted of Brazilian Indians, the descendants of African slaves and Portuguese colonizers, as well immigrants of different nationalities who began to arrive in larger numbers around 1880 – primarily Portuguese, Italians and Spanish, but also Germans, Swiss and North Americans. In spite of a predominantly agrarian-export economy, significant urban and industrial growth occurred in some regions of the country. The state of São Paulo grew by more than 101 per cent, adding more than four million inhabitants between 1900 and 1920. In 1907, 326 factories employed 24,186 workers; by 1920, 4,145 factories employed 83,998 workers.[8]

The situation of Brazilian workers did not differ significantly from that of their European or American counterparts, but four centuries of slavery certainly left its scars. Since the mid-nineteenth century, slaves and free workers laboured side by side in several activities, which influenced the relationship between employers and workers and made it more difficult to organize labour and social movements. The arrival of immigrants in São Paulo played a fundamental role in spurring social reform proposals at the beginning of the new century – a period that witnessed the establishment of the nation state. At this time a labour movement also emerged.

Society debated the role of the government and to what extent it could or should intervene in the life of its inhabitants. Governmental bureaucracy was rudimentary and fluid, with no department or ministry exclusively dedicated to labour issues. Hospitals belonged to private or religious enterprises. The state's role in regard to healthcare was limited to fighting epidemics, controlling the sanitation of cities and ports and regulating medical professionals and midwives, as well as foodstuffs and medicine. Intellectuals, medical doctors, policymakers, bureaucrats, jurists, employers and workers questioned who was responsible for maternity protection, work accidents, health and retirement – whether it should be the state, employers, workers or philanthropists.[9]

Men and women from different social classes and movements struggled to establish social laws in Brazil. They faced strong resistance from the politically hegemonic groups, which forced the incipient state to regard workers' demands as 'a case for the police'. Even the leading elite faced repression when demanding social legislation. In 1917, Representative Mauricio de Lacerda drafted a proposal for social legislation that called for an eight-hour workday, a ban on the employment of children under the age of fourteen, labour rules for apprentices, safe working conditions for women and the creation of daycare centres. The proposal led to his expulsion from the Republican Party and the loss of his mandate.[10] While many proposals were sent to the legislature, only a few became reality, and the laws that did pass generally did not cover all categories of workers throughout the country and were not strictly enforced. The first workers who benefited were public employees from the departments of railroad construction, water supply and transportation.

As for maternal and child protection, some historians consider Brazil to have played a precursor role in this area.[11] This argument is based upon the fact that in 1822, while still under monarchy, Representative José Bonifácio de Andrade e Silva proposed a law to regulate slave labour, including that of pregnant slaves and children. According to the proposed bill, women beyond their third month of pregnancy would be excused from performing heavy or hazardous jobs. After eight months, women's labour would be restricted to the master's house, and after childbirth, they would be allowed a month of rest. The child would stay together with its mother for at least one year. The law also stipulated that slaves up to the age of twelve were not to be employed in unhealthy or excessively demanding jobs.[12] It is also worth mentioning that in 1834 the midwife Mme Durocher sent to the Municipal Chamber of Rio de Janeiro – then the capital of the Brazilian Empire – a project aimed at the examination of wet nurses in order to combat infant mortality.[13] However, because these projects threatened the interests of slave masters, neither was enacted as a law.

A short time after the proclamation of the Republic, Rio de Janeiro became the first city where child labour was regulated.[14] Three years later, in 1894, the sanitary code of the state of São Paulo established some working hygiene rules: age limits for child labour, a ban on night shifts for women and children, sanitary working conditions and mandatory small-pox vaccination for workers. In some cities, beginning in 1910, primary teachers were granted two months' prepaid maternity leave and women were not allowed to work during their last month of pregnancy or the first month after giving birth.[15]

Until the 1920s, regulations concerning salaries, working hours, week-ly working days, vacations, disability, retirement, maternity leave and child labour did not apply to most workers. On a national basis, those benefits, along with female suffrage, were established only in the 1930s and 1940s, during the presidency of Getúlio Vargas.

Women's Status and the Feminist Movement

In an 1892 editorial published in *A Família*, one of the most important newspapers for women in this period, the journalist Josefina A. Azevedo called upon women to organize a federation and to struggle for their rights.[16] In contrast to what occurred in the United States, France, Germany and Britain during the nineteenth century, Brazilian women rarely came together in clubs or religious, philanthropic, educational and re-form societies to discuss matters of common interest.[17] Among the few significant exceptions were abolitionist and charitable associations, liter-ary societies and meetings held at the publishers of women's newspapers and magazines. Various hypotheses that seek to explain the relatively small number of female associations have been introduced, stressing such fac-tors as: Brazilian women's comparative isolation; their lack of educational opportunities; the precarious conditions in the urban areas; unfavour-able social relationships; and the difficulties of obtaining consumer goods (most basic products were still homemade by the women), which resulted in long and tiresome journeys.

However, the number of groups and associations founded, organ-ized and administered by women increased in the late nineteenth and early twentieth century. Until then, Brazilian women's complaints and struggles against social oppression had basically been limited to what they could achieve through publishers and the press. Nísia Floresta, a teacher, was one of the forerunners. In 1832, she translated Mary Wollstonecraft's *Vindication of the Rights of Women* and included some thoughts about the situation of Brazilian women. An author of several other books, Nísia Floresta defended women's moral education and instruction as a means of improving their performance as wives and mothers. She had lived many years in Europe, where she had been in contact with well-known writers of her time, such as George Sand, Alexandre Dumas, Alphonse de Lamartine and Auguste Comte. In Brazil, however, she was neglected and a victim of slander.[18]

Newspapers edited by women began to appear in 1850. They covered different matters and included notes and comments about women's accomplishments in the United States and Europe, informing Brazilians about feminist movements in other countries. Not all the feature writers held the same opinions on all issues, but women's education and the importance of womanhood emerged as the two main topics discussed in the editorials and by the contributors. Women's education was supported because it meant national progress, the development of female intelligence and capabilities, personal achievement, the ability to earn a living in the absence of a father or husband, women's emancipation, or simply better performance as mothers.

Books and newspapers – written and published by women – repeatedly stressed women's importance as mothers. That appreciation had been carefully cultivated in Brazilian society since the mid nineteenth century. Women writers frequently used the image of the slave as a metaphor for the female condition; they defined their struggle as that of overcoming the tyranny of husbands, fathers and brothers, and obtaining recognition of their importance as mothers. Female nature, according to the writers, granted women specific characteristics for motherhood, thus, husband and wife had equally important but different functions, to be fulfilled in separate spheres. The practice of the mother's role was seen as a form of patriotism. In 1852, Joana Paula Manso, in an editorial of the *Jornal das Senhoras*, wrote:

> We know perfectly well that every family needs a head and that the natural head of the family is the man. No doubt there are duties that bind the woman to the household, yet it is precisely from the bosom of her family that she is able to exert a direct influence on the nation, on all humankind.

Likewise, in 1873, Francisca S.M. Diniz, in the paper *O Sexo Feminino*, justified the importance of women's education as follows:

> A woman, having the same faculties as a man, with intelligence and the mind opened up to literature, to the arts and sciences, has to take on the attributes which the cultivated society cannot deny her, to be useful to the country and perform her mission in society, the greatest and sanctified mission, which entirely depends on the family mother. Education for the female sex, my dear patriots![19]

By the turn of the twentieth century, women's importance as mothers was widely acknowledged by both men and women in Brazilian society. The discourse of separate spheres had achieved its goal. Claims regarding 'female nature' had often been used to restrict women to the household and to prevent them from obtaining civil, political, economic, intellectual and social rights. Now they also began to be used for the opposite ends, to encourage women to go beyond their homes, to enter professions compatible with their 'altruistic mission' and even to exercise their political rights by asserting their allegedly unique, moral perspective.[20]

With the founding of the Republic, female newspapers started to support suffrage, and some women vindicated that right by voting. In 1890, the dentist Isabel Dillon registered to vote. She appeared as a candidate for the *Assembléia Constituinte da República* in the pages of *A Família*. Her candidacy was based on the argument that the law, establishing that all literate citizens over the age of twenty-one could vote, did not exclude women. She was also one of the first Brazilian women to propose protective laws for mothers and children, which were items in her campaign.[21]

In the first decades of the twentieth century, social life in Brazil reflected the impact of urbanization, industrialization, of improved education and greater professional opportunities for women. As a result, women's participation in social reforms and political movements increased. For example, both the teacher Anália Franco and the medical doctor Maria Rennotte, collaborators on the paper *A Família*, widened their field of activities to encompass educational and health organizations for women and children. The philanthropic entities created at this time differed from the charitable associations of mid-nineteenth century. While the latter had been organized and administered by clergymen, giving immediate spiritual and material comfort to those in need – especially through donations that involved little contact with the poor themselves – the former were founded and managed by women with different religious beliefs.[22] The organizers worked together with the beneficiaries, and their objective, besides providing immediate material aid, was to improve the social conditions of the beneficiaries.[23]

At the same time, the groups created to support political rights did not restrict themselves to campaigning for women's suffrage. In addition, they struggled for women's legal, social, economic and intellectual emancipation and for the establishment of protective laws for mothers and children. In 1910, the teacher Leolinda Daltro founded what is thought to be the first organized feminist group in Rio de Janeiro.[24]

In general, Brazilian women, regardless of social or ethnic origin, encountered serious difficulties and limitations. Since 1879 women had had access to university education, but they lacked opportunities to be admitted into public secondary schools, the preliminary step for college. The husband was considered the head of the marital partnership, and without his authorization, women could not receive or withdraw an inheritance, practice a profession, buy or sell, incur debts or even choose a legal residence.[25] There were still other legal restrictions: if a widow remarried, she lost her legal authority in relation to her minor children; if she married a foreigner, she lost her Brazilian nationality. Moreover, women workers earned lower salaries performing the same jobs as their male counterparts; they were sexually molested or badly treated at offices; there was no policy for maternity leave or places for breastfeeding; and several public services, including the postal service, did not employ women.

In 1922, the *Federação Brasileira pelo Progresso Feminino* (Brazilian Federation for Female Progress, or FBPF) was founded in Rio de Janeiro. It is considered the most visible female organization of the period, gathering the largest number of members. There were branches in several states, and it remained very active until 1937, when the Getúlio Vargas dictatorship was established. The group consisted mainly of educated women from the middle class and the elite, including women of different political beliefs, many who had already been radicalized on individual level, or were already involved with other social movements or organizations. Working-class teachers, trade workers or typists were also associated with the FBPF.

The founder and main spokeswoman of the FBPF, Bertha Lutz, was one of the first women to occupy a high public position in the country. She had experience in the European and American feminist movements but did not approve of the militant street protests of the British suffragists or striking workers. She supported, with equal conviction, women's economic emancipation, freedom to choose a professional career (regardless of marital status), political rights and the idea that the proper foundation of society was the family. In 1936, Lutz wrote:

> It is not fair, nor logical, to declare that, once voting rights are obtained, the woman abdicates from the place nature granted her. Today, women's domain, we feminists all agree, is the household; yet, the home is no longer restricted to four walls. A home also means the school, factory and office. Home is mainly the parliament, where laws that rule the family and human society are elaborated.[26]

This suggests that, for Lutz, education, work and emancipation were not against or separate from the family and the role of mother and wife, nor did they threaten women's altruistic mission in social and political life.

The objectives of the FBPF were: 1) to promote women's education and improve the level of female instruction; 2) to protect mothers and children; 3) to obtain legal and practical guarantees for female workers; 4) to assist women's initiatives and to guide them in their professional choices; 5) to stimulate sociability and understanding among women and to motivate them in regard to social and public matters; 6) to ensure their political rights and to prepare women to use those rights in an 'intelligent' way; 7) to strengthen friendship with the other American countries, in order to guarantee justice and peace in the Western hemisphere.[27]

Year after year, the FBPF struggled to obtain suffrage and laws that would benefit women, including workers, through legal strategies. The FBPF profited from every opportunity to allow women to perform activities; it promoted debates so as to influence the public opinion on women's rights; it kept the press informed about the movement and its agenda, while replying to critiques of anti-feminists; it asked for support among jurists and politicians. Members tried to register and vote, wrote manifestos and pressured representatives to obtain legislative changes. They also organized feminist congresses, to which they invited important men and women from different Brazilian states and some foreign countries, giving great visibility to the movement.

In 1922, the FBPF organized the First International Feminist Congress in Rio de Janeiro, attended by Carrie Chapman Catt, the American peace advocate and former suffragist. On this occasion, commissions were formed (on work, education, civil and political rights, maternal and child protection) that drew together members of women's professional and philanthropic organizations. Valentina Biosca introduced a report detailing the dismal working conditions of female workers and children in the textile industry: women and children were sexually abused; there was no regulation of work hours; and the salary policy jeopardized women. The report recommended the end of the night shift and the prohibition of hazardous and heavy tasks for women, along with protective measures to allow breastfeeding during working hours, health control of industrial plants, an end to sexual abuse in the workplace and a reduction of the number of hours that workers spent standing.[28]

During the next decade, the FBPF organized the Second International Feminist Congress, held in 1931, also in Rio de Janeiro. The commission promoted a wide array of reforms, including: women's suffrage; changes in women's education to improve their professional opportunities; the organization of women's dormitories in colleges; the creation of a government department for women and children; female inspectors at factories that employed women and children; paid vacations, minimum salary and equal wages for equal work; cafeterias and rest rooms; maternity leave; a female police force; a review of the nationality law for married women; and punishments for crimes committed to avenge honour, or so-called crimes of passion.[29]

A review of the extensive records in the *Arquivo Nacional* of the Brazilian feminist movement in general, and the FBPF in particular, should lead us to reassess the movement. The feminist struggle may not have succeeded in overturning male dominance or in fundamentally challenging the social structure, but that should not diminish the importance of its accomplishments or its legacy. In 1930, a revolution took place in Brazil, and the new government faced pressure to re-establish the constitutional system. Bertha Lutz was nominated to serve on a commission to draft the new constitution. Advised by lawyers associated with the FBPF, Lutz introduced proposals that had been discussed and approved in the Feminist Congress, many of which were ultimately adopted. The proposals incorporated into the 1934 Constitution included: women's right to vote and hold office; the right of women who married foreigners to maintain their birth nationality and pass it on to their children; a minimum wage and an eight-hour workday; paid vacations; maternity leave; accident or disability insurance; retirement; the right of women to hold any position in the public sector, regardless of marital status; and a preference for qualified women to manage and administer social assistance programmes related to maternal and childhood welfare.[30]

Cruzada Pró Infância

Pérola Byington, representing the *Cruzada Pró Infância*, participated in the Second International Feminist Congress organized by the FBPF in Rio de Janeiro. She presented two papers to the commission of Mother and Childhood Protection: 'Pró Infância' and 'Recreios Infantis' ('Breaks for Children'). She made four recommendations: 1) to call upon Brazilian women, since it was their duty to protect and defend children; 2) to have educational and social associations promote 'Children's Week' in October; 3) to implement health and disability insurance and special taxes to fund children's and public health programmes; 4) to establish a minimum wage to help 'alleviate the conditions of labouring classes'.[31]

At the time of the Second Feminist Congress, the *Cruzada* was still in its early stages. Founded in 1930 by a group of women from São Paulo led by Pérola Byington and Maria Antonieta de Castro, its goal was to combat infant mortality through a social assistance programme for both mothers and children. Infant mortality was a worrisome issue for Brazilian elites. Although agrarian and industrial development brought about progress in the cities, a great number of inhabitants did not benefit, and economic inequalities grew during this period. Most of the population suffered under poor working conditions and lack of sanitation. Government campaigns against mortality failed, and the rate of infant mortality, caused by infectious diseases, remained very high.[32] Educated men and women from the middle class and the elite began to call people's attention to the waste of human lives and its impact on the nation. Influenced by the expansionist spirit of the time, they believed that Brazil needed to fill in its empty spaces, and that a larger number of inhabitants would mean more manpower. They also believed that the government needed to invest more in public health and that the future of the nation depended on both the quantity and the physical, moral and educational quality of its population.

The *Cruzada Pró Infância* was created in this context. Maria Antonieta de Castro, president of the *Associação de Educadoras Sanitárias*, and Pérola Byington started a campaign against infant mortality. Within a few months, they brought together a hundred concerned women, and in August 1930 they founded the *Cruzada*, managed solely by women.[33] For more than thirty years until her death in 1963, Pérola Byington remained the managing director, while Maria Antonieta de Castro served as the managing secretary. Both can be considered pillars of the *Cruzada*. Pérola Byington descended from a North American family that had immigrated after the Civil War. She was fifty years old, married to an important entrepreneur and had enjoyed good relations with the elite for fifteen years. However, her social connections were not the only, and certainly not the most important, reason why she was encouraged to play a leadership role.[34] She was an educator with a plan for social reform, and she had extensive experience as a volunteer for the American and Brazilian Red Cross. Maria Antonieta, born in the interior of São Paulo, was single and had played an important role as a teacher, sanitary educator and children's writer. Pérola Byington was Protestant and Maria Antonieta, like most Brazilians, was Catholic.

Both women agreed that they would play different roles. Maria Antonieta wrote the paper that Pérola Byington presented at the Second Feminist Congress. Maria Antonieta, following her sanitary educator's experience, was responsible for the courses on child care, as well as the health and fresh air schools. Pérola Byington advocated proposals such as the *Casa Maternal*, a milk dispensary, maternity allowance, sexual education and the establishment of a female police force. She acquired her knowledge from Brazilian sanitary practitioners. Travelling to the United States, she also visited several philanthropic societies and governmental offices, such as the Children's Bureau in Washington, D.C.

Pérola Byington's proposal at the Second Feminist Congress was actually being developed in São Paulo: a women's organization for a National Pro-Childhood Crusade. The entity took care of a variety of activities, some of which were more urgent, such as providing material, moral, medical, sanitary, home and hospital assistance to mothers and their children. In the long run, projects included child care courses for mothers, campaigning for laws to protect pregnant women and children, ensuring the proper enforcement of these laws, the creation of a research and information centre for childhood, to call on public opinion regarding children and to congregate the different associations and entities working with these issues.[35]

At the beginning of the *Cruzada*'s activities, volunteer work was performed and its associates called on the whole society to collect funds. There was not a fixed meeting place. Among its services, it gave assistance to organizations, families and individuals, helping with clothes, food, medicine, counselling and even complementing government health and educational services. Besides providing assistance, it also acted as an employment agency and family counsellor. Pérola Byington related one of its first actions: offering moral support to a sixteen year old whose parents maltreated her after they had been informed of her pregnancy. She was thrown out of her home and was 'on the brink of committing suicide'. A group of ladies decided to act, securing her parents' forgiveness, the interest of the Juvenile Court, the participation of a priest and the agreement of the parents-in-law for 'a happy ending' marriage.[36]

The proposals of the *Cruzada* were not forgotten: advocacy for the establishment of laws to create programmes and services to protect mother and child and the creation of a knowledge centre. From 1930 to 1945 the entity acquired a professional status. The activities and services were diversified, employing more people. The *Cruzada* built a site, dispensaries (providing general clinical treatment, infant hygiene, prenatal care, physiotherapy, and nutrition) and a *Casa Maternal* that would assist women before and after childbirth. Fresh air schools with psychology assistance were organized, as well as campaigns and courses to spread child care principles. A human milk dispensary for infants was created and in the 1940s daycare centres were founded. The *Cruzada* published its own magazine, actively participated in congresses and seminars gathering experts from different areas, presented papers, undertook and discussed projects, and produced important literature on mother and childhood protection.[37]

Quite often the *Cruzada* tried to influence executive and legislative authorities in order to obtain sponsorship for new programmes favouring mothers and their children. Some of its proposals ran in the same direction as Getúlio Vargas' governmental policies and were therefore approved; others were accepted only years later. For example, during the Second Feminist Congress, participants discussed the need to establish a special female police force. Pérola Byington invited two members of the Women's Police Service, a British voluntary organization, to deliver a lecture in São Paulo, which the Chief Officer of São Paulo's police and the

Judge for Juvenile Cases attended. In 1935, Pérola Byington continued to promote the idea of a female police force in the newspapers. When interviewed, she said that the care of women and adolescents who broke the law 'should be handed over to women, to be perfect'. The objective was to create a female police force as another 'woman's mission' in society, but such service would not be implemented for two decades.[38]

For years, Pérola Byington supported another project: a state allowance for mothers without breadwinners. She contacted governors and representatives to campaign for it, but apparently the project was only implemented in one Brazilian state.[39] According to some health visitors, illegitimacy was one of the causes of infant mortality. Maternity allowances and the *Casa Maternal* were promoted as ways of preventing child abandonment.

The recommended model of the family, and the one that represented a pillar of society during this period, was that formed by a providing husband and a dependent wife, dedicated to the care of her children. But the social reality of most of Brazilian women differed radically. In Pérola Byington's opinion, everyone – the church, government, associations, the media and the public – had to fight for the continuity of the 'sacred dyad, mother and child'.[40] She argued that the Brazilian mother was not protected in the way she ought to be. 'Our social legislation doesn't protect her. And that is depressing. How can we evaluate the degree of progress of a country, if there isn't any efficient organization – service standard for maternity?' She considered it inhuman and against 'natural laws' for mothers to be separated from their children. Yet when such separation occurred, she did not blame women: 'How often does she abandon her child for fear of society's prejudice!' Byington opposed children's homes, suggesting that children could be sheltered in foster households, or that mothers could be helped with an allowance. In her words:

> funds would thoroughly benefit the homes without breadwinning fathers, representing savings for the government. A single mother is obliged to consider her child as a second priority, in order to look for a job. It's obvious, she needs a job, leaves her home to find one, deviating from her mission in detriment to the children who are often put in state homes. The biggest damage, the lack of maternal care during the first years of life, will reflect on the future of mankind. First of all, it's a psychological–social matter. The child has to be raised at home, where it develops its personality, and not in a children's home, making it feel different from those protected by their families.[41]

Byington supported an allowance for fatherless ('headless') homes and in 1932 opened the doors of the *Casa Maternal* for pregnant and single mothers. It is worth mentioning that she used the word 'head' and not 'husband', which suggests that she defended the same rights for both abandoned and single mothers. At the *Casa Maternal*, mothers were assisted until they recovered from childbirth, 'received friendly advice' and could perform some duties. If they were 'good', they were recommended for a job, and the child continued under the *Cruzada*'s care until the mother could earn her own living. There was no infrastructure for childbirth at the site; birthing women were forwarded to a local maternity ward. The *Casa Maternal* also provided temporary shelter for children who had no place to stay while their mothers gave birth.[42] In 1934, the *Cruzada* was asked to accept a 12-year-old pregnant girl, considered 'mentally ill', who had been raped. That same year, according to a report published in the *Diário da Noite*, the Juvenile Court had forwarded four girls under the age of sixteen.[43] The *Casa Maternal* also sheltered poor married women, although there was a selection criterion based on the husband's income. Until 1939, no other public institution or religious entity in São Paulo provided similar services.

The practice of paying women for breast milk was another strategy used to keep poor mothers and their children together. Although Pérola Byington supported breastfeeding, arrangements had to be made in cases involving a mother's illness or death, or a child's abandonment. Therefore in 1940 a lactation campaign was launched. Milk was mechanically obtained and distributed free to needy babies. Donors went through medical examinations and were paid for their milk, so as to provide for their own children.[44]

The education of mothers was one of the most important campaigns developed by the *Cruzada* throughout those years. Ignorance, lack of basic knowledge of child care, irregular habits and inadequate nourishing were the main causes of infant mortality. The educational project of the *Cruzada* included information given during medical consultancy, courses on child care and the promotion of events such as 'Children's Week' and well baby contests.

But very often the educational proposals went beyond the principles of child care and were aimed at the teaching of motherhood rights. In 1933, Pérola Byington participated in the Congress for Children's Protection in Rio de Janeiro, where she delivered her speech on 'Sexual Education and Its Importance: How and When to Teach It'. The proposed sexual education should start in the first year of life, by the mother and at home. However, when 'the mother's education' was not up to the mission, Byington recommended that it should take place at school, by people 'of real intellectual and moral values'. She suggested the government should create a course of Social Hygiene at teaching schools. Its syllabus was to include traditional subjects as natural history, biology, venereal diseases, sexual behaviour, individual duties as for sexual hygiene, hereditary diseases, illegitimacy, pornography, abortion, etc., as well as subjects that are not taught at school even today, such as women and mothers' rights, fatherhood and duties of the state and society towards motherhood, among others.[45]

The *Cruzada* also developed strategies to support working mothers of different social classes, organizing courses for child-nurses and demanding the opening of daycare centres. According to Pérola Byington, the discussion was no longer about ability, or the right of women to act shoulder to shoulder in any field. The big problem was children's safety while mothers were outside their homes. The main duties of women were childbearing and raising within their communities – 'a rather hard task', in Byington's opinion. 'Yet, when a woman needs to work out of her home, when she has to follow her husband on social duties, favouring his success, or when science requires her collaboration, what does society offer her in exchange for almost abandoning her home and children?'

For some years, the *Cruzada* offered a course for child-nurses that prepared girls for housework.[46] In 1941, the number of registered students was smaller than expected, and graduates ended up working in day nurseries instead of family houses. In the 1940s, the *Cruzada* started to campaign for daycare centres and even developed a project in a company. It has to be said that during its first decade the *Cruzada* sheltered small children only in exceptional cases and on a temporary basis, for example when a mother had been abandoned and was staying at the *Casa Maternal*, waiting to be relocated; healthy children of mothers with tuberculosis, waiting for the effect of the vaccine; ill children waiting for a bed in hospital and/or those receiving medical care.[47] Would the struggle for daycare centres mean a change in the entity's principle in relation to what it considered the essential role of women? Documentation suggests that it did not. Emphasizing the 'necessity' (not the right) of mothers to work, the campaigns against child abandonment and for children's education justified the opening of daycare centres. Apparently, Pérola Byington shared the opinion of many social workers, who considered daycare centres a 'necessary evil'.[48]

Conclusion

The history of the *Cruzada Pró Infância* could be analysed from a number of different angles, such as its role in promoting principles of child care and work discipline, the medicalization of childbirth, or even the development of paediatric dermatology. Its promotion of well baby contests and the commemoration of Children's Week could be explored in relation to the rise of eugenics. The parties, bazaars and bridge tournaments – all organized to raise funds – would provide material for a thorough analysis of leisure activities in the city of São Paulo. But the study of the *Cruzada Pró Infância* from the perspective of maternalism sheds some light on a series of fundamental issues, allowing us to rethink the social and political participation of elite and middle-class women in philanthropic organizations during the first half of the twentieth century.

In that period, motherhood began to be considered a social function rather than simply an individual, familial one. Female philanthropists believed that motherhood, women's essential role, would bring social recognition, rights and equality, in spite of women's differences from men. They argued that women's maternal nature qualified them to perform certain tasks, specifically those aimed at enhancing the welfare of women and children, and that it was their patriotic duty to assume this responsibility. Maternalist discourse can be considered 'conservative' and blamed for the perpetuation of women's subordination; it can even be viewed as authoritarian because it not only obliged women to become mothers, but also imposed the dominant class ideology upon poor women. Still, to neglect the importance of maternalism in the first half of the twentieth century is to ignore a major aspect of women's experiences, or to attribute assumptions, proposals and attitudes to women that were different from their own. Such neglect also perpetuates a false and partial analysis of Brazilian society – one that suggests that the women associated with philanthropic organizations did not participate in state-building or the struggle for their rights.

A more detailed analysis of Pérola Byington's proposals demonstrates the complexity of maternalist discourse. Even as the *Cruzada* supported marriage and male-headed households, it protected, assisted and recognized the rights of all mothers, taught them to demand their rights and struggled to ensure that all women received proper maternity care. The education proposed by the *Cruzada* extended beyond teaching women about their maternal duties so that they could keep their babies alive and thereby provide more workers for the state: it also focused on educating mothers about their rights as citizens. The motherhood protection supported by the *Cruzada* covered all women, single and married, non-working and working mothers, including even housemaids and rural workers who had typically been overlooked by social and labour legislation. Considering the stigma that unmarried mothers faced during this period, the *Cruzada*'s foundation of the *Casa Maternal* must have stirred particular controversy. In 1937, a labour attorney was questioned about whether an employer was required to provide 50 per cent salary for an eight-week childbirth leave, as stipulated by the 1932 law. The employer alleged that the worker was single and that the payment would therefore set a 're-pulsive' example – one that demonstrated contempt for honest women and undermined the legitimate family.[49] In an interview, Pérola Byington opposed this view, arguing that withholding the allowance would simply compound 'the wrong', resulting in further social problems.[50]

Evidence suggests that childbirth assistance promoted by the *Cruzada* followed the required quality standards. During a Mothers' Seminar in São Paulo in 1938, Pérola Byington suggested publishing the causes of mortality among mothers in order to improve the services rendered to childbearing women.[51] The idea was discussed, but did not gain unanimous support, revealing how little some members valued women's lives. One of the participants argued that the requested information would violate the privacy of medical doctors and might increase the use of birth control, because the number of women who feared motherhood might rise. In other words, procreation was valued above women's right to adequate maternity care.[52]

Motherhood protection was not the only struggle of the *Cruzada*. Reflecting the broader social needs of the period, the wide variety of proposals from 1930 to 1945, many of which were never adopted, included labour laws for minors, a school-inspector service, the regulation of children's sports practice, traffic rules, compulsory paediatrics courses for all doctors and special film performances for young audiences. Among other proposals, the *Cruzada* also supported a minimum wage, better sanitary conditions, controls for water and milk, lower food prices, and higher salaries for medical doctors and sanitary educators who accepted jobs in the interior of any Brazilian state.

Between 1930 and 1945, the *Cruzada* sent official letters to the legislature, urging that certain measures be adopted and enforced; it demanded several measures from the authorities and society; it created an alliance amongst politicians, philanthropic entities, feminist groups, medical doctors, teachers, educators, psychologists, social assistants and entrepreneurs to launch its projects; it promoted lectures and called on the public opinion through the media. In 1932, when the Constitutional revolution took place in São Paulo, the *Cruzada* participated very closely in the movement, aiding the civilian population, especially the families of the combatants. The organization received financial support from the state, and it established partnerships with the state, entrepreneurs and even with a district association to develop different projects, suggesting that the relationship between it and the assisted members was not always a vertical one. The celebration of 'Children's Week' and the *Casa Maternal* were 'copied' by the government. It can even be said that in some instances the *Cruzada* took the place of the state, especially in regard to dispensaries and fresh-air schools – services that had previously been unavailable or of poor quality.

There was no place for improvisation concerning the *Cruzada*'s development, characteristics and engagements. Middle-class and elite women had organized all that work. Mrs Byington and Maria Antonieta de Castro formed a team to administer the entity, managed the budget, hired personnel and solved, among other problems, matters of labour and employee relations. It is important to remember that the *Cruzada*'s credibility and easy access among the public authorities, elites, entrepreneurs and media was, to a large extent, due to the social background and web of relationships of its leaders.

The study of the *Cruzada*'s development allows us to rethink some statements about the voluntarism of elite women. First, it is simply incorrect to say that philanthropic activity was always a pretext for women to leave their homes and fend off boredom, or that their main objectives were to contribute to their husband's social ascent. Pérola Byington and Maria Antonieta de Castro had a well-defined project to combat infant mortality, which they considered their patriotic duty to implement. Maria Antonieta was single and had a successful career as a writer, teacher and sanitary educator before she started her *Cruzada Pró-Infância*. Thus, she had no husband to promote, nor did she need the organization to justify a professional activity.

Pérola Byington's biography, on the other hand, requires us to reconsider the idea that middle-class and elite women could more easily participate in philanthropic activities once they had been freed from domestic drudgery. The evidence suggests that their domestic demands, coming from the society and themselves, had another meaning. Of course, such women had fewer responsibilities because they relied upon domestic servants. Yet certain familial duties were still considered exclusively theirs. One of her granddaughters tells us that whenever Albert Byington remained at the farm while Pérola was busy in São Paulo, she would return very early the next morning, before breakfast, to bake biscuits to be eaten while still hot. Once, the driver had been late, and when she arrived home she saw that her husband had already had his breakfast and left. Surprised, she asked the cook who had baked the biscuits. When she found out that it had been the maid, Pérola Byington, usually 'so thoughtful and pragmatic', lost her temper and refused to talk to her maid for a month![53]

Notes

I wish to thank Susana E. Götz for the translation and Marina Maluf, Berteke Waaldijk, Rebecca Jo Plant, Marian van der Klein and Nichole Sanders for their helpful comments.

1. J. Hahner. 1990. *Emancipating the Female Sex: The Struggle for Women's Rights in Brazil, 1850–1940*, Durham, NC: Duke University Press, 36; S.K. Besse. 1999. *Modernizando a desigualdade: Reestruturando da ideologia de Gênero no Brasil, 1914–1940*, São Paulo: EdUSP, 167–72; M.R. Schpun. 1997. *Les Années Folles à São Paulo*, Paris: L'Harmattan, 93–100; and J.E. Wasdsworth. 1999. 'Moncorvo Filho e o problema da infância: modelos institucionais e ideológicas da assistência à infância no Brasil', *Revista de História* 19(37), 103–24.

2. M.L.M. Leite. 1984. *A outra face do feminismo: Maria Lacerda de Moura*, São Paulo: Editora Ática; and M.L. Mott. 1986. 'Biografia de uma revoltada: Ercilia Nogueira Cobra', *Cadernos de Pesquisa* 58, 89–104.

3. An earlier version of this article appeared as M.L. Mott. 2002. 'Maternalismo, políticas públicas e benemerência no Brasil', *Cadernos Pagu* 16, 199–234. See also idem, M.E.B. Byington and O.S. Fabergé (eds). 2005. *O gesto que salva: Pérola Byington e a Cruzada Pró-Infância*, São Paulo: Grifo Projetos Históricos e Editoriais.

4. On maternalism and maternal-infant welfare policies, see: S. Koven and S. Michel. 1990. 'Womanly Duties: Maternalist Politics and the Origins of the Welfare States in France, Germany, Great Britain, and the United States, 1880–1920', *American Historical Review* 95(4), 1076–108; G. Bock and P. Thane. 1991. 'Introduction', in idem (eds), *Maternity and Gender Policies: Women and the Rise of the European Welfare States, 1880s–1950s*. London and New York: Routledge; and P. Wilkinson. 1999. 'The Selfless and the Helpless: Maternalist Origins of the U.S. Welfare State', *Feminist Studies* 25(3), 571–97. On philanthropy, see: A. Lindenmeyr. 1993. 'Public Life, Private Virtues: Women in Russian Charity, 1762–1914', *Signs* 18(3), 562–91; P.A. Schell. 1999. '"An Honorable Avocation for Ladies": The Work of the Mexico City *Unión de Damas*, 1912–1926', *Journal of Women's History* 10(4), 78–103; E.K. Abel. 1998. 'Valuing Care: Turn-of-the-Century Conflicts between Charity Workers and Women Clients', *Journal of Women's History* 10(3), 32–52; and T. Deane. 1996. 'Late Nineteenth-Century Philanthropy: The Case of Louisa Twining', in A. Digby and J. Stewart (eds), *Gender, Health and Welfare*, London and New York: Routledge, 122–42.

5. See, for example, P. Scharp. 1999. 'Maternidade: uma visão política', in S. Auad, *Mulher: cinco séculos de desenvolvimento na América*, Belo Horizonte: Federação Internacional de Mulheres da Carreira Jurídica; and O.T. Otovo. 2009. '"To Form a Strong and Populous Nation": Race, Motherhood, and the State in Republican Brazil', Ph.D. diss., Georgetown University.

6. Pérola Byington remained director until her death in 1963. Currently, the *Cruzada* administers ten day care centres in São Paulo, as well as a home for children and adolescents whose families are in crisis.

7. Koven and Michel, 'Womanly Duties'; G. Bock. 1992. 'Pauvraté Feminine, Droits des Mères et États Providence', in F. Thébaud (ed.), *Histoires des Femmes en Occident*, Paris: Plon, 382–409; A. Cova. 1997. *Maternité et droits de femmes en France (XIX-XX siècle)*, Paris: Anthropos.

8. E. Carone. 1975. *A República velha: Instituições e Classes Sociais*, São Paulo: Difel, 76.

9. R. Lima. 1904. *A maternidade*, Rio de Janeiro; and C. Ferreira, 'Obras e fatores de preservação e assistência à infância', *Imprensa Médica* 15(7), 4 October 1907, 117–23.

10. M.-V.J. Pena. 1981. *Mulheres e trabalhadoras: Presença feminina na constituição do sistema fabril*, Rio de Janeiro: Paz e Terra; Carone, *A República velha*; and A.C. Gomes. 1988. *A invenção do trabalhismo*, Rio de Janeiro: IUPERG/Vértice.

11. F. Magalhães. 1922. *A Obstetrícia no Brasil*, Rio de Janeiro: Leite Ribeiro, 213–14.

12. A.M.P. Malheiro. 1976. *A escravidão no Brasil: Ensaio histórico, jurídico, social*, vol. 2, Petrópolis: Vozes/INL, 228–31.
13. M.L. Mott. 1998. *Parto, parteiras e parturientes no século XIX: Mme. Durocher e sua época*, Tese de Doutoramento, Departamento de História, FFLCH/USP.
14. Pena, *Mulheres e trabalhadoras*, 153; and E.L. Blancois. 1977. 'O trabalho da mulher e do menor na indústria paulista, 1880–1920', Dissertação de Mestrado, Departamento de História, FFLCH/USP.
15. A.R. Dordal. 1923. *A proteção da operária grávida: Tese defendida na Faculdade de Medicina e Cirurgia de São Paulo*, São Paulo: P.M. Higgins, 11; and O. Souza, 'Aspecto Social da Assistência Obstétrica: Relatório', *Primeiro Congresso de Ginecologia e Obstetrícia*, 72–8.
16. On the small number of philanthropic associations during the Brazilian Empire, see: T. Ferreira. 1940. *Subsídios a História da Assistência Social em São Paulo (obras do Império)*, Monografia conclusão de curso, Escola de Serviço Social do Centro de Estudos de Ação Social de São Paulo.
17. On the limited opportunities women had to gather in the nineteenth century, see the entries by S. Schumaher and E.V. Brazil. 2000. *Dicionário Mulheres do Brasil de 1500 até a Atualidade*, Rio de Janeiro: J. Zahar.
18. C.L. Duarte. 1989. 'Os primórdios do feminismo no Brasil', in N. Floresta (ed.), *Direitos das Mulheres e Injustiça dos Homens*, São Paulo: Cortez, 99–134.
19. A.M. Almeida. 1985. 'Maternidade e Cidadania: uma encruzilhada para as primeiras feministas', Manuscript, ANPOCS, Águas de São Pedro, 1.
20. F.S.M. Diniz described female suffrage as follows: 'The free expression of our ideas, by right, shouldn't be denied to us … Recall that a woman has to advocate for her cause, i.e., the cause of rights, justice and humanity, remembering that she, as a mother, represents the sanctity of the infinitive love.' F.S.M. Diniz. 1988. 'Igualdade de Direitos: O quinze de novembro do sexo feminino', in M.T.C. Bernardes (ed.), *Mulheres de ontem? Rio de Janeiro – século XIX*, São Paulo: T.A. Queiroz, 152.
21. During the monarchy, Isabel Dillon tried to register and vote. Her argument was based on the Saraiva law that gave graduates in scientific courses the right to vote. B.M. Alves. 1980. *Ideologia e Feminismo: A luta pelo voto no Brasil*, Petrópolis: Vozes, 91.
22. In 1891, Pope Leo XIII, in his encyclical letter *Rerum Novarum*, called on Catholics to get involved in promoting social justice, and influenced Catholic groups engaged in philanthropic activities. Schell, '"An Honorable Avocation for Ladies"', 79.
23. M.M.S.B. Leite. 1997. *Educação, Cultura e Lazer das Mulheres de Elite Em Salvador: 1890–1930*, Dissertação de Mestrado, Salvador, Mestrado em História/UFBA, ch. 4, 110–37.
24. H.A. Marques. 2000. 'A construção da cidadania feminina no Rio de Janeiro', *Revista do Instituto Histórico e Geográfico Brasileiro* 1, 71–77.
25. Pena, *Mulheres e trabalhadoras*.
26. Hahner, *Emancipating the Female Sex*, 149.
27. Information on the *Federação Brasileira pelo Progresso Feminino* was taken from the Arquivo Nacional (National Archives – FBPF, AP 46); H. Saffioti. 1979. *A mulher na sociedade de classes: mito e realidade*, Petrópolis: Vozes, 255–83; Hahner, *Emancipating the Female Sex*, 121–80; Alves, *Ideologia e Feminismo*, 85–118; Besse, *Modernizando a desigualdade*, 184–99; and Schumaher and Brazil, *Dicionário Mulheres do Brasil*, 217–26.
28. Schumaher and Brazil, *Dicionário Mulheres do Brasil*, 518.
29. Arquivo Nacional (FBPF, AP 46, cx.3 e 4); and Besse, *Modernizando a desigualdade*, 189–90.
30. A. Campanhole and H.L. Campanhole. 1984. *Constituições do Brasil*, 7th edn, São Paulo: Atlas, 540–41, 548–9; and Besse, *Modernizando a desigualdade*, 189–90.
31. On the participation of the *Cruzada Pró Infância* in the Second Feminist Congress, see: Arquivo Nacional (FBPF, cx. 38, AP 46).
32. M.A.R. Ribeiro. 1993. *História sem fim … Inventário da Saúde Pública em São Paulo (1880–1930)*, São Paulo: UNESP.

33. Ata da 1ª. Reunião Geral Ordinária Cruzada Pró Infância, 8 December 1930. *Cruzada Pró Infância* Archive.
34. Pérola Ellis McIntyre was born in 1879 in the interior of São Paulo. Her mother, Mary Ellis McIntyre, was a teacher and owner of a school. Pérola's social activities began after her marriage. As a recently graduated teacher in 1901, she was invited to work as a nanny for an elite family in the city of São Paulo. She was then engaged to marry Albert Byington, a young American entrepreneur, and thus did not accept the job. Some years later, her son married a relative of the same family who had invited Pérola to work for them. Alberto Byington was known as the 'crazy American' due to his habit of buying land with waterfalls to build dams that produced electric power, an expanding economic sector at the time. Later on, he also dedicated himself to import trade.
35. Documentation suggests that after having achieved suffrage, the alliances were broken, starting a period of struggles. The *Cruzada* separated from the FBPF, joining Carlota Pereira de Queiroz, Brazil's first female representative, whose vision of welfare policies for mothers and children differed from that of Bertha Lutz, the director of the FBPF.
36. Ata da 1ª. Reunião Geral Ordinária Cruzada Pró Infância, 8 December 1930, *Cruzada Pró Infância* Archive.
37. 'A Cruzada Pró Infância: Histórico, desenvolvimento e realizações de 12/8/30 a 12/8/1949', *Cruzada Pró Infância* Archive. One of these women was 'Commandant' Mary Allen, a controversial figure who ended up joining the British Union of Fascists. The Brazilian press referred to her simply as a member of the 'Women's Police Service', without mentioning her reactionary political views.
38. Which means that she believed that women knew better about the needs of other women and children, 'Assistência à mãe e à criança', *Diário da Noite*, 4 May 1935.
39. Pérola Byington, 'Como melhorar a alimentação na 1ª Infância' (manuscript). From the conference that took place on 22 September 1940: 'Our claims haven't been useless ... the State of Bahia, answering to them, took the positive measure of providing mothers with an allowance for the aid of natural breastfeeding.'
40. 'Inicia-se amanhã a "Semana da Criança"', *Diário da Noite*, 7 October 1938.
41. 'Assistência à mãe e à criança', *Diário da Noite*, 5 April 1935.
42. Other organizations that served similar functions typically provided shelter to small children of mothers in labour. See S. Beauvalet-Boutouyerie. 1999. *Naître à l'hôpital aux XIX siècle*, Paris: Bellin, 76.
43. 'Assistência à mãe e à criança', *Diário da Noite*, 23 August 1934.
44. 'Solenidades comemorativas do "Dia da Criança" nesta capital', *Folha da Noite*, 25 March 1940. The *Cruzada*'s milk bank was the first of its kind in Brazil. J.A.G. de Almeida. 1999. *Amamentação: Um híbrido natureza-cultura*, Rio de Janeiro: Fio-Cruz.
45. P. Byington. 1933. 'Educação Sexual e sua importância: Como e quando ministrá-la', *Anais da Conferência Nacional de Proteção à Infância* 3, 129–39. The programme of sexual education was based on the proposals of Dra. Paulina Luisi, the first woman doctor in Uruguay. She created the National Council for Women (1916); the Alliance of Feminist Women for Women's Rights (1920); and the Association of University Women (1935), in Uruguay. She published several papers on sexual education, child care, women's civil rights, prophylaxis of venereal diseases and the fight against prostitution. She defended sterilization of individuals with genetic and mental problems, as well as abortion in cases of married women who were obliged, under violence, to maintain sexual relationships with their husbands. See A. Silva. 1954. *A primeira médica do Brasil*, Rio de Janeiro: Pongetti, 43–6; and D.J. Guy. 1999. 'Pan American Child Congresses, 1916 to 1942: Child Reform, and the Welfare State in Latin America', *Journal of Family History* 23(3), 272–91.
46. 'Cruzada Pró Infância. P. Byington', Manuscript, December 1944.
47. 'Curso de Pagens', *Folha da Noite*, 14 October 1941.

48. 'Pensões para mães cujos pais não assumem responsabilidade', *Jornal do Comércio*, 19 September 1935.
49. G.U. Telles. 1938. 'As creches como auxiliares das famílias', Monografia de conclusão de curso, Escola de Serviço Social.
50. H.X. Lopes. 1937. 'Consulta, Previdência e Assistência Social', *Boletim do Ministério do Trabalho, Indústria e Comércio* 39, 224–8.
51. 'Cruzada Pró Infância', *Diário de São Paulo*, 23 August 1934.
52. Pérola Byington translated into Portuguese Paul de Kruif's popular book, *Fight for Life* (1938), which described the attempts of obstetrician Herman N. Bundesen to reduce maternal and infant mortality in Chicago. Bundesen had published statistics concerning the causes of mothers' deaths, with the goal of improving maternity care.
53. 'Seminário das Mães', *O Estado de São Paulo*, 22 July 1938.

CHAPTER 10

MATERNALISM IN A PATERNALIST STATE
The National Organization for the Protection of Motherhood and Infancy in Fascist Italy

Elisabetta Vezzosi

In Italy, the fascist state attempted – through activities carried out by women's fascist party groups and the National Organization for the Protection of Motherhood and Infancy (*Opera Nazionale per la Protezione della Maternità e dell'Infanzia*, ONMI) – to bring motherhood and women's caretaking duties into the domain of the state, thereby transforming a common social practice into an 'obligation of female citizenship'.[1] This essay demonstrates how Italian women tried to take advantage of the fascist regime's emphasis on motherhood. In particular, it shows how they combined maternalist and pronatalist policies to obtain social rights as working and non-working mothers, to develop a new sense of entitlement to assistance and to create new female-dominated professions in the field of social assistance.

As Maria Sophia Quine has observed, 'Fascism's family policy was the basis of an agenda for a conservative modernization of Italy in that it aspired both to protect the family and politicize its functions'.[2] Fascist policies sought to shape Italian women's matrimonial choices, procreative behaviour and post-natal care-giving. Within this context, ONMI played an important role in guiding the modernization of social assistance and the professionalization of female-dominated occupations such as nursing, obstetrics and social work. Quine also suggests, perhaps too emphatically,

Notes for this chapter begin on page 202.

that ONMI was the catalyst for what she defines as a 'welfare revolution' for mothers and babies.

I argue that the particular contours of maternalism in fascist Italy, especially the nascent professionalization of women's jobs in the field of social assistance, provided an opportunity for women's empowerment. Definitions of maternalism that imply a strongly active civil society do not work for fascist Italy because civil liberties were greatly restricted, and in the public sphere women were largely relegated to fascist organizations. A broader definition, however, sheds light on how Italian women attempted to use the fascists' politicization of motherhood to achieve their own ends. In this article, I consider 'maternalism' to be the manifestation of mothers' expression of their own needs, encompassing women's unorganized resistance to the regime's pronatalist policies, as well as the indirect influence that recipients exercised in shaping welfare policies.

Created in 1925, three years after the fascist regime attained power, ONMI[3] was the keystone of the government's demographic campaign.[4] The organization's roots are to be found in the assistance programmes developed during the period between the last liberal governments and the advent of fascism, when upper-class Roman women from the National Association of Women (*Associazione Nazionale della Donna*) began to take an interest in the plight of poor and single mothers. One of their projects, established in 1918, was Mothers' Aid for Illegitimate Children and Unwed Mothers (*Assistenza Materna per gli Illegittimi e le Madri Nubili*).[5] This non-governmental programme provided services, subsidies and assistance to poor and single women with children. Sponsors of the programme encouraged single mothers to keep their babies, promoted breastfeeding and urged mothers to avail themselves of the health assistance and childrearing information available at women's and children's consulting clinics (*consultori*). In addition, they lobbied for legislation to establish paternity, obtained official working papers for female factory workers and assisted war widows in securing their widow's pensions.

In some respects, ONMI replicated the activities of Mothers' Aid and other similar programmes established by progressive women's organizations after World War I. In addition, fascist legislation concerning the protection of female workers was clearly continuous with prior provisions, most notably the Maternity Fund (*Cassa di Maternità*).[6] This fund, instituted in July 1910 and activated in 1912 after a long and complicated trek to parliamentary approval, provided maternity insurance for various categories of female workers, though many were excluded (including domestic service, agricultural and seasonal workers).[7] Despite pressures from the women's movement, the fund was insufficient, and few women actually received benefits. Nevertheless, the legislation was pathbreaking for the time, and the United States identified the Italian programme as an important example of a publicly funded maternity provision.[8]

Apart from the Maternity Fund, Italy was generally a latecomer in terms of developing a comprehensive plan for maternity protection. The 1925 law n. 2277, which provided for ONMI, sought to address this deficiency. As Sarogni points out, an examination of the parliamentary debate surrounding the creation of ONMI makes clear that its original purpose was not the extension of rights to women, but rather the improvement of the 'race'.[9] The objectives of this new agency were to strengthen family ties, increase the birth rate, and decrease the high rates of infant and maternal mortality. Mussolini himself elaborated these principles in 1927 in a well-known speech on Ascension Day: 'The demographic capacity of nations is a prior condition for their political and therefore economic and moral strength'.[10] ONMI was slow to get off the ground, and its first years were marked by the growth of a crippling bureaucracy that hindered the realization of its few initiatives.

ONMI was considered very important not only because it filled a long-standing gap in social welfare, but also because the infant mortality rate in Italy had reached alarming levels, due primarily to wretched living conditions among the urban and rural poor. ONMI would never have been able to single-handedly reduce infant mortality rates, which were markedly higher in southern Italy and the islands, but its intense, if uneven, activity during its first years had remarkably little effect. For every 1,000 live births in 1927, 120 babies died within their first year of life; 125 out of every 1,000 babies died in 1929; 106 in 1930; 113 in 1931; and 110 in 1932.[11] In 1939, Italy's infant mortality rate of ninety-seven deaths per 1,000 live births remained higher than that of France (sixty-three per 1,000) and Germany (seventy-two per 1,000) in the 1930s.[12]

The Belgian National Childhood Institute, which had been created in 1919 and administered effectively, served as a model for ONMI's sweeping objectives.[13] At its founding, Italy's institute was designed as a state-controlled entity for the coordination of all public and private institutions assisting mothers and children; in some cases, pre-existing structures were completely incorporated into ONMI. Extensive resources were devoted to disseminating information on the scientific norms and methods of prenatal and infant hygiene. This information was conveyed to both health practitioners and the public through various means, including classes on pregnancy, childbirth, and early childhood for doctors and midwives; practical schools for visiting home health assistants; public seminars and conferences on hygiene and childrearing; and mobile classrooms in rural areas for public education on maternity, childbirth and childrearing. In addition, the organization provided direct assistance through obstetric and paediatric clinics; mothers' kitchens (*refettori*) for women from their sixth month of pregnancy through their seventh month of nursing; mothers' homes to shelter unmarried women during their pregnancies, deliveries and nursing periods; crèches for infants up to three years of age for women working outside of the household; food subsidies and home visits. Indirect services included the provision of wet nurses, foster care, admission to education and training schools, and admission to summer camps and anti-tuberculosis colonies. ONMI also exercised 'moral' guidance, providing assistance with job placement, convincing unmarried fathers to legally claim their children and offering bonuses to cohabiting couples who legalized their 'illegitimate' unions. Finally, ONMI served to regulate and insure the effective application of all the legislative norms and rules for the protection of mothers and children.

The ambitious ONMI programmes were extended not only to unwed mothers, expectant mothers and widows, but also to married mothers and expectant mothers who had been abandoned or lacked support because of their husband's incarceration, hospitalization, or other conditions impeding his maintenance of the family. In order to receive assistance, the mother had to agree to keep and raise the children herself. ONMI officials emphasized the importance of breastfeeding, especially for single mothers, for they believed that breastfeeding would lead them to decide to remain with their babies, and that it was therefore critical for their 'redemption'. Assistance was granted from the end of the eighth month of pregnancy until six weeks after the birth. ONMI also provided aid to children. These beneficiaries included nursing or weaned children up to the age of five; children of parents unable to provide proper care; children of any age from needy families; physically or mentally handicapped minors; and children up to the age of eighteen who were abandoned or delinquent.

The activity of ONMI, which was heavily bureaucratic and characterized by a complex framework of periphery agencies, was managed through provincial associations, and, on a municipal level, benevolence committees. These local entities played a number of roles in organizing and overseeing assistance for mothers and children. For example, they arranged maternity assistance through specialized clinics for mothers, nursing babies and young children. In addition, they oversaw the sanitary, educational and moral conditions for minors under the age of fourteen. They also guaranteed the assistance and protection of children with special needs, abandoned children and adolescents, and denounced infractions of child labour laws. Finally, they undertook all of the relevant initiatives deemed necessary in the individual municipality. By law, the composition of these committees had to be at least one-third 'lay or religious ladies'.[14]

The provincial associations and benevolence committees carried out their work in collaboration with women volunteers who paid home visits to needy women and families. Significantly, it was the home visitor who determined the 'state of need' of the household. Indigence and absolute poverty were not required in order to receive assistance; it was sufficient for a pregnant woman to demonstrate to the visitor that she had no other sources of support, or that the other sources of support were inadequate. The home visitors were patrons from the community, unpaid health aides or paid health aides who were compensated from time to time, usually in agreement with other public bodies such as anti-tuberculosis societies, industrial unions and aide offices from the larger municipalities. In general, they were selected based on their loyalty to fascism and their allegedly maternal qualities. While many health officials sought to promote greater professionalization of these 'lady visitors', in many cases their primary duty continued to be seen as the cultivation of mothers and children for the 'mother country'. It was only in the mid-1930s that training courses provided by the Red Cross became obligatory for home visitors. This was part of a reorganization process initiated in 1932–33 by ONMI President Sileno Fabbri that definitively transformed the voluntary service system.[15] It was actually Fabbri, a firm advocate for the rationalization of assistance and for professionalization of social workers based on the American model, who insisted that the women visitors, following extensive training, should act as the experts of the committees of patrons (*comitati di patronato*).[16]

Yet the regime remained suspicious of the prospect of more emancipated women, especially of women calling for greater access to traditionally male professions. The fascist appeal for women to devote themselves to their maternal roles was directed specifically at such women.[17] Despite the central role that women played in the realm of public assistance, they never occupied leadership positions within ONMI. The office of Royal Commissioner, the highest position attainable and the most influential in terms of shaping policy, was always filled by men.[18] Furthermore, although Title Three of the by-laws set down on 15 April 1926 stipulated that at least two women sit on the Central Committee of the organization, the law of 24 December 1934 made no reference to such a female presence. For the women who had been active in the emancipation movement at the beginning of the 1920s, the rest of the decade was a very discouraging period. Even fascist women were excluded from the new bureaucracy. In 1942, the distribution of jobs among the 670 male and 3,183 female employees of ONMI demonstrates that the former were occupied primarily in management roles, and the latter mostly with service provision.[19]

One of ONMI's tasks was to oversee the implementation of labour laws designed to protect working mothers. With the approval of the Consolidated Act (*Testo Unico*) of 24 September 1923, law n. 2157 coordinated the pre-fascist legislation concerning maternity insurance for female workers, extending the subsidy from 40 to 100 liras. The total allowance was enough to cover the missed wages, but too low to include any type of health assistance. To implement maternity insurance, an annual contribution of seven *liras* (of which four were paid by the factory owner and three by the female worker) was established. For every birth or miscarriage, the state reimbursed the *Cassa di maternità* eighteen liras.

Coverage was extended to women between the ages of fifteen and fifty years who worked in private businesses or in companies subject to child and female labour laws. The latter included craft workers and workers in manufacturing, the building trades and the mining industries. Again, domestic service, agricultural and seasonal workers were excluded.

Table 10.1 Number of women workers and percentage of workers in the total workforce in Italy from 1921–1936

	1921		1931		1936	
	C.a.	%	C.a.	%	C.a.	%
Agriculture	4,236,195	66.7	3,922,063	62.7	4,004,601	58.7
Industry	1,160,141	18.3	1,196,018	19.1	1,311,890	19.2
Services	957,125	15.1	1,140,862	18.2	1,500,607	22.0
Total	**6,353,461**	**100**	**6,258,943**	**100**	**6,817,098**	**100**

Source: O. Vitali, *Aspetti dello sviluppo italiano alla luce della ricostruzione della popolazione attiva*, Università di Roma, Istituto di Demografia, Roma 1970, Tav. 3, 368–71

Maternity insurance was improved and extended through the Labour Charter (*Carta del lavoro*) of April 1927, and two years later the laws for the protection and assistance of motherhood and childhood were integrated with female labour laws by the Royal Legislative Decree (RDL) n. 850 on 13 May 1929. At this point, insurance was extended to all female blue-collar workers and to all female office workers employed in industry and trade who earned less than 800 *liras* monthly. State and public employees also received the benefit unless they were already guaranteed through special regulations an indemnity that exceeded the value of that guaranteed through RDL n. 850. Every insured woman was granted 150 *liras* of compensation upon birth or in the case of a miscarriage. Factory workers were allowed to refrain from work during the last month of pregnancy and could extend their leave for a month after childbirth, with the guarantee that their job would be held for them until their return. In addition, the decree provided for the extension of maternity insurance to some categories of agricultural workers. The law of 26 April 1934, n. 653, prohibited night work for women of all ages and children under the age of sixteen. It also limited the working day to eleven hours for women and ten hours for children. Finally, it stipulated that workers be certified as capable for work by either the Health Office or – with the permission of the Ministry of Corporations (*Ministero delle Corporazioni*) – by physicians from ONMI or other assistance organizations. In the early 1930s, the debate on the protection of working mothers centred on increases in the level of the maternity leave grant and on its extension to other categories of workers, such as rice weeders and female seasonal workers, whose discontinuous employment patterns precluded their accumulation of the working time and contributions required to qualify for maternity insurance.[20]

The Royal Decree of 22 March 1934, no. 654, encompassed all of these concerns, addressing above all the physical and moral protection of women working in sectors that posed increased risks to future and new mothers, or that offered fewer guarantees regarding the women's right to return to their same job after a maternity absence. The decree also extended the length of the obligatory maternity leave from the last month of pregnancy until six weeks after delivery. Factories employing more than fifty women had to provide special 'nursing rooms' (*camere di allattamento*) where mothers could feed their babies, and new mothers were guaranteed two daily rest periods for breastfeeding. Finally, the decree ratified the maternity allowance, which increased to 300 *liras* upon the birth of a child, or 100 *liras* in the case of a miscarriage. There were still no norms protecting women from dismissal or guaranteeing the right of female workers to receive wages equal to men's for the same kinds of work. At that time, women's wages were typically fixed at 50 per cent of men's wages for the same work, a disparity accepted by fascist trade unions.[21]

Despite its limitations, this legislation was a notable improvement from that of the pre-fascist liberal governments. The meaning of this type of legislation, however, was deeply transformed by the fascist objective of discouraging extra-domestic employment. Indeed, domestic helpers, in-home workers and many categories of workers in the agricultural sector were excluded from protection. It was only in 1936, with the RDL no. 1502 of 7 August, that maternity insurance was extended to some categories of agricultural workers. The fascist legislation thus came to be viewed as quite advanced compared to the provisions of other nations, which were almost always cited in disparaging terms. The United States, for example, was strongly criticized for its fragmented system, which reflected the great autonomy of individual states, and for its lack of a federal law on maternity leave.[22]

The increased protection for working mothers is striking, in part because it seemed to contradict the fascist government's growing tendency to expel women from the labour market, even through legislative means. One example, the RDL 5 September 1938, no. 1514, went beyond the repeated and largely ineffective efforts to encourage women to leave the labour market. This decree limited women's presence in public and private enterprises to 10 per cent of the company's personnel.[23] According to many women, this legislation not only led to strong discrimination in the labour market, but also caused a sharp division between married women with children and single women. The former were seen as having privileged access to employment positions, while single women who remained unemployed were perceived as having fewer chances of marrying. The letters sent to Mussolini protesting this legislation demonstrate the increasing hardship that women – even fascist women – faced under the regime, which would only intensify with the passage of the racial laws and the eventual declaration of war on France in 1940.[24]

It does not appear that ONMI made any efforts to keep women engaged in the labour market, and little is known about its abovementioned functions as a job placement agency. In addition, the mandate to create crèches in or nearby factories amounted to very little. These were supposed to have been created as a service to blue-collar women, supplanting the unhygienic 'nursing' rooms ('*camere di allattamento*') that had been required by the law of 10 November 1907, yet were rarely realized.[25] There is also little documentation detailing the degree to which ONMI was effective in protecting working women from dismissal in the weeks prior to, or the months following, their delivery dates. The two most important measures for working-class women were probably the establishment of mothers' kitchens (*refettori materni*) in the nation's cities and towns (which totalled 84,502 in 1935) and the creation of women's workshops (*labouratori femminili*) in depressed urban areas to facilitate women's employment, which were supported by ONMI, the *Fasci Femminili* and other fascist institutions.

Concerns regarding the health of pregnant workers were acute, especially in regard to the risk of miscarriage. References to the 'plague' of miscarriage were frequent.[26] While a worker's miscarriage was grounds enough for dismissal, voluntary abortion was highly criminalized by the 1930 Rocco Penal Code as 'a crime against the health and integrity of the race'.[27] Though abortion could warrant punishment as severe as four years' imprisonment, the pervasiveness of the procedure led many judges to be fairly compassionate and flexible in judging and sentencing of offenders.[28] Significantly, though women's autonomy in the reproductive sphere became evermore restricted, it was in relation to abortion rights that women demonstrated themselves to be formidable, if infrequent, protestors of fascist policies. Perry Willson describes women's response to the arrest of an abortionist in Rho, a small textile city near Milan, in April of 1928. More than 150 women, 8 of whom were arrested, protested outside of the prison where he was incarcerated, bringing him bouquets of flowers, calling for his release and expressing their willingness to resist the policies of the regime.[29] While these episodes should not be underestimated, it would be risky to interpret them as indicative of a strong opposition to the female role proposed by fascism. Anna Muraro's research on the city of Perugia, for instance, reveals that most of the women accused of abortion were unmarried and unable to support a child.[30]

The regime's attitude concerning abortion was consistent with the gender ideology of fascism, and by extension ONMI: a fundamental goal of its assistance policy was the maximum reinforcement of family ties. It was therefore still the family – even if but a 'pseudo-family' – that was reaffirmed and encouraged to be not only prolific, but also 'organically connected to the State, of which it should become an absolute element and instrument'.[31] As women seemed to vanish on the fascist political horizon, it was motherhood, symbolically and socially useful, whether legitimate or illegitimate, that received the highest valorization in the rhetoric of the regime. In the context of aid to delinquents and orphans, 'mothering' was even disconnected from biology and universalized as a moral force, 'active, infallible, and omnipresent'.[32]

In the wake of fascist policies, the family became the explicit partner of the new social state, and systems of punishment and reward were established to encourage 'desirable' behaviour. For example, women who used contraception or had abortions faced strong condemnation, while men who married and fathered children received bonuses and job promotions.[33] Though Italian fascist family policy never reached the extremes of eugenics and racism that led to the politics of extermination in Germany, the prohibition of employment outside of the home and the strong state presence on issues of birth and maternity constituted an unprecedented invasion of the state into Italian family life.[34]

Although the general consensus holds that ONMI only got off the ground after 1930, in some locations it managed to make significant progress in the late 1920s. The services delivered by the Milan federation provide one such example.[35] Between 1927 and 1930, 90,387 mothers were assisted with aid and shelter, 59,650 illegitimate children remained with their birth mother and 88,542 pregnant women received care in obstetrical clinics. The most consistent results were tied to a strong growth in the numbers of women who legally acknowledged their babies, the rise in breastfeeding rates for of babies in assistance programmes, the higher number of single women who kept their babies, a decline in the infant mortality rate and the organization of assistance for children whose mothers worked as rice weeders. In the national context, however, the Milan organization constituted an exception due to the city's long tradition of maternal assistance. In general, ONMI continued to be characterized by a number of deficiencies, especially in rural areas, throughout the 1930s.

Despite concerted efforts to rationalize ONMI, the full development of the assistance programme continued to be strongly hindered by its bureaucratic structure. The limits of the agency were clear to all those concerned: the distribution of services was concentrated in urban areas, the poorly trained health staff rendered the maternal and paediatric clinics highly ineffective and the infant mortality rate fell by just 20 per cent between 1925 and 1940. Furthermore, the measures supporting motherhood and infancy were not designed to provide a permanent level of minimum assistance, but rather to be used as emergency interventions. The circumscribed nature of their application left room for the introduction of family allowances in 1936 and the establishment of fertility prizes in 1939, both of which obfuscated the centrality of women's role in the assistance programmes. The war, for which 'civil mobilization' was declared, further impeded the activity of the organization. Finally, ONMI was subject to ever greater burdens, among them being an increase in the risk factors for infant mortality, which climbed from 97 deaths in the first year of life for every 1,000 live births in 1939 to 202.6 deaths in 1940.[36]

The agency's dysfunction went well beyond objective obstacles such as the war. In the fifteen years following its creation, ONMI had managed to carry out only a small number of its directives. Moreover, despite repeated plans to improve the services that it did deliver, the agency never managed to develop a comprehensive welfare system with well-defined recipients and an effective, efficient distribution structure. As Annalisa Bresci has noted, the grand project of 'absolute social assistance' promoted by fascism exhausted itself above all on the rhetorical front.[37] Because the state hesitated to provide generous financing for many ONMI initiatives, the actual impact of the fascist welfare reforms was often minimal; beyond the larger cities, the agency's presence was limited to its propaganda campaigns. The meagre subsidies offered failed to produce any real improvement in the material conditions of poor urban women and proved even less effective among poor rural women.

Whereas some countries during this period appeared reluctant to extend welfare benefits to unmarried mothers, such women were the principal targets of the fascist assistance policies. The citizenship 'rights' that they acquired through this aid, however, cost them much more dearly than married women. Along with the benefits came the invasion of the state into their private lives, as their morals came under scrutiny. This attempt to police private behaviour was not exclusive to the fascist welfare state, however. The morality of mothers – especially single mothers – was also supervised in the United States, where widows received mothers' pensions from state-funded programmes in the 1910s and 1920s and from the federally funded Aid to Dependent Children programme beginning in the mid-1930s.[38]

In spite of the limitations and restrictions inherent to fascist social policies, women often used the structures created by the fascist regime to achieve their own ends. The assistance programmes led to the creation of networks of women who interpreted social work as a political practice, and fascist social policies led to greater recognition of several predominantly female professions. From the end of the 1920s, the intense push to modernize maternity translated into the training of midwives, health nurses and social workers, through instruction and the completion of courses in specialized professional schools. In 1928, sixteen universities opened training courses in puericulture for midwives and general physicians. At the end of the year, 625 physicians and 240 midwives obtained diplomas. In 1930 the Midwives' National Fascist Union was established, and by 1937 midwives were granted the more scientific title 'obstetrician', indicating that they were supposed to be repositories of scientific knowledge and eugenic practices. In 1938, ONMI developed a two-week-long specialization course for obstetricians. But despite this emphasis on obstetrical training, the number of obstetricians grew by only 2 per cent between 1927 and 1941, from 16,099 to 16,468.[39] In part, the investment of financial resources in training failed because the majority of ONMI's personnel were volunteers, which ran counter to the goal of creating a permanent, professional network of health and social services. As Maria Sophia Quine has observed, 'ONMI certainly took for granted that women would perform selfless service in aid of the fascist welfare revolution ... Fascism's grand project for administrative state-building and modernization was compromised because of the problem of recruitment and employment in the enterprise'.[40]

On the surface, women's initiatives remained stifled by a fascist demographic policy that firmly placed the family at the centre of social policies. Aid came in the form of family allowances (1936) directed to the male household head; the establishment of the Union of Large Families (1937);

and cash bonuses upon the birth of additional children (1939). Women's activism only comes to light through an examination of their informal political strategies, in the small but multiple episodes of resistance they posed to the regime, and particularly in the spaces they managed to carve out for themselves within the realm of the welfare institutions in which they worked. These women were at least partial inheritors of the early 'social laboratories', that is, the 'entirety of the service structures activated by the women's organizations' of liberal, pre-fascist Italy, including the painstakingly achieved Maternity Fund. Many helped to lay the foundations for the modernization of welfare in Italy, formulating their right to services and assistance in terms other than their status as mothers.[41] As Quine stresses, women's assertion of their right to public assistance 'suggests that female clients were not passive recipients of fascist welfare or its ideological trapping ... That women wanted welfare, but not propaganda ... did not preclude the possibility that they would use maternalist ideology and policy to their own advantage'.[42]

A lack of evidence, due to the 'disappearance' of ONMI's central archives, prevents a reconstruction of the relationship between the agency and working and non-working mothers. There are very few remaining letters from women requesting aid, or from women who had been helped by the agency. Thus, there is no known source of information to shed light on the real needs of women during that time, nor to measure their confidence in the welfare institutions of the regime and the 'familiarity' with which they encountered them. We cannot trace, as Maurizio Ferrera puts it, 'the moving borders of the welfare state, that is, the points of state penetration into the numerous spheres of an individual's life'.[43]

Within the fascist social policy system, it was only through biological reproduction that women became legitimate producers of social value, and it was this function above all others that the state attempted to protect. As a consequence, working mothers were never fully legitimized. As Anna Rossi-Doria has argued, it was precisely in the context of employment that the maternalist policies of the regime failed to untangle the difficult relationship between citizenship and maternity.[44] When ONMI became engaged in the supervision and control of female workers through its social policies, the organization's attention was directed above all towards workers in industrial plants. It generally limited its activity to the urban sphere and, despite the entreaties of the regime's propaganda, only occasionally occupied itself with the needs of female agricultural and seasonal workers, such as the rice weeders. The fact that working women received better protection from ONMI's fascist visitors than from their own trade unions is significant, not only for what it reveals about the regime's ambiguous stance on female employment, but also because it highlights the extent to which protective legislation was designed primarily to serve pronatalist objectives.[45]

While it is true, as De Grazia writes, that in fascist Italy there was an enormous difference 'between the propaganda's emphasis on the importance of promoting modern maternity, and the low quality of the services and administration', there were also some clear attempts to rationalize the system of assistance.[46] Furthermore, the innovative training programmes for nurses, obstetricians, social workers and health aides introduced during that period, though marked by constraints and ambiguities, set in motion a process of professionalization process for women in many sectors of maternal and child welfare that would develop further immediately after World War II. There were thus signals, however weak, of a future that went well beyond the regime's original intentions. By means of social policies, Italian women in fact gained new political identities; as Paul Pierson states, 'policy creates politics'.[47] The imperfect modernization of the system of social protection for mothers and children, and the role women played in it as both beneficiaries and professional service providers, opened up post-war opportunities and scenarios for a new kind of female citizenship, the embryo of which was already visible during the fascist period.

Notes

1. R. Pickering-Iazzi (ed.). 1995. *Mothers of Invention: Women, Italian Fascism, and Culture*, Minneapolis: University of Minnesota Press, xvi.
2. M.S. Quine. 2002. *Italy's Social Revolution: Charity and Welfare from Liberalism to Fascism*, Houndmills: Palgrave, 132.
3. The historiography on Italian fascism is extensive. Among the more recent studies, see: A. Del Boca, M. Legnani and M.G. Rossi (eds). 1995. *Il regime fascista*, Rome-Bari: Laterza; A. De Bernardi and S. Guarracino (eds). 1998. *Il fascismo: Dizionario di storia, personaggi, cultura, economia, fonti e dibattito storiografico*, Milan: B. Mondadori; S. Lupo. 2000. *Il fascismo: La politica in un regime totalitario*, Rome: Donzelli; E. Gentile. 2002. *Fascismo: Storia e interpretazione*, Rome-Bari: Laterza; A. De Bernardi. 2006. *Una dittatura moderna: Il fascismo come problema storico*, Milan: B. Mondadori; E. Gentile. 2008. *La via italiana al totalitarismo: Il partito e lo Stato nel regime fascista*, Rome: Carocci; and L. Di Nucci. 2009. *Lo Stato-partito del fascismo: Genesi, evoluzione e crisi 1919–1943*, Bologna: Il Mulino.
4. On ONMI's history, see A. Bresci. 1993. 'L'Opera Nazionale Maternità e Infanzia nel ventennio fascista', *Italia Contemporanea*, 192, 433; V. De Grazia. 1993. *Le donne nel regime fascista*, Venice: Marsilio, 69–111; Quine, *Italy's Social Revolution*, ch. 5; M. Monnanni. 2005. *Per la protezione della stirpe: Il fascismo e l'Opera Nazionale Maternità e Infanzia*, Rome: Sallustiana; M. Bettini. 2008. *Stato e assistenza sociale in Italia: L'Opera Nazionale Maternità e Infanzia, 1925–1975*, Pisa: Erasmo; and M. Minesso. 2007. *Stato e infanzia nell'Italia Contemporanea: Origini, sviluppo e fine dell'ONMI, 1925–1975*, Bologna: Il Mulino; and idem. 2011. *Welfare e minori: L'Italia nel contesto europeo*, Milan: Franco Angeli.
5. E. Modigliani. 1924. *Assistenza materna. Relazione morale sul primo quinquennio di funzionamento (1918–1922) con uno studio sui fattori sociali della maternità illegittima*, Rome:

Opera Nazionale di assistenza alla maternità ed all'infanzia illegittima o bisognosa. Sezione di Roma; and D. Di Robilant. 1937. *L'assistenza obbligatoria agli illegittimi riconosciuti,* Turin: Tipografia Vincenzo Bona.

6. C. Saraceno. 1991. 'Redefining Maternity and Paternity: Gender, Pronatalism and Social Policies in Fascist Italy', in G. Bock and P. Thane (eds), *Maternity and Gender Policies: Women and the European Welfare States 1880s–1950s,* London and New York: Routledge, 202–3.

7. A. Buttafuoco. 1990. *Le origini della Cassa Nazionale di Maternità,* Arezzo: Dipartimento di Studi storico-sociali e filosofici; and idem, 'Motherhood as a Political Strategy: The Role of the Italian Women's Movement in the Creation of the *Cassa Nazionale di Maternità*', in Bock and Thane, *Maternity and Gender Policies,* 170–95.

8. In this regard, see H.J. Harris. 1919. *Maternity Benefit Systems in Certain Foreign Countries,* Washington: Government Printing Office.

9. E. Sarogni. 1995. *La donna italiana: Il lungo cammino verso i diritti, 1861–1994,* Parma: Practiche Editrice.

10. A.R. Santucci. 1940. *L'Opera Nazionale Maternità e Infanzia. Legislazione, scopi e compiti, funzionamento. Lezione introduttiva al corso per visitatrici indetto dalla Federazione Provinciale dei Fasci Femminili,* Empoli, 4.

11. P. Corsi. 1936. *La tutela della Maternità e dell'Infanzia in Italia,* Rome: Novissima, 20.

12. G. Vicarelli. 1997. *Alle radici della politica sanitaria in Italia: Società e salute da Crispi al fascismo,* Bologna: Il Mulino, 22.

13. L. Furlan. 1933. 'La protezione e l'assistenza della maternità e dell'infanzia in Italia', in Federazione delle Donne Giuriste, *La donna e la famiglia nella legislazione fascista,* Naples: 'La Toga', 33–57.

14. Royal Legislative Decree, 15 April 1926, n. 718, Regulations of law 10 December 1925, n. 2277, on protection of and assistance for maternity and infancy, *Gazzetta Ufficiale del Regno d'Italia,* 5 May 1926, n. 104, title 103.

15. Vicarelli, *Alle radici della politica sanitaria in Italia.*

16. S. Fabbri. 1933. *L'Assistenza della maternità e dell'infanzia in Italia (Problemi vecchi e nuovi),* Naples: Chiurazzi.

17. A. Lo M. Aprile. 1937. 'La protezione della madre nutrice come elemento di difesa della razza', *Rivista della Assistenza e Beneficienza* 1 (January).

18. Saraceno, *Redefining Maternity and Paternity,* 200.

19. De Grazia, *Le donne nel regime fascista,* 317.

20. See 'Il coordinamento delle disposizioni sull'assicurazione di maternità nello schema proposto dalla Commissione per la revisione della legislazione del lavoro', *Bollettino del lavoro e della previdenza sociale* 6, 1931, 895–901.

21. M.V. Ballestrero. 1979. *Dalla tutela alla parità: La legislazione italiana sul lavoro delle donne,* Bologna: Il Mulino, 70.

22. L.R. Sanseverino, 'La legislazione fascista sul lavoro femminile', in Federazione delle Donne Giuriste, *La donna e la famiglia nella legislazione fascista,* 119.

23. O. Vitali. 1970. *Aspetti dello sviluppo economico italiano alla luce della ricostruzione della popolazione attiva,* Rome: Pubblicazioni dell'Istituto di demografia.

24. On women's attitudes toward fascism, see H. Dittrich-Johansen. 2002. 'Per la Patria e per il Duce: Storie di fedeltà femminili nell'Italia fascista', *Genesis* 1(1), 125–56.

25. Corsi, *La tutela della Maternità e dell'Infanzia in Italia,* 47.

26. A. Bonora. 1928. *Alcuni problemi sociali considerati soprattutto dal punto di vista ostetrico riguardanti l'Opera Nazionale per la Protezione della Maternità e dell'Infanzia. Relazione compilata per incarico della Federazione Provinciale Forlivese dell'Opera Nazionale per la Protezione della Maternità e dell'Infanzia,* Pesaro, 9–10; and A. Masciotta. 1940. 'L'operaia, donna e madre: Rassegna e considerazioni generali con contributo statistico', *La Ginecologia* 6(12), 619–38.

27. The Rocco Code (*Codice Rocco*) was the new penal code jurist Alfredo Rocco elaborated in 1926. In 1942 the civil code defined the family as a social and political institution and negated all improvements in the legal status of women.

28. D. Detragiache. 1980. 'Un aspect de la politique démographique de l'Italie fasciste: la répression de l'avortement', *Mélanges de l'Ecole Française de Rome* 92(2), 691–735. On the repression of abortion and the status of obstetricians, see A. Gissi. 2006. *Le segrete manovre delle donne. Levatrici in Italia dell'Unità al Fascismo*, Rome: Biblink Editor.

29. P.R. Willson. 1996. 'Flowers for the Doctor: Pro-natalism and Abortion in Fascist Milan', *Modern Italy* 1(2), 44–62; M.S. Quine. 1995. *Population Politics in Twentieth-Century Europe: Fascist Dictatorships and Liberal Democracies*, London: Routledge, 50–51; and L. Passerini. 1984. *Torino operaia e fascismo: Una storia orale*, Rome: Laterza.

30. A. Muraro. 1996–7. 'Donne tra politica e giustizia: La repressione dell'aborto durante il fascismo. Il caso di Perugia', M.A. thesis, University of Siena.

31. Saraceno, 'Redefining Maternity and Paternity', 196, 208.

32. Domenico Soprano. 1933. *Maternità fascista. Conferenza tenuta il 19 marzo 1933 – XI, Salerno,* Salerno: Opera Nazionale per la Protezione della Maternità e dell'Infanzia. Federazione Provinciale di Salerno, 12.

33. A.J. De Grand. 1976. 'Women under Italian Fascism', *Historical Journal* 19(4), 968.

34. G. Bock, 1992. 'Il nazionalsocialismo: politiche di genere e vita delle donne', in Françoise Thébaud (ed.), *Storia delle Donne in Occidente: Il Novecento*, Rome-Bari: Laterza, 176–212.

35. S. Fabbri, *Fra un anno e l'altro di lavoro per la protezione e l'assistenza della Maternità e dell'Infanzia*, Milan: La Stampa periodica italiana, 1930.

36. Statistics quoted in Archivio Centrale dello Stato – Rome (ACS), Presidenza del Consiglio dei Ministri (PCM), box II.10.1001, file 6.187, 1940–41. Lettera del Ministero dell'Interno alla Presidenza del Consiglio dei Ministri, 23 March 1942.

37. Bresci, 'L'Opera Nazionale Maternità e Infanzia nel ventennio fascista', 433.

38. See, among others: L. Gordon. 1994. *Pitied But Not Entitled: Single Mothers and the History of Welfare, 1890–1935*, New York: Free Press; and E. Vezzosi. 2002. *Madri e stato: Politiche sociali negli Stati Uniti del Novecento*, Rome: Carocci.

39. Gissi, '*Avvalendosi del suo mestiere*', 134.

40. Quine, *Italy's Social Revolution*, 158.

41. A. Buttafuoco. 1997. *Questioni di cittadinanza: Donne e diritti sociali nell'italia liberale*, Siena: Protagon, 19–20.

42. Quine, *Italy's Social Revolution*, 162.

43. M. Ferrera. 1993. *Modelli di solidarietà: Politica e riforme sociali nelle democrazie*, Bologna: Il Mulino, 51.

44. A. Rossi-Doria. 1995. 'Maternità e cittadinanza femminile', *Passato e presente* 13(34), 171–7; and De Grazia, *Le donne nel regime fascista*, 245.

45. I. Piva and G. Maddalena. 1982. 'La tutela delle lavoratrici madri nel periodo 1923–1943', in M.L. Betri and A.G. Marchetti (eds), *Salute e classi lavoratrici in Italia dall'Unità al Fascismo*, Milan: F. Angeli, 841.

46. De Grazia, *Le donne nel regime fascista*, 95.

47. P. Pierson. 1994. *Dismantling the Welfare State? Reagan, Thatcher and the Politics of Retrenchment*, Cambridge, MA: Harvard University Press.

CHAPTER 11

MATERNALISM, SOVIET-STYLE
The Working 'Mothers with Many Children' in Post-war Western Ukraine

Yoshie Mitsuyoshi

The existing scholarship on maternalism has encouraged the comparative study of the relationship between gender and the welfare state in diverse geographic, cultural and political settings. From its original focus on Western European and North American countries, this scholarship has recently expanded its horizons beyond the traditional borders of the 'West'. However, until recently these studies have almost completely overlooked the socialist societies of the Soviet Union and Eastern Europe. Maternalism constitutes a very different discourse in a Soviet historical context than in an American or Western European one, where maternalist discourse was intertwined with women's activism, lobbying groups and the ideology of the 'male breadwinner'. In the Soviet Union, in contrast, the society was socialist, not capitalist, and had neither autonomous lobbying groups, nor a feminist movement, nor the notion of the 'male breadwinner'.

Many scholars who have analysed the nature of domination and subordination in socialist societies have interpreted paternalism as endemic to state socialism.[1] For example, Katherine Verdery argues that socialist systems legitimized themselves with the claim that they redistributed everything that was produced in the interest of the general welfare. The Communist Party, in a paternal guise, acted as a 'wise father' and made all the family's allocative decisions as to who should produce what and who

---

should receive what reward, so that rewards were not granted as rights or given in exchange for something else, but provided as amenities. Subjects were presumed not to be politically active, but rather to be the grateful recipients – like small children in a family – of benefits that their rulers had decided to bestow upon them. Emphasizing a quasi-familial dependency, 'socialist paternalism' posited a moral tie linking subjects with the state through their right to a share in the state's redistribution system.[2]

However, socialist paternalism was not without disruptions and modifications. Recent studies have shown the complexities of the encounter between Soviet power and society, an encounter characterized by interplay and negotiation rather than simple domination and subordination. These works have problematized the traditional perception of Soviet society, particularly during the period of Stalinism, as 'monolithic'. Moreover, one of the new thrusts since the 1990s has been the attempt to explain the Soviet experiment in its comparative context and to show that Soviet practices were not totally dissimilar to those of Western democratic societies. Shaped by the experience of World War I, the interwar process that was characterized by the spread of mass culture, mass politics, mass consumption and welfare policies unavoidably affected the Soviet Union.[3] In terms of the types of maternal welfare policies implemented in such fields as hygiene, health, daycare centres, children's allowance and maternity leaves, Stalinist pronatalism appears strikingly similar to strategies pursued in many Western European countries during the interwar period.[4] However, in the Soviet context, these policies were geared towards achieving greater control over labour and maximizing production, regardless of how many children women had. The fundamental premise of Soviet women's policies involved the incorporation of women into the wage labour system, the democratization of the patriarchal family, the communalization of housework and the elimination of gender discrepancies. The feature most clearly distinguishing Soviet policy was the principle of women's paid work, whereas Western European maternalist policies were usually intended to keep women out of wage labour and to strengthen the traditional family with a male breadwinner.

By locating the Soviet welfare programme within maternalist discourse, it becomes possible to offer a new perspective on what has become a familiar discussion concerning maternalism: the comparison between 'strong states' and 'weak states'. According to Seth Koven and Sonya Michel, 'strong states', defined as those with well-developed bureaucracies and traditions of governmental intervention, tended to have weaker women's movements yet developed more comprehensive welfare programmes for women and children. The Western European countries of Germany and France belong to this pattern. Examples of 'weak states', on the other hand, are the United States, and, to a lesser degree, Great Britain, which had more politically powerful women's reform movements and yet ended up with less extensive and generous maternal and child benefits.[5] The dichotomy of the 'strong' and 'weak' states can be rephrased as the differences between 'maternal welfare provision in the paternalistic regimes' and 'maternalist regimes'; however, a line cannot be easily drawn between maternalism and paternalism.[6] Is it possible to describe the paternalist policies in the Soviet Union, one of the strongest states in the world, as 'maternalist'?

Taking advantage of the comparative nature of the scholarship on maternalism and current developments in Soviet social history, this study explores the possibilities and limits of 'maternalism' as a paradigm for Soviet women's history. It begins by examining the transformation of Soviet family codes from the revolutionary 1918 Code to the more conservative 1944 Code, along with various forms of Soviet women's organizations that exemplified the changing Soviet society in the first half of the twentieth century. It then carries the discussion a step further by incorporating a non-Russian perspective through which to explore the Soviet maternalist discourse. The state's policies on mothers and children affected all Soviet women, but their implementation, practice and impact varied in such a diverse society as the Soviet Union. Whereas historians addressing the issues of mothers and children have focused mainly on Russia, this study will look at how the Soviet maternal policies and a pronatalist drive were incorporated into the Soviet modernization of women in Western Ukraine, a new Soviet territory where people had experienced a fierce civil war between Ukrainian nationalists and the Soviet Army throughout World War II. This view from the periphery not only offers fresh insight into Soviet maternalist discourse, but also calls attention to a critical point that is often neglected in the study of Soviet women's history – the fact that Soviet society was indeed multiethnic.

Representing one of the strongest nationalist movements in East Central Europe in the twentieth century, the Ukrainian nationalists traditionally involved women in their underground organizations, as well as working with women's own community movements. While some women chose to devote themselves to the underground rebel movement as patriotic martyrs, others were alienated from the nationalists' paternalistic treatment of women. Upon occupying the region in the wake of the World War II, the newly arrived Soviet authorities launched a 'delayed' Soviet emancipation of women under the slogan of gender equality and sponsored a variety of welfare programmes, even though the rest of the Soviet Union had already retreated into social conservatism and traditional values, a process in which women became 'double-burdened' in the High Stalinist and paternalist Soviet society. Caught in the midst of the civil war, Ukrainian women found themselves at a crossroads where the two opposing political ideologies, Stalinist socialism and Ukrainian nationalism, competed with each other for the recruitment of women. Women's situation was made even more precarious by the fact that, for all their incompatibility, both ideologies embraced patriarchy in gender relations.

Soviet Family Policies and Women's Organizations

The evolution of the Soviet policy towards mothers and children was closely linked to the development of Soviet women's organizations. The first Soviet Family Code in 1918 constituted the era's most progressive legislation for women and families.[7] Imbued with utopian revolutionary visions that assumed that the family would eventually wither away and that marriage would be based purely on love, the Code abolished women's inferior legal status, established marriage as a union between equals and permitted divorce at the request of either spouse. In addition, it swept away centuries of male privilege in property law. The Code abolished illegitimacy and entitled all children to equal status, whether born within or outside of a registered civil marriage. Furthermore, the 1918 Family Code outlawed adoption and foster care, optimistically believing that the state's public institutions could care for children better than foster families, and also assuming that a foster care system would only increase children's unpaid labour in peasant households.[8] The 1918 Family Code was the first step in transferring child care from the family to the state. In 1920, abortion was legalized for the first time in world history. The Women's Department of the Communist Party, the *zhenotdel*, was instrumental in the attempt to realize utopian Bolshevik aspirations. Headed by the most famous female revolutionary, Aleksandra Kollontai, the *zhenotdel* played a central role in implementing the Party's programmes of reforms for women.

Reality, however, quickly belied the promise of the Bolshevik utopia. Overwhelmed by World War I, the Bolshevik Revolution and civil war, the country was left with hundreds of thousands of homeless and orphaned children, whom the new public institutions were unable to accommodate. Pressed by the mounting numbers of homeless children, overcrowded children's institutions and concerns over juvenile crime, the Soviet authorities reinstituted adoption in 1926, a first sign of retreat from the communist dream. From the late 1920s onwards, as Stalin launched two massive initiatives to industrialize the Soviet Union – the collectivization of agriculture and the First Five Year Plan (1928–1932) – policies towards women also began to change. As women increasingly entered the workforce, Stalin's government assumed a new attitude towards them and their role in the family. The 'New Soviet Woman' was to be equal to men in the workplace and society, but she also had to devote herself to her family by caring for her children and providing moral support and a comfortable home for her husband. The image of an equal citizen, full-time worker and housewife – a double-burdened 'superwoman' – appeared in the Soviet public discourse. The New Soviet Women provided valuable economic and social services to a society in which, despite the utopian promise of communalization of household work and institutionalization of child care, consumer goods and social services remained perpetually insufficient. The 1936 Family Code, often called the 'Stalinist Retreat', reflected this shift in that it criminalized abortion, made divorce much more difficult to obtain and initiated a pronatalist drive by providing aid to women with many children. A mother with six children or more henceforth received an annual allowance of 2,000 rubles for five years for each subsequent child.

After the *zhenotdel* was abolished in 1930 for the specious reason that the 'women's question was resolved in the Soviet Union', another type of women's organization appeared that exemplified Stalinist society in the 1930s. The *obshchestvennitsa* was a wives' movement in which mainly housewives were organized according to their husbands' workplaces and positions.[9] They engaged in a variety of socio-cultural, often wifely, activities, such as cleaning workers' dormitories and canteens, improving the quality of workers' food and nutrition, checking the standards of nurseries and kindergartens, and decorating gardens and hospitals. The movement originally began among urban housewives whose husbands worked in industry, usually in prestigious positions, but it gradually spread from urban factories to the countryside. Although their activities had to conform to the party line, women activists often made their own decisions, took initiative without the guidance of the party or trade unions and considered the social work they carried out to be their own achievement. In the process, they gained a sense of self-fulfilment. Scholars have argued that the discourse upon which the *obshchestvennitsa* was based closely resembled the maternalist discourse in Western countries: it held that a woman performed a service to the state by caring for her husband and children, and her official identity was based on her 'dependency' on a husband who earned a family wage. Thus, the *obshchestvennitsa* movement, in which women voluntarily performed additional domestic duties without remuneration, stands in stark contrast to Kollontai's *zhenotdel* in the 1920s, which had sought economic independence and political emancipation for women.[10]

The pronatalist drive initiated by the 1936 Family Code evolved significantly during World War II. The German attack and occupation of the Soviet territories resulted in unprecedented human loss, family separation and large numbers of homeless children and orphans. The statistics suggest that between 27 and 28 million people were killed in the Soviet Union. Most of the victims were male, resulting in a massively imbalanced male–female ratio and lower birth rates during and immediately after the war.[11] The 1944 Family Code represented a direct response to wartime realities.[12] The number of children necessary to qualify for state support payments was lowered from six (in the 1936 Code) to four, and the money was paid in monthly, rather than annual, instalments. Mothers received a one-time payment after the birth of their third and each subsequent child. Maternity leave was extended from 63 days under the 1936 Code to 77 days, including 35 days before the birth and 42 days after the birth. In the case of a difficult birth or the birth of more than two children, post-partum leave was increased to 56 days. Pregnant and nursing mothers were not to be put on overtime or night work. Supplementary rations for mothers were increased. Moreover, for the first time since the Russian Revolution, an unregistered marriage was no longer legally valid, thus creating a clear distinction in birth certificates between legitimate and illegitimate children. Divorce became an even more difficult and complicated procedure that required high fees and a tax was imposed on bachelors over the age of twenty-five.

In addition, the 1944 Code created new honorary titles for mothers who had given birth to five or more children. A mother who gave birth to five children was not only provided with monetary benefits, but also awarded the Motherhood Medal, Class II. Six children earned a Motherhood Medal, Class I. Mothers of seven, eight and nine children were honoured with the Order of Motherhood Glory, Class III, II and I, respectively. The highest honour, the Order of 'Mother Heroine', went to mothers of ten or more children. The introduction of military-style medals for mothers reinforced the notion that giving birth and rearing children was as honourable as engaging in combat. While the 1944 Family Code is often regarded as the culmination of conservative Stalinist gender policies, these pronatalist programmes, with their emphasis on motherhood, were not unique to the Soviet Union. Even the awarding of military-style motherhood medals had many precedents elsewhere. In 1920, the French government introduced an award for mothers with five or more children, and in Franco's Spain a 'large family', defined as a family with four or more children, could draw family allowances and benefits, while a family with twelve children earned an honorary title.[13] In Nazi Germany, mothers with four or more children received the 'Cross of

Honour of the German Mother'.[14] Well after World War II, in the 1960s, Ceausescu's Romania followed in the Soviets' footsteps, introducing a 'Medal of Maternity' and medals to honour the 'Maternal Glory' and 'Heroine Mother'.[15]

Nevertheless, Soviet pronatalism had its own distinctive characteristics. In the Soviet Union, the child allowance was paid to mothers regardless of whether they were single or married, whereas in Italy and Germany, a family allowance was paid to fathers as a supplement to the breadwinner's wage, thus reinforcing male authority within the family. In Nazi Germany, single mothers received a child allowance only if the father of the child was known to the authorities. Also in Nazi Germany and, to a lesser degree, Romania, the pronatalist programmes accompanied drives for 'racial purity'. The Nazis pursued a selective antinatalist policy by imposing sterilization and abortion on Jewish as well as Sinti and Roma (Gypsy) women.[16] Similarly, in Ceausescu's Romania, the government had an unstated preference for increasing the birth rate among 'pure' Romanians, but not 'hyphenated' Romanians, such as Hungarians and Gypsies. In addition, the Soviet legislation defined what constituted a 'child' for 'Mothers with Many Children' quite broadly. To qualify for all mother awards in the Soviet Union, a woman was able to count adopted children, stepchildren or children from different fathers, none of whom qualified in the previous 1936 Family Code.[17] This extended eligibility reflected a new recognition of adoption as a selfless act performed by patriotic Soviet citizens. By contrast, in Romania, children acquired through a second marriage and adoption could not be counted for awards.

The most important aspect of the Soviet form of maternalism is that, for all the emphasis on motherhood and pronatalism, the Soviet state never precluded women's work outside the home, even at the peak of the pronatalist campaign during World War II. Soviet programmes involving mothers and children, such as public institutions for children, generous maternity leaves and communal facilities for housework, were all geared towards achieving greater control over labour and maximizing production. When Soviet maternal policies shifted in the late 1920s, the First Five Year Plan was officially launched, and women started to enter the wage labour force in every sector of the economy to an unprecedented degree. In fact, the actual increase of women workers to 1,268,000 was well beyond the initial figure of 793,000 that Soviet officials estimated.[18] Faced with a labour shortage during this period of rapid industrialization, perpetual shortages of consumer goods and deficient public institutions, officials promoted women's traditional role as housekeeper and nurturer rather than attempting the more difficult task of creating a true welfare state that would assume comprehensive responsibilities for all Soviet citizens.[19] Yet while Soviet social policies towards mothers and children were predicated upon women's traditional nurturing and care-giving role, they were also designed to facilitate women's incorporation into wage labour. The *obshchestvennitsa* movement, in this respect, was a rare example in the Soviet maternalist discourse of a phenomenon that had a Western counterpart. A 'wife-activist' was defined as a married woman, and her identity revolved around her role as her husband's helpmate at home. Dubbed the 'housewife to the nation', the wife-activist was encouraged to believe that her responsibility to husband and children took precedence over her civic obligations.[20]

The unique experiment of Soviet maternalism also explains Soviet historians' discomfort in approaching the state's maternalist discourse. Just as some feminist historians in the West reject the ideas of motherhood and maternalism as incompatible with female emancipation, Soviet historians also appear critical of the maternalist discourse employed by the Soviet state. Scholars are reluctant to assess Soviet maternal policies as empowering, because such policies were clearly incompatible with female emancipation. Instead, they led women to become increasingly 'double-burdened' as mothers and workers within the male-dominated socialist patriarchy. Nonetheless, the Soviet state did in fact reorganize motherhood and gender roles. When the Soviet Family Codes were revised to emphasize motherhood and pronatalism, the state also provided more legislation to ensure good working conditions for working mothers, to provide more public eating facilities and to increase the number of public institutions for children's upbringing. Moreover, relatively early retirement served to make unpaid household labour largely the responsibility of pensioners, who stood in food lines, cared for grandchildren and prepared meals for their working family members. Though still extremely feminized because of the sex imbalance among the elderly, household tasks were, to a certain degree, actually 'geriatrized'.[21]

Furthermore, despite all the emphasis on motherhood and the pronatalist drive, the perception and impact of this campaign varied throughout the vast Soviet Union.[22] While it is true that Soviet maternal policies represented a shift away from an attempt to create a revolutionary utopia and toward support for the maintenance of a neoconservative status quo, this scheme did not apply to the new territories that had become Soviet only recently and never experienced the Bolshevik 'utopia' of the early 1920s. For women in Western Ukraine, who had been isolated from Soviet influences throughout the interwar period, the 1944 Family Code was their first encounter with the Soviet policies regarding mothers and children.

Western Ukraine and Women: A Brief Overview

Western Ukraine, as a unit of historical analysis, holds a unique position in the history of Eastern Europe.[23] Located at the eastern edge of the Habsburg Empire, the Western half of Ukraine was never part of the Russian Empire or the Soviet Union until seized in the wake of World War II. It thus constituted a political, social and cultural world apart from the rest of the Soviet Union. Under the liberal parliamentary Habsburg Empire, within the milieu of the national revival in the nineteenth century, Western Ukrainians benefited from the growth of ethnic nationalism and created a highly developed national culture and political life. In stark contrast, in Eastern Ukraine, the Russian Empire placed harsh restrictions on the public use of the Ukrainian language.[24] After the collapse of the Habsburg Empire in 1918 and the defeat of the national revolution's attempt to unite Eastern and Western Ukraine in 1917–1920, a vast area of Western Ukraine came under the control of the newly independent Polish state.[25] Eastern Ukraine became 'the Ukrainian Soviet Socialist Republic', a part of the USSR. Western Ukrainians continued to fight for their national autonomy while being fiercely persecuted by the Polish authorities, and their struggle eventually led to the creation of a radical right-wing nationalist ideology that emphasized selfless dedication and patriotic volunteerism for the sake of independence.[26] With the secret protocol of the Nazi–Soviet Nonaggression Pact in August 1939, the Western Ukrainian lands were incorporated into the Soviet Ukrainian Republic. Within less than two years, however, Nazi Germany occupied these lands, which it held until the Soviet Army finally expelled the Germans in 1944 and re-established the Soviet regime in Western Ukraine.[27] Throughout the turmoil of World War II and until the early 1950s, the Ukrainian nationalists engaged in a fierce underground partisan struggle against the Poles, the Nazis and the Soviets.

Women in Western Ukraine before 1939 had already developed a remarkable degree of cohesion in their pragmatic, if not explicitly 'feminist', community movement, which involved education, culture, day care centres, a cooperative movement, a women's press and the defence of the Ukrainian Greek Catholic faith. In interwar Poland, the Ukrainian women's organization *Soiuz ukrainok* (Union of Ukrainian Women) involved women from all social classes in the region, encompassing about 500,000 members.[28] Since the majority of the Ukrainian population consisted of the smallholding and landless peasantry, however, middle-class notions of domesticity and female benevolence were of little relevance to the women's activities. Instead, women had to rely on each other to meet their everyday needs. Cooperative movements for trading dairy products were particularly successful and constituted the main part of women's

activities. In Western Ukraine's agricultural society, women were responsible for the cattle and poultry, whose products provided the co-ops with
most of their commodities. The cooperative movements also educated
women about other cultural and political activities. Although well versed
in Western feminist literature, leaders of the movements neither openly
adopted Western feminism nor called themselves 'feminists'. Instead of
calling for equal rights for men and women, they stressed motherhood
and emphasized the socializing role of mothers and their active participation in community life, in which women's right to work outside the home
was an essential element.[29] Thus, the Ukrainian women's movement was
comparable to relational feminism in nineteenth-century Western Europe; its advocates upheld the idea of a uniquely feminine, and especially
maternal, nature, as well as the sexual division of labour in family and society, while at the same time seeking to dismantle patriarchal institutions
and to restructure society.[30] Its aim was to modernize mothers from the
bottom up, not through the state, which was not an option for a stateless Ukrainian people. Without access to political authorities composed
of members of their own ethnic group, they could not pursue political
power by employing maternalist discourse. Moreover, they did not enthusiastically cooperate with the Ukrainian nationalist movement, which
sought to limit women's role to that of the bearers of children, the realm
of domesticity and acceptance of male tutelage. Rather, Ukrainian women
distanced themselves from the male nationalists' political struggles and
tried to maintain their autonomous community network.

Upon the arrival of the Soviet regime, *Soiuz ukrainok* was dissolved,
and the leaders of the movement migrated to the West. The Soviets
launched the building of socialism more than twenty years after they had
done so in the rest of the Soviet Union. While dissociating women from
their interwar 'bourgeois' feminist experiences, the Soviet state also began mobilizing women to support the socialist economy and to establish
a separate women's organization in Western Ukraine,[31] despite the fact
that the rest of the Soviet Union had already retreated to overall social
conservatism and traditional values, and existing women's organizations
been abolished.

The Belated Implementation of Soviet Motherhood

The official women's organizations, *zhinviddily* (*viddily po roboti sered
zhinok*: the Departments of Work among Women), were curious remind-
ers of the Women's Departments of the Communist Party in Moscow, the
zhenotdely. The resurrected Women's Departments in Western Ukraine in

the late 1940s, though they were not born of a women's movement from below, as they had been in the 1920s, followed the overall pattern and organization of the *zhenotdely*. The Women's Departments in Western Ukraine were assigned a variety of tasks, including furthering political education, ending illiteracy and promoting female cadres to important party and administrative posts. The Women's Departments in the eight provinces of Western Ukraine were composed of a chairwoman and a few inspectors. Each inspector supervised several districts and consulted women organizers at the district level. 'Women organizers' were responsible for women's affairs at a district level and had the most direct contact with the local female population. In addition, the Women's Departments organized 'women's councils' (*zhensovety*) at factories, enterprises, schools and administrative offices in order to mobilize the local female population for volunteer work.[32] The Women's Departments were responsible for recruiting women into the work of the women's councils. A women's council consisted of between three to seven women and its work was divided into sections such as culture, education, industry, trade, school, elections, land and sanitation. These councils often included professionals, teachers, physicians, gynaecologists, nurses or librarians. The reports about what kind of work women activists successfully did or did not perform reveal the wide range of their expected duties. In the immediate post-war years, women's councils engaged in volunteer work directly related to social reconstruction: helping families of soldiers with their agricultural work; repairing schools, hospitals, daycare centres and dormitories; and assisting with war orphans. For cultural and educational activities, women's councils read newspapers aloud at factories, prepared wall newspapers, and organized cultural exhibitions, film and theatre presentations and music concerts. While the activities of the Women's Departments and women's councils were not confined to promoting the Soviet pronatalist drive – their duties also included more political activities and participation in the struggle against the Ukrainian nationalist forces – the 1944 Family Code certainly established their guiding principle. In fact, the belated implementation of the Soviet modernization of motherhood in Western Ukraine was based upon the 1944 Family Code.

The Department for the Protection of Motherhood and Infancy (OMM) coordinated the implementation of the 1944 Code throughout the Soviet Union, but in Western Ukraine, Women's Departments functioned as intermediaries between the OMM and the local population. Soviet authorities were well aware that increasing and improving medical facilities was essential in order to encourage women to have more children. As a new Soviet territory, Western Ukraine had poorer medical facilities than those in the rest of the Soviet Union. Many parts of

Western Ukraine lacked enough gynaecologists and other medical personnel to care for the population. Accordingly, thousands of gynaecologists, midwives and nurses were sent to Western Ukraine. In addition, the OMM held a conference of gynaecologists and medical workers to discuss birth and child mortality rates,[33] and the Soviet state increased the building of local medical schools. During the 1945–6 academic year, Western Ukraine had only twelve medical schools, but within just one year, the number had risen to twenty-one.[34]

The new Soviet medical agencies had to struggle not only with inefficient medical facilities, but also with cultural traditions. Having lived in a pre-industrial society until World War II, many Ukrainian women were still not accustomed to going to doctors. The Soviet medical staff, with the help of the Women's Departments, made extensive efforts to educate women and encourage them to go to doctors and give birth in hospitals. The statistics for childbirth in the Lviv province, a central region of Western Ukraine, show different patterns of childbirth in the cities and countryside (see Table 11.1). While most births (over 90 per cent) in the cities were already supported by Soviet medical services, the countryside lagged behind. An especially striking contrast, though not utterly surprising, was that while medical support for Soviet childbirth gradually increased both in the cities and in the countryside, in the cities childbirth in the hospitals steadily increased while home birth decreased, whereas in the countryside, childbirth at home dramatically increased while birth in

Table 11.1 Percentage of childbirths supported by the Soviet medical facilities in the Lviv province, Western Ukraine, 1946–1948

		Year	1946	1947	1948
Cities	A	Percentage of total childbirths supported by the Soviet facilities	91.3	90.6	94
	B	Percentage of A occurring in hospitals	84.3	85.3	90.7
	C	Percentage of A occurring in homes	7.0	5.3	3.3
Countryside	D	Percentage of total childbirths supported by the Soviet facilities	32.3	55.2	74.9
	E	Percentages of D occurring in hospitals	3.5	5.4	6.8
	F	Percentage of D occurring in homes	28.8	49.8	68.2

Source: TsDAVO, f. 342, op. 14, spr. 4071, ark. 9; spr. 4122, ark. 6a.

the hospitals only slowly increased. Officials attributed the low support for childbirth by the Soviet medical agencies in the countryside to the lack of a transportation system, poor sanitary facilities in hospitals and misinformation about the Soviet medical system. Above all, they placed particular blame on the ignorance of local Ukrainian women, who 'lacked a cultural attitude, and kept old customs, and went to see illiterate *babki*' or lay midwives.[35]

The Women's Departments cooperated with the OMM to promote the Soviet view of motherhood among the female population. Seminars on 'mothers and babies', 'problems with child care', 'women's hygiene' and 'children's infectious disease' were held, which emphasized the same themes found in the political seminars on 'What has the Soviet Union given women?' and 'The nature of Ukrainian nationalists'.[36] The women activists helped with mothers' applications for awards and reported to the authorities how many women applied, were accepted, and received awards and medals. The pronatalist drive went hand-in-hand with an anti-abortion campaign. Although the Greek Catholic Church, an influential native religion in Western Ukraine, strongly condemned abortion and contraception, and the interwar women's movement also strongly condemned abortion for ethical reasons, abortion was indeed practiced in Western Ukraine,[37] and the newspapers periodically publicized news about the prosecution of those who had received or performed illegal abortions.[38]

The process of the Sovietization of Western Ukraine, as has been well documented in other studies, generated tremendous resistance and created difficulties for the Soviet regime. The civil war between the Ukrainian nationalist forces and the Soviet army continued well into the 1950s. Because the authorities had to heavily recruit Russians and Eastern Ukrainians to fill the administrative positions in Western Ukraine, the Soviet administration was perceived as an 'alien' regime in the region, and anti-Soviet sentiment among the population increased. The situation was the same for the mobilization of women. The majority of the Women's Departments' activists were recruited from outside of Western Ukraine, mostly from Eastern Ukraine and Russia. Soviet programmes, such as the collectivization of agriculture, industrialization and political education, produced massive resistance and conflict. Women activists who joined the Soviet collective farms were often targeted by the Ukrainian partisan forces as traitors, even when these activists had been recruited from the local population. The awards for mothers, however, were part of a different kind of Soviet campaign; they were entitlements. Caring for children did not require professional training or political education. Mothers who were awarded medals and cash benefits had given birth well before 1944, while still living under the Polish regime or German occupation. Thus, the

awards for mothers were the least 'Soviet-coloured' programme that targeted women in Western Ukraine. Above all, mothers awarded for having
many children were most likely local Ukrainian women, not newcomers
from Eastern Ukraine or Russia, the majority of whom came to Western
Ukraine to work and did not have large families. The available statistics do
not indicate the ethnic composition of the recipient of benefits, but the
campaign for 'Mothers with Many Children' was one of the rare Soviet
programmes in Western Ukraine in which the Women's Departments did
not have to report to the authorities whether or not the awarded mother
was actually a 'local' Ukrainian woman. In all other Soviet programmes,
the officials were always concerned with how many local people had been
recruited to collective farms, the Communist Party or industries.

Representations and Realities of the 'Mothers with Many Children'

Although Soviet policies towards mothers and children were based on
women's traditional nurturing and care-giving roles, the Soviet regime in
Western Ukraine did not simply resort to a traditional notion of women
as mothers or echo the emphasis of the interwar women's movement on
motherhood. When the Soviets provided support for mothers and children, their goal was to foster a uniquely Soviet style of womanhood that
combined female wage labour and domestic obligations. In addition, given
the Soviet presence's unpopularity in the region in this period of social dis-
location and scarcity of consumer goods, Soviet assistance for mothers and
children offered an appealing example of how generously the Soviet state
was taking care of them and securing the future of the entire society.

The first post-war International Women's Day on 8 March 1945 featured the liberation of Ukraine from Germany. At the celebration meetings,
many women received their awards for 'Mothers with Many Children',
including one thirty-three-year-old mother who had recently given birth
to her eighth child. This mother was awarded the order of Motherhood
Glory Class II and received more than 4,000 rubles, which she would
use to buy shoes, clothes and food for her children. She was a housewife,
and her husband worked at a locksmith factory, thus contributing to the
Soviet Union's war effort.[39] Having lived under a foreign regime and war
occupation, and having previously had no rights or entitlements, Western
Ukrainian women made particularly ideal and gracious recipients of the
generous Soviet policies for mothers. Thus, at the celebrations, mothers
thanked Stalin and the Soviet Union for liberating Western Ukraine from
German occupiers: 'only under the Soviet regime do mothers with many

children have the honorary titles of Mother Heroine and receive many state benefits for bringing up children'.[40]

The statistics on the children of 'Mothers with Many Children' demonstrate the dichotomous nature of mothers' status and also reflect the chaotic reality of the post-war Soviet society (see Table 11.2). In 1946, in Lviv province, 6,704 children were born into families that already had at least three children; in other words, they were children of 'Mothers with Many Children'. Of those children, the mothers of 1,798 of them were classified as 'housewives' and were therefore not working outside the home. In contrast, the fact that only ten children were classified as having mothers who were 'collective farm workers' does not necessarily indicate that peasant women had fewer children. These statistics were compiled in 1946 when the collectivization drive in Western Ukraine was still in its early stage, and many non-collectivized peasant women would have been categorized as 'others and unknown'. The same applied to the large number of fathers whose occupations were classified as 'others and unknown'. However, this category, in addition to non-collectivized peasants, included many fathers who had died at the front, did not have a job, or whose whereabouts were not known. This indicates that, as a result of war, many mothers became single parents and, thus, family breadwinners.

Table 11.2 Number of children born in families of 'Mothers with Many Children' and the occupations of their mothers and fathers, in Lviv province, Western Ukraine, 1946

			Father's occupation		
			Workers and white collar employees	Collective farm workers	Others and unknown
Total Number of Children		6,704	2,005	7	4,692
Mother's Occupation	Workers and white-collar employees	232	151	0	81
	Collective farm workers	10	1	6	3
	Housewives	1,798	1,370	1	427
	Others and unknown	4,664	483	0	4,181

Source: DALO, f. R-283, op. 13, spr. 7, ark. 75, 76, 79.

While the statistics show that the mothers of 1,789 children were house-wives, the idyllic image of the *obshchestvennitsa* in the 1930s was far less relevant in post-war Western Ukraine than it was elsewhere in the Soviet Union. Rather, the story of Maria Buiukla, a Mother Heroine with eleven children, exemplified the ideal of Soviet motherhood in Western Ukraine. Three of her sons had fought at the front, and one had not come back. Her youngest son was at the military college. Her three daughters were either working as professionals or studying for professional jobs.[41] She said that in the Soviet Union, women had the chance to pursue a career. Although herself a mother with eleven children, she was not a housewife but worked at the village council, and she hoped her daughters would become profes-sionals. The ideal Soviet woman was not just a 'mother with many children' but a 'working mother with many children'.

In accordance with the overall Soviet maternalist policies that com-bined motherhood and women's participation in the workforce, the new Soviet regime began building public child care facilities. If Soviet policies towards mothers were based on the premise of securing female labour, the authorities had to provide facilities in order not only to encourage mothers to have many children, but also to get the mothers back to work after giving birth. The availability of child care outside the home was vital, and the Soviets strongly committed themselves to providing public child care facilities. This was in stark contrast to the Western countries, where the institutionalization of child care encountered resistance because it was thought to increase the number of working mothers.[42] Soon after the implementation of the 1944 Family Code, the Ukrainian Politburo in November 1944 issued a decree to enlarge the network of child care institutions. When the Fourth Five Year Plan started in 1946 and women began to enter the workforce, the building of daycare centres took on added urgency. The overall qualities of the facilities, however, remained extremely unsatisfactory throughout the period.

Contrary to the official representation of new Soviet mothers in West-ern Ukraine, the reports by the Women's Departments reveal many diffi-culties and problems, including delays in payment, miscalculations, arrears and even overpayments.[43] A local Soviet official once falsified documents for his wife so that she would get extra money.[44] Extra rations for moth-ers and child care institutions often disappeared during the delivery.[45] Extended eligibility increased the complexity of the required paperwork and created long waiting periods for the actual awards or state support. In one extreme case, a local office did not process a file of one 'Mother Heroine' for ten months after it had been first sent to the office at the end of 1945.[46] Although thousands of mothers applied and were accepted as eligible, not all mothers received medals or orders as stipulated in the

Family Code (see Table 11.3). Soviet officials were concerned with the number of actual recipients of medals and orders, not only because of what it revealed about the inefficiency of the Soviet administration, but also because medals and orders symbolized Soviet women's heroic dedication to the country. Statistics also reveal that the granting of medals in Western Ukraine lagged far behind that in the rest of Ukraine.

Table 11.3 Number of 'Mothers with Many Children' and actual recipients of medals and orders in Western Ukraine within the Ukrainian Soviet Republic, 1947–1948

	Western Ukraine, 1947	Western Ukraine, 1948	The Ukrainian Soviet Republic, 1948
Mother Heroine (10 or more children)	209	520	2,525
Motherhood Glory I (9 children)	554	1,070	NA
Motherhood Glory II (8 children)	1,586	2,803	
Motherhood Glory III (7 children)	3,809	6,881	
Motherhood Medal I (6 children)	4,087	9,098	NA
Motherhood Medal II (5 children)	6,047	14,793	
Total women eligible for medals and orders	16,083	34,645	251,947
Recipients of medals and orders	8,999	24,246	196,572
Percentage of recipients among eligible women	55.9%	69.9%	78%

Source: TsDAHO, f. 1, op. 74, spr. 4, ark. 91, 97.

Despite the Soviet officials' intentions, women adopted a pragmatic approach to Soviet pronatalism. Once granted official recognition as 'Mothers with Many Children', mothers tried to get as many benefits as possible in order to survive in the difficult post-war conditions. The reports of Women's Departments show how avidly women pursued material benefits. For example, Maria Pavlovna Pychekha, a 'Mother Heroine' who had emigrated from Poland after the war with her ten children and invalid husband, wrote a letter to Stalin to complain about her material situation. The letter was forwarded to the Women's Department, which investigated her situation. The investigation revealed that Pychekha already had enough material aid: a one-time cash benefit of 6,000 rubles and a monthly allowance of 300 rubles, a house with cattle, coupons for children's shoes, winter coats, sweaters, fabrics, 1,000 kilograms of potatoes, 300 kilograms of cabbage, 200 kilograms of beets, and the list went on. Additionally, the family had been asked to join a collective farm, which would offer them another house.[47] Such letters making excessive requests indicate Ukrainian women's pragmatic approach to Soviet pronatalism.

On the other hand, there were indeed miserable cases in need of immediate help. Anna Ivanovna's case was extreme, for she and her children all had venereal disease and lived in poverty, despite her medal for 'Motherhood Glory'. Her husband had not returned from the war front; her application to join the collective farm had been rejected because of her illness; and her children could not go to school. The case was sent to the first secretary of the Lviv party committee and immediate action was taken. The family was to be provided with necessary medical care, help with their living conditions, school for the children and admittance into a collective farm.[48] Even if a husband had survived the war, he often could not support a family. Another case of a mother with many children involved a husband who had a job but was often drunk and did not work enough to support his family.[49] In the immediate post-war years, life was too difficult for most women to stay home as housewives. Moreover, despite the state's commitment to increasing the birth rate, the war losses were too huge to be recovered quickly. In fact, Ukraine's war losses were so extreme, due to the occupation and civil war, that it did not return to its pre-war population level until 1960.[50] Despite the generous aid for mothers and children and the propaganda and positive representation of 'Mothers with Many Children', the Stalinist pronatalist drive definitely did not achieve its intended aims.

Conclusion

It has been argued that the Soviet modernization of motherhood after 1917 continued along the lines already under way in Imperial Russia.[51] It is perhaps not surprising that a maternalist discourse, evolving out of the traditional notion of women as natural nurturers, would contain a certain degree of historical continuity that transcended changes in political regimes. This was undoubtedly the case in Western Ukraine. The Soviet transformation of motherhood in many respects resembled not only similar developments in other countries, but also those within Western Ukraine itself before the arrival of the Soviet regime. Prior to the war, Western Ukrainian women lived in a predominantly agricultural and traditional patriarchal society, but as the activities of *Soiuz ukrainok* reveal, they had already begun to explore the modernization of motherhood with the limited means available to them.

When compared with the strong maternalist movements in other Western countries, in which women actively voiced their opposition to governments and asserted their right to a mother's allowance, the examples from Western Ukraine, both before and after World War II, appear modest. The prewar Ukrainian women's movement did autonomously act on its members' own initiatives and needs. But as members of a stateless nation in Eastern Europe, Western Ukrainian women could not draw upon maternalist ideology to make demands on the government, nor did they aspire to challenge the patriarchal Ukrainian society.

The Soviet form of maternalism does not fit neatly into either a 'strong state' or a 'weak state'. First, while strong states with a well-developed bureaucratic apparatus generally had politically ineffective women's movements yet provided more comprehensive programmes for women, in the Soviet Union, Women's Departments and activities were explicitly 'politically conscious'. Certainly, however, their activities had to follow the party line, and any independent or non-party groups and movements were not formally permitted. Second, Soviet maternalism never lost its paternalist nature. Yet changes over time in the manner in which maternal assistance was given to mothers in Western Ukraine reveal that even the strongest of paternalist states did not avoid problems. While theoretically the Soviet Union prepared the most comprehensive programmes for mothers and children, the reality was far from ideal. Soviet officials' handling of maternal assistance and medals was often unsatisfactory and tainted by corruption. Consumer goods and facilities for mothers and children were perpetually scarce. Under the circumstances, 'Mothers with Many Children' may have been, at least within official Soviet discourse, grateful recipients, but they did not always behave as 'small children' towards their 'fathers' (the Party), as described by Katherine Verdery. Most of the mothers in Western Ukraine had become mothers well before the coming of the Soviet regime and quickly learned how to exercise their rights in defence of their lives, as the post-war economic conditions simply did not allow women to remain grateful 'children' of the family. Alternatively, some local Ukrainian women took advantage of the new Soviet maternal policies when it was in their interest to do so, thus becoming important if not active agents in the establishment of the Soviet regime.

Moreover, the Stalinist maternalism in Western Ukraine had a different meaning and impact than that of maternalism in the rest of the Soviet Union. The Soviet pronatalist drive, and especially the campaign for 'Mothers with Many Children', served to justify otherwise extremely unpopular Soviet policies in the region. The essentialized gender role of 'mother' was a rare feature of Sovietization that did not require special skills, training or political education, and therefore would not have provoked much resistance or bloodshed. If the Soviet authorities had been able to provide enough consumer goods and adequate material aid, their maternal policies would likely have been the least unpopular Soviet policies in the region.

Ironically, for all the ideological differences and antagonism between Ukrainian nationalists and the Soviets, women living under both ideologies adopted a similar pattern of maternalism that combined the glorification of motherhood and work outside home. In contrast, women in Western countries were urged to return to the home after the war. The Soviet regime implemented its experiment in the modernization of motherhood through more drastic means and on a more extensive scale than its predecessors, but, in essence, both programmes treated women as mothers, and both sought to impose male tutelage and guidance under a patriarchal guise.

Notes

1. L.H. Siegelbaum. 1998. '"Dear Comrade, You Ask What We Need": Socialist Paternalism and Soviet Rural "Notables" in the Mid-1930s', *Slavic Review* 57(1), 107–32.
2. K. Verdery. 1996. *What Was Socialism, and What Comes Next?* Princeton: Princeton University Press, 61–82.
3. This trend of 'no more *Sonderweg* for Soviet Union' (in Laura Engelstein's words) is best exemplified by Stephen Kotkin's works. See S. Kotkin. 2001. 'Modern Times: The Soviet Union and the Interwar Conjuncture', *Kritika: Explorations in Russian and Eurasian History* 2(1), 111–64. See also L. Engelstein. 2000. 'Culture, Culture Everywhere: Interpretations of Modern Russia, across the 1991 Divide', *Kritika: Explorations in Russian and Eurasian History* 2(2), 363–93.
4. D.L. Hoffmann. 2000. 'Mothers in the Motherland: Stalinist Pronatalism in its Pan-European Context', *Journal of Social History* 34(1), 35–54.
5. S. Koven and S. Michel. 1990. 'Womanly Duties: Maternalist Politics and the Origins of Welfare States in France, Germany, Great Britain, and the United States, 1880–1920', *American Historical Review* 95(4), 1077–108.
6. J. Lewis. 1994. 'Women's Agency, Maternalism, and Welfare', *Gender and History* 6(1), 117–23.
7. W.Z. Goldman. 1993. *Women, the State, and Revolution: Soviet Family Policy and Social Life, 1917–1936*, Cambridge: Cambridge University Press. For other studies on Soviet women in the early Soviet years, see Richard Stites. 1978. *The Women's Liberation Movement in Russia: Feminism, Nihilism, and Bolshevism, 1860–1930*, Princeton: Princeton University Press; and E. Wood. 1997. *The Baba and the Comrade: Gender and Politics in Revolutionary Russia*, Bloomington: University of Indiana Press.
8. L. Bernstein. 1997. 'The Evolution of Soviet Adoption Law', *Journal of Family History* 22(2), 204–27; and idem, 'Fostering the Next Generation of Socialists: *Patronirovanie* in the Fledgling Soviet State', *Journal of Family History* 26(1), 66–90.

9. There are several studies on the *obshchestvennitsa*. T.G. Schrand. 1999. 'Soviet "Civic-Minded Women" in the 1930s: Gender, Class, and Industrialization in a Socialist Society', *Journal of Women's History* 11(3), 126–50; M. Buckley. 1996. 'Untold Story of *Obshchestvennitsa* in the 1930s', *Europe-Asia Studies* 48(4), 569–86; and idem. 2000. 'The Soviet 'Wife-Activist' down on the Farm', *Social History* 26(3), 282–98.

10. R.B. Neary. 1999. 'Mothering Socialist Society: The Wife-Activists' Movement and the Soviet Culture of Daily Life, 1934–41', *Russian Review* 58(3), 396–412. As Minister of Social Welfare, Kollontai insisted that equal rights for women were not incompatible with special treatment for mothers and argued for measures to encourage fertility, but historians have emphasized only her advanced ideas on the nature of sex relations under communism. G.W. Lapidus. 1978. *Women in Soviet Society: Equality, Development, and Social Change*, Berkeley: University of California Press, 62.

11. B.A. Anderson and B.D. Silver. 1985. 'Demographic Consequences of World War II on the Non-Russian Nationalities of the USSR', in S. Lintz (ed.), *The Impact of World War II on the Soviet Union*, Totowa, NJ: Rowman and Allaheld, 207–42; and M. Ellman and S. Maksudov. 1994. 'Soviet Death in the Great Patriotic War: A Note', *Europe-Asia Studies* 46(4), 671–80.

12. For its English translation text, see R. Schlesinger (ed.). 1949. *Changing Attitudes in Soviet Russia: The Family in the USSR*. London: Routledge and Kegan Paul, 367–77.

13. M. Nash. 1991. 'Pronatalism and Motherhood in Franco's Spain', in G. Bock and P. Thane (eds), *Maternity and Gender Policies, Women and the Rise of the European Welfare States, 1880s–1950s*, London: Routledge, 160–77.

14. L. Pine. 1997. *Nazi Family Policy 1933–1945*, New York: Berg, 96.

15. G. Kligman. 1992. 'The Politics of Reproduction in Ceausescu's Romania: A Case Study in Political Culture', *East European Politics and Societies* 6(3), 364–418.

16. G. Bock, 'Antinatalism, Maternity and Paternity in National Socialist Racism', in Bock and Thane, *Maternity and Gender Policies*, 233–55.

17. *Vil'na Ukraina*, 23 August 1944, 2; S. Fitzpatrick. 1999. *Everyday Stalinism: Ordinary Life in Extraordinary Times: Soviet Russia in the 1930s*, New York: Oxford University Press, 156.

18. W.Z. Goldman. 2002. *Women at the Gates: Gender and Industry in Stalin's Russia*, Cambridge: Cambridge University Press, 88.

19. C. Chatterjee. 1999. 'Ideology, Gender, and Propaganda in the Soviet Union: A Historical Survey', *Left History* 6(2), 11–26.

20. Neary, 'Mothering Socialist Society', 403.

21. Verdery, *What Was Socialism, and What Comes Next?*, 65.

22. For a study on motherhood and pronatalism in a non-Russian Soviet Islamic republic, see P.A. Michaels. 2001. 'Motherhood, Patriotism, and Ethnicity: Soviet Kazakhstan and the 1936 Abortion Ban', *Feminist Studies* 27(2), 307–33.

23. J.-P. Himka. 1994. 'Western Ukraine in the Interwar Period', *Nationalities Papers* 22(2), 347–63.

24. O. Subtelny. 1988. *Ukraine: A History*, Toronto: University of Toronto Press, 279–306.

25. However, during the interwar period, 'Western Ukraine', mostly under Polish rule, was larger than it had been under the Habsburg Empire because the territories of Volhynia and Polissia from the former Russian empire were incorporated into Poland.

26. On Ukrainian nationalist movements, see J.A. Armstrong. 1990. *Ukrainian Nationalism*, 3rd edn, Englewood, CO: Ukrainian Academic Press; and J. Burds. 1997. 'Agentura: Soviet Informants' Networks and the Ukrainian Underground in Galicia, 1944–1948', *East European Politics and Societies* 11(1), 89–130.

27. On the Soviet regime in Western Ukraine, see Y. Bilinsky. 1964. *The Second Soviet Republic: The Ukraine after World War II*, Brunswick, NJ: Rutgers University Press; D.R. Marples. 1992. *Stalinism in Ukraine in the 1940s*, New York, St. Martin's Press; and R. Szporluk (ed.). 1976. *The Influence of East Europe and the Soviet West on the USSR*, New York: Praeger.

28. M. Bochachevsky-Chomiak. 1988. *Feminists Despite Themselves: Women in Ukrainian Community Life, 1884–1939*, Edmonton, Alberta: Canadian Institute of Ukrainian Studies.

29. Marta Bohachevs'ka – Khomiak (ed.). 1998. *Milena Rudnyts'ka: statti, lysty, dokumenty*, L'viv: Mi-sioner, 227–30.

30. On the definition of relational feminism, see K.M. Offen. 1987. 'The Theory and Practice of Feminism in Nineteenth-Century Europe', in R. Bridenthal, C. Koonz and S. Stuard (eds), *Becoming Visible: Women in European History*, 2nd edn, Boston: Houghton Mifflin, 335–73.

31. See the decree by the Central Committee of the Communist Party of Ukraine on 5 April 1945 in Tsentral'nyi derzhavnyi arkhiv hromads'kykh ob'iednan' Ukrainy (Central State Archive of Public Organizations of Ukraine, hereafter cited as TsDAHO), fond 1, opys 6, sprava 859, ark. 133–6. Hereafter 'f.', 'op.', 'spr.', and 'ark' stand for 'fond' (fund), 'opis' (section), 'sprava' (file), and 'ark' (page), respectively.

32. In fact, this volunteer work was the first form of *zhensovety* (women's councils) in the Soviet Union, which would become an all-Union phenomenon in the 1960s and 1970s under Khrushchev. According to Genia Browning, *zhensovety* were set up in 1950s, but some of the earliest models were formed during the war. My archival sources suggest that the earliest form of *zhensovety* was founded in Western Ukraine. G.K. Browning. 1987. *Women and Politics in the USSR: Consciousness Raising and Soviet Women's Groups*, New York: St Martin's Press.

33. Tsentral'nyi derzhavnyi arkhiv vyshchykh orhaniv vlady i derzhavnoho upravlinnia Ukrainy (Central State Archive of the Higher Organs of Power and Government of Ukraine, hereafter cited as TsDAVO), f. 342, op. 14, spr. 494, ark 43.

34. TsDAVO, f. 342, op. 14, spr. 494, ark 2–6.

35. TsDAVO, f. 342, op. 14, spr. 407, ark 1–9.

36. TsDAVO, f. 342, op. 14, spr. 494, ark 2.

37. A. Krawchuk. 1997. *Christian Social Ethics in Ukraine: The Legacy of Andrei Sheptytsky*, Edmonton, Alberta: Canadian Institute of Ukranian Studies Press, 147–50; and Bohachevsky-Chomiak, *Feminists Despite Themselves*, 192.

38. *Vil'na Ukraina*, 25 January 1941, 6; 1 February 1941, 6.

39. *Vil'na Ukraina*, 16 March 1945, 3.

40. Derzhavnyi Arkhiv L'vivskoi oblasti (State Archive of Lviv Oblast, hereafter cited as DALO), f. P-3, op. 3, spr. 139, ark 143.

41. *Buduemo nove zyttia: zbirnyk* (Ukrains'ka vydavnytstvo: Kyiv, 1947), 22–4.

42. S. Michel. 1993. 'The Limits of Maternalism: Policies toward American Wage-Earning Mothers during the Progressive Era', in S. Koven and S. Michel (eds), *Mothers of a New World: Maternalist Politics and the Origins of Welfare States*, New York and London: Routledge, 280.

43. DALO, f. P-3, op. 2, spr. 523, ark 192.

44. TsDAHO, f. 1, op. 23, spr. 4581, ark 153.

45. *Vil'na Ukraina*, 24 October 1945, 2.

46. DALO, f. P-3, op. 2, spr. 290, ark 101.

47. DALO, f. P-3, op. 2, spr. 287, ark 68–9.

48. DALO, f. P-3, op. 2, spr. 287, ark 45.

49. DALO, f. P-3, op. 2, spr. 287, ark 42.

50. B. Krawchenko. 1987. *Social Change and National Consciousness in Twentieth-Century Ukraine*, Edmonton, Alberta: Canadian Institute of Ukranian Studies Press, 171.

51. E. Waters. 1992. 'The Modernization of Russian Motherhood, 1917–1937', *Soviet Studies* 44(1), 123–35. As for maternalism in Imperial Russia, see Adele Lindenmeyr. 1993. 'Public Life, Private Virtues: Women in Russian Charity, 1762–1914', *Signs* 18(3), 562–91; and idem, 'Maternalism and Child Welfare in Late Imperial Russia', *Journal of Women's History* 5(2), 114–25.

CHAPTER 12

THE ORIGINS AND TRANSFORMATIONS OF THE INFANT-MATERNITY HEALTH AND NUTRITIONAL PROGRAMMES IN ARGENTINA

Alma Idiart

Early twentieth-century governments in Argentina provided welfare for the poor largely through funding female-headed beneficent organizations. Members of groups such as the *Sociedad de Beneficencia* tended to be maternalists, emphasizing the social role mothers played in their children's lives. Mothers did not merely give birth to their children; they raised and educated them. It was through their pivotal role in the socialization process that many women claimed a political voice. Maternalism as a social and political force in Argentina, however, diminished in strength and importance over the twentieth century. While mothers remain central to welfare programming, their social responsibilities have been curtailed and gradually replaced by an emphasis on their biological function as mothers. An examination of current Maternal Child Health and Nutrition Programmes and their historical antecedents will show how public policy transformations redefined and globalized maternalism in Argentina, leading to a more limited, biological definition of motherhood.

According to Jane Lewis's early review of the literature, maternalism constitutes a very slippery concept that may refer to policies that are for women and by women, policies for improving maternal and child wel-

---

Notes for this chapter begin on page 240.

fare, or policies for organizing a feminist strategy to improve women's social and political rights.[1] Referring to the Argentine context, historian Karen Mead argues that maternalism is 'any organized activism on the part of women who claim that they possess gendered qualifications to understand less fortunate women and, especially, children'.[2] Maternalism, therefore, is often understood in two different ways. First, maternalism has a political dimension, that is, the specific policies resulting from political demands and subsequent governmental responses with respect to the well-being of mothers and children. Maternalism, however, also has an ideological dimension, evident in rhetorical appeals that focus on supporting or protecting motherhood, as well as the strategies utilized by women's groups (which may or may not include feminist organizations). Historically, such rhetoric articulated women's allegedly unique virtues – their capacity for nurturing, selflessness and unconditional love – to justify women's demands for social provisions for women and children.[3]

In Argentina, the state-sponsored Infant-Maternity Programmes that began in the 1930s constituted maternalist social provisions in the political sense, as defined above, but shifted decisively away from the ideological maternalism of the female-headed charities of the nineteenth century. The programmes' central goal was to improve health by reducing the levels of malnutrition in mothers, pregnant women and infants through the provision of free milk, and, in some cases, formula. The state was able to monitor beneficiaries' health by forcing them to undergo periodic health examinations and receive vaccinations in exchange for free milk and formula.

The origins and implementation of Argentina's federal Infant-Maternity Programme (1937) had roots in both private and state initiatives. The welfare state that emerged during the 1930s built its foundation on charity provided by nineteenth-century women's organizations. As Mead has shown, the *Sociedad de Beneficencia* – a female-run, private and state-funded charitable institution created in 1823 – was the dominant (indeed, almost hegemonic) entity charged with organizing both charitable activities and welfare and health provisions for mothers, children and the destitute from its founding until 1946. In contrast, the specific federal maternal and child health and nutrition provisions launched during the second half of 1930s were designed and implemented by male legislators and predominantly male public health professionals (e.g. medical doctors and hygienists).

This chapter examines Argentina's Infant-Maternity Programmes from their origins in the 1930s to their recent transformations resulting from the implementation of market liberalization reforms in the 1990s.[4] Argentina's Infant-Maternity Programmes have not been studied in any systematic way until the late twentieth century, in large part because of the programmes' relative inability to substantially improve maternal and child health throughout the twentieth century. The evolution of infant mortality rates during the second half of the twentieth century has been unsatisfying (though it is possible to observe considerable long-term improvements), especially when compared to neighbour countries with similar, or even lower, levels of public health and social service expenditures.[5] The lack of uniform success of the Argentine welfare state can partially be attributed to twentieth-century Argentina's political instability and low institutional capacity for formulating and implementing social protection programmes. An analysis of maternal and child provisions shows that women's welfare organizations and activities in the late nineteenth and early twentieth centuries were central factors that paved the way for future developments of the welfare state and, consequently, state-led maternal and child provisions at the national level.[6]

Social Policy and Maternal and Child Health Programmes in Argentina

Research in the area of gender and social policy in Latin America constitutes a relatively young endeavour. Until the 1990s, and following research agendas on the origins of the welfare state for advanced industrialized countries, the influence of women's and feminist movements on social policy had not informed scholarship's theoretical framework, nor had it been the subject of extensive historical research.[7]

For Argentina, traditional research on welfare state development up to the late 1980s followed Carmelo Mesa-Lago's model of analysis of the development of the social security system. Mesa-Lago assigns a central role to pressure groups for explaining the introduction and evolution of social policy in Latin America. His explanatory framework includes not only the role and the bargaining power of pressure groups but also the nature and the role of the state, as well as the interaction between state structures and the pressure groups. In a similar vein, and building on Mesa-Lago's models, other scholars have pointed to the clientelistic relationship between, on the one hand, the populist state and, on the other hand, political constituencies and organized social sectors – a relationship not explicitly theorized in Mesa-Lago's works. In summary, the expansion of social security policies did not result from a universal or coherent approach, but was rather developed in a piecemeal form as special benefits for certain sectors of the working class.[8] During the 1990s, works on social policy development in Argentina integrated Gøsta Esping-Andersen's typology of welfare state regimes into their theoretical frameworks.[9] But remarkably, research based on Mesa-Lago's classic framework focuses on traditionally defined pressure groups – such as political parties, corporations, trade unions – and neglects to explore the influence of women's organizations and feminist groups.

Historical works have employed a gendered perspective to explore the role of the women's movement in creating policies such as protective labour legislation. Research devoted to the specific analysis of maternalist movements and the implementation of infant-maternity programmes in Argentina, however, is scarce, especially for the late twentieth century.[10] Argentina has a long tradition of social policy implementation, being along with Uruguay and Chile among the pioneers in Latin America for the development of a system of social programmes. Sources describing Argentina's traditional Infant-Maternity Programme are both rare and hard to find in a regular, organized manner: the library and archives of the Federal Ministry of Health and Social Action vanished while moving offices in 1992. Scarcity of information – both written records and oral histories – has been the dominant challenge faced by researchers.[11]

What we do know is that Argentina's *Programa Nacional Materno-Infantil* (PMI) was established with the passage of the Mother and Child's Bill (Bill 12,341, 1936). In 1937, the new Office of Maternity and Infancy developed the first National Infant-Maternity Programme (PMI). After the creation of the Ministry of Health in 1946, the programme was consolidated and began distributing milk to its beneficiaries shortly thereafter, in 1948.[12] The PMI changed over the twentieth century, going through three distinct periods: an initial period of pre-universalistic programmes (up to the mid-1930s); a second period of universalistic programmes (from the mid-1930s to the mid-1980s); and a third period of hybrid programmes (from the mid-1980s onwards). The characteristics of each period responded to the predominant role of the state in social policy, the features of social programmes themselves and the evolution of public social expenditures.[13]

Pre-Universalistic Programmes (1820s–1940s)

The pre-universalistic period is characterized by the multiplicity of philanthropic organizations charged with providing social assistance to the poor. The main organization created by a state initiative in the nineteenth century, the previously mentioned *Sociedad de Beneficencia*, provided private social assistance.[14] During the second half of the nineteenth century, the *Sociedad* monopolized publicly funded social assistance as well.[15] In the late nineteenth century, mutual aid societies (based on both ethnicity and trade) increased the myriad types of private organizations that provided social assistance for their members as well.

This particular arrangement for administering social policy was a predecessor of current non-governmental (or quasi-governmental) organizations: private, non-profit organizations with volunteers that received considerable funds through the state. Along with its links to the Catholic Church, a particular characteristic of the *Sociedad* was its feminine composition: powerful elite women composed its administration. In fact, according to Mead, early Argentine maternalist groups represented by the *socias* of the *Sociedad* played a key role in initiating strong demands for the expansion of government social provisions. Early maternalists took advantage of available political opportunities from a developing, relatively weak central state and a rhetoric that linked gender with national progress and order.

Several other private philanthropic institutions dedicated to maternal-infant well-being existed until the mid-1930s: the *Sociedad de Damas de Caridad* and the *Patronato de la Infancia*, created in 1912. In addition, a public institution in the city of Buenos Aires that had been founded in 1883, *Asistencia Pública*, created an office dealing specifically with infant and maternal well-being. Programmes known as *Gotas de leche* (Drops of Milk) developed everywhere after 1905, though their geographical dispersion was irregular within the country. Geographical dispersion as well as regional disparities characterized social provisions up to this date.[16] What these organizations had in common, however, was a clear understanding of the social role mothers played in society. The early maternalists working through groups like the *Sociedad* saw mothers as crucial to the development of a strong Argentina.

Starting in 1910, the multiplicity of organizations and agencies, the lack of uniformity in efforts to protect infant-maternal health and the lack of coordination among services allowed predominantly male medical professionals to argue for a unified, centralized office to provide general guidelines and coordination of infant-maternal health services. According to Dr Aráoz Alfaro, a renowned paediatrician, expert on maternal and child health and National Director of Hygiene at the time, the strong intervention of the *Sociedad* and other philanthropic institutions in matters concerning maternal and child health posed obstacles for providing high-quality maternal and child benefits. In his opinion, the solution was the creation of a centralized state agency for maternal and child services.[17] Doctors and other health and welfare professionals, rather than female volunteers, would staff and manage the agency.

Between 1920 and the mid-1940s, the organization of state welfare was characterized by the implementation of numerous state initiatives, marking the transition from private charity to the creation of a welfare state. This period showed increasing state participation in the design, administration and financing of social programmes. In addition, the coexistence of private social organizations generated conflict between state institutions and the traditional *Sociedad* over the monopolization of the social protection network.[18] New federal-level organizations were created, first to increase controls over social spending through the *Sociedad* and later to organize a more coherent social policy.

At the end of 1936, the legislature passed the Mother and Child's Bill, which created the new Bureau of Maternity and Infancy (hereafter the Bureau), under the supervision of the National Department of Hygiene.[19] The main goal of this office was 'perfecting future generations ... by diminishing all causes of infant mortality as well as protecting women as mothers or future mothers'. Among the functions of the Bureau was the oversight of public and private institutions related to infant-maternal health, the development of agreements between the National Government (federal level) and the provinces (state level) to design and enact activities within the general PMI, and technical assistance to provinces for the implementation of the programme. The Bureau not only supervised and monitored activities, but also sought to identify irregularities in the implementation of PMI's subsidies.[20]

Women's organizations, according to Mead, influenced social policy less and less during this period, largely because of increasing internal divisions among and within the various private women's organizations (e.g. Catholic women's organizations, *socias* and *universitarias*) that negatively affected their capacity to articulate and influence social policy implementation.[21] Simultaneously, the consolidation of the nation state reduced political opportunities and leverage for such women's organizations. Both Mead and historian Asunción Lavrin, who has written a comparative study on feminism in Argentina and other countries, discuss the declining influence of women's organizations. According to Lavrin, 'by the 1930s the state had become a surrogate father through the services of male physicians, whose loving attention to babies and their mothers, was free of unwanted advice from women's groups'.[22]

All the activities developed in the 1930s were originally centralized through the Bureau. For almost forty years, this programme maintained the same institutional structure and design, although its resources (technical and budgetary) suffered periodic reductions as a result of institutional incapacities, chronic political instability and the state's recurrent economic and fiscal crises.[23] It is important to note that the Federal Ministry of Health historically had a secondary role within the structure of the state apparatus. Its functions and responsibilities were periodically restricted, first by the Ministry of Labour (and its Secretary of Social Provision) and later on by the Secretary of Social Security. When the Ministry absorbed the activities dealing with social provision (and became the Ministry of Health and Social Action), the health dimension assumed a lower organizational rank, down to the Secretary of Health (sometimes being even the Undersecretary of Health). The profile of this Ministry expressed the subordination of healthcare to welfare policies.[24]

It was this centralizing government that sponsored maternal and child health and nutrition policies, such as the creation of both a National Programme for Maternal and Child Health (1937), and the Federal Ministry of Health (1946) that initially resulted in the extension of the Infant-Maternity Programme, towards the universalization of coverage.[25]

Universalistic Programmes (1950s to the mid-1980s)

The universalistic period was characterized by a welfare state organized according to a more traditional social insurance system that was created to complement a nationalist economic policy – Import Substitution Industrialization (ISI). ISI argued for a strong state presence in the economy and linked protectionism to economic expansion. Proponents of ISI believed that industrialization (rather than the previous export-led economic model) was the key to domestic growth and that industrialization was best achieved through a partnership with the state. Universal programmes (e.g. public healthcare and public education systems, social security, family allowances, maternity benefits) were seen as part of this policy and sought to unify pre-existing and fragmented partial programmes for the whole population. The main goal of social policy in this period was to adequately meet the needs of the whole population, even though 'the whole' generally meant those employed in the formal wage system, at least until the mid-1960s. Coverage beyond the formal wage system expanded in the mid to late 1960s.[26]

During the period of democratic government, from 1963–6, national sanitary and social policy emphasized actions to control infant mortality rates and ameliorate the socio-economic conditions contributing to high infant mortality rates. The formulation of a new PMI, with similar goals to the programme established in the 1930s and 1940s, emphasized the required integration and coordination with other social programmes.[27]

In 1973, however, the Secretary of Public Health developed a new National Maternal and Child Plan, which had comparable goals of protecting infants' and mothers' health and of providing food assistance to the same group with an emphasis on the improvement of the primary healthcare system for those at risk of having unhealthy babies. This was part of the government's triennial plan (1973–6) that also attempted to create daycare centres, though the law for the creation of these centres was never passed.[28] Distribution of powdered milk to provinces as a specific institutionalized sub-programme within the PMI began at this time.

Towards the late 1970s and the early 1980s this now 'traditional' social protection network entered a critical stage. The crisis of the old-age and pension system resulted not only from factors endogenous to the social protection network, but from the fiscal crisis of the state and the exhaustion of the model for economic development as well. The expansion of services and coverage levels, and the subsequent expansion of social and fiscal public expenditures, was not accompanied by a coherent financing strategy. Such structural deficiency, in addition to the collapse of the Import-Substitution Industrialization, marked the exhaustion of this strategy for social provisions as well.

During the last military government (1976–83), public health policy discourse emphasized primary care and infant-maternal health in order to increase legitimacy for the military government, but the number of effective state-run health policies actually decreased.[29] According to sociologist and historian Susana Belmartino, this was due to rationalization and sanitary zoning, which were justified in order to avoid the overlap of resources. In 1980, with the creation of the *Programa Unico de Salud*, the supplementary feeding subprogramme was completed and initiated transfers of funds to provinces, which started in 1981.

While many of the programmes instituted under the universal stage had faults, the premise underlying the system was one of equal access. All Argentines deserved access to public healthcare, education and other welfare services. While specific policies targeted women, they were to have access to programmes because they were citizens, not specifically because they were mothers. This represented a shift away from the maternalism of the pre-universal period. The new economic model, however, would bring mothers back into the picture as a focus of state policy.

Hybrid Programmes and the Role of Neoliberalism (mid-1980s onwards)

The period following the mid-1980s crisis was characterized by numerous attempts to reform social policy. In the 1990s, neoliberalism became a central component of social policy, emphasizing privatization, decentralization and selectivity (or targeting) of social provisions.

Privatization refers to transformations from public social provisions to public/private and private programmes, in different degrees. Decentralization refers to the transfers of responsibilities, administration and/ or implementation of social programmes from the national (federal) to provincial (state), municipal (county) levels and private providers. Targeting, a tendency strongly favoured by international financial institutions, is one of the most developed social policy proposals implemented through structural adjustment reforms in the past two decades. Targeting refers to transformations from relatively solidaristic, universalistic programmes benefiting the entire population (regardless of any specific socio-economic characteristic) towards more selective, targeted, 'means-tested' programmes for the structurally poor. This is a movement away from previously hegemonic discourse that initiated traditional universalistic policies – arguing that all citizens had the right to universal access to social programming. Targeted anti-poverty programmes assisted vulnerable groups as well, e.g. food-distribution programmes, labour emergency programmes, old-age assistance programmes, community-based programmes and educational programmes. Selective targeting meant targeting poor women as biological mothers, ignoring the structural reasons for their poverty.

During President Raul Alfonsin's new democratic government (after the collapse of the military dictatorship), the PMI was reformulated under the Bureau's guidelines in 1984. The reforms attempted to preserve the universalistic component of infant-maternity programmes. Simultaneously, an unprecedented social programme, the first federal feeding programme targeted to the poor sectors of the population, the *Programa Alimentario Nacional (PAN)*, was enacted.

By the late 1980s, the goal of the PMI, though defined more specifically than before, remained basically the same: 'to control the development and the nutritional status of children under six years of age, and pregnant and nursing women'.[30] In order to fulfil such a goal, unified criteria and procedures were required. In terms of the population covered by the PMI, the programme traditionally presented a universalistic character, initially providing health coverage to all women and children in Argentina. The population of beneficiaries, however, was redefined to provide health and nutrition services to pregnant women, nursing mothers and children under six years of age. In 1990, teenagers were added to the beneficiaries. In terms of nutrition services, the target population was defined as pregnant women, nursing women, children under two years of age and undernourished children under six years of age. Beside this element, there was no additional targeting instrument, and in practice the programme operated on a more self-selective basis: that is, programme provisions were given according to demand to those people who went to the health centres for the provision of benefits.

During the 1990s Argentina began to work in greater cooperation with international agencies not only to gain technical expertise, but funding as well. New programmes implemented during this period coexist with the pre-existing universalistic model in an uncoordinated manner. A combination between universal remnants from the traditional welfare state and new targeting criteria has dominated the design, administration and implementation of social policy at the federal level during the entire decade. The state still finances, designs and implements pre-existing universal programmes. All these activities, though, are organized within a context of budgetary crises and long-lasting administrative deficiencies, in turn generating a process of de-financing of public social provisions (e.g. public education and healthcare sectors). In addition, decentralization, combined with targeting and privatising efforts, favours the state financing of private and voluntary initiatives to implement social assistance, with an increasing emphasis once again on non-governmental organizations, non-profit and religious organizations as central collective actors. The multiplicity of voluntary organizations seems to take the implementation of social assistance back to pre-universal times, completing in this way a sort of 'historic' circle.[31]

By the mid-1990s, increasing demands for social protection overflowed the capacity of the state to satisfy needs, or even to provide a minimum provision that would ameliorate the poverty that a large and increasing proportion of the Argentine population suffered. A deep and long-lasting economic recession began in 1996 and 1997, leading to an unprecedented economic, social and political crisis that resulted in proposals for higher levels of state participation and institutional strengthening (e.g. regulatory capacity).

PROMIN and the Globalization of Maternalism

Between 1991 and 1992, the Peronist government ordered a study to provide an overview the health and nutritional conditions of mothers and infants and, indirectly, to evaluate the traditional PMI. The final report, written by experts from outside government agencies, particularly UNICEF, provided a baseline for the development of a new infant-maternity programme named the Maternal and Child Health and Nutrition Programme (*Programa Materno-Infantil y Nutricional*, hereafter PROMIN). This new programme did not replace the traditional PMI, but it stood apart from it, albeit still within the orbit of the Federal Ministry of Health. This programme had external multilateral financing by the World Bank and the Inter-American Development Bank, accounting for about 60 to 70 per cent of its total budget, and operated within a limited time frame, originally from 1993 to 2003.

PROMIN's ending date was twice extended to facilitate the implementation of the Health Emergency Plan following the crisis in 2001–2, first until 31 December 2004 and then until 31 December 2005.[32]

The programme represented a shift not only in regard to the services provided, but also in terms of the criteria for determining the population eligible to be covered. With a strong and definitive emphasis on strict targeting criteria, the programme only benefits mothers, pregnant women and children under conditions of structural poverty. The programme presents double criteria for targeting: a geographical target – regions in which the population has unsatisfied basic needs; and a demographic target – mothers, pregnant women and children up to five years of age. The main goal of the programme is to improve the basic life quality indicators of the structurally poor.

In addition, a shift from direct curative and preventive care of the targeted population to the provision of basic infrastructure (e.g. building small preventive and primary care clinics) altered the basic configuration of the original infant-maternity programmes. At the same time, this programme did not completely replace the old PMI, which it is still in place, though with extremely reduced budgetary resources and a considerable loss in prestige and technical personnel because of this new 'modern' programme. Despite the original plan, there has been no coordination between these two infant-maternity programmes for most of the decade.[33]

PROMIN constitutes a relatively young infant-maternity programme designed according to new, modern criteria for implementing social provisions: targeting, decentralization, community participation, and integration both within the healthcare sector and among social sectors. With relatively strong financial capacities provided through multilateral lending (relatively strong when compared to the traditional and federally underfunded PMI), PROMIN appears to be the government's flagship programme for the transformation of both primary healthcare and federal social programmes as a whole.

PROMIN programming, then, appears to respond to an international consensus on the definition of motherhood. Maternalism continues to be defined in political rather than ideological terms, and this definition has its roots in domestic welfare policy as well as international policy. Over time the programme has performed well, with positive indicators regarding effectiveness, coverage and efficacy for programme implementation. Several internal and external programme-monitoring actions, however, point to problems.[34] Despite the original idea of an integrated coordination between these two programmes, effective institutional instances for programme coordination took longer to materialize than originally planned. Only by late 1998, five years after the creation of PROMIN, was a coordinating committee under the orbit of the Federal Ministry of Health organized. Only under the new federal administration (c. 2000) did the government officially create the Coordinating Unit to Execute Maternal Child Health and Nutrition Programmes (*Unidad Coordinadora Ejecutora de Programas Materno Infantiles y Nutricionales*) under the supervision of the Federal Ministry of Health.[35] This fact expresses the political decision to support coordinating activities while pointing at political and institutional difficulties in effectively fulfilling PROMIN's goals. Effective unification of PMI and PROMIN in Argentina took place during the final years (2002–3), formally consolidating as one national programme at the end of PROMIN around 2004–5.[36]

Infant-Maternity Programmes in Argentina over Sixty Years

Since the 1940s, infant mortality rates, an indicator of welfare programmes' success, have decreased in Argentina, though not as sharply as in neighbouring Chile. According to my comparative research of Infant-Maternity Programmes in Argentina and Chile, Argentina presents a high number of similar specific social programmes at the national level, thus indicating programme proliferation and policy fragmentation. Consequently, Argentina shows increasing problems, associated with the state's administrative gaps in regulatory capacity, to overseeing the implementation of these programmes. These factors, in turn, generate higher levels of inefficiency.[37] Finally, implicit and explicit tensions between the principles of universalism and targeting are present within the design and administration of the programmes. In several cases, despite strict targeting criteria at the time of programme design (as exemplified by PROMIN's targeting guidelines), the effective reception of programme's benefits does not correspond to the targeting criteria as strictly defined.

Argentina's relative position within Latin America has worsened in recent years. Despite the increasing financial resources and the multiplicity of infant-maternity programmes available, the Argentinian programmes have not efficiently addressed maternal and child health. Problems such as under-coverage – meaning that there are needy people not covered by any of the programmes – and 'leaks' in benefits – meaning that people receive benefits, even though they do not meet the targeting criteria in terms of basic needs, or that they receive similar benefits from several different infant-maternity programmes – are due to inefficiency or capacity gaps. The inability of the Argentinian programmes to record an accurate list of beneficiaries – systematically proclaimed by successive administrations – reflects insufficient administrative capacities and deficient monitoring and coordination among programmes. In terms of finances, there were traditionally numerous and frequent delays of the transference of funds allocated to infant-maternity programmes (especially for the PMI). This situation makes programme implementation increasingly difficult at the provincial level.

Argentina shows increasing problems associated with the state's administrative and regulatory capacities to oversee the implementation of these programmes. These factors, in turn, generate higher levels of inefficiency. The lack of information for programmes' evaluation and policy decision-making is a central problem not only for these two social programmes, but for social policy in Argentina more generally. The main problem, however, resides not within the programme itself but at the core of the Argentine social policy network, expressing again one of the recurrent characteristics – and failures – of Argentinian social policy: overlapping, competition and lack of coordination among social programmes both within social sectors (e.g. national, state and county) and between social sectors (e.g. interaction between health and education initiatives).

Conclusion

Prior to the formation of the welfare state, women played an important role in forcing the political agenda towards gender-related issues through the hegemonic role of the *Sociedad,* later through feminist groups such as the *Asociacion Universitarias Argentinas* (Argentine Association of University Women), created in 1904, and even through their participation in the Pan-American Child Congresses. But despite this historical tradition, since the late 1930s and 1940s, their role has been invisible regarding the process of implementation of social policy at the national level.[38] Social legislation that aims to protect maternal and child health and nutrition has been passed and designed by male professionals: medical doctors, public health experts, hygienists and lawyers. Male professionals in middle- and high-ranking positions at the national levels have dominated the effective implementation of these programmes, with female participation concentrated at the level of day-to-day programming since the 1930s and 1940s. Only more recently have a few women assumed leadership positions at the Bureau. When women's organizations were pushed out, male reformers capitalized on broad notions of 'need' to institutionalize universal welfare programmes. Additionally, neoliberal practices such as targeting served to further reduce women's roles as mothers to the strictest biological sense. Rather than having access to healthcare or nutrition programmes as part of a universal welfare system, women could now have access to programmes solely through their biological role as mothers. Mothers, not women, could access medical and nutritional programmes.

PROMIN, working in partnership with international financial agencies, shows the weaknesses of neo-liberal welfare restructuring. The tension between the 'traditional', universalistic model of social assistance and the newer, 'modern' target model (PROMIN) has contributed to the persistence of a certain amount of inefficiency in social welfare provision. The tension also highlights the need for historical specificity and context when discussing maternalism. Recent Argentine debates seem to echo, on the one hand, the earlier discourses of the Pan-American Child Congresses (as shown by Sanders in Chapter 8), and on the other, debates within and regarding private charitable foundations (such as the female-headed organizations discussed by Mott in Chapter 9). 'Modern' versus 'traditional' has come full circle. With the rise of populist, anti-globalization movements in Latin America in recent years, maternalism is sure to be redefined and politically and ideologically redeployed once again.

Notes

Funding to support several stages of this research has been provided by generous grants from the Graduate School of Arts and Sciences of Emory University and by a fellowship from CONICET, Argentina.

1. J. Lewis. 1994. 'Women's Agency, Maternalism and Welfare', *Gender and History* 6(1), 120. Regarding these types of policies, see T. Skocpol. 1992. *Protecting Soldiers and Mothers: The Political Origins of Social Policy in the United States*, Cambridge, MA: Harvard University Press; P. Baker. 1984. 'The Domestication of Politics: Women and the American Political Society, 1780–1920', *American Historical Review* 89(3), 620–47; S. Koven and S. Michel (eds), *Mothers of a New World: Maternalist Politics and the Origins of Welfare States*, New York and London: Routledge; and idem. 1990. 'Womanly Duties: Maternalist Politics and The Origins of Welfare States in France, Germany, Great Britain, and the United States, 1880–1920', *American Historical Review* 95(4) 1076–106.
2. K. Mead. 2000. 'Beneficent Maternalism: Argentine Motherhood in Comparative Perspective, 1880–1920', *Journal of Women's History* 12(3), 120.
3. K.K. Barker. 1997. 'Federal Maternal Policy and Gender Politics', *Journal of Women's History* 9(2), 183.
4. A. Idiart. 2002. 'Neo-Liberal Experiments, State Reform, and Social Policy in the 1980s and the 1990s: The Cases of Argentina and Chile', Ph.D. diss., Emory University. Unless indicated, comparative references for Argentina and Chile are drawn on this source.
5. Divergent evolutionary patterns are impressive: whereas in the early 1950s, the infant mortality rate in Chile was more than double that of Argentina, by 2000, the infant mortality rate in Chile represented barely 54 per cent of that of Argentina. Even though Argentina's infant mortality rate improved in the long term, the nation's position in relation to other Latin American countries (with even lower relative public health expenditures, such as Chile and Uruguay) had worsened by the end of the millennium. Idiart, 'Neo-Liberal Experiments', chs 1 and 3.

6. This is in line with Karen Mead's research on maternalism and voluntary social work in Argentina. Mead, 'Beneficent Maternalism', 138.

7. Koven and Michel (eds), *Mothers of a New World*; Koven and Michel, 'Womanly Duties'; L. Gordon. 1988. 'What Does Welfare Regulate?' *Social Research* 55(4), 609–30; L. Gordon (ed.). 1990. *Women, The State, and Welfare*, Madison: University of Wisconsin; Skocpol, *Protecting Motherhood*; and G. Bock and P. Thane (eds). 1991. *Maternity and Gender Politics: Women and the Rise of European Welfare States 1880s–1950s*, London and New York: Routledge. The shift away from viewing women as passive victims (merely policy recipients) and toward seeing as active agents has required a revision of social welfare history. See Koven and Michel, 'Womanly Duties', 1084; Gordon, 'What Does Welfare Regulate?'; and Koven and Michel (eds), *Mothers of a New World*, 24, 29. On feminism in Latin America, see A. Lavrin, *Women, Feminism, and Social Change in Argentina, Chile, and Uruguay, 1890–1940*, Lincoln: University of Nebraska Press, 1995.

8. C. Mesa-Lago. 1989. *Ascent to Bankruptcy: Financing Social Security in Latin America*, Pittsburgh: University of Pittsburgh Press; idem. 1978. *Social Security in Latin America: Pressure Groups, Stratification and Inequality*, Pittsburgh: University of Pittsburgh Press; S. Borzutzky. 1993. 'Social Security and Health Policies in Latin America: The Changing Roles of the State and the Private Sector', *Latin America Research Review* 28(2), 246–56; A.C. Barbeito and R.M. Lo Vuolo. 1993. *La Modernización Excluyente: Transformación económica y Estado de Bienestar en Argentina*, Buenos Aires: UNICEF, CIEPP, LOSADA; and E.A. Isuani. 1985. *Los Orígenes Conflictivos de la Seguridad Social en Argentina*, Buenos Aires: Centro Editor de América Latina.

9. G.V. Alonso. 2000. *Política y seguridad social en la Argentina de los noventa*, Buenos Aires: FLACSO, Miño y Dávila Editores.

10. Most research on the relationship between the women's movement and public policy in Argentina refers to issues such as civic (voting) rights and protective labour legislation. See D.J. Guy. 1998. 'The Pan American Child Congress, 1916 to 1942: Pan Americanism, Child Reform, and the Welfare State in Latin America', *Journal of Family and History* 23(3), 272–92; and idem. 2000. 'La "verdadera" historia de la Sociedad de Beneficencia', in J.L. Moreno (ed.), *La política social antes de la política social*, Buenos Aires: Trama Editorial/Prometeo Libros. On the relationship between maternalism, feminism, and public policy, see M. Nari. 1988. 'Feminismo, maternidad y derechos de las mujeres, 1920–1940', *V Jornadas de Historia de las Mujeres y Estudios de Género*, Universidad Nacional de La Pampa; idem. 2000. 'El Feminismo frente a la cuestion de la mujer en los primeras decadas del siglo XX' in J. Suriano (ed.), *La Cuestión Social en la Argentina 1870–1943*, Buenos Aires: La Colmena; idem. 2004. *Políticas de la maternidad y maternalismo político: Buenos Aires 1890–1940*, Buenos Aires: Biblos; and M. Lobato. 2000. 'Entre la protección y la exclusión: Discurso maternal y protección de la mujer obrera argentina 1890–1934', in Suriano, *La Cuestión Social*.

11. For a historical study of maternalism in Argentina (1880–1920), see Mead, 'Beneficent Maternalism'. For a recent and ongoing work on the historical formation of the Infant-Maternity Programme, see C. Biernat and K. Ramacciotti. 2008. 'Las madres y sus hijos en foco', in C. Barry, K. Ramacciotti and A. Valobra (eds), *La Fundación Eva Perón y las mujeres: entre la provocación y la inclusión*, Buenos Aires: Biblos, 51–76.

12. R. Giraldez and V. Ruiz. 1997. 'Evaluando por productos: Decisiones y acciones en la búsqueda de un programa social más eficiente', in J. Capitanich, R. Giraldez and V. Ruiz (eds), *La eficiencia del gasto social*, Buenos Aires: BPR; and Biernat and Ramacciotti, 'Las madres y sus hijos en foco'.

13. Idiart, 'Neo-Liberal Experiments', ch. 4.

14. This secularized provision was coherent, with predominant local ideologies modelled on late eighteenth- and nineteenth-century European liberalism. Moreno, *La Política Social*; and Mead, 'Beneficent Maternalism'.

15. Initially (in the mid-1820s), the *Sociedad* was in charge of supervising the education of

young girls and administering charitable institutions for women and children that had previously been run by religious orders. During the second half of the nineteenth century, the number and types of institutions administered by the *Sociedad* increased: the Asylum for Insane Women (*Hospital Nacional de Alienadas*); the Orphan Children's Asylum; the Eye Hospital; the Children's Hospital (later renamed Ricardo Gutierrez Hospital); and the Poor Population Fund. The organization was definitively dissolved on 18 September 1947 (decree 28,752); the state assumed direct supervision of the *Sociedad*'s multiple organizations. See Guy, 'La "verdadera" historia', 338. For a comprehensive history of the *Sociedad*, see C.C. Luna. 1923. *La Sociedad de Beneficencia de la Capital: Su origen y desenvolvimiento, 1823–1923*, Buenos Aires. For specific contemporary studies on social policy and the *Sociedad*, see Thompson, *Público y Privado*; Moreno, *La Política Social*; and Mead, 'Beneficent Maternalism'. Funding for the *Sociedad* traditionally had a disproportionate component from public finances, becoming the most considerable financial source.

16. *Gotas de leche* programmes were well developed in the capital (Buenos Aires), as well as in the province of Tucumán, which developed the first official and coordinated campaign against infant mortality. However, the interior of the country lacked sufficient services to provide for the population of mothers and infants. Aráoz Alfaro denounced the deficiency of infant-maternity services in the early 1930s, even within Buenos Aires. See G. Aráoz Alfaro. 1936. *Por Nuestros Niños y por las Madres: Protección, Higiene y Asistencia Social*, Buenos Aires, 146–8. See Carolina B. and K. Ramacciotti, 'Las madres y sus hijos en foco'. Extreme regional disparities on infant mortality rates are emphasized in writings during the 1930s and persist up to the present. For indicators and information, see Aráoz Alfaro, *Por Nuestros Niños*, 161–2. For the historic evolution of infant mortality rates in Argentina, see Idiart, 'Neo-Liberal Experiments', ch. 3.

17. In writings and public addresses, Dr Aráoz Alfaro called for both a national infant-maternity law and for the creation of a national infant-maternity programme. Alfaro, 'Por Nuestros Niños', address to the Argentine Association of Pediatrics, 1933, in idem, *Por Nuestros niños*, 154–5. See also Oficina Sanitaria Panamericana, *Actas de la Décima Conferencia Sanitaria Panamericana*, Bogotá, 1939, 335, cited in Guy, 'La "verdadera" historia'; and Biernat and Ramacciotti, 'Las madres y sus hijos en foco'.

18. Mead, 'Beneficent Maternalism'.

19. Law 12,341 (known as Palacios' Law) was passed on 21 December 1936 and promulgated on 31 December 1936 (Official Bulletin, 11 January 1937). The Bureau had varying organizational hierarchies within the structure of the National Public Administration through the years.

20. Law 12,341 defined the central goals and activities of the Bureau. Among these goals were: 1) the study of infants' social hygiene; 2) development of a permanent registry of private and public institutions related to the protection of mothers and infants (institutional coordination); 3) implementation of public media campaigns to disseminate information regarding social hygiene for mothers and infants; and 4) implementation and administration of public and private institutions.

21. *Universitarias* were 'ideologically stranded with scientific discourse that alienated other maternalists, and a claim to nurture that, in the opinion of hygienists, qualified them to volunteer but not to take on paid professional roles ... the Beneficent Society remained an impregnable fortress, but one that was increasingly less central to the defense of the state'. Mead, 'Beneficent Maternalism', 138.

22. Ibid.; and Lavrin, *Women, Feminism, and Social Change*, 124.

23. In early 1960s, the PMI was under the supervision of the National Ministry of Social Assistance and Public Health. Its main goals appear to be very similar to the ones originally specified in Palacios' Law (1936), but the definition of specific goals and activities was more precise than before: coordination with provinces for the creation of PMI at the provincial levels; development of a national infant-maternity health plan; definition of goals

and priorities; opening of health centres, especially to provide treatment for diarrhoea; and collection of statistical information on newborns' health. See Ministerio de Acción Social y Salud Pública. 1966. *Política Sanitaria y Social. Argentina: Poder Ejecutivo Nacional, Buenos Aires,* Buenos Aires, 455, and Ministerio de Acción Social y Salud Pública, *Salud Pública,* 48–9.

24. S. Belmartino. 1991. 'Políticas de salud en Argentina: Perspectiva histórica', *Cuadernos Médico-Sociales,* 55, 32.

25. The Bureau was regulated by decree 5,520 (1938) and was charged with the following functions: 1) hygiene and social service (research and sanitary statistics), public campaigns, and social services; 2) inspection (monitoring) and legislation; 3) eugenics and maternity (protection of women as mothers and future mothers, involving prenatal assistance, maternity insurance, breastfeeding subsidies, etc); 4) early infancy (children younger than two and a half years); 5) 'secondary' infancy (children between two and a half and six years of age); 6) sick, abnormal and needy children; and 7) dental assistance. See S. Novick. 1993. *Mujer, Estado y Políticas Sociales,* Buenos Aires: Centro Editor de América Latina, 99.

26. For specifics on the social insurance system and the massification of privileges, see Mesa-Lago, *Social Security,* 15–16; and Idiart, 'Neo-Liberal Experiment', ch. 1.

27. Ministerio de Acción Social y Salud Pública, *Política Sanitaria y Social,* 455.

28. *Programa Nacional de la Madre y el Niño,* Law 20, 445/73; E. Moreno. 1974. 'Reportajes: El Plan Nacional de Salud Materno Infantil, interview with Dr Elsa Moreno, National Director of Infant-Maternal Health', *Administración Hospitalaria* 11(11), 8–10; and Novik, *Mujer, Estado y Políticas Sociales.*

29. For example, public health expenditures decreased from 6 to 2.5 per cent of total public expenditures between 1975 and 1983. Belmartino, 'Políticas de Salud', 23.

30. Dirección de Salud Materno Infantil, *Manual Metodológico de Capacitación del Equipo de Salud en Crecimiento y Nutrición de Madres y Niños,* Ministerio de Salud y Acción Social, 1996. The 1985 Proposal for Supplementary Feeding Norms is the only national regulation of the PMI besides the Palacios' Law (12,341) of 1936. Promotion of breastfeeding, Law 23,056/84, Regulatory Decree 908/84.

31. Moreno, *La Política Social.*

32. World Bank, *Implementation Completion Report on a Loan in The Amount of US $100 Million to the Argentine Republic for a Second Maternal and Child Health and Nutrition Project (PROMIN II),* Report No.: 36544-AR, June 2006.

33. For specific analyses on PROMIN's design, organization, effective implementation and monitoring, see Idiart, 'Neo-Liberal Experiments', ch. 5.

34. Ibid., ch. 7 and conclusion.

35. Secretaria de Hacienda, *Cuenta de Inversión,* Buenos Aires, 2000, 275.

36. World Bank, *Implementation Completion*; Dirección de Nacional de Salud Materno Infantil, *Informe de Cierre del PROMIN II,* Buenos Aires, December 2005.

37. SIEMPRO. 2000. *La situación de la infancia: Análisis de los últimos diez años,* Buenos Aires: Subsecretaria de Desarrollo Social, Ministerio de Desarrollo Social y Medio Ambiente.

38. On features of *Universitarias'* feminism, see Lavrin, *Women, Feminism, and Social Change,* 26–32; and Mead, 'Beneficent Maternalism', 135–6.

CHAPTER 13

AFTERWORD
Maternalism Today

Rebecca Jo Plant

Sociologist Ann Shola Orloff has recently argued that wealthy democracies in Western Europe, North America and the Antipodes are in the midst of a series of 'farewells to maternalism'. By this, she means that policymaking is shifting decisively away from a model in which mothers were expected to stay home and care for children toward a new model that encourages 'employment for all'. As she puts it, the 'explicitly gender-differentiated maternalist logic of politically recognizing, and financially supporting mothers' care-giving' has been losing ground to 'ostensibly gender-neutral notions' that attempt to foster independence through workplace participation. At the same time, she argues, maternalism as a political ideology is 'on the decline among advocates of women's equality'.[1] Orloff presents a compelling analysis that, in its general contours, is borne out by developments in numerous countries. But it is worth pausing here to briefly note some countervailing trends, both within and beyond the nations that she analysed.

Perhaps most striking is the rise of proposals to address growing concerns over 'depopulation' – a trend evident in nations as diverse as South Korea, Russia, Greece and Japan.[2] As women have seized new opportunities in education and employment, they have in many cases elected not to have children or to bear only one child; in other cases, they have reluctantly remained childless because of the difficulty of combining work and motherhood. Today, most wealthy nations have fertility rates well below

Notes for this chapter begin on page 248.

replacement level, leading to fears that the young will be burdened with the support of a larger, rapidly aging population.[3] The obvious solution to this problem – large-scale immigration – is highly controversial, since so many people in wealthy nations still define national identities in exclusionary ethnic and racial terms. As a result, policymakers in many countries have enacted measures designed to boost fertility among the 'right' kind of people. In Western Europe, for instance, the stigma that has adhered to explicit pronatalism since the end of World War II appears to be fading.

It remains to be seen whether this wave of pronatalism will be accompanied by renewed efforts to define all women as potential mothers or to connect women's citizenship more tightly to their reproductive capacities. But there are some disturbing signs that such classic formulations are indeed being revived. For instance, today in Russia, one can see numerous billboards that amount to pronatalist propaganda, like one with a young woman and three children that reads: 'Love for your nation starts with love for family'.[4] The Prime Minister of Turkey, Recep Ayyip Erdogan of the conservative Justice and Development Party, has become increasingly bold in voicing his belief that all Turkish women should bear at least three children.[5] Likewise, in a report aired on the radio in 2005, the Australian Treasurer Peter Costello (of the Liberal Party) urged women to do their national duty by producing three children apiece: 'If you can have children,' he stated, 'you should have one for your husband, one for your wife, and one for the country.'[6] In nations that had witnessed a decisive shift away from biologically based conceptions of female citizenship, the re-emergence of such rhetoric is jarring, to the say the least.[7]

At the same time, in certain parts of the world, women themselves continue to embrace maternalist politics to retain or acquire welfare benefits. This has been particularly notable in Eastern Europe, where, under socialism, 'feminism' became widely associated with state-backed efforts to compel women to enter the workforce. In these countries, women have often espoused maternalist arguments as a way of legitimizing their public influence and asserting their political independence. For instance, Angela Argent has shown how feminists in the newly established Czech Republic articulated a form of maternalist feminism in the 1990s as a way of legitimizing their claims to power. These women recognized the public's antipathy for the ideal of the 'superwoman' who worked full time while still performing the vast majority of housework – a model that, under state socialism, had served to legitimize the heavy burdens placed on women. Moreover, they understood that, given the special importance of the private realm during socialist times, a political language that emphasized women's private roles as mothers would resonate more strongly than an 'equal rights' discourse that had become widely discredited due to its association with the former regime. By arguing that women alone possessed the 'moral virtue and life sustaining energies' needed to regenerate society – because they alone had remained distant from state power in socialist times – Czech feminists insisted that women should play a prominent role in the emergent political order.[8]

Resistance to a more gender neutral, neo-liberal model is also evident Eastern Europe on a policy level. Indeed, according to Christy Glass and Éva Fodor, the widespread 'farewell to maternalism' that Orloff has charted is not occurring in Hungary and Poland, where policy regimes 'show marked continuity with socialist era maternalism, which supported women's extended retreat from paid work following childbirth'.[9] In her impressive study of Hungary, sociologist Lynne Haney has charted how the socialist government's maternalist policies in effect helped to create a nascent political constituency of mothers– one that mobilized in 1995–6 when the new government proposed a restructuring of the nation's comparatively generous system of maternity and family leave. Middle-class women, who opposed the shift from a universal to a needs-based system, protested outside welfare agencies in Budapest, shouting 'We are still mothers!' Subsequently, maternalist ideology proved effective in uniting conservative and liberal Hungarian women, who have joined together to protest a proposed reduction in maternity benefits from three to two years.[10]

If maternalism appeals to many Eastern Europeans who hoped to protect welfare benefits, women in the United States have in recent years invoked maternalist arguments as a way of protesting the lack of a nationwide system of paid maternity (and paternity) leave, affordable healthcare, subsidized child care and other benefits. One might even argue that, since around 2000, the U.S. has been witnessing a new wave of 'neo-maternalism'; it is no longer accurate to say, as Lisa Brush observed in 1996, that 'Maternalism is ... remarkably absent from current debates if by maternalism we mean a claim that motherhood should among other things empower women within the state and that the state should help support motherhood'.[11] Anne Crittenden advanced precisely these arguments in her surprise bestseller, *The Price of Motherhood: Why the Most Important Job in the World is Still the Least Valued*, which detailed the financial losses (she called it the 'mommy tax') that American women incur by becoming mothers. Strikingly, Crittenden even resurrected the analogy between mothering and soldiering, claiming, as did so many early twentieth-century maternalists, that mothers 'render an indispensable national service to their country' and therefore ought to be materially rewarded.[12] Australian Anne Manne made a similar splash with her book *Motherhood: How Should We Care for Our Children*.[13] Criticizing the 'neo-liberal' approach, Manne argued that policies designed to return new mothers as quickly as possible to the labour market are bad for children and many mothers as well. According to Manne, feminists who have made 'the workplace the arena of women's liberation' are out of step with the majority of parents, who overwhelmingly prefer for mothers to remain at home when children are very young.[14]

Of course, most feminists are still committed to deconstructing gender roles and de-gendering care work so that women can participate in employment and public life on equal terms with men, and many remain highly sceptical of maternalist approaches. Yet in the face of stubborn realities– the fact that women still perform the vast majority of care-giving and still, in sheer economic terms, pay a high price for doing so – some have cast aside their reservations about reviving maternalist approaches in a strategic manner. American political theorist Eileen McDonagh's recent book, *The Motherless State: Women's Political Leadership and American Democracy*, exemplifies this trend. Concerned with understanding why American women remain so badly underrepresented in government, she argues that the explanation resides in fact that the U.S. state is so 'un-motherly'. According to McDonagh, in nations that have a more robust welfare system, people tend to perceive the state in more 'maternal' terms; as a result, women are more likely to be seen as having an important role to play in governing. McDonagh anticipates the feminist objection to her argument, namely: why must 'care-giving' be associated with 'maternal' rather than 'paternal' or 'parental'? And why should women pursue a strategy that reinforces the tendency to conflate the idea of 'woman' with that of 'mother' when they have long sought to challenge such thinking? Her response, in essence, is that so long as women are still perceived as caregivers, strategies to increase their political power simply have to take such perceptions into account in order to be effective.[15]

The progressive netroots group MomsRising has apparently arrived at a similar calculation, for it deploys the cultural role of 'mom' (rather than a gender-neutral identity of parent or caregiver) to lobby for 'family-friendly' policies, such as paid maternity and paternity leaves and flexible work options. When asked why she wrote a 'Motherhood Manifesto' rather than a 'Parenthood Manifesto', one of the group's cofounders, Joan Blades, bypassed the issue of ideology and instead referred to the specific disadvantages that mothers face, especially discrimination in the workplace. Clearly, this organization has chosen to focus on 'real-life', practical problems, rather than addressing the underlying issue of how 'motherhood' is conceptualized and defined.[16]

Perhaps today's neo-maternalists feel less ambivalent about maternalist politics than an earlier generation of feminists because women have made significant headway in breaking down barriers in the public realm.

In affluent democracies, the fear of being reduced to the role of wife and mother is no longer as palpable as it is was for second-wave feminists; indeed, many working mothers, particularly in the U.S., long for more flexible work schedules that would allow them to devote more time to family life. It remains to be seen whether these initiatives are the beginning of a lasting trend that will result in significant political or cultural change. Still, it seems that caution is in order. If there is one thing that the history of maternalism tells us, it is surely that motherhood is often a precarious basis on which to stake political claims. The idea of recognizing and compensating mothers is always accompanied by a broader political agenda, and that agenda can all too easily shift from a progressive ideal of more inclusive social citizenship to a reactionary one of state-enforced gender conformity.

Notes

1. A.S. Orloff. 2006. 'From Maternalism to "Employment for All": State Policies to Promote Women's Employment across the Affluent Democracies', in J. Levy (ed.), *The State After Statism: New State Activities in the Age of Liberalization*, Cambridge, MA: Harvard University Press, 230–68. Rianne Mahon has shown how the OECD has promoted two different 'post-maternalist' paths in R. Mahon, 'The OECD and the Reconciliation Agenda: Competing Blueprints', Occasional Paper 20, Child Resource and Research Unit, July 2005. Retrieved from http://www.childcarecanada.org/pubs/op20/index.html on 25 July 2011.

2. To cite just a few examples: South Korea recently passed a law that included a raft of measures to bolster fertility rates, including financial assistance to couples undergoing IVF; Japan introduced a new child allowance without an income cap; and Russia recently enacted incentive payments for second births. C. Haub, 'Did South Korea's Population Policy Work Too Well?' Population Reference Bureau. Retrieved from http://www.prb.org/Articles/2010/koreafertility.aspx on 2 February 2011; and 'Population Decline Worsening', *Japan Times*, 15 January 2010. Retrieved on http://search.japantimes.co.jp/cgi-bin/ed20100115a2.html on 2 February 2011. For an analysis of pronatalist ideology and policies in contemporary Greece, see: H. Paxson. 2004. *Making Modern Mothers: Ethics and Family Planning in Urban Greece*, Berkeley: University of California Press. Whereas some of these measures are similar to longstanding family allowance policies in post-World War II Germany and Scandinavia, laws in these countries tended to be framed as support for children, rather than in explicitly pronatalist terms.

3. See, for example: P. Longman. 2004. *The Empty Cradle: How Falling Birthrates Threaten World Prosperity and What to Do About It*, New York: Basic Books, 2004. For a less polemical, though still somewhat alarmist analysis, see J. Grant and S. Hoorens. 2006. 'The New Pronatalism? The Policy Consequences of Population Ageing', *Public Policy Research* 13(1), 13–25.

4. 'Natural Population Decline in Russia Down by 31% in 2009', *Ria Novosti*, 2 February 2010. Retrieved from http://en.rian.ru/russia/20100216/157906438.html on 2 February 2011.

5. Erdogan appears to have first expressed this view at speech delivered, ironically enough, during a celebration of International Women's Day in 2008. His remarks have met with

criticism from numerous quarters, but he continues to call repeatedly upon Turkish women to bear three children each. 'Society Reacts to PM's Call for Couples to have 3 Kids', *Today's Zaman*, 5 September 2010. Retrieved from http://www.todayszaman.com/tz-web/detaylar.do?load=detay&link=139512 on 2 February 2011.

6. The same programme went on to quote the conservative Australian Prime Minister John Howard, who exhorted women: 'Come on, come on, your nation needs you'. F.M. Clarke, Comment, Berkshire Conference of Women Historians, June 2005.

7. In some contexts, pronatalism has long been a prominent aspect of social and political discourse. For instance, Rhoda Ann Kanaaneh discusses the ways in which some Palestinian women living in Galilee conceptualize their fecundity as a way of protesting Israeli policies toward Palestinians in R.A. Kanaaneh. 2002. *Birthing the Nation: Strategies of Palestinian Women in Israel*, Berkeley: University of California Press.

8. A. Argent. 2008. 'Hatching Feminisms: Czech Feminist Aspirations in the 1990s', *Gender and History* 20(1), 86–104.

9. C. Glass and E. Fodor. 2007. 'From Public to Private Maternalism? Gender and Welfare in Poland and Hungary after 1989', *Social Politics* 14(3), 323–50. Glass and Fodor argue that post-socialist Hungary has developed a form of 'public maternalism' in which women's maternal caregiving is supported and subsidized by the state. In contrast, Poland – where a strong labour movement and a powerful Catholic Church played a major role in shaping policy – developed a type of 'private maternalism', in which the government promoted policies that would support male breadwinners and allow women to 'return to their rightful roles as wives and mothers'. (Glass and Fodor use the term 'private maternalism' as a way of identifying the government's shift toward privileging women's roles as mothers rather than workers. It is worth noting, however, that Theda Skocpol would presumably characterize this kind of approach as 'paternalist'.) For a general overview of the ways in which post-Soviet bloc countries have reformed their welfare systems since 1989, see G. Pascall and N. Manning. 2000. 'Gender and Social Policy: Comparing Welfare States in Central and Eastern Europe and the Former Soviet Union', *Journal of European Social Policy* 10(3), 240–66.

10. L. Haney. 2002. *Inventing the Needy: Gender and Politics in Hungary*, Berkeley: University of California Press; and E. Kispeter. 2010. 'Family Policy Debates in Post-State Socialist Hungary: From Maternalism to Gender Equality', in M. Verloo and S. Walby (eds), Final WHY Report, Quality in Gender + Equality Policies, European Commission Sixth Framework Programme Integrated Project, Institut für die Wissenschaften vom Menschen. Retrieved 25 July 2011 from http://www.quing.eu/files/results/final_why_report.pdf.

11. L.D. Brush. 1996. 'Love, Toil, and Trouble: Motherhood and Feminist Politics', *Signs* 21(2), 453.

12. A. Crittenden. 2001. *The Price of Motherhood: Why the Most Important Job in the World is Still the Least Valued*, New York: Metropolitan Books, 7–9.

13. A. Manne. 2005. *Motherhood: How Should We Care for Our Children?* Crows Nest, NSW: Allen and Unwin.

14. See also idem. 2008. 'Love and Money: The Family and the Free Market', *Quarterly Essay*, 29, 1–90. Somewhat similarly, the legal scholar Joan Williams has argued that the 'full-commodification model' – based on the idea that women will enter the workforce on equal terms with men, while delegating child care to the marketplace – has not succeeded in redressing the power imbalance between men and the majority of women who become mothers. She sees the solution residing in a shift toward 'reconstructive feminism' that 'pins hopes for women's equality on a restructuring of market work and family entitlements'. Williams believes that reconstructive feminism holds the potential to revive a stagnating movement, particularly by allowing for greater coalition building with working-class women who have remained alienated from liberal feminism. J. Williams. 1999. *Unbending Gender: Why Family and Work Conflict and What to Do about It*, New York: Oxford University Press, 41. Laura T. Kessler has used the term 'legal maternalism' to describe the

views of Williams and several other feminist legal scholars in L.T. Kessler. 2002. 'Transgressive Caregiving', in M.A. Fineman, J.E. Jackson and A.P. Romero (eds), *Feminist and Queer Legal Theory: Intimate Encounters, Uncomfortable Conversations*, Surrey: Ashgate, 349–72.

15. E. McDonagh. 2009. *The Motherless State: Women's Political Leadership and American Democracy*, Chicago: University of Chicago Press.

16. J. Blades and K. Rowe-Finkbeiner. 2006. *The Motherhood Manifesto: What America's Moms Want and What to Do About It*, New York: Nation Books. For a critical assessment, see N. Mezey and C.T.L. Pillard, 'Rethinking the New Maternalism', 2010. Retrieved 2 February 2011 from http://works.bepress.com/naomi_mezey/2.

SELECT BIBLIOGRAPHY

Abel, E.K. 1998. 'Valuing Care: Turn-of-the-Century Conflicts between Charity Workers and Women Clients', *Journal of Women's History* 10(3), 32–52.

Accampo, E.A., R.G. Fuchs and M.L. Stewart (eds). 1995. *Gender and the Politics of Social Reform in France, 1870–1914*, Baltimore: Johns Hopkins University Press.

Adams, C. 2005. 'Maternal Societies in France: Private Charity before the Welfare State', *Journal of Women's History* 17(1), 87–111.

_____. 2010. *Poverty, Charity, and Motherhood: Maternal Societies in Nineteenth-Century France*, Champaign: University of Illinois Press.

Adams, Julia and Tasleem Padamsee. 2001. 'Signs and Regimes: Rereading Feminist Work on Welfare States', *Social Politics* 8(1), 1–23.

Allen, A.T. 1991. *Feminism and Motherhood in Germany, 1800–1914*, New Brunswick: Rutgers University Press.

_____. 2005. *Feminism and Motherhood in Western Europe, 1890–1970: The Maternal Dilemma*, New York: Palgrave MacMillan.

Allman, J. 1994. 'Making Mothers: Missionaries, Medical Officers, and Women's Work in Colonial Asante, 1924–45', *History Workshop Journal* 38, 23–47.

Argent. A. 2008. 'Hatching Feminisms: Czech Feminist Aspirations in the 1990s', *Gender and History* 20(1), 86–104.

Baker, P. 1984. 'The Domestication of Politics: Women and American Political Society, 1780–1920', *American Historical Review* 89(3), 620–47.

Baldwin, P. 2005. 'Beyond Weak and Strong: Rethinking the State in Comparative Policy History', *Journal of Policy History* 17(1), 12–33.

Barker, K.K. 1997. 'Federal Maternal Policy and Gender Politics: Comparative Insights', *Journal of Women's History* 9(2), 183–91.

Bergmann, E.L. (ed.). 1990. *Women, Culture and Politics in Latin America*, Los Angeles: University of California Press.

Bernstein, L. 1997. 'The Evolution of Soviet Adoption Law', *Journal of Family History* 22(2), 204–27.

_____. 2001. 'Fostering the Next Generation of Socialists: *Patronirovanie* in the Fledgling Soviet State', *Journal of Family History* 26(1), 66–90.

Bettini, M. 2008. *Stato e assistenza sociale in Italia: L'Opera Nazionale Maternità e Infanzia, 1925–1975*, Pisa: Erasmo.

'Beyond Maternalism: Special Issue.' 2000. *Social Politics: International Studies in Gender, State, and Society* 7(1).

Biernat, C. and K. Ramacciotti. 2008. 'Las madres y sus hijos en foco', in C. Barry, K. Ramacciotti and A. Valobra (eds), *La Fundación Eva Perón y las mujeres: entre la provocación y la inclusión*, Buenos Aires: Biblos, 51–76.

Blades, J. and K. Rowe-Finkbeiner. 2006. *The Motherhood Manifesto: What America's Moms Want and What to Do About It*, New York: Nation Books.

Blum, A. 2009. *Domestic Economies: Family, Work, and Welfare in Mexico City, 1884–1943*, Lincoln: University of Nebraska Press.

Blum, E. 2008. *Love Canal Revisited: Race, Class, and Gender in Environmental Activism*, Lawrence: University of Kansas Press.

Bock, G. and P. Thane (eds). 1991. *Maternity and Gender Policies: Women and the Rise of the European Welfare States, 1880s–1950s*, London and New York: Routledge.

_____. 1994. 'Poverty and Mothers' Rights in the Emerging Welfare States', in F. Thébaud (ed.), G. Duby and M. Perrot (series eds), A. Goldhammer (trans.), *A History of Women in the West: Toward a Cultural Identity in the Twentieth Century*, Cambridge, MA: Harvard University Press.

Boris, E. 1994. *Home to Work: Motherhood and the Politics of Industrial Homework in the United States*, New York: Cambridge University Press.

_____. 1993. 'What About the Working of the Working Mother?' *Journal of Women's History* 5(2), 104–7.

_____. and S.J. Kleinberg. 2003. 'Mothers and Other Workers: (Re)Conceiving Labor, Maternalism, and the State', *Journal of Women's History* 15(3), 90–117.

_____. and S. Michel. 2001. 'Social Citizenship and Women's Right to Work in Postwar America', in P. Grimshaw, K. Holmes and M. Lake (eds), *Women's Rights and Human Rights: International Historical Perspectives*, Basingstoke and New York, 199–219.

_____. 2005. 'On the Importance of Naming: Gender, Race, and the Writing of Policy History', *Journal of Policy History* 17(1), 75–92.

Bouvard, M.G. 1994. *Revolutionizing Motherhood: The Mothers of the Plaza de Mayo*. Wilmington, DE: Scholarly Resources.

Bresci, A. 1993. 'L'Opera Nazionale Maternità e Infanzia nel ventennio fascista', *Italia Contemporanea*, 192, 421–42.

Brown, E.B. 1989 'Womanist Consciousness: Maggie Lena Walker and the Independent Order of St. Luke', *Signs* 14(3), 610–33.

Browning, G.K. 1987. *Women and Politics in the USSR: Consciousness Raising and Soviet Women's Groups*, New York: Prentice Hall.

Brush, L.D. 2002. 'Changing the Subject: Gender and Welfare Regime Studies', *Social Politics* 9(2), 161–86.

_____. 2003. *Gender and Governance*, Lanham, MD: AltaMira Press.

_____. 1996. 'Love, Toil, and Trouble: Motherhood and Feminist Politics', *Signs* 21(2), 429–55.

_____. 1997. 'Worthy Widows, Welfare Cheats: Proper Womanhood in Expert Needs Talk about Single Mothers in the United States, 1900 to 1998', *Gender and Society* 11(6), 720–46.

Bryder, L. 2003. *A Voice for Mothers: The Plunket Society and Infant Welfare, 1907–2000*, Auckland: Auckland University Press.

Buck, S.A. 2002. 'Activists and Mothers: Feminist and Maternalist Politics in Mexico, 1923–1953', Ph.D. diss., Rutgers University.

_____. 2008. 'Constructing a Historiography of Mexican Women and Gender', *Gender and History* 20(1), 152–60.

Buckley, M. 2000. 'The Soviet "Wife-Activist" down on the Farm', *Social History* 26(3), 282–98.

_____. 1996. 'Untold Story of *Obshchestvennitsa* in the 1930s', *Europe-Asia Studies* 48(4), 569–86.

Burton, A.M. 1994. *Burdens of History: British Feminists, Indian Women, and Imperial Culture*, Chapel Hill: University of North Carolina Press.

_____. 1990. 'The White Woman's Burden: British Feminists and the Indian Woman, 1865–1915', *Women's Studies International Forum* 13(12), 295–308.

Burton, R.D.E. 1993. 'Maman-France Doudo: Family Images in French Colonial Discourse', *Diacritics* 23(3), 69–90.

Bussemaker, J. and R. Voet (eds). 1998. *Gender, Participation and Citizenship in the Netherlands*, Brookfield, Hampshire: Ashgate.

Buttafuoco, A. 1990. *Le origini della Cassa Nazionale di Maternità*, Arezzo: Dipartimento di Studi storico-sociali e filosofici.

_____. 1997. *Questioni di cittadinanza: Donne e diritti sociali nell'italia liberale*, Siena: Protagon.

Campbell, L. 2009. *Respectable Citizens: Gender, Family, and Unemployment in Ontario's Great Depression*, Toronto: University of Toronto Press.

Christie, N. 2000. *Engendering the State: Family, Work and Welfare in Canada*, Toronto: University of Toronto Press.

Chunn, D. 1992. *From Punishment to Doing Good: Family Courts and Socialized Justice in Ontario, 1880–1940*, Toronto: University of Toronto Press.

Clark, L.L. 2000. 'Feminist Maternalists and the French State: Two Inspectresses-General in the pre-World War I Third Republic', *Journal of Women's History* 12(1), 32–61.

Cohen, D. 2001. *The War Come Home: Disabled Veterans in Britain and Germany, 1914–1939*, Berkeley: University of California Press.

Cooper, N. J. 2008. 'Gendering the Colonial Enterprise: La Mère-Patrie and Maternalism in France and French Indochina', in H. Fischer-Tiné and S. Gehrmann (eds), *Empires and Boundaries: Rethinking Race, Class, and Gender in Colonial Settings*, New York: Routledge, 129–45.

Costa, M. and S. James. 1975. *The Power of Women and the Subversion of the Community*, Bristol: Wages for Housework.

Cott, N.F. 1987. *The Grounding of Modern Feminism*, New Haven: Yale University Press.

Cova, A. 1997. *Maternité et droits de femmes en France (XIX–XX siècle)*, Paris: Anthropos.

Cox, R.H. 1993. *The Development of the Dutch Welfare State: From Workers' Insurance to Universal Entitlement*, Pittsburgh and London: University of Pittsburgh Press.

Crittenden, A. 2001. *The Price of Motherhood: Why the Most Important Job in the World is Still the Least Valued*, New York: Metropolitan Books.

Cruikshank, B. 1999. *The Will to Empower: Democratic Citizens and Other Subjects*, Ithaca, NY: Cornell University Press.

Curry, L. 1999. *Modern Mothers in the Heartland: Gender, Health and Progress in Illinois, 1990–1930*, Columbus: Ohio State University Press.

Davin, A. 1978. 'Imperialism and Motherhood', *History Workshop Journal* 5(1), 9–66.

De Alwis, M. 2001. 'Ambivalent Maternalisms: Cursing as Public Protest in Sri Lanka', in M. Turshen, S. Meintjes and A. Pillay (eds), *The Aftermath: Women in Post-war Reconstruction*, London: Zed Books, 210–24.

De Grand, A.J. 1976. 'Women under Italian Fascism', *Historical Journal* 19(4), 947–68.

De Grazia, V. 1992. *How Fascism Ruled Women: Italy, 1922–1945*, Los Angeles: University of California Press.

de Swaan, A. 1988. *In Care of the State: Health Care, Education and Welfare in Europe and the USA in the Modern Era*, New York: Oxford University Press.

Deane, T. 1996. 'Late Nineteenth-Century Philanthropy: The Case of Louisa Twining', in A. Digby and J. Stewart (eds), *Gender, Health and Welfare*, London and New York: Routledge, 122–42.

Dittrich-Johansen, H. 2002. 'Per la Patria e per il Duce: Storie di fedeltà femminili nell'Italia fascista', *Genesis* 1(1), 125–56.

Dore, E. (ed.). 1997. *Gender Politics in Latin America: Debates in Theory and Practice*, New York: Monthly Review Press.

Erickson, C.K. 2004. '"So Much for Men": Conservative Women and National Defense in the 1920 and 1930s', *American Studies* 45(1), 85–102.

Esping-Andersen, G. 1990. *The Three Worlds of Welfare Capitalism*, Princeton: Princeton University Press.

_____. 1999. *Social Foundations of Postindustrial Economies*, Oxford: Oxford University Press.

Evans, P.M. and G.R. Wekerle (eds). 1997. *Women and the Canadian Welfare State: Challenges and Change*, Toronto: University of Toronto Press.

Feldstein, R. 2000. *Motherhood in Black and White: Race and Sex in American Liberalism, 1930–1965*, New York: Cornell University Press.

Frader, L. 2008. *Breadwinners and Citizens: Gender in the Making of the French Social Model*, Durham, NC: Duke University Press.

Fraser, N. 1997. *Justice Interruptus: Critical Reflections on the 'Postsocialist' Condition*, New York: Routledge.

_____. and L. Gordon. 1992. 'Contract vs. Charity: Why Is There No Social Citizenship in the United States?' *Socialist Review* 22(3), 52–6.

Fuchs, R. 1990. *Poor and Pregnant in Paris: Strategies for Survival in the Nineteenth Century*, New Brunswick: Rutgers University Press.

Glass, C. and E. Fodor. 2007. 'From Public to Private Maternalism? Gender and Welfare in Poland and Hungary after 1989', *Social Politics* 14(3), 323–50.

Goldman, W.Z. 1993. *Women, the State, and Revolution: Soviet Family Policy and Social Life, 1917–1936*, Cambridge: Cambridge University Press.

_____. 2002. *Women at the Gates: Gender and Industry in Stalin's Russia*, Cambridge: Cambridge University Press.

González, V. and K. Kampwirth (eds). 2001. *Radical Women in Latin America: Left and Right*, University Park: Penn State University Press.

Goodwin, J.L. 1992. 'An American Experiment in Paid Motherhood: The Implementation of Mothers' Pensions in Early Twentieth-Century Chicago', *Gender and History* 4(3), 323–42.

_____. 1997. *Gender and the Politics of Welfare Reform: Mothers' Pensions in Chicago, 1911–1929*, Chicago: University of Chicago Press.

Gordon, L. 1991. 'Black and White Visions of Welfare: Women's Welfare Activism, 1890–1945', *Journal of American History* 78(2), 559–90.

_____. 1993. 'Gender, State and Society: A Debate with Theda Skocpol', *Contention*, 2(3), 113–57.

_____. 2002. *Heroes of their Own Lives: The Politics and History of Family Violence*, Chicago: University of Illinois Press.

_____. 1994. *Pitied But Not Entitled: Single Mothers and the History of Welfare, 1890–1935*, New York: Free Press.

_____. 1992. 'Social Insurance and Public Assistance: The Influence of Gender in Welfare Thought in the United States, 1890-1935', *American Historical Review* 97(1), 19–54.

_____. 1988. 'What Does Welfare Regulate?' *Social Research* 55(4), 609–30.

_____. (ed.). 1990. *Women, the State, and Welfare*, Madison: University of Wisconsin Press.

Gouda, F. 1995. *Poverty and Political Culture: The Rhetoric of Social Welfare in the Netherlands, 1815–1954*, Boston: Rowman and Littlefield.

Guest, D. 1985. *The Emergence of Social Security in Canada*, Vancouver: University of British Columbia Press.

Guy, D.J. 1998. 'The Pan American Child Congresses, 1916 to 1942: Pan American-ism, Child Reform, and the Welfare State in Latin America', *Journal of Family and History* 23(3), 272–92.

_____. 1998. 'The Politics of Pan-American Cooperation: Maternalist Feminism and the Child Rights Movement, 1913–1960', *Gender and History* 10(3), 449–69.

_____. 2000. 'La "verdadera" historia de la Sociedad de Beneficencia', in J.L. Moreno (ed.), *La política social antes de la política social*, Buenos Aires: Trama Editorial/ Prometeo Libros, 321–41.

_____. 2000. *White Slavery and Mothers Alive and Dead: The Troubled Meeting of Sex, Gender, Public Health and Progress in Latin America*, Lincoln: University of Nebraska Press.

Hagemann, G. (ed.). 2007. *Reciprocity and Redistribution: Work and Welfare Recon-sidered*, Pisa: Pisa University Press.

Hagemann, K., S. Michel and G. Budde (eds). 2008. *Civil Society and Gender Jus-tice: Historical and Comparative Perspectives*, Oxford and New York: Berghahn Books.

Hahner, J. 1990. *Emancipating the Female Sex: The Struggle for Women's Rights in Brazil, 1850–1940*, Durham, NC: Duke University Press.

Haney, L. and L. Pollard (eds). 2003. *Families of a New World: Gender, Politics, and State Development in a Global Context*, New York: Routledge.

Haney, L. 2002. *Inventing the Needy: Gender and the Politics of Welfare in Hungary*, Berkeley: University of California Press.

Heineman, E. 2001. 'Whose Mothers?: Generational Difference, War, and the Nazi Cult of Motherhood', *Journal of Women's History* 12(4), 139–64.

Hering, S. and B. Waaldijk (eds). 2003. *History of Social Work in Europe (1900–1960): Female Pioneers and Their Influence on the Development of International Social Organizations*, Opladen: Leske + Budrich.

Hickel, W. 2000. 'War, Region, and Social Welfare: Federal Aid to Servicemen's Depend-ents in the South, 1917–1921', *Journal of American History* 87(4), 1363–91.

Higginbotham, E.B. 1993. *Righteous Discontent: The Women's Movement in the Black Baptist Church, 1880–1920*, Cambridge, MA: Harvard University Press.

Hodges, S. 2008. *Conception, Colonialism, and Commerce: Birth Control in South India, 1920–1940*, Hampshire: Ashgate.

Hoffmann, D.L. 2000. 'Mothers in the Motherland: Stalinist Pronatalism in its Pan-European Context', *Journal of Social History* 34(1), 35–54.

Howard, I. 1988. 'The Mothers' Council of Vancouver: Holding the Fort for the Unemployed, 1935–38', *BC Studies* 69–70, 249–87.

Howe, S.E. 2006. 'The *Madres de la Plaza de Mayo*: Asserting Motherhood; Rejecting Feminism?' *Journal of International Women's Studies* 7(3), 43–50.

Idiart, A. 'Neo-Liberal Experiments, State Reform, and Social Policy in the 1980s and the 1990s: The Cases of Argentina and Chile', Ph.D. Diss., Emory University, 2002.

Jacobs, M.D. 2009. *White Mother to a Dark Race: Settler Colonialism, Maternalism, and the Removal of Indigenous Children in the American West and Australia, 1880–1940*, Lincoln: University of Nebraska Press.

Kanaaneh, R.A. 2002. *Birthing the Nation: Strategies of Palestinian Women in Israel*, Berkeley: University of California Press.

Kashani-Sabet, K. 2011. *Conceiving Citizens: Women and the Politics of Motherhood in Iran*, New York.

_____. 2006. 'The Politics of Reproduction: Maternalism and Women's Hygiene in Iran, 1896-1941', *International Journal of Middle Eastern Studies* 38(1), 1–29.

Kealey, L. (ed.). 1979. *A Not Unreasonable Claim: Women and Reform in Canada, 1880s–1920s*, Toronto: The Women's Press.

Kenney, A.R. 1984 *Women's Suffrage and Social Policy in Third Republic France*, Princeton: Princeton University Press.

Kessler-Harris, A. 1995. 'Designing Women and Old Fools: The Construction of the Social Security Amendments of 1939', in L.K. Kerber, A. Kessler-Harris and K.K. Sklar (eds), *U.S. History as Women's History*, Chapel Hill: University of North Carolina Press, 87–106.

_____. 1999. 'In the Nation's Image: The Gendered Limits of Social Citizenship in the Depression Era', *Journal of American History* 86(3), 1251–80.

_____. 2001. *In Pursuit of Equity: Women, Men, and the Quest for Economic Citizenship in 20th-Century America*, New York: Oxford University Press.

King, L. 1998. 'France Needs Children: Pronatalism, Nationalism and Women's Equity', *Sociological Quarterly* 39(1), 33–52.

Kispeter, E. 2010. 'Family Policy Debates in Post-State Socialist Hungary: From Maternalism to Gender Equality', in M. Verloo and S. Walby (eds), Final WHY Report, Quality in Gender + Equality Policies, European Commission Sixth Framework Programme Integrated Project, Institut für die Wissenschaften vom Menschen. Retrieved 25 July 2011 from http://www.quing.eu/files/results/final_why_report.pdf.

Klaus, A. 1993. *Every Child a Lion: The Origins of Maternal and Infant Health Policy in the U.S. and France, 1890–1920*, Ithaca, NY: Cornell University Press.

Kligman, G. 1992. 'The Politics of Reproduction in Ceausescu's Romania: A Case Study in Political Culture', *East European Politics and Societies* 6(3), 364–418.

Knijn, T. and M. Kremer. 1997. 'Gender and the Caring Dimension of Welfare States: Toward Inclusive Citizenship', *Social Politics* 4(3), 328–61.

Knotter, A., B. Altena and D. Damsma (eds). 1997. *Labour, Social Policy and the Welfare State*, Amsterdam: Aksant Academic Publishers.

Kornbluh, F.A. 1996. 'The New Literature on Gender and the Welfare State: The U.S. Case', *Feminist Studies* 22(1), 171–97.

Koven, S. 1994. 'Remembering and Dismemberment: Crippled Children, Wounded Soldiers, and the Great War in Great Britain', *American Historical Review* 99(4), 1167–202.

Koven, S. and S. Michel (eds). 1993. *Mothers of a New World: Maternalist Politics and the Origins of Welfare States*, New York and London: Routledge.

_____. 1990. 'Womanly Duties: Maternalist Politics and the Origins of the Welfare States in France, Germany, Great Britain, and the United States, 1880–1920', *American Historical Review* 95(4), 1076–108.

Ladd-Taylor, M. 1994. *Mother-Work: Women, Child Welfare and the State, 1880–1930*, Urbana: University of Illinois Press.

_____. and L. Umansky (eds). 1998. *'Bad' Mothers: The Politics of Blame in Twentieth-Century America*, New York: New York University Press.

Lapidus, G.W. 1978. *Women in Soviet Society: Equality, Development, and Social Change*, Berkeley: University of California Press.

Larsen, Eirinn. 1997. 'The American Introduction of "Maternalism" as a Historical Concept', *Nordic Journal of Feminist and Gender Research* 5(1), 14–25.

_____. 1996. 'Gender and the Welfare State: Maternalism – a New Historical Concept?' University of Bergen, Norway, http://www.ub.uib.no/elpub/1996/h/506002/eirinn/eirinn.html.

Lavrin, A. 1995. *Women, Feminism, and Social Change in Argentina, Chile, and Uruguay, 1890–1940*, Lincoln: University of Nebraska Press.

Lemons, J.S. 1973. *The Woman Citizen: Social Feminism in the 1920s*, Urbana: University of Illinois Press.

Lewis, J. 1992. 'Gender and the Development of Welfare Regimes', *Journal of European Social Policy* 2(3), 159–73.

_____. 1994. 'Gender, the Family and Women's Agency in the Building of "Welfare States": The British Case', *Social History* 19(1), 37–56.

_____. 1994. 'Women's Agency, Maternalism, and Welfare', *Gender and History* 6(1), 117–23.

Lindenmeyr, A. 1993. 'Public Life, Private Virtues: Women in Russian Charity, 1762–1914', *Signs* 18(3), 562–91.

Lister, R., F. Williams, A. Anttonen, J. Bussemaker, U. Gerhard, J. Heinen, S. Johansson, A. Leira, B. Siim and C. Tobio, with A. Gavanas. 2007. *Gender Citizenship in Western Europe: New Challenges for Citizenship Research in a Cross-National Context*, Bristol: Policy Press.

Little, M. 1999. 'The Limits of Canadian Democracy: The Citizenship Rights of Poor Women', *Canadian Review of Social Policy* 43, 59–76.

_____. 1998. *'No Car, No Radio, No Liquor Permit': The Moral Regulation of Single Mothers in Ontario, 1920–1997*, Toronto and New York: Oxford University Press.

Lobato, M. 2000. 'Entre la protección y la exclusión: Discurso maternal y protección de la mujer obrera argentina 1890–1934', in J. Suriano (ed.), *La Cuestión Social en la Argentina, 1870–1943*, Buenos Aires: La Colmena.

Lovett, L. 2000. 'Land Reclamation as Family Reclamation: The Family Ideal in George Maxwell's Reclamation and Resettlement Campaign', *Social Politics* 7(1), 80–100.

Luna, L.G. 2003. 'Los movimientos de mujeres en América Latina y la renovación de la historia política', Centro de Estudios de Género Mujer y Sociedad, Universidad del Valle, La Manzana de la Discordia, Cali, Colombia.

Lutkehaus, N.C. 1999. 'Missionary Maternalism: Gendered Images of the Holy Spirit Sisters in Colonial New Guinea', in M.T. Huber and N.C. Lutkehaus (eds), *Gendered Missions: Women and Men in Missionary Discourse and Practice*, Ann Arbor: University of Michigan Press.

Macias, A. 1982. *Against All Odds: The Feminist Movement in Mexico to 1940*, Westport, CT: Greenwood.

Mahon, R. 2002. 'Child Care: Toward What Kind of Social Europe?' *Social Politics* 3(9), 343–79.

_____. 2005. 'The OECD and the Reconciliation Agenda: Competing Blueprints', Occasional Paper 20, Child Resource and Research Unit, July. Retrieved from http://www.childcarecanada.org/pubs/op20/index.html on 25 July 2011.

Manne, A. 2008. 'Love and Money: The Family and the Free Market', *Quarterly Essay* 29, 1–90.

_____. 2005. *Motherhood: How Should We Care for Our Children?* Crows Nest, NSW: Allen and Unwin.

May, M. 1985. 'Bread Before Roses: American Workingmen, Labor Unions and the Family Wage', in R. Milkman (ed.), *Women, Work and Protest: A Century of U.S. Women's Labor History*, London and New York: Routledge, 1–21.

Marshall, T.H. 1992 (orig. 1950). *Citizenship and Social Class*, London: Verso, 1992.

McDonagh, E. 2009. *The Motherless State: Women's Political Leadership and American Democracy*, Chicago: University of Chicago Press.

Mead, K. 2000. 'Beneficent Maternalism: Argentine Motherhood in Comparative Perspective, 1880–1920', *Journal of Women's History* 12(3), 120–45.

Meagher, S.M. and P. DiQuinzio (eds). 2005. *Women and Children First: Feminism, Rhetoric, and Public Policy*, Albany: State University of New York Press.

Mezey, N. and C.T.L. Pillard. 2010. 'Rethinking the New Maternalism', http://works.bepress.com/naomi_mezey/2.

Michaels, P.A. 2001. 'Motherhood, Patriotism, and Ethnicity: Soviet Kazakhstan and the 1936 Abortion Ban', *Feminist Studies* 27(2), 307–33.

Michel, S. 2000. *Children's Interests/Mothers' Rights: The Shaping of America's Child Care Policy*, New Haven: Yale University Press.

_____. 2000. 'Claiming the Right to Care', in M.H. Meyer (ed.), *Care Work: Gender, Labor, and the Welfare State*, New York: Routledge, 37–44.

_____. and Rianne Mahon (eds). 2002. *Child Care Policy at the Crossroads: Gender and Welfare State Restructuring*, New York: Routledge.

_____. and R. Rosen. 1992. 'The Paradox of Maternalism: Elizabeth Lowell Putnam and the American Welfare State', *Gender and History* 3(4), 364–86.

Minesso, M. 2007. *Stato e infanzia nell'Italia Contemporanea: Origini, sviluppo e fine dell'ONMI, 1925–1975*, Bologna: Il Mulino.

Mink, G. 1995. *The Wages of Motherhood: Inequality in the Welfare State, 1917–1942*, Ithaca, NY: Cornell University Press.

Monnanni, M. 2005. *Per la protezione della stirpe: Il fascismo e l'Opera Nazionale Maternità e Infanzia*, Rome: Sallustiana.

Muncy, R. 1991. *Creating a Dominion in American Female Reform, 1890–1935*, New York: Oxford University Press.

_____. 2000. 'The Citizenship of Mothers in the United States', *Journal of Women's History* 11(4), 157–65.

Nari, M. 2000. 'El Feminismo frente a la cuestion de la mujer en los primeras decadas del siglo XX', in J. Suriano (ed.), *La Cuestión Social en la Argentina, 1870–1943*, Buenos Aires: La Colmena.

_____. 2004. *Políticas de la maternidad y maternalismo político: Buenos Aires 1890–1940*, Buenos Aires: Biblos.

Neary, R.B. 1999. 'Mothering Socialist Society: The Wife-Activists' Movement and the Soviet Culture of Daily Life, 1934–41', *Russian Review* 58(3), 396–412.

Nord, P. 1994. 'The Welfare State in France, 1870–1914', *French Historical Studies* 18(3), 821–38.

O'Connor, J.S., A.S. Orloff and S. Shaver. 1999. *States, Markets, Families: Gender, Liberalism, and Social Policy in Australia, Canada, Great Britain and the United States*, Cambridge: Cambridge University Press.

Offen, K. 1998 'Defining Feminism: A Comparative Historical Approach', *Signs* 14(1), 119–57.

_____. 2000. 'Feminism, Anti-feminism and National Family Politics in Third Republic France', in M.J. Boxer and J.H. Quartaert (eds), *Connecting Spheres: European Women in a Globalizing World*, Oxford: Oxford University Press.

_____. 1984. 'Depopulation, Nationalism and Feminism in Fin-de-Siècle France', *American Historical Review* 89 (3), 648–76.

J. Olcott. 2011. "Introduction: Researching and Rethinking the Labors of Love', *Hispanic American Historical Review* 91(1), 1–27.

_____. 2005. *Revolutionary Women in Postrevolutionary Mexico*, Durham, NC: Duke University Press.

_____. 2002. '"Worthy Wives and Mothers": State-Sponsored Women's Organizing in Postrevolutionary Mexico', *Journal of Women's History* 13(4), 106–31.

Orleck, A.S. 1993. '"We are that Mythical Thing Called the Public": Militant Housewives During the Great Depression', *Feminist Studies* 19(1), 147–72.

Orloff, A.S. 2006. 'From Maternalism to "Employment for All": State Policies to Promote Women's Employment across the Affluent Democracies', in J. Levy (ed.), *The State After Statism: New State Activities in the Age of Liberalization*, Cambridge, MA: Harvard University Press, 230–68.

_____. 1991. 'Gender in Early U.S. Social Policy', *Journal of Policy History* 3(3), 249–82.

Otovo, O.T. 2009. '"To Form a Strong and Populous Nation": Race, Motherhood, and the State in Republican Brazil', Ph.D. diss., Georgetown University.

Pascall, G. and N. Manning. 2000. 'Gender and Social Policy: Comparing Welfare States in Central and Eastern Europe and the Former Soviet Union', *Journal of European Social Policy* 10(3), 240–66.

Paxson, H. 2004. *Making Modern Mothers: Ethics and Family Planning in Urban Greece*, Berkeley: University of California Press.

Pedersen, S. 2004. *Eleanor Rathbone and the Politics of Conscience*, New Haven: Yale University Press.

_____. 1993. *Family, Dependence, and the Origins of the Welfare State: Britain and France, 1914–1945*, Cambridge: Cambridge University Press.

_____. 1990. 'Gender, Welfare and Citizenship in Britain during the Great War', *American Historical Review* 95(4), 983–1006.

_____. 2001. 'The Maternalist Moment in British Colonial Policy: The Controversy of "Child Slavery" in Hong Kong', *Past and Present* 171(1), 161–202.

_____. 1991. 'Natural Body, Unspeakable Acts: The Sexual Politics of Colonial Policy Making', *Journal of Modern History* 63(4), 647–80.

Pederson, J.E. 2003. *Legislating the French Family: Feminism, Theater, and Republican Politics, 1870–1920*, New Brunswick: Rutgers University Press.

Pickering-Iazzi, R. (ed.). 1995. *Mothers of Invention: Women, Italian Fascism, and Culture*, Minneapolis: University of Minnesota Press.

Pierson, P. 1994. *Dismantling the Welfare State? Reagan, Thatcher and the Politics of Retrenchment*, Cambridge: Cambridge University Press.

Pierson, R.R. 1990. 'Gender and the Unemployment Insurance Debates in Canada, 1934–1940', *Labour/Le Travail* 25, 77–103

Pine, L. 1997. *Nazi Family Policy 1933–1945*, New York, Berg.

Pollard, L. 2005. *Nurturing the Nation: The Family and Politics of Modernizing, Colonizing and Liberating Egypt, 1805–1923*, Berkeley: University of California Press.

Quine, M.S. 2002. *Italy's Social Revolution: Charity and Welfare from Liberalism to Fascism*, Houndmills: Palgrave.

_____. 1996. *Population Politics in Twentieth-Century Europe: Fascist Dictatorships and Liberal Democracies*, London: Routledge.

Rakowski, C.A. 2003. 'Women as Political Actors: The Move from Maternalism to Citizenship Rights and Power', *Latin American Research Review* 38(2), 180–94.

Ramusack, B.N. 1990. 'Cultural Missionaries, Maternal Imperialists, Feminist Allies: British Women Activists in India, 1865–1945', *Women's Studies International Forum* 13(12), 295–308.

Razavi, S. 2008. 'Maternalist Politics in Norway and the Islamic Republic of Iran', in N. Kabeer and A. Stark, with E. Magnus (eds), *Global Perspectives on Gender Equality: Reversing the Gaze*, Oxford: Routledge, 64–86.

Rosemblatt, K.A. 2000. *Gendered Compromises: Political Cultures and the State in Chile, 1920–1950*, Chapel Hill: University of North Carolina Press.

Ross, E. 1995. 'New Thoughts on "the Oldest Vocation": Mothers and Motherhood in Recent Feminist Scholarship', *Signs* 20(2), 397–413.

Rossi-Doria, A. 1995. 'Maternità e cittadinanza femminile', *Passato e presente* 13(34), 171–7.

Rothbart, R. 1989. '"Homes are What Any Strike is About": Immigrant Labor and the Family Wage', *Journal of Social History* 23(2), 267–84.

Sainsbury, D. 2001. 'Gender and the Making of Welfare States: Norway and Sweden', *Social Politics* 8(1), 113–43.

Sangster, J. 1989. *Dreams of Equality: Women on the Canadian Left, 1920–1950*, Toronto: McClelland and Stewart.

Scharp, P. 1999. 'Maternidade: uma visão política' in S. Auad, *Mulher: cinco séculos de desenvolvimento na América*, Belo Horizonte: Federação Internacional de Mulheres da Carreira Jurídica.

Schell, P. 1999. '"An Honorable Avocation for Ladies": The Work of the Mexico City *Unión de Damas*, 1912–1926', *Journal of Women's History* 10(4), 78–103.

Schrand, T.G. 1999. 'Soviet "Civic-Minded Women" in the 1930s: Gender, Class, and Industrialization in a Socialist Society', *Journal of Women's History* 11(3), 126–50.

Siim, B. 2000. *Gender and Citizenship: Politics and Agency in France, Britain and Denmark*, Cambridge: Cambridge University Press.

Siegelbaum, L.H. 1998. '"Dear Comrade, You Ask What We Need": Socialist Paternalism and Soviet Rural "Notables" in the Mid-1930s', *Slavic Review* 57(1), 107–32.

Sklar, K.K. 1995. *Florence Kelley and the Nation's Work: The Rise of Women's Political Culture, 1830–1930*, New Haven: Yale University Press.

——, A. Schüler and S. Strasser (eds). 1998. *Social Justice Feminists in the United States and Germany: A Dialogue in Documents, 1885–1933*, Ithaca, NY: Cornell University Press.

Skocpol, T. 1992. *Protecting Soldiers and Mothers: The Political Origins of Social Policy in the United States*. Cambridge, MA: Harvard University Press.

——. 1993. 'Soldiers, Workers and Mothers: Gendered Identities in Early U.S. Social Policy', *Contention* 2(3), 157–83.

Stadum, B.A. 1992. *Poor Women and Their Families: Hard Working Charity Cases, 1900–1930*, Albany: State University of New York Press.

Stewart, M.L. 1983. 'Protecting Infants: The French Campaign for Maternity Leaves, 1890–1913', *French Historical Studies* 13, 79–105.

——. 1989. *Women, Work and the French State: Labour Protection and Social Patriarchy, 1879–1919*, Ontario: McGill Queen's University Press.

Stites, R. 1978. *The Women's Liberation Movement in Russia: Feminism, Nihilism, and Bolshevism, 1860–1930*, Princeton: University of Princeton Press.

Storrs, L.R.Y. 1998. 'Gender and the Development of the Regulatory State: The Controversy over Restricting Women's Night Work in the Depression-Era South', *Journal of Policy History* 10(2), 179–206.

Strong-Boag, V. 1979–80. 'Wages for Housework: Mothers' Allowance and the Beginning of Social Security in Canada', *Journal of Canadian Studies* 14(1), 24–34.

——. M. Gleason, A. Perry and M.L. Gleason (eds). 2002. *Rethinking Canada: The Promise of Women's History*, 4th edn, Toronto: Oxford University Press.

Struthers, J. 1994. *The Limits of Affluence: Welfare in Ontario, 1920–1970*, Toronto: University of Toronto Press.

——. 1983. *No Fault of Their Own: Unemployment and the Canadian Welfare State, 1914–41*, Toronto: University of Toronto Press.

Swerdlow, A. 1993. *Women Strike for Peace: Traditional Motherhood and Radical Politics in the 1960s*, Chicago: University of Chicago Press.

Thomson, R.G. 1996. 'Benevolent Maternalism and Physically Disabled Figures: Dilemmas of Female Embodiment in Stowe, Davis and Phelps', *American Literature* 68(3), 555–86.

Toupin, L. 1996. 'Des "usages" de la maternité en histoire féminisme', *Recherches féminists* 9(2), 113–35.

Valverde, M. 1992. '"When the Mother of the Race is Free": Race, Reproduction, and Sexuality in First-Wave Feminism', in F. Iacovetta and M. Valverde (eds), *Gender Conflicts: New Essays in Women's History*, Toronto: University of Toronto Press.

van der Klein, M. 2003. 'The Widows of the Gasworks: Gendered Path Dependency and the Early Dutch Welfare State', *Social Politics* 10(1), 1–25.

van Drenth, A. and F. de Haan. 1999. *The Rise of Caring Power: Elizabeth Fry and Josephine Butler in Britain and the Netherlands*, Amsterdam: Amsterdam University Press.

Verdery, K. 1996. *What Was Socialism, and What Comes Next?* Princeton: Princeton University Press.

Vezzosi, E. 2002. *Madri e stato: Politiche sociali negli Stati Uniti del Novecento*, Rome: Carocci.

Waaldijk, B. 1996. *Het Amerika der Vrouw: Sekse en geschiedenis van maatschappelijk werk in Nederland en de Verenigde Staten*, Groningen: Wolters-Noordhoff.

Wall, R. and J. Winter (eds). 1988. *The Upheaval of War: Family, Work and Welfare in Europe, 1914–18*, Cambridge: Cambridge University Press.

Waters, E. 1992. 'The Modernization of Russian Motherhood, 1917–1937', *Soviet Studies* 44(1), 123–35.

Weiner, L.Y. 1994. 'Reconstructing Motherhood: The La Leche League in Postwar America', *Journal of American History* 80(4), 1357–81.

_____. A.T. Allen, E. Boris, M. Ladd-Taylor, A. Lindenmeyr and K.S. Uno. 1993. 'Maternalism as Paradigm: Defining the Issues', *Journal of Women's History* 5(2), 96–130.

Wilkinson, P. 1999. 'The Selfless and the Helpless: Maternalist Origins of the U.S. Welfare State', *Feminist Studies* 25(3), 571–97.

Williams, J. 1999. *Unbending Gender: Why Family and Work Conflict and What to Do about It*, New York: Oxford University Press.

Willson, P.R. 1996. 'Flowers for the Doctor: Pro-natalism and Abortion in Fascist Milan', *Modern Italy* 1(2), 44–62.

Wood, E. 1997. *The Baba and the Comrade: Gender and Politics in Revolutionary Russia*, Bloomington: University of Indiana Press.

Woodroofe, K. 1962. *From Charity Organization to Social Work in England and the United States*, London: Routledge and Kegan Paul.

Zeiger, S. 1996. 'She Didn't Raise Her Boy to Be a Slacker: Motherhood, Conscription, and the Culture of the First World War', *Feminist Studies* 22(1), 6–39.

Notes on Contributors

Lara Campbell is an Associate Professor in the Department of Gender, Sexuality and Women's Studies at Simon Fraser University in Vancouver, British Columbia, Canada. Her book *Respectable Citizens: Gender, Family, and Unemployment in Ontario's Great Depression* (University of Toronto Press, 2009) received an Honourable Mention for the prestigious Sir John A. Macdonald Prize. She is currently working on a book about women, gender and Vietnam War resisters in Canada.

Alma Idiart graduated from the University of Buenos Aires, Argentina, and completed her M.A. and Ph.D. in Sociology at Emory University. She works in the area of Political Sociology, Public Policy and Comparative Social Policy. She is an Assistant Researcher at the National Research Council (CONICET), Gino Germani Institute (IIGG/UBA) in Argentina. She has been a Visiting Professor in the Sociology Department and the Huber Program of Global Health at Emory University and in the Department of Government at Georgetown University. From 2003 to 2007, she served as Assistant Professor and the Academic Coordinator for the Policy and Development Management Program for Georgetown University/National University of San Martin in Buenos Aires. Currently, she works on comparative historical and contemporary studies of maternal and child health and nutrition programmes.

Marian van der Klein organized the workshop upon which this volume is based at the International Institute for Social History. She holds a Ph.D. in Social Sciences (Amsterdam University, 2005) and an M.A. in Social and Economic History (Utrecht University, 1989). Her main research interests are gender, social history and welfare states, especially the impact of social policy on the socio-economic position of women. Her dissertation, 'Risks of Labor, Women and Social Insurance, 1890–1940', explores the Dutch case in an international context. At present she is senior researcher at the Verwey-Jonker Institute.

Sonya Michel is co-editor, with Seth Koven, of *Mothers of a New World: Maternalist Politics and the Origins of Welfare States* (Routledge, 1993) and author of numerous books and articles on women and social policy, including *Children's Interests/Mothers' Rights: The Shaping of America's Child Care Policy* (Yale, 1999). She is a founding co-editor of the journal *Social Politics: International Studies in Gender, State, and Society* and is now completing a study entitled *Old Age Insecurity: Inequality and Instability in U.S. Retirement Provision, 1945 to the Present*. She has been Director of United States Studies for the Woodrow Wilson International Center for Scholars in Washington, D.C. She is currently Professor of History at the University of Maryland, College Park, where she has also served as Director of the Nathan and Jeanette Miller Centre for Historical Studies.

Yoshie Mitsuyoshi received her Ph.D. from the University of Alberta, Canada, and currently teaches courses on European and Russian history at Fukuoka University and Seinan University in Japan. Her research interests include the experience of Ukrainian women during the Second World War, Stalinist gender politics and historical memories in Ukraine. She has published articles in both Japanese and European academic journals, including *Jahrbücher für Geschichte Osteuropas*. Her latest article, 'The Zhenotdel Resurrected: Soviet Women's Organizations in Postwar Western Ukraine', appeared in the *Journal of Ukrainian Studies* in 2011.

Maria Lúcia Mott held a Ph.D. in History and was a researcher at the Instituto Butantan in São Paulo, Brazil. She published widely on issues relating to the history of philanthropy, women health workers, feminism and maternal-child healthcare in Brazil. Sadly, she died on June 26, 2011, after a long battle with lung cancer.

Rebecca Jo Plant is an Associate Professor in the History Department at the University of California, San Diego. She focuses on gender history and the history of psychiatry in the twentieth-century United States. Her book *Mom: The Transformation of Motherhood in Modern America* (University of Chicago Press) was published in 2010.

Nichole Sanders is currently Associate Professor of History at Lynchburg College in Virginia. Her research focuses on issues of gender, state formation and economic development. Her book, *Gender and Welfare in Mexico: The Consolidation of a Postrevolutionary State*, was published by Pennsylvania State University Press in 2011.

Elisabetta Vezzosi is Full Professor of American History at the University of Trieste in Italy. She is President of the Italian Association of Women Historians and a member of the editorial board of *Social Policy*. Her publications include: *Madri e stato: Politiche sociali negli Stati Uniti del Novecento* (*Mothers and State: Social Policy in the United States in the Twentieth Century*) (Carocci, 2002) and, with Roberta Nunin, *Donne e famiglie nei sistemi di welfare* (*Women and Families in Welfare Systems*) (Carocci, 2007). Her current research focuses on African American women in decision-making positions and international relations.

Berteke Waaldijk is a gender historian and Full Professor of Language and Culture Studies at the Faculty of Humanities of Utrecht University. Her research focuses on gender, culture and citizenship. She has published on the colonial context of the Dutch women's movement and on histories of gender and social work in the Netherlands, Europe and the United States. With Maria Grever, she co-authored *Transforming the Public Sphere: The Dutch National Exhibition of Women's Labor in 1898* (Duke University Press, 2005). In 2007 she published 'Beyond Social Citizenship: New Approaches in Comparative European Welfare History' in Gro Hagemann (ed.), *Reciprocity and Redistribution: Work and Welfare Reconsidered* (Pisa University Press, 2007).

Lori R. Weintrob is Chair and Associate Professor, History Department, at Wagner College in New York City. Her research on French civil society, gender and public policy has been published in the collected volumes *Démocratie, Solidarité et Mutualité: Autour de la loi de 1898* (Economica, 1999) and *Le Social dans la Ville en France et en Europe, 1750–1914* (Éditions de l'Atelier, 1996). Dedicated to civic engagement in local immigrant communities, she has also co-authored, with Phillip Papas, *Port Richmond* (Arcadia, 2009) and co-edited, with Kenneth Gold, *Discovering Staten Island* (History Press, 2011). She received her B.A. from Princeton University and her Ph.D. from the University of California, Los Angeles.

INDEX

Note: page numbers followed by 't' indicate tables.